Mississippian Mortuary Practices

Florida Museum of Natural History: Ripley P. Bullen Series

UNIVERSITY PRESS OF FLORIDA

Florida A&M University, Tallahassee
Florida Atlantic University, Boca Raton
Florida Gulf Coast University, Ft. Myers
Florida International University, Miami
Florida State University, Tallahassee
New College of Florida, Sarasota
University of Central Florida, Orlando
University of Florida, Gainesville
University of North Florida, Jacksonville
University of South Florida, Tampa
University of West Florida, Pensacola

Copyright 2010 by Lynne P. Sullivan and Robert C. Mainfort Jr.
All rights reserved
Printed in the United States of America. This book is printed on Glatfelter Natures Book, a paper certified under the standards of the Forestry Stewardship Council (FSC). It is a recycled stock that contains 30 percent post-consumer waste and is acid-free.

First cloth printing, 2010
First paperback printing, 2012

Library of Congress Cataloging-in-Publication Data
Sullivan, Lynne P.
Mississippian mortuary practices: beyond hierarchy and the representationist perspective/Lynne P. Sullivan and Robert C. Mainfort, Jr.
p. cm.—(Florida Museum of Natural History: Ripley P. Bullen series)
Includes bibliographical references and index.
ISBN 978-0-8130-3426-3 (cloth: alk. paper)
ISBN 978-0-8130-4201-5 (pbk.)
1. Mississippian culture—Southern States. 2. Mississippian culture—Middle West. 3. Claflin-Emerson Expedition—Funeral customs and rites—Southern States—History. 4. Indians of North America—Funeral customs and rites—Middle West—History. 5. Social archaeology—Southern States. 6. Social archaeology—Middle West. 7. Indians of North America—Southern States—Antiquities. 8. Indians of North America—Middle West—Antiquities. 9. Southern States—Antiquities. 10. Middle West—Antiquities. I. Mainfort, Robert C., 1948– II. Title.
E99.M6815S85 2010
975.'019–dc22   2009038763

The University Press of Florida is the scholarly publishing agency for the State University System of Florida, comprising Florida A&M University, Florida Atlantic University, Florida Gulf Coast University, Florida International University, Florida State University, New College of Florida, University of Central Florida, University of Florida, University of North Florida, University of South Florida, and University of West Florida.

University Press of Florida
15 Northwest 15th Street
Gainesville, FL 32611-2079
http://www.upf.com

Mississippian Mortuary Practices

Beyond Hierarchy and the Representationist Perspective

EDITED BY

Lynne P. Sullivan and Robert C. Mainfort Jr.

University Press of Florida
Gainesville/Tallahassee/Tampa/Boca Raton
Pensacola/Orlando/Miami/Jacksonville/Ft. Myers/Sarasota

Contents

List of Figures   vii
List of Tables   xi
Preface   xiii

1. Mississippian Mortuary Practices and the Quest for Interpretation   1
   Lynne P. Sullivan and Robert C. Mainfort Jr.

2. The Missing Persons in Mississippian Mortuaries   14
   Timothy R. Pauketat

3. Cosmological Layouts of Secondary Burials as Political Instruments   30
   James A. Brown

4. Multiple Groups, Overlapping Symbols, and the Creation of a Sacred Space at Etowah's Mound C   54
   Adam King

5. Social and Spatial Dimensions of Moundville Mortuary Practices   74
   Gregory D. Wilson, Vincas P. Steponaitis, and Keith Jacobi

6. Aztalan Mortuary Practices Revisited   90
   Lynne G. Goldstein

7. Mississippian Dimensions of a Fort Ancient Mortuary Program: The Development of Authority and Spatial Grammar at SunWatch Village   113
   Robert A. Cook

8. Temporal Changes in Mortuary Behavior: Evidence from the Middle and Upper Nodena Sites, Arkansas   128
   Robert C. Mainfort Jr. and Rita Fisher-Carroll

9. The Materialization of Status and Social Structure at Koger's Island Cemetery, Alabama   145
   Jon Bernard Marcoux

10. Pecan Point as the "Capital" of Pacaha: A Mortuary Perspective   174
    Rita Fisher-Carroll and Robert C. Mainfort Jr.

11. Mound Construction and Community Changes within the Mississippian Community at Town Creek   195
    Edmond A. Boudreaux III

12. Mortuary Practices and Cultural Identity at the Turn of the Sixteenth Century in Eastern Tennessee   234
    Lynne P. Sullivan and Michaelyn S. Harle

13. The Mortuary Assemblage from the Holliston Mills Site, a Mississippian Town in Upper East Tennessee   250
    Jay D. Franklin, Elizabeth K. Price, and Lucinda M. Langston

14. Caves as Mortuary Contexts in the Southeast   270
    Jan F. Simek and Alan Cressler

References Cited   293

Contributors   341

Index   345

Figures

1.1. Locations of Archaeological Sites Discussed in this Volume   2
2.1. Plan Map of Cahokia and Mound 66   20
2.2. Feature 205 in Cahokia's Mound 72   23
3.1. Fatherland Site Mound C Shrine Summit   35
3.2. Section Through the North End of the Great Mortuary   37
3.3. Great Mortuary Plan with Rows   41
3.4. Drawing of the Outer Surface of Craig B Cup 229   47
3.5. Spiro Mound Group as a Solsticial Organization   49
3.6. Detail of Burials at Cahokia Mound 72 Submound 1   50
4.1. Plan Map of the Etowah Site   55
4.2. Burials Excavated by Larson at Mound C   56
4.3. Mound C Construction Stages   58
4.4. Late Wilbanks Burial Groupings   61
4.5. Creek Square Ground Structure   62
4.6. Northern Georgia Mississippian House Floor Plan   63
4.7. Centering Motifs in Engraved Shell and Complicated Stamped Pottery   64
4.8. The Lobe Burials at Mound C   67
4.9. Profile Showing the Relationship of the Lobe Burials   68
5.1. The Moundville Site Featuring the 1939 and 1940 Roadway Excavations   76
5.2. Selected Mississippian Cemeteries from the Moundville Roadway Excavations   78
5.3. Phase-Based Chronology for the Black Warrior Valley Featuring Diachronic Changes in the Frequency of Burials for the Moundville Roadway Excavations and the Entire Moundville Site   79
5.4. Sheratt Diagram for the Roadway Excavations at the Moundville Site   82
5.5. Number of Artifacts per Individual Burial for the Roadway Excavations at the Moundville Site   84
5.6. Burial RW 2884, Man over 50 years Old Located in the Center of a Cemetery in Moundville Roadway Block 48+65   85
5.7. Moundville II–III Cemetery Superimposing Moundville I Residential Group (Roadway blocks 48+00 to 49+00)   86

5.8. Detail of the Moundville II–III Cemetery Shown in Figure 5.7 (Roadway Blocks 48+00 to 48+50)   87
5.9. Spatial Comparison of Mississippian Structure Floor Areas to Burial Clusters in the Moundville Roadway   88
6.1. Location of the Aztalan Site in the State of Wisconsin   91
6.2. Increase A. Lapham's Detailed 1855 Map of the Aztalan Site   92
6.3. An Outline Map of General Activity Areas at Aztalan Indicating Michigan State University's 2000 and 2001 Research Activity Locations   100
6.4. Cross-Sections of Two of the Large Pits in the Sculptuary Area   102
6.5. The Sculptuary as Seen from the Ground   103
6.6. Map of the Sculptuary Location, Outline of the Feature, and Michigan State University Excavations in Relation to the Northwest Platform Mound   105
6.7. Location of Articulated Burials, Nonarticulated Human Remains, and Structures at the Aztalan Site   107
7.1. Study Region for the SunWatch Site   115
7.2. SunWatch Site Map Highlighting Burial Group Locations and Solar Alignments   118
7.3. Photo of the Complete Whelk Shell from SunWatch   119
7.4. SunWatch Burial Cluster Locations   120
7.5. Mortuary and Lithic Production Relationships Between the South and West Portions of SunWatch   122
7.6. Reconstructions of SunWatch and a Mississippian Village   125
8.1. Location of the Middle and Upper Nodena and Nearby Sites   129
9.1. Areal Map Showing the Location of the Koger's Island Cemetery   146
9.2. Plan Map Depicting the Excavated Burials and Features at the Koger's Island Cemetery   147
9.3. NAT Analysis at Koger's Island   161
9.4. Age and Sex Distribution of Selected Artifact Types from the Koger's Island Cemetery   162
9.5. Plan Map Depicting the Cemetery Row Structure Put Forth by Peebles   164
9.6. Plan Map Depicting Koger's Island Cemetery Sections Resulting from Simple Visual Inspection and Cluster Analysis   165
9.7. Plot Depicting the Results of a K-Means Cluster Analysis (3-Cluster Solution) Conducted on the Spatial Location of Burials at the Koger's Island Cemetery   166
9.8. Comparison of Age-Group Frequencies in the Three Cemetery Sections at the Koger's Island Cemetery   167

9.9. Comparison of Sex Frequencies in the Three Cemetery Sections at the Koger's Island Cemetery   167
9.10. Comparison of Burial Type Frequencies in the Three Cemetery Sections at the Koger's Island Cemetery   168
9.11. Comparison of the Presence of Funerary Objects in the Three Cemetery Sections at the Koger's Island Cemetery   168
9.12. Plan Map Depicting Burials Associated with Concentrations of High-Status Items at Koger's Island Cemetery   170
10.1. Location of Pecan Point and Nearby Sites   175
10.2. The Pecan Point Site and Vicinity in 1912   177
11.1. Map Showing the Location of the Town Creek Site   197
11.2. Identified Architectural Elements at Town Creek   198
11.3. Early Town Creek Phase Architectural Elements   202
11.4. Burials in Small Circular Structures at Town Creek   203
11.5. Premound Public Buildings and Associated Burials at Town Creek   204
11.6. Burials Associated with Structures 4a and 24 at Town Creek   205
11.7. Late Town Creek–Early Leak Phase Architectural Elements   217
11.8. Structures on Mound Summits Dating to the Late Town Creek Phase (Structures 45a and 45b) and Early Leak Phase (Structures 46a and 46b)   218
11.9. Burials Associated with Enclosure 1 and Structure 51 at Town Creek   219
11.10. Burials in Enclosed Circular Structures at Town Creek   220
11.11. Burials in Large Rectangular Structure at Town Creek   221
11.12. Histograms of NAT for Early Town Creek and Late Town Creek–Leak Phase Burials with Grave Goods   226
11.13. Bar Chart Showing Percentages of Burials with Artifacts by Structure Type or Burial Area at Town Creek   227
11.14. NAT Density (NAT/Number of Burials) by Structure Type or Burial Area at Town Creek   227
11.15. Town Creek Burial 59/Mg2   228
11.16. Town Creek Burial 20/Mg3   229
12.1. Ledford Island Site Plan   240
12.2. Fains Island Site Plan   241
12.3. Comparison of the Demographic Profiles of the Ledford Island and Fains Island Burials   242
12.4. Burial Deposition at Ledford Island Plaza Cemetery and Fains Island Mound   244

12.5. Occurrence of Funerary Objects by Age and Sex at Ledford Island and Fains Island 245
12.6. Occurrence of Objects by Age and Sex in the Fains Island Mound and the Ledford Island Plaza Cemeteries 245
12.7. Occurrence of Ornaments by Age and Sex in the Fains Island Mound and Three Mouse Creek Phase Sites 246
13.1. Location of the Holliston Mills Site 251
13.2. Plan View Map of the Holliston Mills Site 251
13.3. Distribution of Burials with Grave Goods vis-à-vis Burials Without Grave Goods at Holliston Mills 258
13.4. Other Mississippian Period Sites in the Immediate Vicinity of Holliston Mills 263
13.5. Prominent Mississippian Period Sites in the Region Surrounding Holliston Mills 264
13.6. Modeled Appliqué Face Cord-Marked Sherd from Holliston Mills 268
14.1. Drawing by Constantine Rafinesque of a Prehistoric Mummy from Short Cave, Kentucky, and Woven Fiber Artifacts Found with It 273
14.2. Late Woodland Period Woven Fiber Bag from Big Bone Cave, Tennessee 274
14.3. Illustrations from E. F. Hassler's Description of a Tennessee Burial Cave 277
14.4. Map of Glover's Cave Burials 278
14.5. Map of Prehistoric Burials in Coleman Cave, Tennessee 279
14.6. Count of Burial Caves Known Today by Time Period 281
14.7. Count of Burial Caves Known Today by State 282
14.8. Examples of the Toothy Mouth Motif from Caves Discussed in the Text 285
14.9. Petroglyphs from 38th Unnamed Cave, Tennessee 289
14.10. Petroglyphs from 12th Unnamed Cave, Tennessee 290

Tables

2.1. Known or Likely Ridgetop Mounds in the Greater Cahokia Region 21
3.1. Number of Individuals Placed on the Great Mortuary Floor 51
4.1. Selected Artifacts in the Late Wilbanks Burials 59
4.2. Artifact Richness in the Late Wilbanks Burials 60
4.3. Demographic Summary of Late Wilbanks Burials 60
5.1. Inventory of Age and Sex Data for the Moundville Roadway Burials 80
7.1. Cluster Analysis Results of SunWatch Burials 119
7.2. Characteristics of Site Planning and Architecture for a Selection of Mississippian Villages and Fort Ancient Villages in Southwest Ohio 126
8.1. Burial Depths 134
8.2. Burial Orientations 135
8.3. Number of Pottery Vessels per Grave 137
8.4. Selected Locations of Ceramic Vessels at Upper Nodena and Middle Nodena 137
8.5. Frequency of Vessel Forms at Middle Nodena and Upper Nodena (data from the Alabama and Arkansas excavations) 138
8.6. Middle Nodena Burials with Stone Discoidals 139
8.7. Upper Nodena Burials with Stone Discoidals 139
8.8. Middle Nodena Burials with Shell Earplugs 140
8.9. Upper Nodena Burials with Shell Earplugs 140
8.10. Middle Nodena Burials with Pipes 141
8.11. Upper Nodena Burials with Pipes 141
8.12. Burial Diversity Scores for Middle Nodena and Upper Nodena 142
9.1. Koger's Island Burials 152
9.2. Comparison of Artifact Types Between Cemetery Sections at Koger's Island 169
10.1. Burials at Pecan Point with a Diversity Score of 3 and at Least One Nonceramic Funerary Object 182
10.2. Burials at Pecan Point with a Diversity Score of 4 183
10.3. Burials at Pecan Point with a Diversity Score of 5 183
10.4. Burials at Pecan Point with a Diversity Score of 6 184
10.5. Burial Diversity Scores for Pecan Point, Upper Nodena, and Middle Nodena 184

10.6. Structure of Burials at Pecan Point Accompanied by Bird Wings   186
10.7. Structure of Burials at Pecan Point with Stone Discoidals   187
10.8. Structure of Burials at Pecan Point with Shell Bead Necklaces   187
10.9. Structure of Burials at Pecan Point with Shell Gorgets   188
10.10. Structure of Burials at Pecan Point with Shell Earplugs   189
10.11. Percentage of Burials with 0, 1, 2, 3, and 4+ Ceramic Vessels at Pecan Point, Upper Nodena, and Middle Nodena   191
11.1. Mortuary Data from Mississippian Contexts at Town Creek   206
12.1. Dates for the Ledford Island and Fains Island Sites   238
13.1. Radiocarbon (AMS) Determinations from the Holliston Mills Site   253
13.2. Overall Burial Population Structure at Holliston Mills by Age and Sex   255
13.3. Mortuary Indicators of Dallas Social Status   256
13.4. General Distribution of Burial Items at Holliston Mills by Age and Sex   257
13.5. General Age/Sex Distributions of Individuals at Holliston Mills Without Burial Items   257
13.6. General Distribution of Burials at Holliston Mills with Shell Beads   259
13.7. Age and Sex Distributions of Burials at Holliston Mills with Columella Beads   259
13.8. Holliston Mills Burials with Shell Gorgets   261
13.9. Burial Items Recovered from the Plum Grove Site   266
13.10. Mississippian Political Economy Structures   268

Preface

The mortuary practices of the Mississippi Period have been instrumental in inspiring archaeological interpretations of late prehistoric cultures in the southeastern and midwestern United States. The well-crafted artwork often interred with individuals of this time period and other evidence of complex societies, such as large towns with earthen pyramidal mounds, naturally raised questions for anyone who observed these antiquities–questions about the ancient peoples who had farmed and built towns along the region's fertile river valleys, long before European explorers intruded and forever disrupted these peoples' ways of life. After many decades of study, the diversity in the cultural practices of "Mississippian" peoples is only now beginning to come into focus. And the study of their mortuary practices is once again at the forefront of new, nuanced understandings of how these peoples organized their lives and communities as well as their beliefs, rituals, and symbols. Our goal for this collection of essays was to provide a sampling of these new ideas across the entire geographic area inhabited by these late prehistoric peoples. We believe that to a large extent we have succeeded in this endeavor, but there are of course many areas in which more work needs to be conducted or in which relevant studies have been done that we were unaware of. We offer our encouragement to those doing research in the former category and our apologies to those in the latter.

This volume was inspired several years ago by Meredith Morris-Babb, director of the University Press of Florida. Meredith suggested to the editors that a book focused on Mississippian mortuary practices was needed and would be well received by the archaeology community. So we put this project on our respective to-do lists and in 2006 were able to begin work by organizing a symposium for the annual Southeastern Archaeological Conference (SEAC) in Little Rock. We thank Meredith for the inspiration and all of the participants in the SEAC session for getting this book project off the ground.

Most of the presentations in the 2006 session have now been transformed into the chapters in this book, with a few exceptions. The papers by Tony Boudreaux, Lynne Goldstein, and Jon Marcoux were added after the conference session. Mainfort and Rita Fisher-Carroll added a second essay and both of their essays are quite different from the original SEAC presentation with Douglas Bird. Christopher Rodning and David Moore were unable to transform their SEAC presentation, which included an intriguing pioneering study of Pisgah mortuary practices, into a book chapter given the time constraints. We look forward to seeing their developed study of this topic in another venue.

We also hope that continued study of mortuary practices can be conducted in a way that enhances the understanding of these earlier times by the descendants of these prehistoric peoples. Much more needs to be done to improve interpretations through involvement of today's native peoples, with their respective cultural traditions and memories, so that they may help shed light on the ritual practices of long ago. Our fervent wish is that the next iteration of mortuary studies will reflect the fruits of such collaborations.

Finally, we wish to thank all of the contributors to this volume for their patience and promptness during the editorial process and the staff of the University Press of Florida for their usual unfailing good humor and assistance. Thanks also to Michaelyn Harle who assisted with manuscript preparation. Our respective home institutions, the Frank H. McClung Museum at the University of Tennessee and the Arkansas Archeological Survey at the University of Arkansas, also deserve mention for their support of this project.

1

Mississippian Mortuary Practices and the Quest for Interpretation

LYNNE P. SULLIVAN AND ROBERT C. MAINFORT JR.

Mississippian Period (ca. A.D. 900–1500) native peoples in the southeastern and midwestern United States are known for towns that typically include platform mounds and plazas and for elaborate and well-crafted copper and shell ornaments, pottery vessels, and stonework. Some of these objects were socially valued goods that often were placed in ritual contexts, such as graves, within or near Mississippian towns. The funerary context of these artifacts has sparked considerable study and debate among archaeologists, raising questions about the place in society of the individuals interred with such items as well as the nature of the Mississippian societies in which these ancient people lived.

The intellectual bridges that connect archaeologically observed mortuary practices with the social behaviors of past populations are of significant interest to archaeologists, and the study of Mississippian mortuary sites was instrumental in the development of archaeological mortuary theory. Notable examples include publications by Brown (1971, 1981a), Goldstein (1980, 1981), Peebles (1971), and Peebles and Kus (1977). These studies were among the first to break from the old school archaeological axiom that "one cannot dig up a social system." While this old saw technically is true, pioneering researchers realized that Kroeber's (1927) long-standing argument that mortuary behavior could not be connected with other aspects of society was flawed and that mortuary sites could indeed provide data sets relevant to the organization and operation of past social systems. Furthermore, these data could be used to develop ideas and models based on observations rather than on speculation or solely upon ethnographic analogy. The social dimensions of mortuary practices thus have become an important arena of study, and these studies have had a significant impact on how archaeologists envision and interpret the late prehistoric Mississippian societies of the eastern United States.

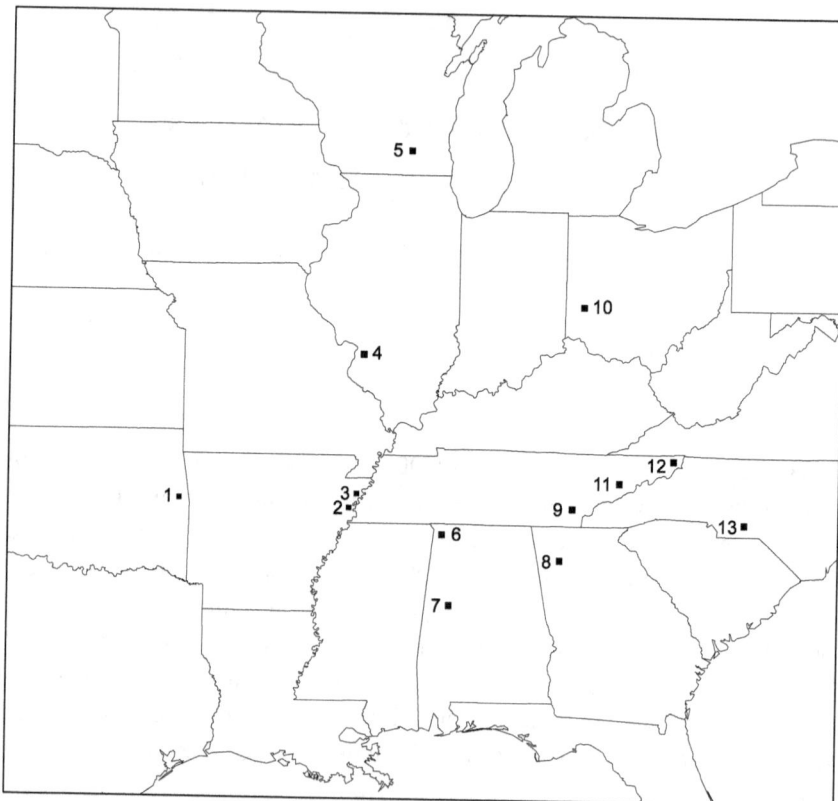

Figure 1.1. Locations of Archaeological Sites Discussed in this Volume. 1. Spiro; 2. Pecan Point; 3. Nodena; 4. Cahokia; 5. Aztalan; 6. Koger's Island; 7. Moundville; 8. Etowah; 9. Ledford Island; 10. SunWatch; 11. Fains Island; 12. Holliston Mills; 13. Town Creek.

Theoretical perspectives and principles for interpreting archaeological mortuary data continue to evolve, as do theoretical perspectives in the discipline as a whole. New perspectives are facilitating new ideas and insights into the operation and diversity of Mississippian ritual, symbolism, and social systems. The collection of essays in this volume showcases some of these new theoretical and analytical currents from a geographically diverse set of Mississippian contexts (Figure 1.1). As a context for these studies, we take the opportunity in this chapter to discuss previous studies of Mississippian mortuary practices as well as current trends and look at how new studies, including those in this volume, are changing perceptions and interpretations of the late prehistoric peoples subsumed under the rubric "Mississippian."

Beyond Representation: The Pursuit of Theoretical Perspectives

The interment of elaborate funerary objects with some Mississippian individuals naturally led scholars to ask questions about social inequities in Mississippian societies. The search for intimations of social hierarchy, typically tied to the cultural evolutionary schemes of Fried (1967) and Service (1962, 1975), was a major focus of many archaeological mortuary studies that appeared in the late 1960s, 70s, and 80s, many of which used data from Mississippian contexts (e.g., Brown 1981a; Decker 1969; Greber 1976; Goldstein 1980; King 1976; Mainfort 1985; Peebles 1971; Rothschild 1979; S. Shennan 1975; Shryock 1987; Stickel 1968; Sullivan 1986; Tainter 1975a, 1975b, 1977; Tainter and Cordy 1977). This approach stemmed from the theoretical foundations of the "new archaeology," namely the materialist evolutionary perspectives of Marvin Harris (e.g., 1968, 1979), Elman Service (1962, 1975), and Julian Steward (e.g., 1955). These views sought overarching principals, explanations, or "laws" of human social behavior and cultural variation that were to be discovered through empirical research using strict scientific methods.

In a particularly influential study, Arthur Saxe (1970) employed these materialist principals and provisionally tested a number of hypotheses regarding various aspects of mortuary practices and their relationships to societal contexts and organization. The notion of representation is embedded in Saxe's view that funerary rites in some way represent the deceased individual's place in society. Drawing on role theory (Goodenough 1965), Saxe (1970: 4–6) viewed funerary rites as a final occasion when survivors discharge their duty-status relationships with the deceased, bringing to the fore the broad range of the decedent's social identities. In short, the representationist perspective views nonrandom variation in mortuary ritual as *representative* of the deceased's role in the social structure.

Two of the Saxe's hypotheses specifically spell out this representationist concept. His hypothesis 1 states: "The components of a given disposal domain cooperate in a partitioning of the universe, the resulting combinations representing different social personae" (Saxe 1970: 65). Hypothesis 4, which places some limits on the first, states: "The greater the social significance of the deceased, the greater will be the tendency for the social persona represented at death to contain social identities congruent with that higher position at the expense of other (and less socially significant identities) the deceased may have had in life, and conversely" (Saxe 1970: 71).

Although his own study was based on ethnographic data, Saxe (1970: 4) claimed: "When archaeologists excavate a set of burials they are not merely excavating individuals, but a coherent social personality." Implicit in this statement seems to be the assumption that Saxe felt that his hypotheses and conclusions were applicable to archaeological mortuary remains in a fairly straightforward manner, but in his conclusions he points out that the methods he used cannot be directly mapped onto archaeological data (Saxe 1970: 235). In their zeal to derive sociological information from mortuary remains, many archaeologists seemingly overlooked this important cautionary comment. As Brown has succinctly noted, Saxe's approach to mortuary studies is "only suitable for a behavioral model and not to untranslated archaeological data" (1981a: 30).

The other cornerstone of the representationist perspective is a 1971 article by Lewis Binford. Like Saxe, Binford adopted role theory as a vehicle for analysis and relied on ethnographic data, in this case rather cursory information drawn from the Human Relations Area File, some of which dated well back into the 1800s (Binford 1971: 19). After tabulating data from 40 societies, Binford claimed to have demonstrated two key points: first, that both the number and the specific dimensions of the social persona symbolized during mortuary ritual vary according to the organizational complexity of a society; and second, that the form of mortuary ritual is determined by the dimensions of the social persona being symbolized. In fact, only four of Binford's (1971: 20) tabulated observations regarding the first point are statistically significant (O'Shea 1984: 6). Problems regarding data and interpretations aside, Binford was able to make a plausible case that mortuary differentiation is broadly related to the organization of a society.

The conclusions Saxe (1970) and Binford (1971) reached were amplified by Tainter (1978: 113), who claimed that "mortuary ritual is basically a communication system in which certain symbols are employed to convey information about the status of the deceased." Operationally, this means that within the burial rites prescribed by a given society, different attributes (in the broadest sense) representing social identities are called forth on the occasion of death and that these attributes in particular combinations represent (i.e., symbolize) the social persona of the deceased and mandate specific burial treatments appropriate to each social persona. This rather narrow view of funerary rites has been called into question by researchers who have shown that some mortuary traditions actually mask social distinctions (e.g., Parker Pearson 1982; Trinkaus 1984).

Underlying the work of Saxe and Binford and studies that derive from their work is the assumption that as the number of social identities held by an individual increases, so does the number of symbolic representations of these identities (see Howell and Kintigh 1996). A second key assumption is that the corresponding symbols would be reflected accurately and unambiguously in forms of mortuary treatment and funerary objects. We must note that by no means did Saxe and Binford make their claims in an anthropological vacuum. For instance, writing around the same time, cultural anthropologist William Douglas (1969: 219) stated, "Not only does death serve to activate the various levels of social organization, but on each level it occasions the widest expression of such relationships. . . . To a significant degree, it is through death that the social relationships of the living are defined and expressed."

Obviously lacking from the Saxe-Binford perspective are the active role of the living in funeral rites (Gillespie 2001) and consideration of the roles that economics (e.g., Brown 1995; McGuire 1992; Precourt 1984) and politics (e.g., Metcalf and Huntington 1991) often play in mortuary ritual (see Pauketat this volume). Rituals surrounding disposal of the dead, including interment, clearly entail more than a final exercise of duty-status relationships, and these rituals, by their very nature, embody more than conveying "information about the status of the deceased." This theme is well represented and elaborated upon in the contributions in this volume. For example, Pauketat notes in chapter 2 that archaeological mortuary studies too often assume "that a single purpose, meaning, or mortuary program resulted in the material remains excavated." Brown (chapter 3) specifically demonstrates that the representationist view (as in discerning individual identities) "do[es] not make sense as a starting point for analyzing secondary burials." Both Brown and King (chapter 4) show the powerful connections between ideology and mortuary displays and how such displays can be used to create sacred space. In a similar vein, in her analysis of mortuary variation at the Aztalan site, Goldstein (chapter 6) remarks that "mortuary variability and patterning in a site encompass more than social statuses or economic elements . . . . For a variety of reasons, past interpretations [of mortuary practices] largely ignore the use and construction of space and ideas and the importance of collective memory and site planning." King further comments that funerals are "about negotiating ideology, interacting with tradition, creating or recreating society." He continues, "In all burial rites, the death of the individual becomes part of the larger community's efforts to influence the natural and supernatural worlds. In fact, in some instances, the dead essentially become sacra manipulated for the living, thereby losing their individual status to the good of the community."

Despite their obvious shortcomings, the initial formulations of archaeological mortuary theory led to important advances in theoretical perspectives. One of the most important consequences of the early studies is that they encouraged archaeologists to search for structure within cemeteries and beyond. Saxe and Binford provided a major impetus for moving beyond trait-oriented generalizations about archaeological mortuary remains (e.g., Dragoo 1963;

Ford 1963; Lewis and Kneberg 1946; Webb and Snow 1945) and for systematically investigating mortuary variability. That individuals receive different mortuary treatments based on a number of factors is indisputable. Even today, the representationist perspective of Saxe and Binford should not be dismissed out of hand (see Brown 1995), and in fact, more recent cross-cultural surveys (e.g., Carr 1995; Kamp 1998) generally support propositions Saxe and Binford advanced.

Donnan (1995) provides an outstanding example of the value of the representationist perspective in specific instances. Unlike most representationist studies, however, Donnan focuses not on inferring social ranks or the degree of social complexity but rather on explicating a shared funerary tradition among the Peruvian Moche that is characterized by structured variation in specific dimensions of mortuary treatment. In this volume, Marcoux uses the Saxe-Binford approach to formulate an alternative to Peebles's (1971) interpretation, which used the same approach, of social structure at Koger's Island cemetery in Alabama. Marcoux's interpretation is based on ethnohistoric models from southeastern rather than the Polynesian chiefdom models that influenced Peebles and a generation of archaeologists studying Mississippian mortuary practices (as we discuss below).

The Search for Hierarchy and the Discovery of Variation and Complexity

In conjunction with the representationist perspective, the popularity of cultural evolutionary schemes (Service 1962, 1975; Fried 1967) had an enormous impact on interpretations of Mississippian mortuary practices and hence of Mississippian societal organization. Although "chiefdom" and "ranked society" models derived mainly from Polynesian societies, these became de rigueur for modeling Mississippian societies. Coupled with the intimations of social hierarchy that appeared in the chronicles of the sixteenth-century Soto expedition, these concepts quickly became a dominant interpretive framework across the Southeast (e.g., Anderson 1994; Cobb 2003; Hatch 1974, 1976a; House 1991; Peebles 1971, 1974, 1978; Peebles and Kus 1977; Scarry 1996; Steponaitis 1983; Welch 1991). Analogies drawn from more closely related groups (i.e., the American Indians of the Southeast and Midwest) were considered inappropriate because European contact was thought to have essentially destroyed traditional social structures by the time they could be recorded. Exceptions were thought to be lower Mississippi valley groups, such as the Natchez, whose social hierarchies and rituals appeared congruent with findings at major Mississippian sites (Steponaitis 1978: 421–423; also see Hally 2008: chapter 2).

The landmark study of Mississippian mortuary practices at Moundville by Christopher Peebles and Susan Kus (1977) set in place notions about hierarchical organization that continue to influence many interpretations today. Their model for Moundville society included hereditary ranking with ranked tiers within a chiefdom society (*sensu* Service 1962 and Fried 1967; see Marcoux this volume). In another contemporary study that focused on a region with smaller mound centers, James Hatch (1974, 1976a) studied the mortuary practices of the Dallas phase, a late Mississippian complex in eastern Tennessee that includes multiple mound sites throughout a 200-mile swath of the Tennessee Valley. He found what he interpreted as less evidence of hereditary ranking in eastern Tennessee than Peebles and Kus did for the evidence at Moundville, but he nonetheless followed the modus operandi of the time and arranged these sites into chiefly hierarchies. More recent studies of Moundville and related sites (Knight and Steponaitis 1998; Wilson, Steponaitis, and Jacobi this volume) and of the eastern Tennessee sites (Sullivan 2007a, 2007b, 2008; Sullivan and Harle this volume) show that both earlier studies suffered from lack of chronological control and thus conflated temporal changes with social differentiation.

As research has progressed with various Mississippian phases and sites, more recent findings indicate that at best the chiefdom model has masked diversity, variation, and thus complexity in regions with major mound centers (Pauketat 2007; Wilson 2007). At worst, it is inapplicable for many areas, especially those with smaller sites (Boudreaux 2007a, this volume; Fisher-Carroll and Mainfort 2000; Mainfort and Fisher-Carroll this volume; Franklin this volume; Hammerstedt 2005a, 2005b). Mainfort and Fisher-Carroll's (chapter 8) examination of mortuary data from the Pecan Point site in Arkansas provides an example of how traditional interpretations of large mound centers as apical sites within an inferred hierarchical, chiefly settlement system (e.g., D. Morse 1989, 1990; P. Morse 1981, 1990; Morse and Morse 1983) do not necessarily hold up under closer scrutiny. Mainfort and Fisher-Carroll do not embrace the "chiefdom" model but rather elected to assess mortuary data within the framework that gave rise to the original interpretation of the site. Boudreaux (chapter 11) and Franklin, Price, and Langston (chapter 13) also make similar points with data sets from the North Carolina piedmont and northeastern Tennessee.

New ideas about the organization of Mississippian Period societies are being offered and debated by archaeologists across the Southeast (e.g., Brown

2006a; Boudreaux 2007a; Cobb 2003; King 2003; Knight 2007; Knight and Steponaitis 1998; Pauketat 2007; Sullivan 2001, 2006; Wilson 2007). Distinct intraregional variation among Mississippian Period societies and their organizational schemes now is apparent, and interpretations that are cast in the language of social evolution as well as in the normative "chiefdom" notion are being replaced by models relying more on ethnohistorically known southeastern and midwestern native groups (e.g., Barker 2004; Brown 2003, 2006; Eastman 2001; King this volume; Marcoux this volume; Rodning 2001; Sullivan 2001, 2006; Welch 2006a). The focus of research has shifted to emphasize segmentary kinship structures and notions of contextualized and overlapping power heterarchies (Ehrenreich et al. 1995) rather than the strict, primarily vertical relations of hierarchies inherent in the chiefdom model. Heterarchy has become a particularly useful concept for emphasizing horizontal relations embedded in gender, age, and lineage (Crumley 1987).

As Cobb (2003: 75) notes,

> Recent mortuary research–combined with data on settlements, landscape and labor–has begun to paint complexity as a multidimensional phenomenon. Individuals and interest groups often did hold superordinate positions that were hierarchical, and the reproduction of hierarchy involved both material and ideological dimensions. Yet people also assumed multiple identities that extended to gender, clan, and age-group affiliations. These social roles provided alternative frameworks for the negotiation of power relationships acted out daily on stages within the household and other venues. Such arenas did not necessarily involve the direct intervention of chiefs or similar positions that we traditionally link to status and institutionalized power. Whether involving elites or not, power is not an abstract essence; it is made manifest through relations that may be codified by institutions or rationalized through kinship and other means.

Boudreaux provides an example of this approach in his reanalysis of the Town Creek site in North Carolina (chapter 11). At Town Creek, "it seems that the absence of intense economic, political, and social competition meant that public buildings were not exclusively associated with particular leaders. Instead, a heterarchical political organization and the use of the platform mound as an integrative facility that remained a symbol of group identity seem to have persisted throughout the existence of the Town Creek community."

Ideology is yet another arena in which the discovery of diversity and complexity is changing long-held interpretations and general models of Mississippian societies. Many of the elaborate objects interred with Mississippian burials were once thought to be associated with a shared religious or ideological complex termed the "Southern Cult" (Waring and Holder 1945), later renamed the "Southeastern Ceremonial Complex" to divest it from the connotation of a cult (Brown 1976; King 2007). Brown (1976) coupled the artifacts and motifs of this complex with hierarchical ranking structures within chiefdoms. As understanding of the art styles and contexts of these objects has improved (e.g., Brown 1996; Townsend et al. 2004), distinctive subregional styles have been recognized and coupled with a variety of meanings. This variation is so extreme that Knight (2006) has argued that the term "Southeastern Ceremonial Complex" should be dropped altogether. Furthermore, as several studies in this volume demonstrate (e.g., Brown, King, Pauketat), the emplacement of these objects with certain individuals has less to do with their personal status than with the collective display of ritual, or spectacles, intended to connect the entire community to the worlds of the ancestors and the cosmos.

Sightings of Mississippian Societies from Multiple Vantage Points

Diverse theoretical paradigms that offer and investigate a multiplicity of views and aspects of Mississippian societies are replacing the overused chiefdom model. New perspectives, such as the notions of cultural pluralism that inform the interpretation of diverse ethnic groups bound together at Cahokia (Alt 2006; Emerson and Hargrave 2000) or interpretations of burial rituals as theatrical ideological tableaus (Brown 1996, 2003, 2006, this volume; King this volume), are influencing the interpretations of Mississippian social practices, and reinterpretations of mortuary practices are making important contributions to this rethinking.

The incorporation of agency theory into the archaeological theoretical arsenal also is playing a role in the freshened interpretations. A new emphasis on "the behavior of people" rather than on "adaptive systems" and social institutions is leading southeastern archaeologists to look for meaningful actions of social groups that were conditioned by the acts of other social agents within Mississippian societies (Welch and Butler 2006: 6). For example, rather than discovering the "lawlike generalizations" sought by the "new archaeology" of the 1970s, the new paradigm requires scholars to think through how, given specific settings and circumstances, certain social groups or segments may have orchestrated or resisted change.

The concepts of the continuity of culture as manifested in tradition and the manipulation of tradition to serve perceived needs is another element of human behavior under scrutiny (e.g., Pauketat 2001a). Few cultural traditions are as conservative and resistant to change as are mortuary practices (see

Mainfort and Fisher-Carroll this volume; Sullivan and Harle this volume). The degree to which a person or group has the ability to manipulate mortuary practices is thus a particularly robust barometer of social power and influence. The ostentatious Cahokian mortuary remains uncovered at Mound 72 (Pauketat and Brown this volume) may reflect more than funerary rites and offerings for a chiefly leader, as once thought (e.g., Fowler et al. 1999). Instead, when viewed from the vantage of those who orchestrated them, these rituals show the immense power and control over others by the living elite. From another vantage, studies such as the one offered by Wilson, Steponaitis, and Jacobi of Moundville in chapter 5 show that interpretations based solely on mound interments miss significant aspects of a society's mortuary program and thus aspects of the society itself. The small cemeteries at Moundville are manifestations of the degree to which "small corporate kin groups exerted certain social and spatial claims within the Moundville polity" (Wilson, Steponaitis, and Jacobi this volume).

Changes in traditions are not, however, always related to manipulation by powerful social entities. Nuanced temporal change in traditions is the topic of Mainfort and Fisher-Carroll's study of Nodena phase mortuary practices (this volume). Similarities in material culture between the Middle and Upper Nodena sites suggest no differences in ethnicity or group identity, but the juxtaposition of close proximity and similarities in material culture with quantifiable contrasts in mortuary behavior lead Mainfort and Fisher-Carroll to suggest that the sites represent sequent occupations by the same social group. Cook (chapter 7) relates changes in regional mortuary (and other) practices to direct interaction between culturally disparate groups. He describes "a co-evolutionary process" that led to hybridization of Fort Ancient and Mississippian groups with concomitant changes in traditions. Franklin, Price, and Langston (chapter 13) also suggest hybridization of Pisgah and Dallas phase groups in northeastern Tennessee; the circumstances that may have led to such a fusion are as yet elusive but likely involved trading relationships.

Gender relationships are yet another vantage from which power, as manifested in mortuary practices, is being investigated in Mississippian contexts. Evidence from both the archaeological and ethnohistoric records indicates that women could hold power as both "chiefs" (Trocolli 2002) or as heads of kin groups (Perdue 1998). Mortuary patterns at southern Appalachian Mississippian towns echo those of early Cherokee towns, where older women are buried in domestic structures and male leaders in or near community buildings. These patterns suggest that women's power may have been vested in kin groups whereas men's power may have been linked more to the larger town itself (Sullivan 2001, 2006; Sullivan and Rodning 2001).

Ethnicity and identity are other social dimensions of mortuary practices that are gaining increased attention among scholars of Mississippian Period societies (Emerson and Hargrave 2000; Hally and Kelly 1998; Sullivan and Harle this volume). Sullivan and Harle note that "cultural identity can be correlated with suites of cultural practices or traditions, especially those related to ritual and symbolic practices" and thus "data concerning mortuary practices are well suited for making observations related to cultural identity." Continuity of traditions across space and time might suggest shared identity, but problems arise when direct cultural interaction and some shared technologies, ideologies, or symbolism, such as among Mississippian groups, make the recognition of significant and important differences difficult (see Cook this volume; and Franklin, Price, and Langston this volume). Sullivan and Harle (chapter 12) caution that studies of cultural identity must focus on comparisons of cultural practices for which constellations of material culture are the signature instead of on direct comparisons of material culture traits. Mainfort and Fisher-Carroll (chapter 8) also note that similarities in ritual behavior, specifically disposal of the dead and the manipulation of symbols, are more likely to reflect group identity than are simple similarities between material culture (e.g., Barth 1969; Jones 1997). Sullivan and Harle's examination (chapter 12) of pronounced contemporary differences in mortuary practices within eastern Tennessee leads them to suggest that differences in cultural identity indeed likely existed.

The house society model pioneered by Levi-Strauss but recently reworked by Carsten and Hugh-Jones (1995) and Joyce and Gillespie (2000) is finding some utility among scholars of the Mississippian Period (e.g., Beck 2007; Brown 2007a; Knight 2007). House societies consist of enduring social groups, often but not exclusively bound by kinship, who are materially represented by a physical building and its contents with a designated place on the landscape (Gillespie 2000: 2–3). Residential burial (interment in or around houses) is a mortuary practice that can be linked to house societies (Adams and King 2010), and the presence of deceased ancestors can be important in creating a social memory or identity for the domestic group (Hodder and Cressford 2004). Sullivan and Rodning (2007; Sullivan and Rodning 2010) further connect a tradition of residential burial among Mississippian and early Cherokee societies in the southern Appalachians to spatial symbolism of gendered power relationships. They further argue that differences in the implementation of these burial practices among neighboring archaeological complexes, especially when these differences relate to gender dynamics, may reflect differing cultural identities (Sullivan and Rodning 2010). In this volume Wilson, Steponaitis, and Jacobi (chapter 5) link small-scale social groups to space, buildings, and cemeteries but do not generalize these practices to a house society model, which like the chiefdom model could mask actual practice and variation. Wilson, Steponaitis, and Jacobi do note that small, nonmound but spatially discrete cemeteries at Moundville were constructed in exactly the same locations "previously occupied by equally discrete residential groups. . . . Indeed, some clues in the organization of these cemeteries indicate that their spatial arrangements intentionally referenced [the] early Mississippian residential past" (chapter 5, this volume). They argue that "it is not unreasonable to speculate that these cemeteries served as a metaphor for a house that embodied kin group identity while maintaining continuity with the residential origin and history of kin groups at Moundville."

The ritual landscape provides yet another perspective for viewing Mississippian mortuary practices (Brown 2003, 2006). Goldstein (chapter 6) observes that "relationships of power and influence come to the forefront when one views the landscape as an ideologically manipulated arena." Her analysis of mortuary practices at the Aztalan site in Wisconsin places varied mortuary practices in a spatial context that also contextualizes the dispersed and cut human bones found at this site–not as evidence of subsistence-based cannibalism as thought by early investigators but as part of a larger, multifaceted mortuary program. This program, with its dispersed and varied treatments, likely gave form to a ritual landscape at Aztalan that imbued everyday life and places with meaning and memory based in ideology.

Simek and Cressler's work with cave archaeology and the mortuary practices associated with caves (chapter 14) also deals with the ritual landscape. They demonstrate that while cave burial is a long and continuous tradition in the Southeast, there are no obvious indicators, such as age or sex, that particular people were selected over others for underground mortuary treatment. Simek and Cressler then raise what is perhaps one of the most intriguing questions about mortuary treatments in the Southeast: "Exactly who was it that warranted eternal rest at the gateways to the underworld?" The answer to this question undoubtedly relates to the ritual landscape and how cave burial may represent a materialization of ideology through ritual, as does the mortuary program at Mound 72 at Cahokia.

A final perspective that has only begun to appear in the literature on Mississippian mortuary practices and that only tangentially appears in this volume is the archaeology of the body and personhood (Fowler 2004; Joyce 2005). The body itself can be seen as a construction of personal identity but "as metaphor for society, as instrument of lived experience, and as surface of inscription" (Joyce 2005: 140). Sullivan and Harle (chapter 12) note the connections between body ornamentation and cultural identity, while Pauketat (chapter 2) broaches this topic in a collective sense by interpreting the Mound 72 rituals as assigning new meaning or identities to human bodies. Study and interpretation of individuals in Mississippian societies clearly is an area that could benefit from a collaboration of biological anthropologists and archaeologists interested in mortuary practices. It is somewhat ironic that this particular perspective, in a very different way, views the body and associated ritual in a mortuary setting as representative of personal identity and society.

Studies of Mississippian mortuary practices continue to offer many innovative and enlightening interpretations of the past. The rich diversity of the cultures of this time period is coming into focus because of new theoretical perspectives that no longer seek to fit this fascinating variation into a single chief model. The chapters in this volume provide only a partial view of the breadth and depth of this exciting research.

2

The Missing Persons in Mississippian Mortuaries

TIMOTHY R. PAUKETAT

Mortuary studies in archaeology frequently focus on inferring the function or meaning of some burial program in society. The results, I believe, are often inconclusive or deceptive, since the procedure typically involves assuming that a single purpose, meaning, or mortuary program resulted in the material remains excavated. Too rarely do archaeologists consider the idea that the mortuary practices themselves were generative of cultural change (but see Parker Pearson 1982, 2000).

In this essay, I pose a simple question concerning how we understand those mortuary practices: Who is missing? For present purposes, I do not provide a complete answer based on a thorough analysis of data. I merely argue that since specific mortuary rites and emplaced remembrances doubtless had lasting effects for living people (contingent on scale, content, context, and audience), archaeologists need to seek answers to this all-important question in every instance.

Background

I suggest that around Cahokia, the precocious granddaddy of Mississippian political capitals and religious centers, the lasting effects of key mortuary practices involved a transformation of personal and corporate identities. Beyond the Cahokia region, across the eastern Woodlands, I suspect that the pre-Columbian cultural phenomenon known to archaeologists as "Mississippian" was closely related to specific mortuary events and related cultural practices. Beginning at about A.D. 1050, according to the current synthesis, a large pre-Mississippian settlement (Old Cahokia) was rebuilt into a planned Indian city (New Cahokia). At that time, what had been an intermittent stream of migrants from outlying regions became a flood, bringing the attendant transformations of the regional landscape, agricultural economy, and social order (Alt 2002; Dalan et al. 2003; Emerson 1997; Pauketat 1994, 2004, 2007). At or shortly after this time, elements of Mississippian culture appeared in lands distant from Cahokia.

Importantly, a series of unusual mortuaries are associated with this early Cahokian era (ca. A.D. 1050–1200) (Pauketat 2004). Within greater Cahokia, these took the form of ridgetop mounds, most famously known from the over 260 interments of Mound 72 (Fowler et al. 1999). As far as we know, these ridgetop tumuli had no historical antecedents and (with one possible exception) no known successors. Similarly unprecedented group mortuaries are known outside greater Cahokia that may be related to the Cahokian mortuary program. But what might explain such widespread (pan-eastern) relationships?

To explain the Cahokia and Cahokia-related mortuary phenomena relative to the dramatic founding events of the early eleventh century, I draw on notions of performance and theatricality, as found in the writings of Geertz (1980) and others (e.g., Inomata and Coben 2006), including archaeologists who have interpreted aspects of Mound 72 at Cahokia, beginning with Paula Porubcan (2000, but see also Brown 2006a; Emerson and Pauketat 2002; Hall 2000; Kehoe 2002). I also draw on two other theoretical concepts. The first is a contemporary sense of personhood, a socially constructed cultural identity that bridges theories of agency and identity and allows us to triangulate to explanations of larger-order cultural change (Fowler 2004; Gillespie 2001). The second is the notion of citation, which I will use generically to refer to a practice that references another or an abstract idea without necessarily reproducing that practice, its referent, or its meaning (see Joyce 2000, following Butler 1993).

My present tack is different than the strategies of those who have previously noted that mounds were theatrical spaces where cultural tableaus or schemas were enacted or where age-old mythical heroes were celebrated (e.g., Brown 2003, 2006a). Such a view assumes that there was one Mississippian narrative. This is highly problematic, as it fails to recognize that the locus of cultural change might well lie in the diversity of narratives and divergent or contested experiences of the local and relocated populations in particular Mississippian regions (especially Cahokia; see Alt 2006; Pauketat and Alt 2003; Pauketat 2003, 2007). Yes, mortuary monuments were emplacements of the cosmos, embodiments of a greater macrocommunity as it was coming into being, and—not incidentally at Cahokia—inaugurations of rulers who were actively claiming legitimacy (see Blom and Janusek 2004; Cobb 2005; Dillehay 1995). But to understand the relationship of mortuary practices to larger-order political-historical changes, we must examine the convergence of the living with the dead (and the human with the nonhuman agents).

I argue that the specificities of audience participation in any mortuary spectacle transformed local senses of personhood as well as the consciousness of audiences (see Parker Pearson 2000). Agency and self were redefined by and for everybody involved in the gatherings, not just once-influential and now-dead persons. Such an argument helps explain the Mississippianization of ancient eastern North America (Pauketat 2007).

Agents and Persons

Certain approaches to human agency allow us to envision how cultural patterns, places, memories, identities, and dispositions were constructed through (among other things) social experience, habitual practice, or grand performance (for a range of views, see Inomata and Coben 2006; Gillespie 2001; Joyce 2005; Pauketat 2000, 2001a). These approaches do more than merely invoke specific human individuals or their "strategies" as explanations of some cultural change (contra Clark and Blake 1994; Maschner 1996); they lead us to investigate the causal relationships between social experience, cultural practice, or political performance and the larger contours of human history and landscapes by focusing on the genealogies and webs of the social relationships wherein change originated (see Dobres and Robb 2000; Dornan 2002; Pauketat and Alt 2005).

In other words, human agency is a social rather than an individual phenomenon. Agency theory should not be misconstrued as an appeal to great man theories of history or to a dominant ideology thesis (cf. Brown 2006a; Schroeder 2004). Agency itself is contingent on the histories and genealogies of cultural practices, the movements of bodies, the productions and distributions of objects, and the experiences of places rather than on the innate tendencies of a few actors to strategize, aggrandize, or dominate (Pauketat 2001a). Indeed, agency might be better understood as distributed or dispersed such that people are constrained by the material and spatial dimensions of their own social experiences, which is to say the objects and the landscapes wherein objects, places, and people are distributed (Pauketat 2009, following Chapman 2000; Gell 1998; Meskell 2004). Some would go so far as to say that things have agency (following Latour 1999), which is similar to saying that culture is physically manifested and has recursive qualities. For the moment, it is sufficient to note that agency cannot be contained entirely within the human body (see Dobres 2000; Meskell and Joyce 2003; Meskell 2004).

Certainly persons do not necessarily correspond to individual human beings (Fowler 2004, Gillespie 2001, and Heckenberger 2004, following Strathern 1988). This is because contrary to commonsense uses today, personhood and selfhood need to be understood as malleable social constructs. In one case, multiple people might consider themselves parts of a single collective "person" while in another case, personal identities might be tethered to seemingly inanimate objects, spirits, or unseen forces (see Fowler 2004; Gillespie 2001; Kammerer and Tannenbaum 2003). Human beings in some cultural contexts might even be unable to conceive of themselves using personal pronouns (I, me, you) or western notions of self. Likewise, human beings in such contexts might view as animate, living, or powerful that which others, especially in today's western world, see as inanimate and powerless (Gell 1998).

Ready examples of such animistic sensibilities are to be found among Prairie-Plains and eastern Woodlands Indians at contact. Members of these groups believed that agency—or the power to effect history—was vested in many things, distributed among human bodies, celestial phenomena, earthly substances, and invisible forces (Bailey 1995; Dorsey 1997; Fletcher and LaFlesche 1992; Hall 1997; McCleary 1997; McGee 1897; Weltfish 1977). For instance, medicine bundles containing objects or substances collected from people, places, things, or nonhuman organisms constituted powerful agents in their own right. They were handled with care and reverence. Likewise, special wooden poles marked community identities and, in places, were venerated as actual persons or apical ancestors who could intercede in the affairs of the living. They were offered prayers and gifts.

Even dead persons were not powerless. Indeed, it was not uncommon for the living to "keep" the souls of the dead in material objects. Mourners might "adopt" the spirits of the dead (e.g., Brown 1953). In such ways, a deceased being was not completely gone and the dead could be reincarnated (Hall 1997, 2000).

Thus, personhood was not a given but (like all identities) was always instantiated by living people, whose experiences were thick with history. Merely by moving through spaces, around some things and alongside others, living people engaged entire social fields. Piling up earth or burning a certain substance might constitute a power-laden act with profound historical consequences, sometimes amounting to a "gathering," an "emplacement," or a centralization of agentic "powers" that were otherwise dispersed among things, landscapes, and bodies (Pauketat 2009, following Barrett 1999, Chapman 2000, Gell 1998, Latour 1999, Strathern 1988, and Wagner 1991).

The upshot is that human bodies (living and dead) and inanimate things associated with those bodies could assume the qualities of persons in part or totally, depending on the scale, content, context, and participants of mortuary practices (Fowler 2004; Gillespie 2001; Hallam and Hockey 2001). With that in mind, I turn now to a brief examination of a series of remarkable mortuary contexts and associated commemorative practices at early Mississippian places, giving most of my attention to greater Cahokia's ridgetop mounds. These mortuary contexts, I argue, are among the most significant causes of the Mississippian phenomenon as a differentially experienced and interpreted political-religious development that spanned the eastern United States.

Early Mississippian Entombments

Several early Mississippian places in eastern North America are associated with unusual mortuary features, singular interments, log tombs, or vertical-post structures that sometimes appear to have contained the remains of multiple bodies. Unfortunately, details are few for many of these, which were excavated in the nineteenth or early twentieth centuries. Among the examples are eleventh-century log-lined pit burials at Macon Plateau, Georgia (Fairbanks 2003), Kincaid, Illinois (Cole et al. 1951: 108–109), and Shiloh (Mound C), Tennessee (Welch 2006b: 10–13). Elsewhere, in the Illinois River valley at Dickson Mounds, Yokem, and Schild, charnel houses appear to have been dismantled and covered or commemorated with primary or secondary burials (Goldstein 1980; Harn 1980; Perino 1971a). Another well-known single-set post building on a platform mound at Aztalan, Wisconsin, contained the bodies of several people, including possible foreigners (Price et al. 2007; Rowe 1958a).

Also at Aztalan was a special burial, dubbed the Princess Burial, associated with one of the unusual "ceremonial pole" mounds, a row of conical mound substructures that supported large vertical wooden posts (Barrett 1933: 231–243). In one of these was the skeleton of a supine female "with the arms placed naturally at the sides and with the legs extended full length" (Barrett 1933: 243). "It was evident that the corpse had been carefully wrapped for burial and that about the outside of the bundle had been wound three belts woven of, or at least richly decorated with . . . [marine] shell beads" (Barrett 1933: 242–243).

As it turns out, a similar eleventh-century burial of one or more individuals seems evident in northern Illinois at the John Chapman site. Many marine-shell beads and human bones were reported from that site's principal mound after one particularly destructive mechanized plowing event (Phillip Millhouse, personal communication, 2003). Another well-known singular burial of four headless men at Dickson Mounds is thought to date to the twelfth century and to reference, rather specifically, four sacrificed men in Cahokia's Mound 72 (Hall 2000; Harn 1991).

Ridgetop Mounds

Clearly, early Mississippian mortuary practices varied in the midcontinent. Of the few noted above, inhumations and secondary disposals were associated with corporate charnel houses, and single individuals or multiple sacrificial victims were inhumed. At least one of the latter was wrapped and interred in association with a large wooden post. Interestingly, all of these treatments are known from Cahokia in a series of anomalous ridgetop mounds (see also Goldstein 2000; Milner 1984). Importantly, these ridgetops are among the largest earthen monuments in eastern North America and are known almost exclusively from the greater Cahokia region in southwestern Illinois and eastern Missouri (Pauketat 2004). The only likely example of a ridgetop mound outside greater Cahokia is Mound C at Shiloh (mentioned earlier), which contained at least three human skeletons and a carved Cahokia sculpture pipe (see Emerson, Hargrave, and Hedman 2003; Welch 2006b).

At one time, there were at least eight and as many as 17 of these special mounds at Cahokia and its suburbs or outliers, including three of the largest tumuli in the region (Figure 2.1; Table 2.1). Based on the contents of several mounds that were excavated or salvaged since the nineteenth century, they were *not* all contemporaneous but date to a 150- to 200-year-span—the late eleventh to early thirteenth centuries C.E., the heyday of Cahokia. The well-known case of Mound 72, which Melvin Fowler excavated in the late 1960s and early 1970s, dates to the late eleventh century and possibly stretches into the early twelfth century (Fowler et al. 1999). Other large ridgetops—the Powell Mound, the Junkyard Mound, the Cemetery Mound at East St. Louis, and probably others—were most likely constructed during the twelfth century; this assumption is based on associated artifacts and nearby or superimposed pre-mound deposits (see Ahler and DePuydt 1987; Alt and Pauketat 2007; Kelly 1994). Finally, the large Mitchell mound—if not also the so-called Big Mound in St. Louis—probably dates to the end of that span and perhaps into the early thirteenth century (Brown and Kelly 2000; Milner 1998; Pauketat 2008).

Given this admittedly rough and incomplete chronology, we may have our first clue to the larger historical significance of these tumuli. A two-century span of time covers approximately 10 human generations of 20 years each. Thus, if these mounds were sequential constructions, as seems plausible, then there might have been one or two ridgetop mounds for every generation within Cahokia's 150- to 200-year reign as eastern North America's cultural and political powerhouse.

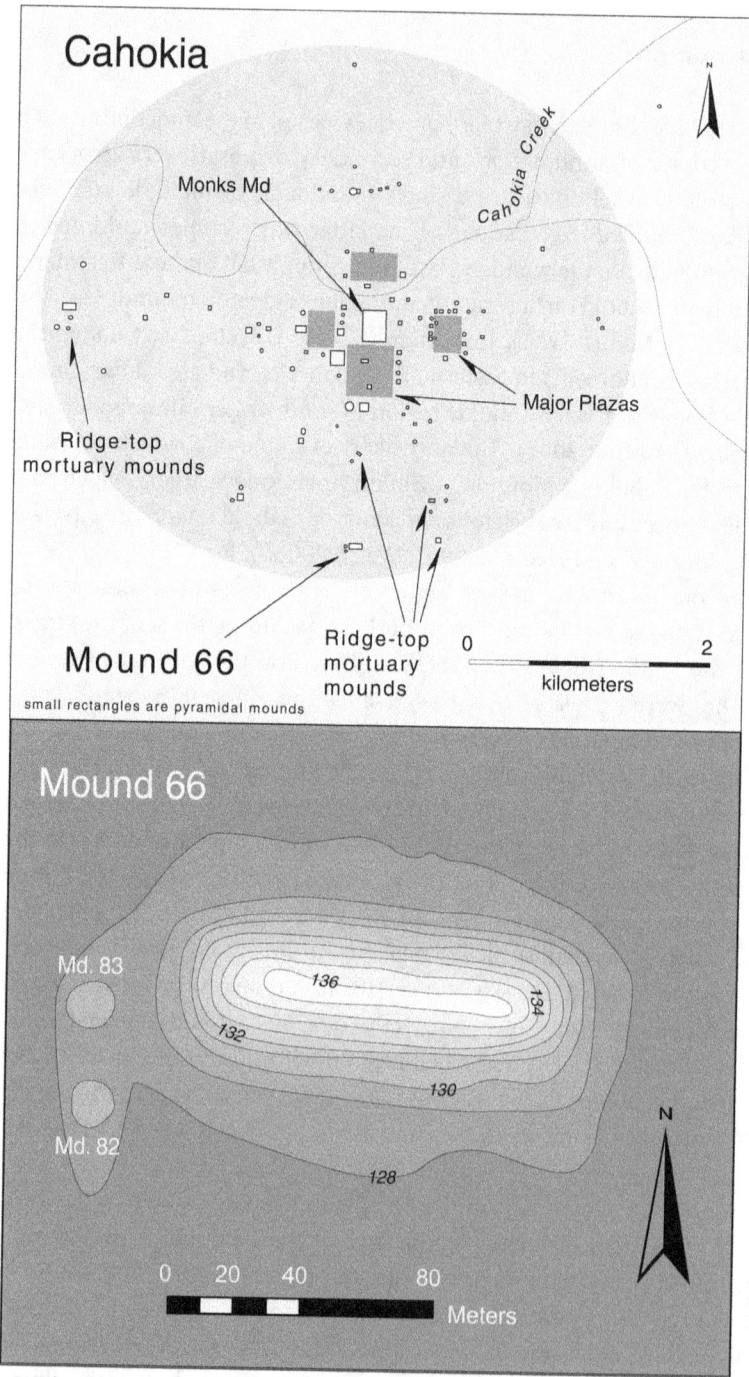

Figure 2.1. Plan Map of Cahokia and Mound 66. Also known as the Harding or "Rattlesnake" mound, adapted from Fowler 1997: Figure 6.21. Contours are pre-1927 projections in meters above sea level.

Table 2.1. Known or Likely Ridgetop Mounds in the Greater Cahokia Region

Mound	Other Name	Chronological Assignation	Condition	Reference
Cahokia Mound 2*[a]	--	unknown	plowed down	Fowler 1997
Cahokia Mound 49*	Red Mound	Lohmann phase	intact	Fowler 1997; Pauketat and Rees 1996
Cahokia Mound 64	True Rattlesnake Mound	unknown	intact beneath railroad grade	Fowler 1997
Cahokia Mound 65	--	unknown	intact	Fowler 1997; Pauketat and Barker 2000
Cahokia Mound 66	Rattlesnake or Harding Mound	unknown	intact, trenched by W. K. Moorehead in 1927	Fowler 1997; Pauketat and Barker 2000
Cahokia Mound 72	Red Pottery Mound	Lohmann–Early Stirling phases	mostly excavated	Fowler et al. 1999
Cahokia Mound 79*	Jondro Mound	unknown	plowed down, trenched by W. K. Moorehead	Fowler 1997
Cahokia Mound 81*	--	unknown	plowed down	Fowler 1997
Cahokia Mound 85*	--	unknown	destroyed in the 1960s	Fowler 1997
Cahokia Mound 86	Powell or Hayrick Mound	Stirling phase	destroyed in the 1930s	Ahler and DePuydt 1987
Cahokia Mound 88*	--	unknown	destroyed in the 1930s	Fowler 1997
Cahokia Mound 95*	--	unknown	plowed down	Fowler 1997
unnumbered Cahokia mound*	--	unknown	plowed down, NE of Mound 6	Preston Holder, notebooks on file at University of Michigan Museum of Anthropology
Junkyard Mound	Wilson Mound	Late Stirling–Early Moorehead phase	destroyed in 1954–1955, partially salvaged	Alt and Pauketat 2007

continued

Table 2.1.—Continued

Mound	Other Name	Chronological Assignation	Condition	Reference
East St. Louis Cemetery Mound	--	Late Stirling–Early Moorehead phases	destroyed in the 1870s	Kelly 1994; Pauketat, editor 2005b
St. Louis Big Mound	Le Grange Terre	Stirling–Moorehead phases	destroyed in the 1870s	Kelly 1994; Marshall 1992
Mitchell Mound*	--	Stirling–Moorehead phases	destroyed in the 1870s	Howland 1877

Note: ªAsterisks indicate likely sites.

Unfortunately, we know only spotty and anecdotal details from the largest of the ridgetop mounds, four of which were destroyed during the period 1869–1930 (Kelly 1994; Pauketat 2004). However, based on scattered excavation details and accounts of the destruction of the St. Louis, East St. Louis, and Mitchell ridgetops, we can make two primary observations (necessarily kept brief for present purposes):

1. Each mound may have been associated with an ancestral temple (Milner 1984). Indeed, in the case of the well-known Mound 72 and probably the lesser-known Junkyard Mound, mortuary events might have been initiated when temples were decommissioned and dismantled (Alt and Pauketat 2007; Emerson and Pauketat 2002; Fowler et al. 1999). At Mound 72, the dismantling of the temple also involved piling bodies and bones on the former floor, removing an oversized marker post, and sacrificing human beings. Construction ended for all intents and purposes with the building of a ridgetop summit on each mound, which was perhaps intended to look like the hipped roof of a temple, albeit an earthen rather than thatched roof. Commemoration of the dead probably did not end there, if the ramps up the final and earlier stages of Mound 72 are any clue.
2. There were principal burials and mass graves in virtually every ridgetop mound. The former were laid on a special surface, often the summit of a flat-topped pyramid, before being covered over with the new earthen ridgetop caps. The latter mass graves included two modes. Some were piles of long bones and skulls of the long dead, which were gathered from

a former charnel house, wrapped in shrouds, and arranged on a soon-to-be-buried surface (e.g., Alt and Pauketat 2007; Fowler et al. 1999; Pauketat and Barker 2000). Others, based on known details of Mound 72 and the sketchy details from the now-destroyed St. Louis, East St. Louis, and Mitchell mounds (Fowler et al. 1999; Kelly 1994; Pauketat 2004), were inhumations—including sacrificed women—entombed in large wooden vaults or arranged on surfaces (Figure 2.2). In several of the known cases, marine shells and beads were heaped over the top of the multiple bodies or disarticulated piles of bones.

In each case, the bodies that were buried in or under these ridgetop mounds and have been identified as "principal" were interred with copper ear ornaments, marine shells, arrows or arrowheads, bead necklaces and beaded garments or capes, Cahokia-style chunkey or "gaming" stones, and bundled or piled objects that, following Robert Hall (1997) and James Brown (2003), I have interpreted as "pieces" of a heroic narrative, perhaps an ancient archetype of the masculine hero twin stories known from Siouan- and Caddoan-speaking peoples of the historic period (Pauketat 2005a, 2009; see also Radin

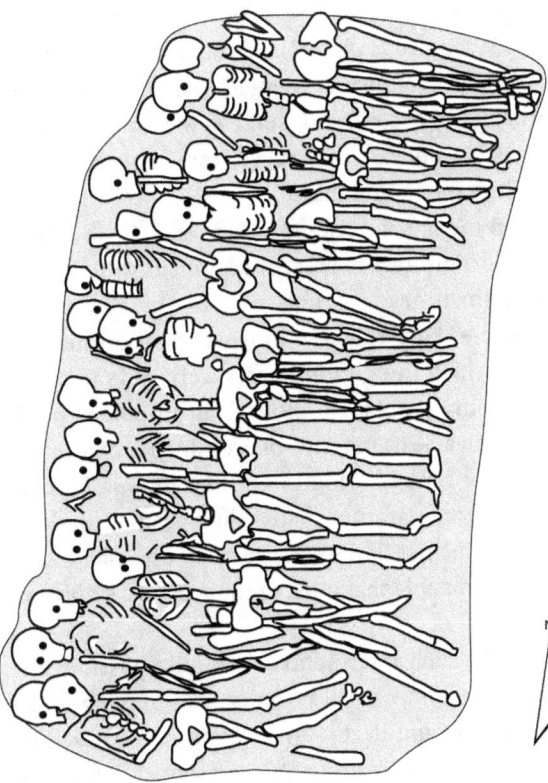

Figure 2.2. Feature 205 in Cahokia's Mound 72. A sand-lined pit 3.4 meters in length containing 22 burials, possibly all females in their 20s. Adapted from Fowler et al. 1999: Figure 6.3.

1948). A series of women in Mound 72 might have impersonated a particular corn goddess or, as argued by Robert Hall (2000), might have been sacrificed to the idea of a masculine Morning Star deity. Incidentally, in at least two other cases, object caches were interred with the human remains that included pots, axes, and beads. One mound at Mitchell also contained bundled objects: copper objects, chipped-stone knives, and an imitation tortoiseshell rattle made from copper wrapped in rabbit skins. The East St. Louis mound contained at least one crystal, and the St. Louis tumulus contained a pair of little shield-shaped human-head earrings made from copper worn on the ears of the larger of a pair of skeletons, as recorded in 1870 (Williams and Goggin 1956).

The so-called "beaded burial" complex in Mound 72, with its bead-studded shroud or cape and various associated objects and celestial referents, appears to best exemplify the Morning Star god-man if not also his Thunderer twin, who was buried beneath the first man (contrast Brown 2003 with Hall 2000 or Pauketat 2008). Alongside the two were other bodies, including a group of seven who if they did not also represent the stars or "seven brothers" of either the big dipper or the Pleiades, were probably oriented to cite one or another summer or winter solstice sunrise or sunset, as were one or two objects that are possibly copper staffs or chunkey sticks and two groups of arrows (Pauketat 2008, citing Fowler et al. 1999; see also Hall 1997). Young and Fowler (2000) suspect that the men of the beaded cape were oriented to cite the solstices, as perhaps were other interments in the mound, such as the bodies of four beheaded and behanded men or the bodies of sacrificed women buried in pits or wooden tombs and, ultimately, the mound itself.

However one might interpret the specific bodies associated with any single mortuary event, it is more important for my present argument to recognize that the beads, beaded capes, human-head earrings, arrows, chunkey stones, and crystals in Mound 72 and the other ridgetop mortuaries of greater Cahokia hint at scripted events at which things and bodies were laid out in the open as props atop soon-to-be-buried platform mounds or in other prominent locations. A similar argument, at least in terms of prominence of location or association, might be made for Shiloh's Mound C tomb burial, Dickson Mounds' foursome, Aztalan's princess, and (perhaps) the burial at the John Chapman site. Because of the specificities of the construction, associations, or contents of these interments, it is possible that most of them cited a Cahokian genealogy.

In the case of Cahokia, that is, such interments were quite possibly elements of theatrical spectacles where forces of the cosmos—day and night, sky and earth, male and female, and life and death—were emplaced at Cahokia through entombment. I say "emplaced" here and not "represented," of course, because the latter fails to adequately describe the historical priority and possible causal relationship in the Cahokian case. Clearly the Cahokia mounds are unusual and probably not representative of a cross-section of society. Given that, we should not confuse the corporate appearance and the dead superhuman impersonators of any one ridgetop mortuary ritual with evidence of traditional "nonhierarchical . . . society" and shared beliefs (contrast Brown 2006a: 205 with Milner 1984). I am not sure we can interpret the "meaning" of something like an elaborate ridgetop mortuary because there were probably as many meanings as there were living and dead participants in the mortuary theatre.

Who Is Missing?

However, if we can't interpret meaning, *we can nevertheless understand how meanings were being produced*. Archaeologists need to move beyond outmoded notions of normative cultures or cultural tableaus in order to disentangle how the dispersed agents— people, places, and things—of larger referential fields were cited in specific historical moments. Toward that end, we should recognize that such citational practices would have included a host of what we can call "missing persons." To explain what I mean, I turn first to a second ridgetop mound just outside the official limits of Cahokia (Alt and Pauketat 2007).

Preston Holder salvaged portions of the Junkyard Mound in 1954 as it was being bulldozed. Holder uncovered a mass interment of 175 skeletons atop a low platform mound stage, mostly secondary "pile" burials, groups of long bones and skulls that had presumably been kept in a charnel house up to the time of burial (see Rose 1999). And while many groups or piles seem to have been wrapped in shrouds and showered with marine shells and beads, there were also eight or nine primary inhumations: adult females, adolescents, and infants. One of the adult women, who wore copper earspools, had died or been killed during childbirth, the fetus in utero, her phalanges drawn up as if in extreme pain at the moment of death. An adjacent adult female—exhibiting what seems to be postmortem removal of the cranium—had been buried with an infant atop her and an unsexed adolescent to her side. Another adolescent was nearby, as was a dog. At least one other female and one or two infant inhumations were found elsewhere amid the wrapped piles of bones. Missing, Holder recognized, were deceased male primaries, which is why Susan Alt and I (2007) have recently suggested that the event—dated via ceramics to the middle to late twelfth century—might have served to eliminate the reproductive members of some honored but rival kin group.

Most of the interments in Mound 72 were also groups of female sacrifices with no associated male interments. Two of these even predate the burial of the twin men. These first Mound 72 features followed the decommissioning of that submound temple and the removal of an adjacent large marker post. Importantly, the removal of the post was followed closely by the sacrifice of 22 young adult women, whose bodies were placed two deep into a pit that had been dug into the location where the post had earlier stood. Around the same time, a second pit was dug five meters south of the temple and filled with 19 more women, including two juveniles, also in two layers (Rose 1999).

Following the interment of the twin men and their retainers, additional pits of sacrificed women were buried in pits or wooden tombs, each burial enlarging the mound, both the female bodies and the mound enlargements now reoriented to reference both the men and solsticial alignments. Various mound stages had ramps up the sides to afford access to the stage summit, hinting at continued use of the location to link the present with the past and (if the solsticial alignments are any clue) to link this world with the greater cosmos (Watson 2000).

Given that there are four excavated pits and at least one more unexcavated pit of sacrificed women among the other interments in Mound 72 and given that at least two of these precede the men and one appears to commemorate the former location of a post and its nearby temple, and then given other suggestive associations here and in the other ridgetop mounds, it is not unreasonable to suggest that like many elaborate mortuary rites around the world, the ridgetop events were not as much about disposal of the dead as they were a definition of the living (Chapman 2000; Dillehay 1995; Hallam and Hockey 2003). But who precisely?

The citations to material things and celestial powers were many and seem to include homage to posts that (to argue from analogy) may have marked identity or (more specifically) have personified great if not also masculine ancestors. It is not unimportant to note that such giant posts were features of central town sites, particularly Cahokia, and that these posts were frequently emplaced and replaced with a regularity that bespeaks the practical (or ritual) "enchainment" of people and posts, which is to say a series of linked citations (see Chapman 2000). It is furthermore important to note that this enchainment as played out in ridgetop mounds also involved citations to masculine bodies, such as the beaded men, as if they embodied ancestral or legendary figures. Finally, it is important to recognize that given that these were performances with a high degree of visibility, living actors and audiences participated in the spectacles.

Presumably among the living were mourners, some of whom—in native Prairie-Plains fashion—might have assumed or "adopted" the soul of the dead person in a virtual act of reincarnation. Such mourning practices are exemplified by, among other examples, the Siouan character Honga, a forward-looking impersonator of the "ancient one" who was invoked in a variety of stories, songs, and rituals (see Hall 1997). These practices are also exemplified by other acts of soul adoption. Father Gabriel Sagard witnessed one such event around 1630 among the Iroquois. In this case, soul adoption doubled as the reincarnation of a leader. After carrying in the bones of a dead chief, the living actors

> all stand upright, except the one who is to raise the dead; on him they impose the name of the deceased, and all, placing their hands down low, feign to raise him back to life in the person of this other man. The latter stands up, and after loud acclamations from the people he receives the gifts offered by those who were present, who . . . thenceforth regard him as if he were the deceased person whom he represented. (Hall 1997: 35, quoting Sagard)

Given such historic-period practices, any interpretation of the beaded burial complex in Mound 72, the buried Junkyard Mound temple, or any of the other ridgetop mound mortuaries, if not other burials at Dickson Mounds, Aztalan, or the John Chapman site, cannot ignore the possibility that the primary actors involved, the ones who would sacrifice those buried or assume a heroic identity, were living. Indeed, the commonalities noted for the other ridgetop mounds suggest that in some important sense, these were the inauguration mounds of living rulers who were, in turn, the reincarnations of their predecessors. Ridgetop inauguration rites, that is, would have joined the present to the past (Bradley 1998), producing what we might reasonably call "founders' cults" (Pauketat 2009, following Kammerer and Tannenbaum 2000).

However one might interpret the principal burials in any one of these contexts, it would be a mistake to end here, concluding that personhood in the Mississippian world involved twin Thunderer god-men or (perhaps) sacrificed god-women (see papers in Townsend, ed., 2005). What particularly concerns me is the genealogy of sacrificial practices, where women and (less frequently) men and children were periodically immolated. Osteological and isotopic evidence indicates that at least some of the sacrificed women in Mound 72 were from lower-status and genetically foreign populations (Ambrose et al. 2003). While this may mean that captives were sacrificed, we now know that foreign immigrants or their immediate descendants were living in and around Cahokia proper, especially in the decades following A.D. 1050 (Alt 2002; Emerson and Hargrave 2000; Pauketat 2003). And in at least one outlying village, the immigrant farmers also appear to have been of low status.

Who were the mourners of these low-status foreigners or recent immigrants sacrificed in Cahokia's ridgetop mounds? And did mourning them, like the American Indian cases of mourning, reincarnation, and political succession, also construct new personal and gender identities among the living? That is, did the periodic gathering of women for theatrical sacrifices involve a "keeping" of their souls in this ridgetop temple of the dead? Did their deaths and emplaced bodies construct new associations among the audiences, some of whom may well have been closely related to the sacrificial victims?

I suspect—based on overwhelming regional settlement evidence—that the answer is yes. That evidence consists of a series of abrupt and coincident alterations of domestic and corporate spaces and practices at or shortly after A.D. 1050. At that time, as I have argued at length elsewhere, pre-Mississippian corporate groups were transmogrified into or replaced by discrete household groups at and around early Cahokia (Pauketat 1994, 2004). Entire neighborhoods at Cahokia may have focused on certain activities more than others, and large-scale ceremonial events in plazas seem to have involved feasts, religious objects, ancestral bones, craft production, temple renewals, wooden-post emplacements and removals, and (probably) mound construction (based on evidence in Pauketat et al. 2002).

More to the point, however, is new evidence presented by Thomas Emerson, Eve Hargrave, and Kris Hedman (2003) from four rural, early-Cahokia-period cemeteries of a practice unknown in the preceding late Woodland era in the region: actual formal cemeteries. In pre-Cahokian times, they note, "mortuary rituals . . . focused on the exposure and natural deterioration of corpses" (Emerson, Hargrave, and Hedman 2003: 177). But with rise of Cahokia and the onset of ridgetop spectacles beginning in the mid-eleventh century, the dead were treated very differently in both ridgetop mounds and in rural farming villages.

Conclusion: The Agency of Audiences

In short, it seems that shortly after A.D. 1050, human bodies in relation to places began to assume new meaning in the greater Cahokia region. Although the details remain spotty, I suspect that there were dramatic changes in the relations and corporate or personal identities of all participants in the central mortuary rites of Cahokia, not just those of the primary players or the newly inaugurated. That is, the spectacles living people witnessed beginning in the late eleventh century probably then enabled, if not required, them to reimagine, talk about, and understand anew their own identities through what must have been inherently powerful gatherings and enchainments of bodies, things, and superhuman forces. Such transformative experiences would have been ongoing over the course of more than 10 Cahokian generations.

In conclusion, if "embodiment is the life-long process of the construction of personal identity from birth up to death" (Chapman 2000: 132), then ridgetop mound commemorations were the process whereby identities—both personal and communal—were emplaced and thereby extended "beyond one life" to become the body politic (Hallam and Hockey 2001). The challenge, as always, is to focus not on personhood and identity but on their construction, which, as it turns out, means separating agents from persons and examining how human and nonhuman agents were articulated in space to construct persons and places by citing, referencing, or memorializing dispersed agentic forces. We cannot start or end our explanations, therefore, with personhood or underestimate the agency of audiences, who would have also assumed some awareness of their own variable personhood via their enchainment to ridgetop mortuary emplacements. Understanding the relationships between identity, agency, and materiality is in a sense, then, about locating the missing persons of the past.

3

Cosmological Layouts of Secondary Burials as Political Instruments

JAMES A. BROWN

Secondary burials offer a fertile field for research that has barely been tapped. The very diversity of secondary burial treatments allow us cultural insights that offer surprising rewards when coupled with fresh analytical perspectives. When we reflect on the deep and myriad cultural connections that bones have as an essence of human life, we can readily recognize the extent to which hard organic residues of life constitute a potent cultural resource in ancient societies. From this observation one can conclude that an important role of bones is to aid in the reproduction of social life. Core structural schemas become acted upon, including notions of how the universe perpetuates itself (Williamson and Farrar 1992). The goal of this chapter is to identify ways that secondary interments can actively portray visions about the cosmos in the pre-contact Americas. My point of departure will be the storied Great Mortuary located in one of the mounds at the Spiro site of eastern Oklahoma. Although this burial display has garnered most of its fame from the sheer volume of graphic art material, the provocative mortuary context is what makes this burial display such fertile ground for the following analysis. Of particular relevance is the unprecedented scale of the piles of scarce artifacts that were amassed among secondary burials. One could slot this feature into ready-made customary categories, but there are too many unique aspects to the feature to make this operation credible. Instead, I advocate detailed comparisons of collective mortuary displays. The burial display from the summit of Submound 1 of Mound 72, Cahokia, which looks very different from others, is the focus of this essay. This approach throws diverse cultural priorities into relief.

Social Display and Secondary Burials

The principle that sometimes human bones are employed as a social resource without any necessary connection to actual social identity is relatively new to southeastern archaeology. That resource can become an instrument for what can be termed a *social display*. What I have in mind is an analogy with a floral display in which the component elements and their arrangement are consciously chosen for an intended effect. Social display is as worthy a subject for analysis as individual identities are. However, the implied disconnect with specific individuals makes for an awkward fit with perspectives that start with arguments about the social identities of individual interments (Parker Pearson 1999). Secondary burials draw upon a much larger social field than that of the identity of a particular individual (Goldstein 1989).

Reburials of all kinds lend themselves to political uses that largely sidestep considerations grounded in the practical disposal of the dead. This has led some scholars to draw the conclusion that politics underlies nearly all mortuary treatments (Parker Pearson 1999). Whatever advantages this all-embracing view of the pervasiveness of politics may have, it does little to uncover connections to what Wolf (2001) terms *structural power*, which commonly acts through broadly supported cultural conventions that are ostensibly power neutral (Bloch and Parry 1982).

Although social identities have been central to the perspective of burial sociology, they have little to do with the symbolism involved in shaping the treatment and disposal of burials. Typically these symbolic expressions have been consigned to the workings of culture in the abstract with little further analysis. In large part this disinclination is a response to the weak and often ambiguous cultural patterning incorporated in displays of secondary burials. For instance, critiques of the cultural-historical school of thought have repeatedly shown that no particular form of burial is a sign for a specific fact about society, culture, or ethnicity. This avenue of analysis has long been discredited (Binford 1971). For these reasons a direct or "self-evident" reading of secondary burials raises more problems than analysis can resolve. A different tack is mandated, and I have adopted an approach that grounds itself in comparing mortuary displays.

Instrumental Uses of Burials

Heretofore, burial analysis has emphasized the social identities of individual interments as the primary vehicle for analysis (Brown 1971, 1975, 1981b; Peebles and Kus 1977). But individual identities do not make sense as a starting point for analyzing secondary burials. Any number of other considerations can assert priority. Whereas age, gender, and wealth have been instrumental in translating individual burials into social identities, the number of analytical considerations prompted by secondary burial, particularly when multiple burials are involved, make age and sex determinations just two of many potentially significant attributes of any "graveyard" population. The placement of burials upon the platform of Submound 1 of Cahokia Mound 72 illustrates the instrumental use of the dead (Brown 2003, 2006a; Byers 2006). This is the same perspective that was applied outside the field of archaeology in an article about the so-called abandoned ruins of the Pueblo Southwest (Colwell-Chanthaphonh and Ferguson 2006). The authors argued persuasively that in this architectural example the principle of instrumentality succeeds where function-based interpretations fall short.

Secondary Burials as Representations of Cosmologic Vision

Various archaeologists have argued that bones were used instrumentally in the Submound 1 burials in Mound 72. Carefully placed human bones were displayed, so to speak, in juxtaposition with specific types of gaming artifacts in order to graphically reference a mythic performance that ordained the cosmos and guaranteed its perpetuation. In this case performance was modeled as a rite of renewal of human life that reenacted the mythic career of the Morning Star spirit or god (Brown 2007a; Brown and Dye 2007; Reilly 2004). The same instrumental perspective can be applied rewardingly to the case of the Great Mortuary of Spiro. Here, the same use of bone as a resource is exemplified, although the manner in which the bones were deployed took on a distinctly different appearance. The Great Mortuary embodies a fundamentally different cosmological plan that represents different kinds of social relationships. While the same collective social function can be identified, the organizational principles differ markedly. In both instances human bone was used in ways that conform to the ideological conventions that dominated each society.

Cosmological Aspects in Secondary Burial Displays

Conceptions about the cosmos commonly influence the burial display of human bones. By that I mean that the deployment of secondary human interments into conceptual designs replays key features of how the universe is organized, how it originated, and the plotlines contained in myths that charter access to spiritual power (Williamson and Farrar 1992). In short, they constituted what Sewell has called structural schemas (Sewell 2005; Beck et al. 2007). When viewed from the perspective of a layout, it is plausible that these remains were keyed to one or more significant solar, lunar, or stellar bearing that exemplified local cosmological principles—cosmovision (e.g., Chappell 2002; Kay and Sabo 2006; Knight 1998).

To articulate these principles, I will examine three major elements: 1) the overwhelming frequency of secondary interments; 2) the formal uniformity of those interments; and 3) the orientation of interments in the direction of one or more external points on the landscape or the horizon.

First, interment in Submound 1 was by secondary burial almost exclusively. The staging of the mortuary display was *independent* of the deaths of the participants. The dead were thus used as a resource for enacting a ceremony. The death of a single individual, however, may have been contemporary with the display.

Second, multiple interments were laid out in accordance with a readily comprehendible plan or design. These dead took on designated "roles" constructed entirely for the purpose of collectively restating a cosmic principle. One could argue that the enlistment of bones of the group's dead for group ritual facilitated the return to the living all of the honor, prestige, and fame attached to the ancestors. Such a connection implies a group's belief in the continuity of history.

Third, the dead were laid out with reference to one or more heavenly bodies. Burial orientation declares an origin or destination after death (e.g., a mountaintop or solar rising point). In the cases described below, the burial furniture and/or the principle burials were oriented either with respect to a cardinally oriented grid or to a post that marked a point within a solar circle or henge monument.

What was excluded at this submound was the simple warehousing of the dead that fits the internal layout of a charnel house. Logically, the disposition of the bones of the dead in such facilities should fit the internal geometry of the enclosing structure. John White's painting of the "Carolinas" charnel house interior exemplifies a pattern that complies with notion of "efficient storage" of the dead (Lorant 1946). Archaeological examples abound from Illinois; examples include the Galley Pond site (Binford 1964, 1972: 390–420), the Schild site (Goldstein 1980), Yokem mound 2 (Perino 1971b), Morton Mound 14 (Strezewski 2003), Cahokia Mound 72 (Fowler et al. 1999), and the Wilson Mound sites (Alt and Pauketat 2007; Milner 1984). The dead at these sites were subordinated to the space dedicated to their storage although the orientation of outer walls or a doorway might have determined orientation as well. Yokem Mound 2 may constitute such an instance, although we do not know enough about it to say so unequivocally. The orientation of the burials at these sites was not independent of other burials and facilities.

The archaeology of the Fatherland site provides useful insights. Excavations into the summit of Fatherland Mound C disclosed the remains of the famous chiefly shrine, which has been described in historical testimony (Neitzel 1965:

Figure 10). It had a significant solar orientation (Brown 1990), but this orientation was not reproduced in the treatment of the dead that were interred deeply within the mound (Figure 3.1). French observers reported that the skeletonized remains—presumably of the Natchez elite—were placed in baskets kept within the principal shrine (Swanton 1911). However, the relatively articulated burials in the contact period summit floor of this mound were evidently never exhumed. They were not disinterred, processed, and converted into treatments of bone resembling the bundles that historic observers have described (Brown 1971; Lorant 1946; Lorenz 1997, 2000). But however one interprets the deposition of skeletons and grave goods at the summit of the postcontact Natchez Mound C, it is clear that the remains were not ordered in any discernable way. The burial assemblage offers no hint of organization; it does not seem to have been dedicated to a narrative or cosmological message. This lack of order contrasts with the burial displays under consideration.

The Spiro Site

In contradistinction to these examples, the imprint of an overriding order is clearly evident in the burials and grave deposits from the Great Mortuary at Spiro. But before turning to the organizing principles encoded in this feature, some context is necessary.

Shortly after A.D. 1400, the local residents of the Arkansas Valley Caddoan culture constructed the Great Mortuary complex at what was the base of the northern and most massive of a continuous line of four cones that form the Craig Mound (Brown 1996: 85–103). Many of the forms of display had been present in the local tradition for several centuries. But the Great Mortuary was unique in its scale and in the way particular burial forms were used together. This unique pattern probably accompanied significant social change and possibly even change in the structural schema that took place between the Spiro and Fort Coffee phases (Rogers 2006). Hence the social moment of this collective representation potentially belongs to a structural event (Beck et al. 2007).

Details of internal organization point to cosmological principles. A clean flooring of split cane pole laid side by side established a special orientation that was repeated in the succeeding arrangement of burials. This flooring underlaid several layers of burials and was surrounded by a 2-meter-high earthen berm that was presumably square to rectangular in form. The complex enclosed approximately 190 m^2. A cross-section of the eastern arm of this berm is clearly shown in a profile exposure north of the Great Mortuary (Figure 3.2). Similar embankment constructions enclosed specialized structures in areas

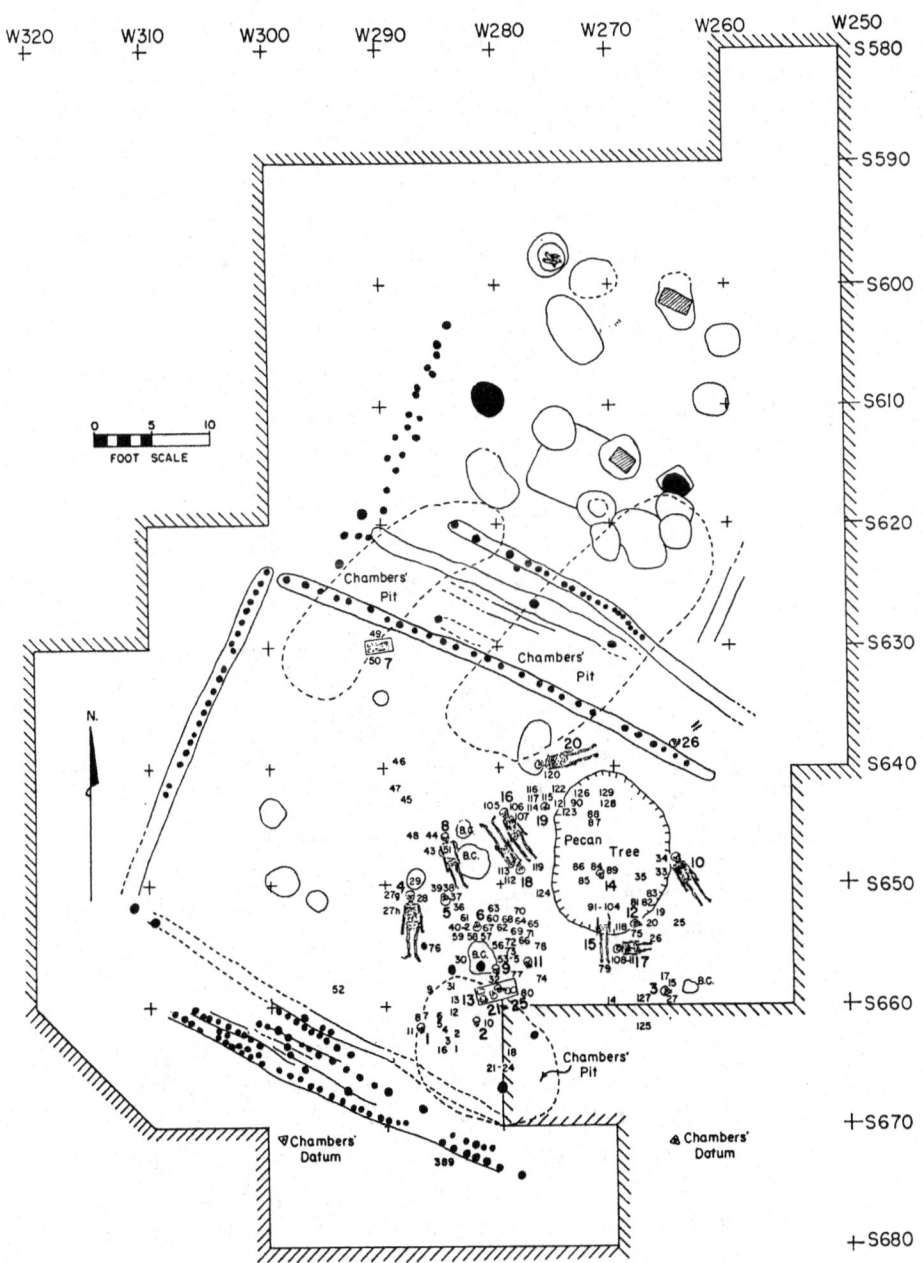

Figure 3.1. Fatherland Site Mound C Shrine Summit. From Neitzel 1965: Figure 10.

other than the northern Caddoan area (Sabo 1998). Apparently the principal axis of the ossuary was oriented a few degrees west of north. Other structures in the Craig Mound neighborhood that were contemporaneous with the Great Mortuary also used this orientation (Brown 1996). We have no information about whether the space was ever completely enclosed or even roofed. Essentially, the Great Mortuary was a giant ossuary of bones and grave goods that as far as we can determine was a unique event. Its construction, one can argue, was a direct outcome of major shifts that were taking place in local society. The creation of the entire deposit was situational, in the sense that it can be thought of as a local response to specific events.

Conditions Prior to the Great Mortuary Event

To gain an idea of what that set of events might be, it is useful to review the main periods in the history of Spiro. The first clearly defined occupation consisted of a local ritual center with an attached village. This period lasted from approximately A.D. 900 to A.D. 1000. During this time, Spiro participated in the Plum Bayou culture network, the hub of which centered on the Toltec site, located over 200 km downstream in the Arkansas River valley (Rolingson 1998). The local expression of this cultural network is called the Evans phase and encompasses the Spiro IA set of features. The subsequent Spiro IB set continued previously established burial practices that persisted until around 1200 or even 1250 during the Harlan phase.[1]

Sometime around 1200 some changes took place in ceramics and burial practices that represented a shift toward greater cultural complexity. The interaction with Cahokia and perhaps other centers is implicated by the small quantities of items from Cahokia that entered the record of Spiro grave goods (e.g., Powell Plain ceramics, Cahokia tri-notched projectile points, Cahokia polished-flint ax heads, and fire clay sculptures retrofitted as pipes) (Brown 1996: 523). The most graphic of these Cahokia presences is the appearance of marine-shell cups and gorgets displaying both Classic and Late Braden styles of engraving. The strength of this connection is communicated through the appearance of a derivative style called Craig A (Brown 2004a). The stylistic similarity between the Classic Braden and Craig A engraving is indicated by the subtle differences researchers used to identify the two as separate entities (Phillips and Brown 1978).

This period of intense connection with Cahokia is represented by the Spiro III grave lots and probably by some of those from Spiro II. Both are now recognized as probably contemporary, although they are formally distinct.

Figure 3.2. Section Through the North End of the Great Mortuary. The location is Row 20 left and Row 20½ right; the filled-in central cavity is in the middle distance. Note the upright cedar poles. The eastern berm is clearly shown on the right; the main tunnel in the center led to the now-filled central cavity. The Great Mortuary floor zone is revealed at the base of the side tunnel with a post protruding. From Brown 1996: Figure 117c.

This period is estimated to have existed between 1200 or 1250 and 1300. The indigenous Craig style developed into the Craig C form around 1300 (Brown 2007c). With the exception of the Great Mortuary itself, copper and shell artifacts of all kinds reached their highest densities per individual interment during this period.

The century from 1300 to 1400 is difficult to pin down primarily because it falls between the period of intense Cahokia connections in the thirteenth century and the creation of the Great Mortuary. Later, around 1400, Spiro made a leap toward greater cultural complexity when it became the center of a dispersion of settlements within a 2 km neighborhood. Only at this time is there evidence for more than a single type of house construction. In contrast to the form of interment in the Great Mortuary and the burials in the overlying cone, inhumations at Spiro were made in flat cemeteries in the surrounding neighborhood. This period appears to be relatively brief, possibly extending to about 1450. Occupation of neighboring sites continued into the Fort Coffee phase.[2] Dated features, housing, and burials point to continued occupation until around 1500 (Rogers 2006; Rohrbaugh 1982, 1984).

The Great Mortuary as a Cosmogram

Human bone and artifacts in the Great Mortuary were distributed in such a way as to define a unique cosmogram that exemplified culturally specific cosmological principles. The sacred significance of the distributional patterns is underscored by a concentration of cedar uprights located in the center of the Great Mortuary deposit without any discernable support function (Figure 3.2). These posts were four to six inches in diameter and were planted in such a manner as to be a hindrance to free movement among the litters and other interments (Brown 1996; Duffield 1973; Hamilton 1952).

Duffield (1973) drew attention to the "anomalous" placement of the posts in the layout of the Great Mortuary and sought to explain them by referring to ethnographic examples from elsewhere in the Southeast. His basic argument is plausible—these posts implemented a plan to provide the tangible means for connecting those using the steadily mounting surface of the overlying mound cap with the powerful sacra entombed beneath as the Great Mortuary tableau (Duffield 1973). As an integrated tableau, the remains piled within this ossuary deposit conveyed power up through the poles erected above the Great Mortuary. The potentially instrumental uses of the poles studding the mound are self-evident.

What are some of the cosmological dimensions of this deposit? Multiple sources of information allow us to assemble a composite picture of the Great Mortuary. Despite the limitations of the excavations and the recovery techniques employed, the systematic work of employees of the Works Progress Administration (WPA) provided much-needed contextual information, sparse and relatively inadequate as it is. This work operated under severe limitations because a relic-mining operation had devastated the center of the display floor, which was the best-preserved portion and constituted 14 percent (25 m^2) of the 190 m^2 total. Statements elicited from the relic miners that were integrated with the records compiled by the WPA-sponsored excavation partially compensated for this handicap. Although the exploits of relic hunters have spawned many misimpressions about the Great Mortuary, a certain amount of substantial detail can be retrieved by careful reevaluation of the available information (Brown 1996). This is not to say that the conclusions are completely satisfactory. Follow-up investigations sponsored by the WPA did not adopt advanced professional record keeping, even by the standards of the day. Sifting screens were used only occasionally, and items contained within a grave lot were logged to a central location within an ad hoc cluster of artifacts and bones. Hence, detailed information on the precise locations of artifacts was frustratingly weak. Grave lots were defined by clusters of objects that included human remains, and context within the earthwork was not systematically recorded (Brown 1996). Consequently, we are forced to rely on photographs and circumstantial details (where these resources were available) for crucial stratigraphic information.

These shortcomings aside, the overall pattern of burial treatment at the Spiro Great Mortuary is strikingly different from the "standard" view of Mississippian Period mortuary practices in which the deceased were typically interred individually in purpose-built pits. Primary articulated skeletons were placed in an extended supine position, often accompanied by one or more ceramic vessels and less frequently accompanied by other grave goods. Rarely has this form of treatment been observed in Eastern Oklahoma prior to 1400, but it is conspicuous in the near-contemporaneous cemeteries near Spiro in the Fort Coffee area. The Moore and Braden Schoolhouse sites stand out as excellent examples (Orr 1946; Rohrbaugh 1982, 1984).

The cosmographic content of the Great Mortuary complies with the criteria listed above. Foremost, and very strongly represented, was the ossuary treatment of disarticulated human remains. Williamson and Pfeiffer (2003; Hutchinson and Aragon 2002; Ubelaker 1974) have reviewed this kind of treatment of human remains in other archaeological contexts. At Spiro, collective representation in burial was marked first by a scattering of bones commingled with broken artifacts. Indeed, in many instances it would be proper to speak of bones alone. But even in disarticulation, bone patterning revealed that the dead were treated in diverse ways (Brown 1971, 1996). The Great Mortuary was composed of at least two layers of interments in which the first or lower osseous mass of disarticulated bone was mixed with broken artifacts. This basal layer was evidently retrieved from preexisting graves with little regard for their original integrity as individuals. The human bone was heavily mineralized through immersion beneath the water table, and grayish-green clay was clinging to some of the bone and artifacts (Brown 1981b). This clay was observed during lab processing of the human bone. It was also documented on the one wooden human figure known from the Great Mortuary (Brose et al. 1985, Plate 96; Brown 1975, Figure 8; Hamilton 1952, Plate 26 left). Since the time that Henry Hamilton (1952: 40) photographed this wooden sculpture, it has been cleaned to reveal a carefully carved figure (Brose et al. 1985).

Grave wealth and artifacts with potential residual sacred power were smashed and the fragments broadcast among the piles of bone. Collective principles clearly prevailed in the scattering of broken engraved and unengraved shell cups and other artifacts, such as jars, bowls, and bottles. In his review of Iroquoian practices, Spence (1994) considers such mixing to be a defining criterion of ossuary treatment. Cross-mends of engraved marine shell and decorated pottery document the scattering of potsherds, engraved marine shell fragments, and other materials (Brown 1996: 72). Unusual natural objects (e.g., a mastodon molar) were subjected to the same treatment.

Superimposed upon these bones were three categories of formally defined burials and numerous deposits of artifacts of different kinds—litter burials, extended rearticulated burials, and burials in a small container.

These superordinate graves consisted of an estimated 14 litters constructed of cedar poles. The litter burials were composed of incomplete skeletons, often of token bones. Disarticulated remains were placed within a litter, which was constructed on the spot and in a way that does not suggest that they were portable.

A second mode of interment was composed of nine partly articulated (and even rearticulated) extended skeletons. These relatively articulated individuals were distributed without apparent order within the litters and boxes. Although these excarnated burials showed limited articulosis, ample evidence of advanced postmortem decay was present in the loss of bones, particularly the extremities (Ubelaker 1974; Brown 1996). The single possible exception to this pattern of secondary treatment was the well-preserved skull complete with a woven headband that relic hunters removed from the hollow cavity above the center of the Great Mortuary (Brown 1996: Figure 2.10 a–c).[3] The well-preserved skull showed no sign of the mineralization that is diagnostic of a history of immersion in waterlogged soils.

The third mode is composed of the 18 or so lidded twillwork boxed "burials" that were interments in the sense that some contained human teeth and small bones. Brown (1996: 311) cited them as a third burial mode although they can be thought of more usefully as ceremonial bundles (see below). Labels make a difference here because "ritual bundles" draws attention to spiritual involvement that is absent from the more socially abstract term "interment types."

A symbolic display of burials superimposed upon a large number of nondistinct ones constitutes a powerful statement of hierarchy (Figure 3.3). When an arrangement in distinctly defined rows is added to this image, there is little room for considering this burial display as anything less than a cosmological formulation. The rows are dominated by an antique funerary bier— in this case a litter—interspersed with more up-to-date extended treatments. In between these high-status burials lay the sacred bundles housed in floatweave baskets. The litter burials, an arguably long-superseded form of burial treatment by A.D. 1400, were arranged in three rows from north to south according to descending size (4 m^2 to 0.5 m^2), in what amounts to the subordination of the ancestral dead to an orthogonal grid.

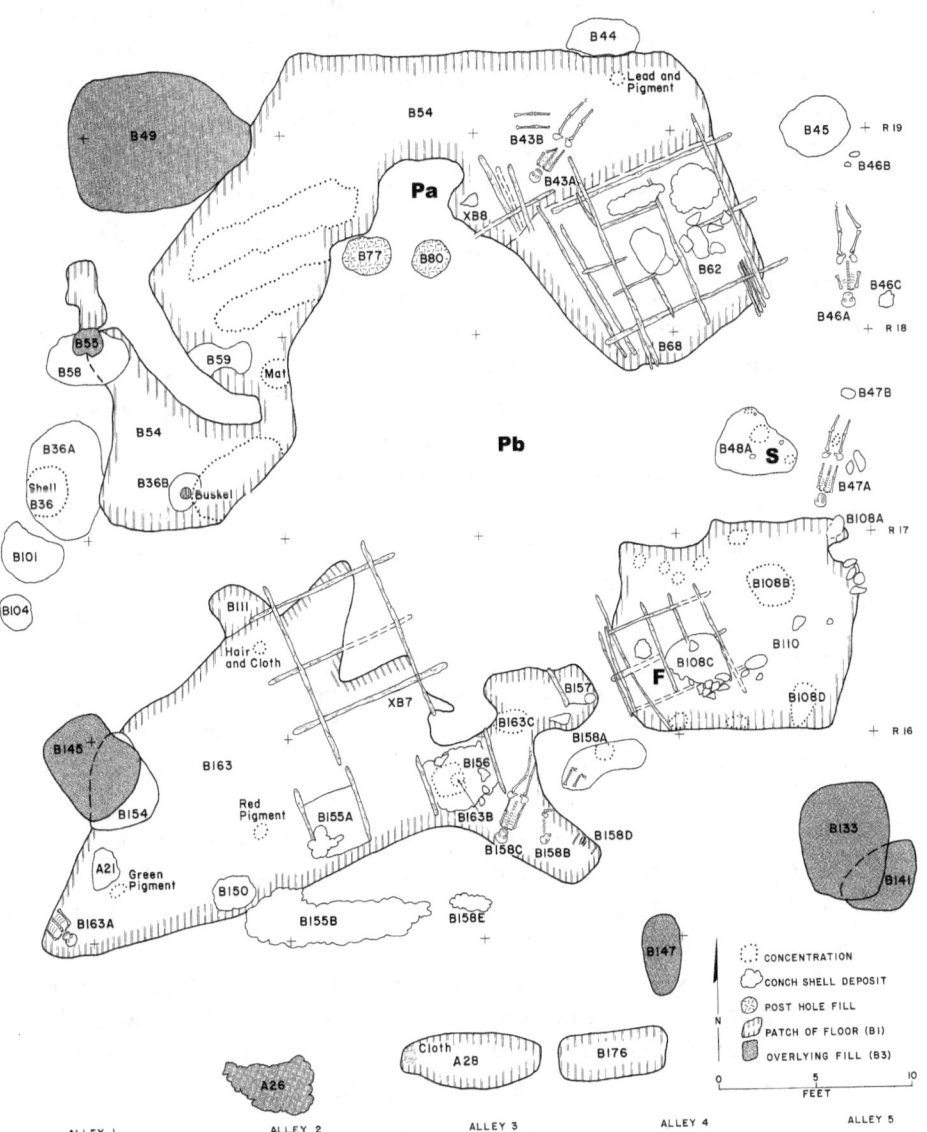

Figure 3.3. Great Mortuary Plan with Rows. Area S denotes the location of the cache of *Olivella dama* shells. Area Pa denotes the location of the red claystone Birdman pipe and the red catlinite snake elbow. Area Pb denotes the location of the white Earth Mother pipe and the dark gray "bird over recumbent human" pipe. Area F denotes the location of the set of wooden mortuary figurines. After Brown 1996: Figure 1.30.

Sacred Bundles

The burial category of basket box refers to lidded floatweave baskets that contained human remains. One particularly well-preserved example in the collections of the University of Arkansas Museum (UAM 37-1-151) serves as an exemplar of its type since other examples are less well preserved. Its description comes from the report by Brown (1996: 414–415, Figures 2-46). The construction of the rectangular body is twillwork of split cane in a floatweave pattern. It measures about 48 cm long, 29 cm wide, and 9.5 cm high. The lid is a complicated double-layer affair stiffened by heavy cane splints inserted into the broad square panels of twillwork in a floatweave pattern . A colorful outer surface was created by dividing the lid into six blocks of floatweave squares that appear to have been dyed black. The lid is either a separate part that telescopes over a box or is somehow a woven extension of one side of the box. It measures about 54.5 cm long, 29 cm wide, and 3.2 cm deep.

The contents remaining within this basket are illustrative of what one might expect in a bundle (Brown 1996: 416). A large hole of decay in the bottom of the basket means that any inventory is incomplete because of losses as the basket was removed from the ground. What remains is a delicate set of objects. Through cautious examination the following could be identified: 1) one broken wooden-handled copper ax; 2) many broken pieces of copper plate (including at least one instance of work in repoussé); 3) one bone pin inserted in a copper hair ornament; 4) three sections of bone pins; 5) one broken Busycon shell pendant; 6) many marine-shell beads (both disc and convexocylindrical); and 7) pearl beads.

Hamilton's so-called Shield, a flattened box separated from its lid, is another notable specimen of baskets of this type; it is housed in the collection at the Smithsonian Institution National Museum of Natural History (Hamilton 1952: Pl. 67). Another noteworthy example of a floatweave basket is the bottom of a basket preserved beneath a cache of wooden-handled copper axes of the "woodpecker head" form, located at the Smithsonian's National Museum of the American Indian (Burnett 1945). Other instances caught the attention of the relic collectors. On the western side of the hollowed chamber was a "straw or reed basket containing thirty human head masks made of wood and covered with copper" (Hamilton 1952: 30, Plates 5, 27, 28a). On the east side were "ten 'copper covered reed baskets' and four breast plates of copper" (Hamilton 1952: 30).[4] Outside the hollow chamber portion of the Great Mortuary, copper was present that clearly helped preserve the underlying basketry. These include the copper-headed axes and the stacks of copper plates. The importance of copper as a preservative is shown by the ghost images on the surfaces of some plates. Under the dome of the Great Mortuary, such aids to preservation were not required because the location was protected from moisture. Indeed, black-dyed sections of twillwork revealing elaborate floatweave designs were well preserved (Brown 1996).

For some time I regarded these twillwork boxes as merely specialized receptacles for bones—a smaller version of the bone boxes that early depictions show to have been used to store the cleaned remains of the elite dead. I was influenced by John White's intriguing illustration of bone baskets stacked inside the mortuaries of the Carolinian tidewater (Lorant 1946). Yet the presence at Spiro of many isolated floatweave basket lids, sides, and isolated scraps considerably complicates the applicability of the Carolinian example for this location (Brown 1996: Figure 2.46).[5] Whether human remains ever accompanied these parts is not known; nevertheless all of these boxes have to be regarded as sacred bundles. It is certainly problematic to assume that the former social identity of the deceased was signaled by the occasional inclusion of human bone. Consequently, these bundles constitute excellent examples of the instrumental use of human bone.

Artifacts of Collective Representation

In addition to the (usually broken) artifacts commingled with human bone, the Great Mortuary contained highly visible stacks, piles, and baskets of specific artifacts. Conspicuous among these were the four stacks of cloth kilts, capes, and other garments that were meticulously folded and placed one on top of the other. Relic hunters often noted these textiles in their accounts of the contents of the protected cave-like space over the floor of the Great Mortuary (Brown 1996; Hamilton 1952). In this context they were protected from percolating ground water (Brown 1996; Hamilton 1952).

At least four thickly piled stacks of extraordinarily well-preserved textiles were placed at separate locations within the central "hollow" portion of the Great Mortuary. Piles of marine-shell beads were placed on top of each stack. According to Jenna Kuttruff (1993), special display features were encoded in these textiles, which were likely to have been newly woven for the event.

The caches of marine-shell beads used at this site include over 20 different shapes and sizes. Pearl beads were numerous, and their fine condition inspired dreams of riches in the imagination of relic hunters (Clements 1945). Elsewhere, marine-shell beads filled Busycon cup containers. In this and other instances, the arrangement and placement of objects in the Great Mortuary are arguably restatements of principles that are obscure to us, at least for the present. For instance, cardinality appears to be relevant to placement (Figure

3.3). According to Hamilton's (1952) research, a claystone figure of Birdman was positioned at the extreme north of the Great Mortuary.[6] At the opposite end the wooden mortuary figurines were placed more or less in a single group. The eastern and western positions were occupied by the baskets noted previously.

More comprehendible are the distributions that can be read as allocations of wealth. Items of display wealth were piled in direct proportion to the size of the litters, which act as status-declaring funeral biers (Brown 1996: 189). At least some of the floatweave box bundles held copper plates and copper-headed axes. Baskets contained copper-headed wooden axes, beads, crumpled copper plates, and other artifacts.

The presence of exotic materials declared connections with distant geographical areas. A round-bottomed basket containing over 400 Pacific Coast beads of *Olivella dama* was positioned among other items without association with any specific individual ([LfCrI B48–1], Brown 1996: 721, Figure 9, 2004b; Kozuch 2002). A cloth of cotton was sandwiched between a layer of cane twillwork and a stack of copper plates (King and Gardner 1981). This cloth example was found in Gravelot A6 located north of the Great Mortuary but lying at the same elevation (Brown 1981b, 1996: 672). Both date from the fourteenth century, and cross-mends connect them as well. Physical associations support the conclusion that a cane floatweave box bundle enclosed the cloth-wrapped plates (Brown and Rogers 1999). Another exotic item was an obsidian scraper reported to have been found lying on the floor of the major tunnel the relic hunters plundered (Barker et al. 2002: 204–5). This tunnel led into the Great Mortuary directly from the north and at the same elevation (Hamilton 1952: Plate 1; Merriam and Merriam 2004: Photograph 18). While this context provides only a circumstantial association, it fits most comfortably with the pattern established by the circa A.D. 1400 timeline of the *Olivella* beads and the cotton cloth.[7]

Objects that logically embodied sacred forces received special treatment. Rather than being smashed, they were carefully interred in ritually significant locations. One was a large red claystone ("flint clay") figurine-cum-pipe of Birdman (the so-called Big Boy pipe) that was completely intact; other figurines of the same mineral had deliberately been broken (Brown 1996: 522–523; Emerson and Hughes 1999; Emerson, Hargrave, and Hedman 2003). Also in the northern locations was a red-stemmed pipe with a monstrous ("dog") head at the prow and a rattlesnake image on its underside (Hamilton 1952: 39, Plate 22b). Two additional massive pipes were placed near the center—one of Earth Mother, the other of the raptor over recumbent human (Hamilton 1952: Pls. 6, 15). Both were unbroken. Five or more seemingly intact carved wooden statues (Brown 1975, 1996: 531, 2001; Hamilton 1952: 40) were placed together in the southeastern quadrant of the mortuary floor, probably on or near litter B-108 (Figure 3.3).

Collective principles prevailed at the Great Mortuary: with the exception of one burial, single individuals did not seem to have a clear association with objects and hence are without grave goods. Objects of a single kind are piled together, quite contrary to the usual pattern of distributive association of artifacts with burials, as is so clearly exemplified in the Etowah Mound C elite burials (Larson 1971). At the Great Mortuary, both skeletons and artifacts were scattered as fragments rather than as complete entities.

Burial Treatments of Collective Representation

The Great Mortuary exemplifies collective action in many ways. The material signatures are the following:

1) Absence of identity markings for burials;
2) Arbitrary allocation of bits of skeletons and artifacts in the burial spaces;
3) Incorporation of human remains within sacred bundles; and
4) Superimposition over the massive ossuary of reinterred human bone by formal burials (litter and extended).

By themselves, human bones lose their individual identity. In a commingled state human remains have a suppressed identity, particularly when represented either by a handful of bone and teeth in a litter or box burial or by a mixture of bone with artifacts. Even the scraps of bone enclosed within grave facilities could easily have lost their original identity after they had been separated from graves that yielded the bone that contributed to the commingled mass (Brown 1996). The central chamber yielded an exception, cited above, in the form of a well-preserved skull (with hair) wearing a woven headband in place. Just what might have been associated with this skull in the sense used here is difficult to evaluate and the reported association is too tenuous to constitute an exception. In one of the extended burials, grave goods were placed on the skeleton in the form of a copper "chisel" ax head (Brown 1996: 692–3).

At the Great Mortuary, human remains are anonymous in several ways. Most obviously, the bones contained within sacred bundles retain potency while remaining concealed. The scattering of remains over the surface of the Great Mortuary floor is another example of anonymity. Many of these bones are fragmentary rather than complete. Other expressions of anonymity are subsumed within distinctive interment practices. Litter burials, for example, are sparsely provided with bones. In one case (B62) at least two individuals are present. The "single" extended treatment is less straightforward. The individual interred as an extended burial is partly disarticulated. It could have become excarnated through exposure to the elements. The clearest instance of this treatment comes from the Brown Mound (BrB3/5) (Brown 1996: Figure 2–6a). The collective principles exemplified by the disarticulated burials are reinforced by the superposition of the formal burials (litter and extended burials) upon the massive layers of scattered remains.

The Great Mortuary as a Cosmogram

The Great Mortuary possessed an apparent design that amounted to a culturally coded message that reiterated the principle of collectivity. The burials for the most part were exhumed remains with consequently suppressed identities. Their grave goods were deliberately dispersed as an expression of collective solidarity. They seemed to be placed in accord with notions of suitable distribution that was current at the time of construction.

The organization of the Great Mortuary becomes more clear in comparison to a much earlier (Spiro II grave period) shaft grave in the nearby Brown Mound (BrB6). Here, at least 13 flexed individuals were massed at the base of the grave with few identifiable grave goods (Brown 1996). Centered on top of this mass was a small litter grave that held the fragmentary remains of a single cremated adult individual. Twenty-five unengraved Busycon shell cups were place within this apical funeral bier. Shamanic charms were present—fire-shattered quartz and siderite crystals were mixed with the cremated remains, and an owl-effigy staff of wood was associated with the burial. If we treat the Brown Mound example as a precedent for the Great Mortuary, then we have the earlier presence of a simpler expression of the principle of superposition and the association of shell cups with the uppermost litter burial.

Cosmological principles can be detected in at least five respects.

1. Individual identities of the dead were submerged within a collective whole. Personhood was lost (Brown 2003). The ossuary of bone was accompanied by smashed and scattered pieces of objects of high value. Copper objects were folded or crumpled. In contrast, sacred bundles, through which spiritual powers were derived, and a select number of other artifacts remained intact. One explanation for this dichotomy is the operation of a distinction between corporate versus individual possessions. Bundles could logically fall into the former category and all other items (including natural curiosities) into the latter.[8]

2. The square shape of the litters is reiterated by organizing the ritual space into a quadrilateral of litters arranged in rows. An artistic composition that is present on at least two of the engraved shell cups exemplifies this quadrilateral conception of the universe. One cup in the Craig B style has a square center flanked by winged rattlesnakes arranged in the four quarters (Figure 3.4). Here as well as elsewhere in the Southeast these winged snakes are linked with the lord of souls in its nighttime sky mode (Lankford 2007c). The principle of the four quarters is replicated by this composition. A parallel likewise exists with the square-sided litter.
3. The litter burials were few in number and ordered by decreasing size from north to south. A cosmic rule would seem to operating, although one should not exclude the concept of the memory of a succession of leaders or individuals of outstanding spiritual attainment. Of course, both a memory of history and cosmic rule may have been the faces of the same underlying belief and practice.

Figure 3.4. Drawing of the Outer Surface of Craig B Cup 229. Winged rattlesnakes arranged in four directions around a central square; from Philip Phillips and James A. Brown, *Pre-Columbian Shell Engraving from the Craig Mound at Spiro, Oklahoma*, part 2, paperback edition, Peabody Museum Press, copyright 1978 by the President and Fellows of Harvard College. Plate 229.

4. The passage of time is established conceptually by the intermingling of old forms of interment (litter burial) with contemporaneous (extended) ones.
5. The Great Mortuary can be regarded as a social sandwich in which the higher orders lie on top of the lower orders, symbolized by the disarticulated remains scattered over the floor. The higher order possesses ideologically charged identity but not personal identity.

The major message conveyed by the cosmogram is the subordination of the collectivity to a stable conception of the cosmos, which was dominated by an ordered hierarchy and was graded within orders by rank. The increase in litter size from south to north grades each row. Potentially, this position with respect to north marks rank and possibly historical order as well. Such an order emerges from the contrast of old forms of interment (litters) intermingled with contemporaneous (extended) ones.

The Spiro Mound Group Cosmogram

Cosmological principles are found embedded in many town plans, and no more so than in the design of Cahokia (Chappell 2002; Fowler 1996) and Moundville (Knight 1998). Solar references appear to be paramount at Spiro. The placement of ritual structures at Spiro exemplifies these principles (Brown 1996; Sherrod and Rolingson 1987). The axial orientation of the Great Mortuary appears to be determined by equinoctial or some other type of observation (Figure 3.5). The same solar observations have been argued for in the Goforth Saindon case (Kay and Sabo 2006). Beginning with the tenth century, solar observations are strongly implicated at Spiro by the orientations of shrine doorways to the equinox and to the summer and winter sunrises/sunsets. Other kinds of social and/or spiritual origins are implied by the placement of mounded structures on the settlement landscape. Prominent landmarks and other features appear to have been used as sightlines to position these structures around a plaza (Figure 3.5; Brown 1996). That principle finds parallel expression within the Great Mortuary, where litter burials are ranked north to south by size and position. All of this was contained within a thoroughly implemented set of practices to submerge the individual identities of the dead.

Comparative Cosmologies

A very different pattern is present in the disposition of burials on the platform of the first mound stage of Submound 1 in Cahokia Mound 72. There,

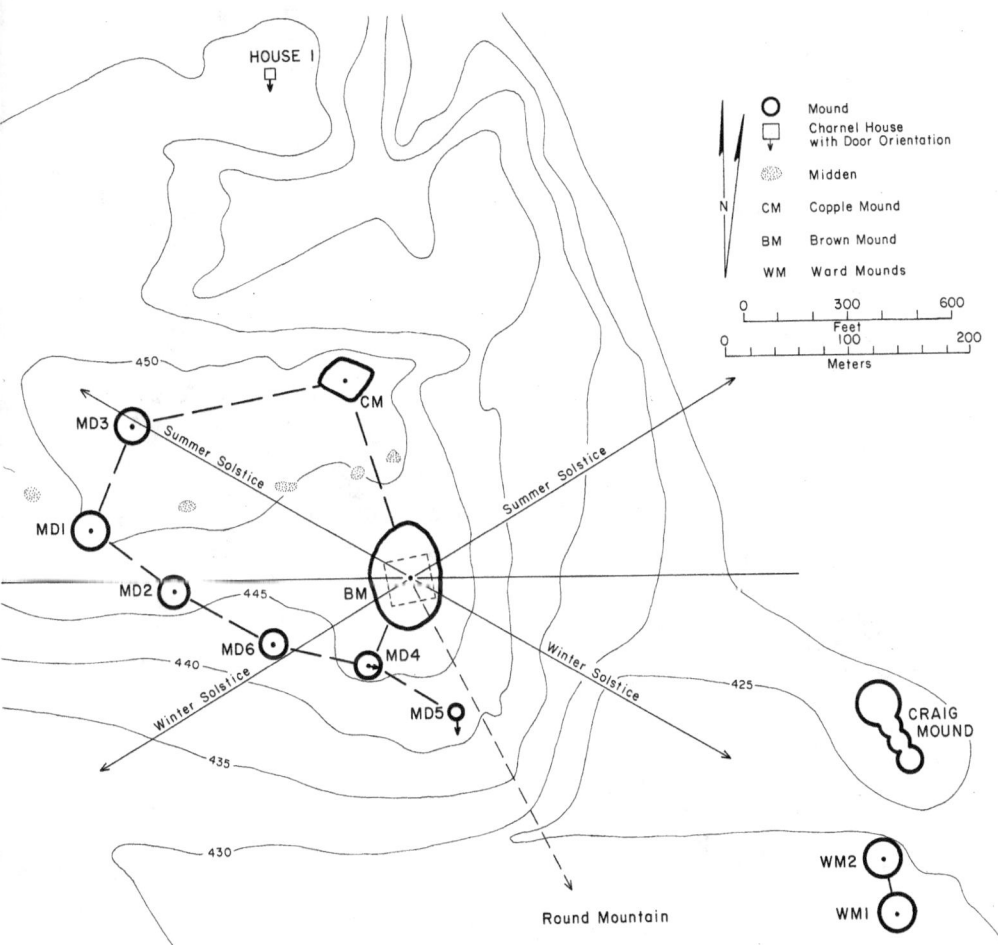

Figure 3.5. Spiro Mound Group as a Solsticial Organization. From Brown 1996: Figure 1.6.

the treatment of the dead is not dominated by multiple ways of subordinating the identities of the dead to the cosmos. Bones and corpses are arranged as actors in a drama, obviously one that referenced cosmic principles. The ideographic arrangement of the dead on this level surface was qualitatively different from the more typical allocation of a specific grave created for the interment of one or two dead individuals (Figure 3.6). Whereas the burials underlying Mound 72 played out an epic narrative around a focal mythic identity (the beaded burial), the Spiro Great Mortuary used bones and objects reclaimed largely from disinterred graves to elaborate a cosmological model of the North Caddoan social body. Rank, hierarchy, and privilege are exemplified by the ordered rows of burial biers of the hallowed dead, sized and oriented to

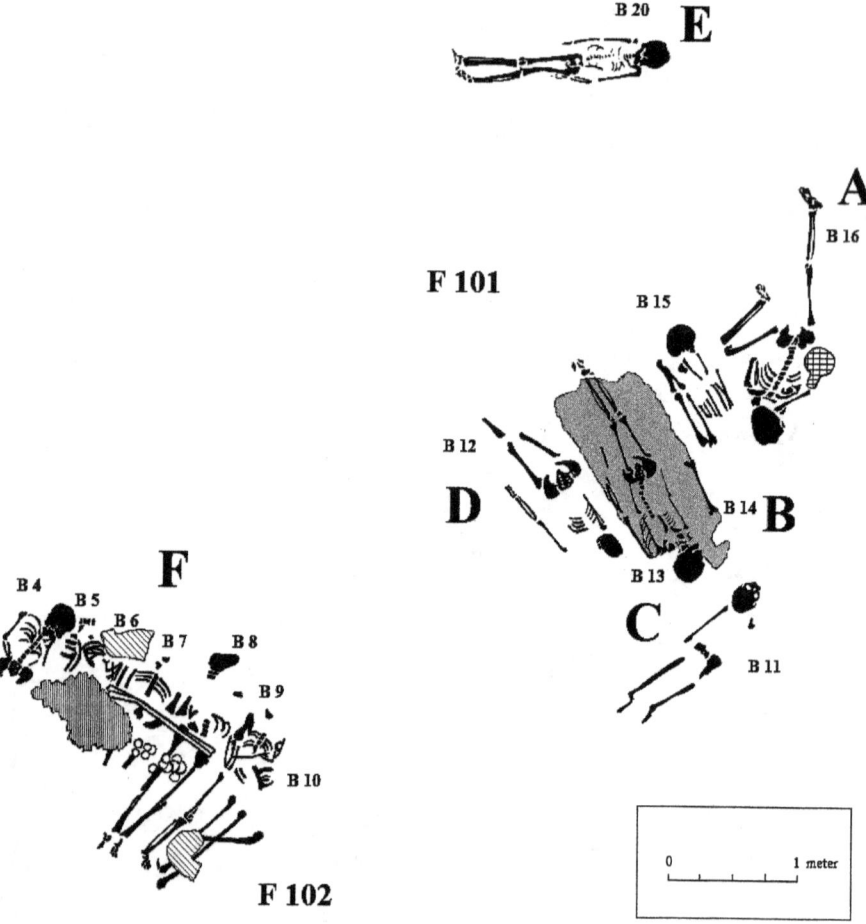

Figure 3.6. Detail of Burials at Cahokia Mound 72 Submound 1. Inset shows layout of the surface of Submound 1. From Brown 2006a: Figures 10.1 and 10.2.

emphasize privilege. That privilege is not necessarily social but more likely is spiritual. The wide scattering of broken artifacts among isolated disarticulated remains nullifies any overt attempt to memorialize the dead as individuals. This treatment of bones and objects is more compatible with an emphasis on spiritual connections and the ideology of the sacred order (Parker Pearson 1999: 94). Consequently, a hierarchy of adepts in accessing spiritual power ("shamans") is implied that has weak political implications. No narrative of collective purpose is present here, only a social map of the cosmos, presumably one laid down initially in times long past (Table 3.1).

Table 3.1. Number of Individuals Placed on the Great Mortuary Floor

	WPA[a]	Hamilton	Estimated Additional[b]	Totals
Upper Layer:				
Buried on Litters	3	1	10	14
Extended Position	9	1	--	10
Buried in Boxes	2	10	6	18
Basal Layer:	37	--	14	41

Source: Brown 1996.
Notes: [a]By field count. See Brown 1996 for details.
[b]By osteological count of Dr. Alice Brues.

The number of dead involved with the Great Mortuary constitutes an important point when comparing tableaus. The actual count for the WPA work is substantial, but it could easily have been much higher if the observed density of human remains extended to the potted area of the Great Mortuary, for which we do not have credible observations. As a point of comparison, high populations have been estimated for other excavated ossuaries. The famous Huron Feast of the Dead grave pit of 1636 that Brébeuf described contained parts of at least 1,000 dead by the excavator's estimation (Kidd 1953: 363). The pit was 7.3 m deep, and the ossuary mass was 1.5 m thick at its maximum.

The number of dead at Submound 1 of Cahokia Mound 72 appears to differ dramatically from that of the Great Mortuary. The burial count is small (8 in F#101 and F#103; 7 in F#102). But if these dead correspond to only the upper burials in the Great Mortuary, then the identification of a logical lower burial component in the Mound 72 case would alter the comparison between the two cases. Contemporary burial features from the opposite, northern end of Mound 72 could constitute a conceptual equivalent to the basal layer of the Great Mortuary (Goldstein 2000: 197). One large collective burial pit (F#237) includes 19 individuals, and the other pit of similar size and function (F#214) yielded 24 (Brown 2003; Porubcan 2000). When these pit burials are conceptualized as equivalent to the Great Mortuary basal layer, the ratio of "upper" Submound 1 dead to "lower" massed pit burials approximates the ratio between upper and lower burial layers of the Great Mortuary.

The differences in the layout of burials and the distribution of grave offerings of Submound 1 of Cahokia Mound 72 and the Spiro Great Mortuary contribute to the distinctiveness of each. But what looks at first judgment to be another difference becomes upon plausible adjustment a similarity in proportional pattern in the treatment of the dead. The possibility that the Great Mortuary pattern and that of Submound 1 are structurally similar raises new directions for research. An argument can be advanced that unites their social purposes as divergent ways of achieving the same goal of social reproduction. That said, the ways in which the two examples conceived of reproduction was about as different as one could suppose. How much of this difference is due to the gap in time (at least two centuries) is difficult to assess with the scanty comparative evidence available. Even bearing in mind the temporal separation, a cultural gulf nevertheless seems to have separated the two examples.

Conclusion

The clearly exhibitory manner in which secondary burials were displayed in the Great Mortuary help frame the ways this chapter has conceived of the potential for secondary burial treatments to tap into insights that archaeological cosmograms provide. I have argued that cosmological principles were applied redundantly in Spiro society in about A.D. 1400 to achieve the display that is known archaeologically. The cosmological beliefs of a particular community are exemplified in the format in which disarticulated bones and skeletal segments are used together with artifacts.

This analysis could have been accomplished only with a focus on the placement of human remains in a tableau of sorts. This perspective has connections with approaches that seek landscapes of the dead and that place great stress on the role of performance in the treatment of the dead. One of the fruits of this approach is the capacity to isolate the culturally perceived priorities different societies seek through collective action. While both Submound 1 of Cahokia Mound 72 and the Spiro Great Mortuary burials are collective in nominal terms, they differ in their priorities and their cultural heritage, and these aspects can be detected in the ways that secondary remains were displayed.

Although patterns of secondary burial disposition are very different in each case, both represent the effect of social action to create and enhance political change through the deployment of burials in a cosmological plan or cosmogram. In neither case can it be shown that differences in social rank are the identities that are being marked by material means.

While relatively little literature has been devoted to the symbolic aspect of burial record, the manner in which human bones are displayed obviously takes on the forms that are significant to specific cultural formations—whether they be small scale in the case of individual communities or very large where major religious traditions operate. The cosmological format of the mortuary event at the Spiro site in eastern Oklahoma called the Great Mortuary is a case in point. The specificity of that format is brought into relief by comparison with comparable formats in other places during the Mississippi Period.

Notes

1. The Evans phase is commonly not set off from the Harlan phase, thereby making later interregional connections even more of a mystery than is necessary (e.g., Kay and Sabo 2006; Rogers 1996).

2. For additional insight we have to draw upon ceramic cross-ties to directly dated sites in the neighboring Fort Coffee area. Stylistic similarities in ceramics suggest a cutoff date of around 1450 (Rogers 2006).

3. Dellinger wrote a letter to Hamilton reporting that he had bought this skull and other items on site from the diggers themselves. At the time they were bringing objects out of the entry tunnel from their work in the hollow chamber (Hamilton 1952: 33).

4. This is a reference to the four exceptionally large copper plates that formerly were part of the A. T. Werhle Collection and are now at the Ohio Historical Society. Before they were cleaned they were covered with ghost impressions of patterned twillwork. All were folded, and two were also covered with the ghost image of other plates in the batch. They appear to have been included in one or two baskets.

5. The largest collection of floatweave pieces and other fiber artifacts was amassed by MacDannald and is now deposited in the Houston Museum of Natural Science.

6. Hamilton's plan views of the hollow chamber layout are oriented incorrectly. The entryway tunnels actually are oriented due north (see Figure 3.2). Once the orientation is corrected, the position of these complete objects aligns with the cardinal directions.

7. Note that this tunnel (judged from photographs to be somewhere around 1.5 m high and 1.2 m wide) shows up in the center of Figure 3.2, where it intrudes into the floor level of the Great Mortuary. A unique obsidian scraper that was donated to the Smithsonian by collector and dealer J. C. Braecklein was picked up on the floor of a tunnel, according to the label he made out (Barker et al. 2002). Undoubtedly this tunnel was the one that provided the most comfortable access for visitors (although it was very daunting for Dellinger; Hamilton 1952: 33).

8. One potentially interesting interpretation is that the complete objects were involved directly in the ritual activities connected with the installation of the Great Mortuary, whereas the broken-up majority of objects were essentially fixtures in the construction of the elaborate burial display.

4

Multiple Groups, Overlapping Symbols, and the Creation of a Sacred Space at Etowah's Mound C

ADAM KING

There is a long tradition in the in the scholarship on the Southeast to interpret mortuary treatment as a way to understand ranking systems and the social status of individuals. This tradition is based on the presumption of a direct relationship between investment in mortuary treatment and social status—a proposal that derives from seminal works by Saxe (1970) and Binford (1971). The application of this so-called Binford-Saxe paradigm in the Southeast was first seen in an influential volume edited by James Brown (1971) containing not only papers by Binford (1971) and Saxe (1971), but also papers on Spiro (Brown 1971), Moundville (Peebles 1971), and Etowah (Larson 1971). The paradigm gained popularity through influential works by Jim Hatch (1974, 1976a, 1976b) on the Dallas area of Tennessee, Chris Peebles's work on Moundville (Peebles and Kus 1977), and George Milner's (1984) writing about the American Bottom. A look at the pages of this volume or recent issues of *Southeastern Archaeology* will show that this approach to exploring mortuary behavior continues to be used productively in the Southeast region.

Critiques of the Binford-Saxe paradigm abound (see McGuire 1992 for a review). They all center on the realization that the material world is part of social action and that material manifestations of death must be viewed as part of the actions of the living. From this perspective, although investment in mortuary treatment may be related to social status, the relationship is not always a direct one. In some cases, the material may be used to mask social inequality rather than reflect it (McGuire 1988). In order to ensure that we do not misinterpret the past or miss opportunities for interpretation, it is important to understand that funerals are as much about the living as they are about the dead—about negotiating ideology, interacting with tradition, creating or recreating society. In all burial rites, the death of the individual becomes part of the larger community's efforts to influence the natural and supernatural worlds. In fact, in

Multiple Groups, Overlapping Symbols, and a Sacred Space   55

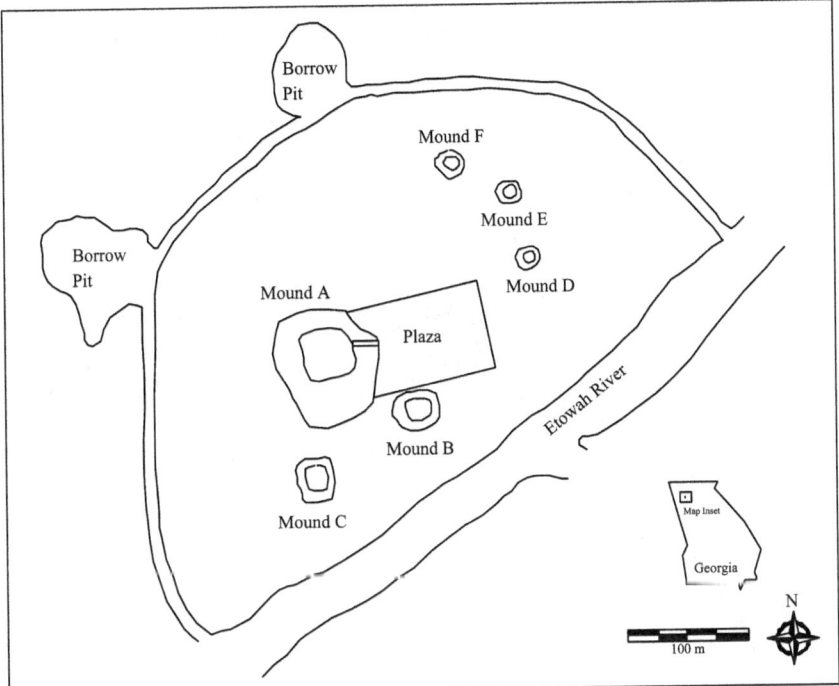

Figure 4.1. Plan Map of the Etowah Site.

some instances, the dead essentially become sacra manipulated for the living, thereby losing their individual status to the good of the community.

The contribution of Lewis H. Larson, Jr. to Brown's edited volume (1971) used the burial record from Mound C at the Etowah site to argue for the presence of social ranking at Etowah and for chiefdoms in the Southeast (Figure 4.1). No one doubts that the burial record of Mound C shows differential burial treatments that are linked to differences in social status in Etowah society. However, as Larson (1971, 1989, 1993) and others (Barker 2004; Brain and Phillips 1996; Brown 2007a; King 2004) have shown, the Mound C record contains information on much more than differential social ranking. Looking beyond Binford-Saxe presents important possibilities for exploring the mortuary data contained in Mound C.

It has long been noted that in addition to differential investment in burial treatment, Mound C contains evidence that multiple groups were buried in the mound. While King (2004) recently has made a case for this in the graves of Mound C from the Early Wilbanks phase (A.D. 1250–1325), Larson (1971; Kelly and Larson 1957) noted spatially discrete burial groupings in the Late

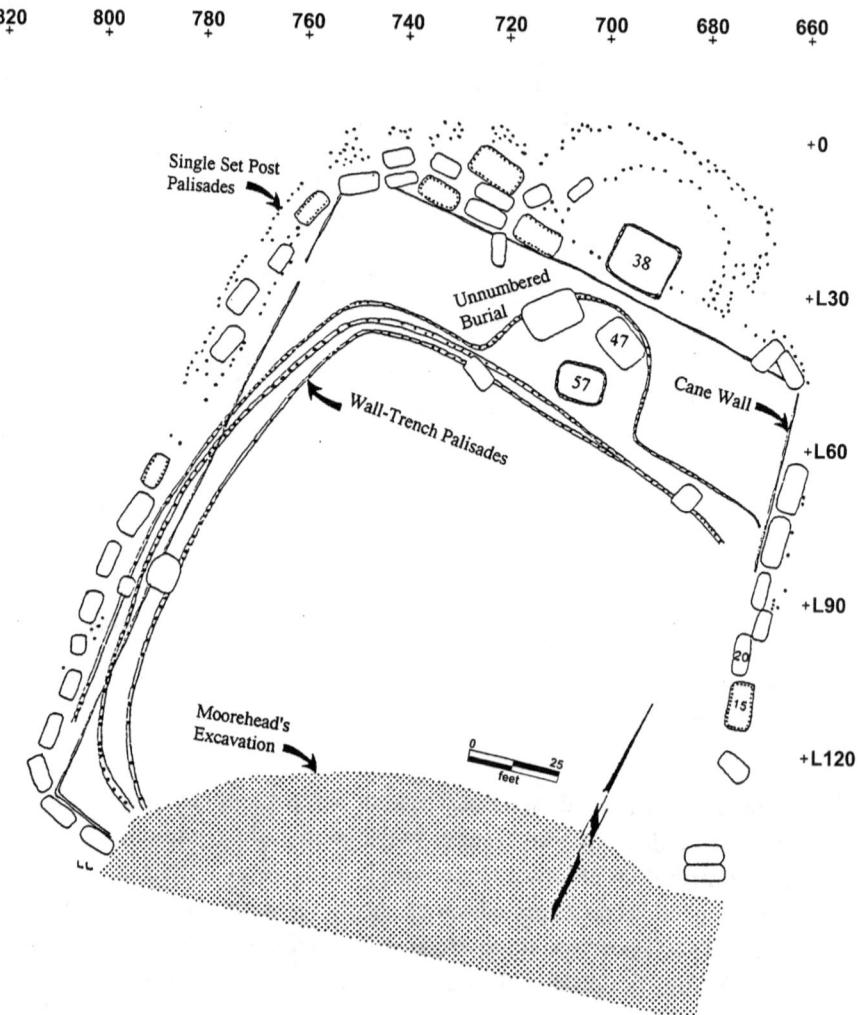

Figure 4.2. Burials Excavated by Larson at Mound C. Adapted from Larson 1971: Figure 2.

Wilbanks phase burials as he excavated them in 1950s and 1960s (Figure 4.2). Brain and Phillips (1996) also discussed the possible interpretations of those groupings in their volume on shell gorget styles. More recently, Jim Brown (2007a) has suggested that those burial groupings may have closely matched Levi-Strauss's idea of the social house. Most influential for this essay is a paper by Alex Barker (2004) that demonstrates a striking correspondence between the burials in the final stage of Mound C at Etowah and the Osage clan structure and mythic cosmology. Barker chooses to use a different arrangement of burials than the one I have reconstructed (King 2004). Despite this difference, his argument that burials in Mound C reflect more than the social status of the individuals buried is compelling.

In this essay my goal is to explore the Late Wilbanks phase portion of the Mound C burial record and particularly to use demographic and artifactual information to more closely examine the nature of the spatial groupings noted so long ago. While I see these groups as containing key information about the nature of elite status at Etowah, I will examine them here as a means of exploring how burial in Mound C was manipulated to meet the ends of the living.

Mound C Excavations and Structure

Before I examine the distribution of artifacts, I review how Mound C was excavated and how I interpret its construction and burial history. Etowah's Mound C has been completely excavated and now stands reconstructed at the site. Those excavations occurred as part of three separate projects spanning the period from 1884 to 1961. John Rogan was the first to work at Mound C, where he investigated a small portion of the summit (Thomas 1894). Warren K. Moorehead's (1932) excavations lasted from 1925 to 1927, during which time his crews removed all of the mound's summits. Finally, Lewis Larson (1971, 1989) began work in 1954 and continued, with a break for graduate school, until 1961. During the course of these excavations, some 350 burials were recorded and excavated. They contained an impressive collection of southeastern artwork associated with a widespread set of styles and themes known as the Southeastern Ceremonial Complex.

For a very long time the complete mortuary data set from Mound C has been relatively inaccessible. This is largely because the field and recording methods used during the three projects were markedly different, making it very difficult to combine the respective data sets. Thanks to the wonders of Geographic Information Systems, we are beginning to unite the data from those three excavations and treat the Mound C data set as a whole.

By combining information from all three excavations, I (King 2003, 2004, 2007) have argued that Mound C was constructed in seven stages (Figure 4.3). The first three date to the Early Wilbanks phase, and the last four were built during the Late Wilbanks phase. The Early Wilbanks graves were placed in the first three summits and around the periphery of the first three stages of the mound. By the Late Wilbanks phase, summit burial had been abandoned. Several key burials were placed along the northern margin of the mound and covered by small appendages or lobes. These lobes will figure prominently in the discussion later. The practice of burying the dead around the base of the

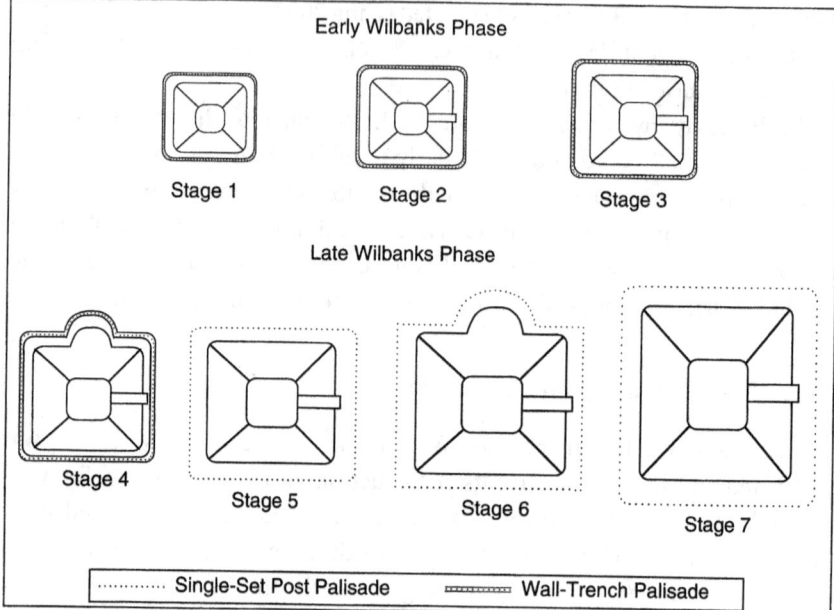

Figure 4.3. Mound C Construction Stages.

mound continued in the Late Wilbanks phase, and this essay focuses on the final set of burials ringing the Late Wilbanks construction stages.

Multiple Groups in Mound C

As noted above, the spatially discrete groupings of the burials of the Late Wilbanks phase have been recognized for some time. In an effort to explore these groupings, I begin by examining the distribution of different kinds of artifacts found in them. To facilitate comparison, I have named each group after its position around the margins of Mound C (NW, NE, SW, and SE; see Figure 4.4).

One of the most elaborate of objects found in these burials are the headdresses made of a wood or bone frame, often covered with hawk skin and feathers and ultimately decorated with copper ornaments (Larson 1959). In the Late Wilbanks contexts (Table 4.1), these clearly appear in multiple burials in each discrete cluster. The same applies to the so-called paint palettes, which Steponaitis (2004) has argued actually are portable altars. The copper celts have a slightly different distribution in that the Northeast group has none. Stone celts, monolithic axes, and chert blades are other examples of artifacts

Table 4.1. Selected Artifacts in the Late Wilbanks Burials

Artifact Type	NW	NE	SW	SE	Lobe	Association
Stone Celt	5	1				North
Chert Blade			2	4		South
Monolithic Axe		1		3		East
Copper Headdress	3	3	2	3	4	All
Stone Palette	2	1	1	1	1	All
Copper Celt	2		1	3	2	All but NE

found in only certain places. The stone celts are found only in the northern groupings, the chert blades only in the southern groupings, and monolithic axes only in groups on the eastern side.

Taken together, these artifacts suggest a series of similarly constituted groups that each contains one or more burials with headdresses decorated with copper, a portable altar, and possibly also a copper celt. At some level these artifacts must refer to some shared status, quality, or association. There are differences among the groups, but, interestingly, individual groups are not distinguished by the presence or absence of specific kinds of artifacts. Instead, particular artifacts are associated with cardinal directions. This almost certainly somehow relates back to cosmological references made by these artifacts or the associated groups.

The fifth grouping in the Late Wilbanks burials—the one associated with the lobes—stands out as different. The location of those lobes, which are appended to the northern side of the mound, is unique and must have some special meaning. Artifactually, the interesting thing about the lobe burials is that contrary to conventional wisdom, they are not the richest in the mound. Compared to the richest burials in the other four clusters, those found in the lobes have a lower diversity of artifacts (Table 4.2). Although they contain the same kinds of objects present in all the other groups (headdresses, copper celts, and portable altars), they lack other kinds of objects that are commonly found in the remaining groups as well as those that seem to distinguish elements of directionality.

The lobe grouping also is distinctive demographically, particularly in its departure from the striking homogeneity of the other groupings (Table 4.3). Each of the four nonlobe clusters contains 11 to 14 graves that include from 12 to 17 people. Adult males dominate each of the four nonlobe clusters; women and non-adults are clearly underrepresented. However, the burials in the lobe cluster are dominated by women; men are distinctly underrepresented.

Table 4.2. Artifact Richness in the Late Wilbanks Burials

Burial	Lobe 57	Lobe 38	SE 109	SW 67	NE 28	NW 45
Headdress w/Copper Plate	X	—	X	X	X	—
Headdress w/Copper Ornament	—	X	X	X	—	X
Other Plate	X	—	—	—	—	—
Copper Celt	X	X	X	—	X	—
Stone Celt	—	—	—	—	X	X
Monolithic Axe	—	—	X	—	—	—
Chert Blade	—	—	X	—	—	—
Copper Ornament	—	—	—	X	X	—
Mica Ornament	—	—	X	X	X	X
Tortoiseshell Ornament	—	—	—	—	—	X
Pottery Vessel	—	—	—	—	X	—
Conch-Shell Vessel	X	—	X	X	—	—
Shell Gorget	X	—	—	—	—	—
Copper Gorget	—	—	—	X	—	—
Portable Stone Altar	—	X	X	—	—	X
Pottery Pipe	—	—	—	—	X	X
Stone Discoidal	—	—	—	—	—	X
Sharks' Teeth	—	—	—	—	—	X
Score	5	3	8	6	8	7

In summary, I think it is reasonable to suggest that there are five distinct groupings in the Late Wilbanks burials. Four of these (NE, NW, SW, and SE in Figure 4.4) likely represent socially redundant corporate kin groups. Demographically and artifactually, there is little to distinguish them. The fifth group (the lobe) is distinct demographically: it has fewer people, and all of them are women.

Table 4.3. Demographic Summary of Late Wilbanks Burials

	NW	SW	NE	SE	Lobes
Graves (N)	14	11	12	11	4
Individuals (N)	17	12	12	11	15
Adult (%)	41	67	75	71	53
Adolescent (%)	18	0	17	0	0
Unknown (%)	41	33	8	29	47
Male (%)	53	50	42	43	6
Female (%)	6	8	16	28.5	47
Unknown (%)	41	42	42	28.5	47
Average Male	35	51	54	40.0	—

Source: Age and sex information for all Mound C burials from analysis completed by Robert Blakely, on file at the Antonio J. Waring Jr., Archaeological Laboratory, University of West Georgia, Carrollton, Georgia.

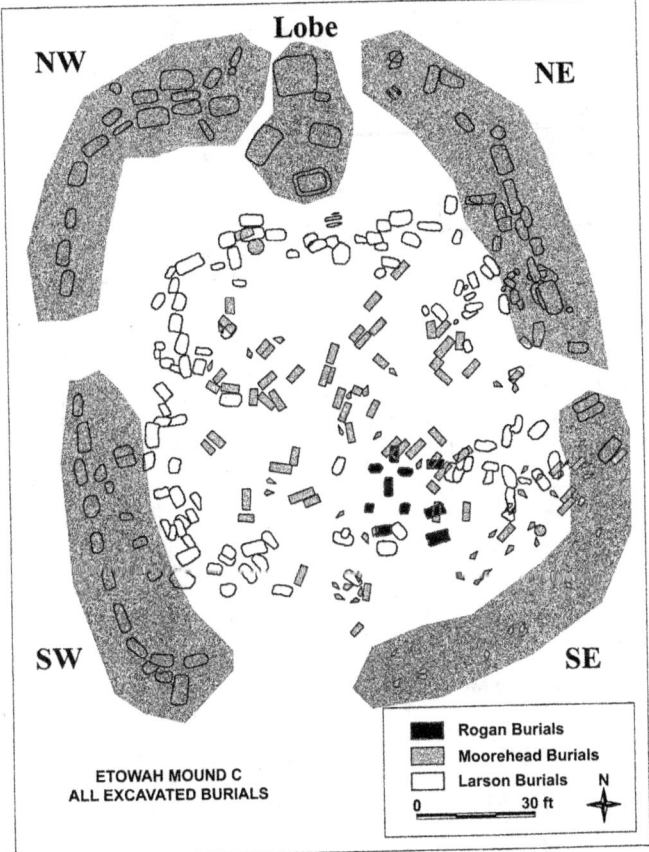

Figure 4.4. Late Wilbanks Burial Groupings.

A Historically Connected and Culturally Appropriate Model

In his article "The Southern Cult and Muskhogean Ceremonial," Antonio Waring (1968) provides us with the beginnings of a useful model for Mound C. In that essay, he notes that one of the primary Creek terms for the Square Ground—where important ceremonies, including the Busk, took place—was translated as "the big house" (Waring 1968: 55). The elements of the Creek Square Ground are well described (Howard 1968; Swanton 1928; Waring 1968) and appear to have been used fairly consistently across groups (Figure 4.5). The Square Ground consists of a specialized space, often defined by a low berm, within which is a central hearth, surrounded by an open space that is in turn flanked at the cardinal directions by covered seating. During ceremonies, the area that is defined by the berm and that is centered on the hearth becomes

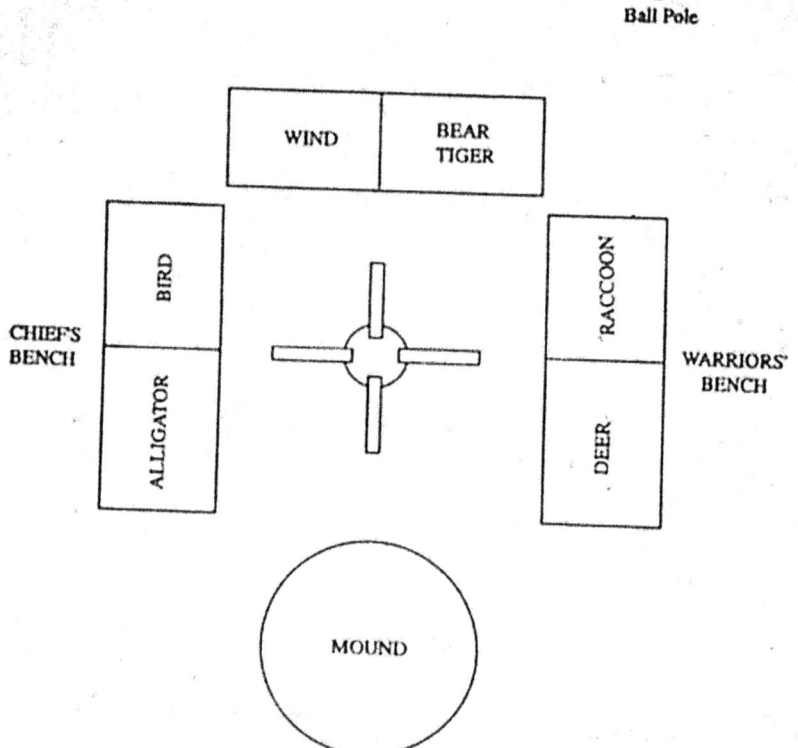

Figure 4.5. Creek Square Ground Structure.

a sacred space. The hearth contains a fire, whose column of smoke creates an axis mundi linking two different realms of the Muskogean cosmos: the Above World where the sun resides and This World where its earthly representative, fire, exists.

As the linguistic link to the house might indicate, the layout of the Square Ground parallels the structure of Mississippian houses in Georgia and eastern Tennessee, the likely homeland of the Upper Creeks (Waselkov and Smith 2000). Square or round (Figure 4.6), residential buildings have a central hearth surrounded by an open space flanked by beds or benches along the walls used for seating, sleeping, and storage (Hally and Kelly 1998; Polhemus 1990; Sullivan 1995). As Waring (1968: 55) also notes, the term used for the benches along the walls of a house was also used to describe the seating areas at the Square Ground. While Waring uses this connection to argue that the historic-period Square Ground had its origins in enclosed spaces or large buildings, I take it to indicate an important ideological principle. The Square Ground was a place where important ritual was conducted and decisions were made. At those events, members of all social segments had a place in the ceremonial space and took part in the activities conducted there. In essence, naming the Square Ground the big house emphasized the communal nature of the exercise of power and the conduct of ritual. The reality might have been different, but the name served to mask the inequality that lay at the heart of society and decision-making and ritual. This same strategy was likely the reason why the League of the Iroquois conceived of that confederation as a great long house.

No less interesting is the fact that this same structure appears to apply to the layout of most large Mississippian communities in the area. Those communities had an open space or plaza at their center that was surrounded by a residential zone containing buildings. Often the entire community was enclosed by a palisade, but in other instances only the plaza and other key features such as mounds were enclosed within the palisade. Often the remains of one or more very large posts are found at the center of the plaza (Hally and Kelly 1998; Polhemus 1990; Sullivan 1995).

As others have argued (Howard 1968; Lankford 1987, 2006a), these arrangements of features and spaces in essence map out important relationships of the cosmos as viewed by Muskogean speakers—they are cosmograms. Similar representations can be found in shell gorget engravings and complicated stamped-pottery designs of northern Georgia and eastern Tennessee (Figure 4.7). Some of the earliest gorgets found in the region exhibit variations of

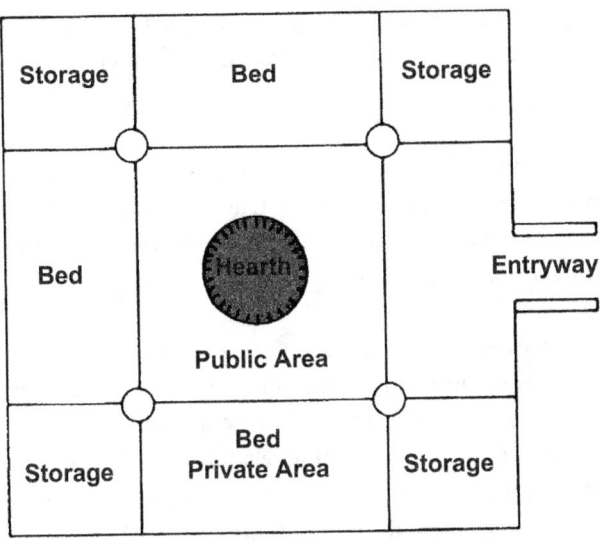

Figure 4.6. Northern Georgia Mississippian House Floor Plan. From Polhemus 1986.

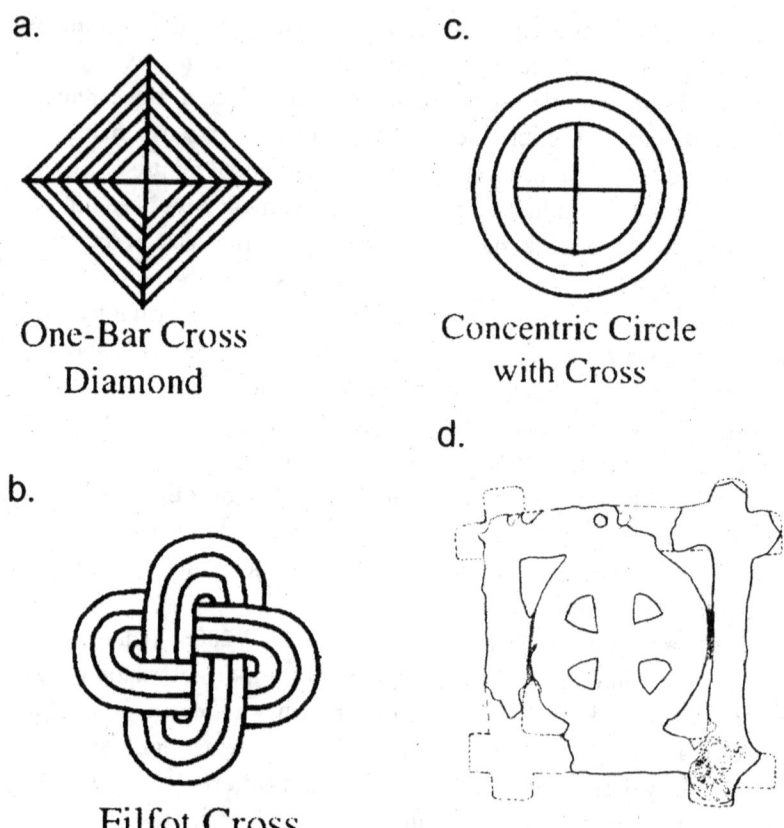

Figure 4.7. Centering Motifs in Northern Georgia Complicated Stamped Pottery (a–c) and Engraved Shell Gorget (d) from Mound C at Etowah. Motif d drawn by Johann Sawyer, used with permission.

the cross-in-circle motif (Sullivan 2007b), which references the same kind of centering of the cosmos seen in the Square Ground structure. Motifs stamped into the wet clay of unfired vessels in the region show the same kind of principle, as seen in the concentric diamond, concentric circle, and filfot cross motifs (Hally and Langford 1988).

This simple structure, most elaborately seen in the Square Ground layout, is repeated on multiple scales in the arrangement of people, space, and architecture. It also has a long history in representational art and domestic pottery design. The overlapping and redundant use of these relationships suggests that they have a deep history and that they represent an important organizational principle. At one level, this arrangement makes reference to important aspects of the cosmos as viewed by Muskogean speakers, and as such it may have functioned as a cosmogram. At another level, this arrangement not only reflects the ordering of the cosmos but creates the circumstances for interaction among the realms of the cosmos. Presumably when the axis mundi was activated through proper ritual, the open area around it—just like in the Square Ground—could become sacred space where interaction with the supernatural can take place. This creates the possibility that the open area in a house or the plaza in a community could be transformed into sacred space, just like in the Square Ground, for different kinds of purposes.

If we ignore the Early Wilbanks graves, then the layout of Mound C replicates that same cosmogram. My reconstruction of the Mound C record (King 2003, 2007) shows that burial in the summits of the mound had ceased by the Late Wilbanks phase. At the minimum, what was left was a ring of graves around the flanks of the mound surrounded by a palisade. The summit had no burials, creating an open space similar to those evident in houses, in the Square Ground, and in communities. Unfortunately, Moorehead (1932) removed almost all of the summits of Mound C, so it is not known whether there was a building, a post, or a hearth at its center. On a remnant of an earlier summit, Larson (1971) found a small segment of wall suggesting that some summits supported buildings. If we go so far as to assume that not only was there a building on Mound C but that it was a temple like those described historically, then the temple building with its central fire would have served as an axis mundi.

Here, then, is a historically connected, regionally specific model that may help explain some aspects of the Mound C record. Mound C, at least its final incarnation, was structured to serve as a replication of the structure of the cosmos.

The Meaning of the Groups around Mound C

Using this model, the summit of Mound C was a sacred space centered on an axis mundi and surrounded by groups of burials. Logically, the burials ringing the mound at the base would have been the equivalent of the seating in the Square Ground or benches in houses. The seating areas in the Square Ground were positioned at the cardinal directions and were designated for specific clans. The people in discrete sets of burials around Mound C would have been the equivalent of the clans around the Square Ground or the family members in the household. The archaeological data is not inconsistent with the notion that burial groupings around Mound C were corporate kin groups.

The exact nature of those groups is difficult to pin down, but several possibilities are worth exploring. One possibility is that these groups represent the clans of Etowah society. We know that during the historic period, there were more than four clans among groups like the Creeks (Swanton 1928). It is possible that the groups represent a limited set of the clans. We also know from the historic period that clans were ranked with respect to one another, so those represented in Mound C may be a subset of the total number of clans present, possibly the highest ranked. It is also possible that those four groupings represent phratries. There is little evidence that phratries were common among groups such as the Creeks, but we simply do not know enough to say the same for an earlier time. Another possibility is that these groups represent social houses as defined by Levi-Strauss (see Brown 2007a). Not unlike the royal houses of Europe, these houses began as kin-based organizations such as clans or lineages. However, they grew to include non-kin by attracting craftspeople, warriors, and others to the house and its wealth and power.

The fifth grouping, comprised of the burials in the two lobes, has the same kinds of artifacts found with burials as other groups but is demographically quite different. While this grouping may represent a corporate kin group, as I argue for the other four, another interpretation becomes more appealing upon closer examination (Figures 4.8 and 4.9).

This lobe grouping actually consists of burials placed under two sequentially created lobes appended to the northern side of Mound C. The first of these lobes contains Burials 47 and 57 and an unnumbered grave. In my reconstruction of the history of Mound C, Burial 57 and this first lobe represent the first construction and burial activity associated with the Late Wilbanks phase. It was added to the northern side of the last Early Wilbanks phase stage and is followed by a major new construction effort. After the placement of the graves under the first lobe, the entire mound was surrounded by a cane fence and then covered—lobe and all—by a new mantle of earth. After the addition of the new stage, a new palisade wall was built to enclose the entire mound.

Based on the sequence of palisade walls, Burial 38 may have been the first of the Late Wilbanks graves to be interred. Burial 38 and its lobe were enclosed by two palisade lines. The first is superimposed by graves in the northwestern grouping, suggesting that it came before those burials were dug. The second palisade enclosing Burial 38 appears to be part of the same line that rings the entire mound and all four other burial groupings. To the extent that my interpretation of the Mound C record is correct, it seems reasonable to consider the first lobe burials as part of a separate mortuary and construction effort that preceded the one that created the final burial ring.

Burial 38 contained the remains of five women, all arranged in a very large pit. Four of the women were placed along the four sides of the tomb—at the cardinal directions—and each of these four was accompanied by a headdress

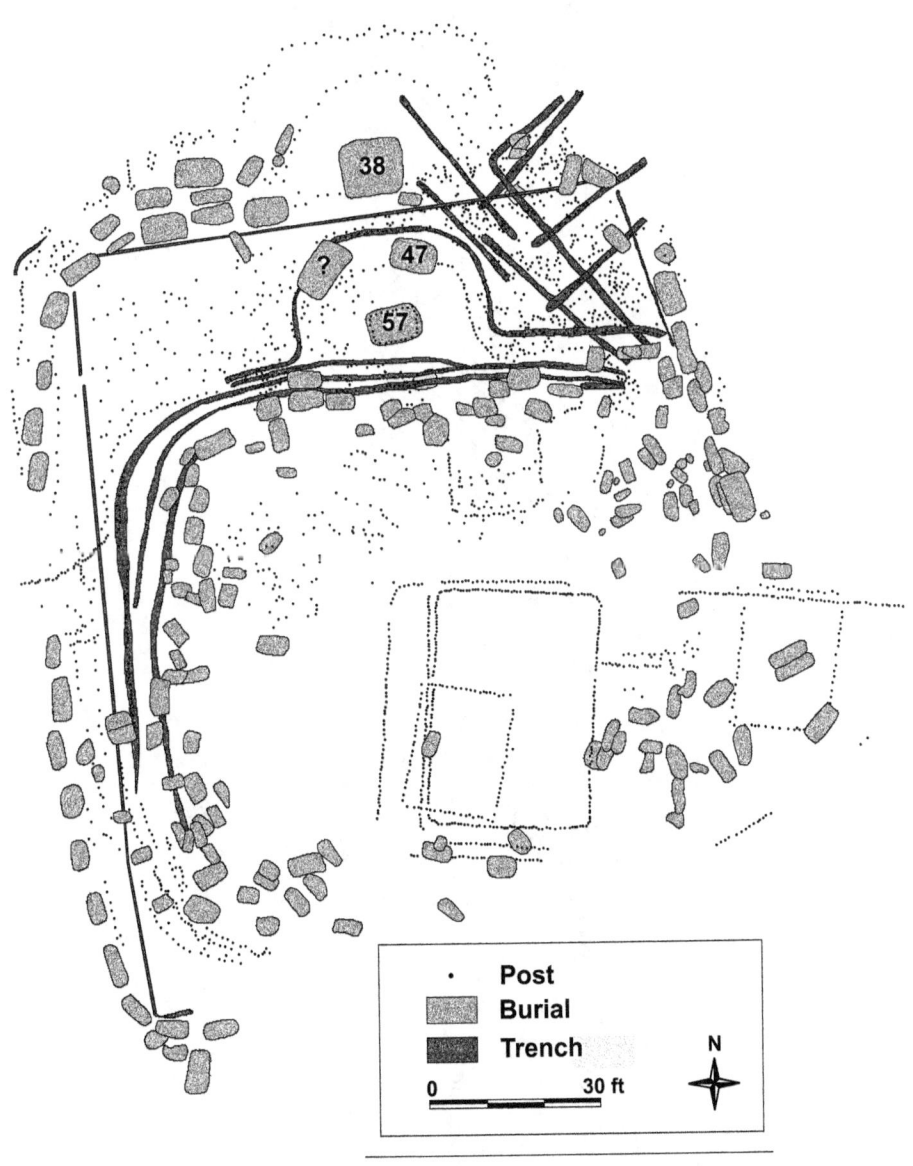

Figure 4.8. The Lobe Burials at Mound C.

Figure 4.9. Profile Showing the Relationship of the Lobe Burials.

with copper ornaments, a copper celt, and copper-covered earspools. The fifth woman was positioned in the middle of the grave; she wore the earspools and had the copper celt, but there was a portable altar close to her instead of a headdress.

These women occupied a unique place in the final burial ring, suggesting that they constituted at least a unique if not important group of people. Southeastern societies were and still are matrilineal, suggesting that they might have had something to do with matrilineal social segments. It also must be meaningful that the number of women buried around the margins of the grave matches the number of discrete groupings identified in the Late Wilbanks burial set. It is tempting to interpret these women as representatives of distinct matrilineal corporate kin groups buried with the Mississippian equivalent of a sacred bundle—a headdress. If this is the case, their presence in Burial 38 made concrete a social order where multiple groups had access to burial in Mound C and chartered the use of space by individual social segments in Mound C.

It is possible that Burial 38 was itself a replication of the sacred space model. In this theory, the four women at the cardinal directions represented the beds of the Square Ground or household, while the fifth woman placed in the middle functioned as the axis mundi. This finds some support in the fact that the central woman was buried with a portable altar. Steponaitis (2004) has argued that tabular pieces of stone served as altars on which things such as medicines could be created in sacred space—in essence serving the same function, albeit on a smaller scale, as the axis mundi and open space at the Square Ground.

Inferences: The Creation of a Sacred Space

As I noted above, there is a striking consistency in the demographic makeup of the four groups positioned at the corners of Mound C. Such consistency from group to group in the number of people and in sex and age distribution could only result from selectively burying individuals who were chosen based on predetermined criteria. The same conclusion can be drawn about the women interred in Burial 38.

In order to complete the pattern apparent at Mound C, the inhabitants of Etowah had three choices. One was to wait until a person of the appropriate age and sex from the appropriate social segment died. Unless the pool of potential candidates was quite large, this approach could take decades or longer. My best estimate for the length of time it took to create and use the Late Wilbanks stages of Mound C is on the order of 75 years (King 2003). That estimate ultimately is derived from radiocarbon dates, which cannot measure time more finely than 50 to 100 years. I suspect that the Late Wilbanks stages of Mound C were used for a generation or less. The fact that the burials are laid neatly end to end with little overlap suggests that a short period of time separated their placement.

A second option would have been to rebury already deceased individuals to complete the groupings. There are no bundled burials or other obvious evidence of secondary burials in the final ring, suggesting that this approach was not taken. This leaves one final possibility. At least some of the people buried in the final ring of burials at Mound C were chosen from the living to die and be buried.

If this logic is accepted, it is possible to argue that the creation of the final ring of burials at Mound C was an event rather than a drawn-out process. That event had a predetermined plan of what was to be produced and involved manipulating the dead and even death itself. Based on the model I outlined above, I think that the predetermined plan was designed to create a sacred space using Mound C, sacred objects, and the dead.

I will posit that this was not just any sacred space but the sacred space through which the dead of Etowah began their journey along the path of souls (Lankford 2006b). Appropriately, it required an elaborate and grand effort to create that sacred space, and given other aspects of Late Wilbanks Etowah, that effort was not out of scale. During this phase the area east of Mound A was converted from a residential zone to a large, paved plaza that created a grand space at the base of the enormous Mound A (King 2003). To connect that space to the summit of Mound A, a large staircase with log risers and clay landings was built on a ramp on the eastern side of the mound (King 2003). At the summit of Mound A, several buildings were constructed, including two that were over 15 m on each side (Sharp et al. 2006). Clearly grand displays were a hallmark of this period in Etowah's history.

This was a major event in the history of Etowah, and for its trigger I turn to Larson (2004), who has argued that the two lobes and associated burials were created over a short period of time—on the order of two to three weeks—and that this event was initiated by the death of the man interred in Burial 57. Burial 57 was a large, log-lined tomb that contained the remains of a 25-year-old male and a 20-year-old female. The plan map made during excavation clearly shows the adult male and associated grave goods, but the body of the female is not readily apparent. According to Larson's field notes, the man was buried wearing a headdress composed of copper ornaments, a garment embroidered with pearls, a feather robe, and a collar of shell beads. Other grave goods included a Hightower-style gorget depicting the anthropomorphic theme, eight conch-shell cups, five or six embossed copper plates, two copper celts, a pair of copper-covered ear disks, a copper bead, and numerous shell beads. It is difficult to understand the relationship of the woman to the other grave goods or to the man interred in Burial 57.

After completion, Burial 57 was covered by a small mound of earth and surrounded by a palisade wall. Subsequently another log tomb, Burial 47, was excavated through this palisade line, covered by an extension of the lobe, and enclosed by yet another palisade line, this time made in a wall-trench. This burial contained the remains of a 50–year-old woman interred with shell beads and a plain local pottery bowl. Finally, a large shallow burial pit (unnumbered burial) was dug through this wall-trench palisade and the flank of the lobe. Larson (2004:137) described the burial floor as being covered with a "thin layer of crushed and badly preserved bone material." The number of sets of tooth crowns indicated that at least seven people were placed in the grave (Larson 1971). More recently, Larson (2004) has suggested that this grave held as many as 11 people. The burial itself was so shallow that Larson suggested that its occupants had been placed on the ground surface. Their state of preservation was so bad that he suggested that the individuals had lain exposed for a period of time before being covered or that they had been subjected to heavy foot traffic after burial. This new grave, like Burial 47, was covered by an extension of the lobe placed around and over Burial 57.

First, the regalia and symbols of the man placed in Burial 57 indicate that he might have been the Birdman (see Brown 2007b) depicted in imagery of the Classic Braden and Hightower styles. The feather robe, the Hightower-style gorget depicting a version of the Birdman, and the embossed copper plates are particularly important. Detailed photographic work on one of those plates done by David Dye suggests that this plate also depicts the Birdman depicted artistically in the Classic Braden style.

Also, the excavators initially missed the fact that a female was present in Burial 57, suggesting that she (or at least some part of her) may have been part of the grave goods or at the least was included in the grave to accompany the man. In a similar vein, the seven somewhat anonymous individuals buried in the unmarked grave seem also to have been accompaniments—possibly even sacrifices. The relative youth of the man and woman in Burial 57 also hint that something other than natural death may have brought them to the grave.

Considering all of this together leaves two possible explanations for the graves in the first lobe. Given that fact that the man in Burial 57 seems to occupy the preeminent place in this set (centrally located, accompanied by elaborate offerings), it is possible that the entire collection of people and things was created to commemorate his death. In this scenario, the women in Burials 47 and 57 and in the unnumbered burial met their end as part of the mortuary activities associated with the death of that man. Extending this argument, the death of the man in Burial 57 set into motion the creation of the final ring of burials at Mound C and the transformation of the mound into a sacred space. Possibly that sacred space was created specifically to provide that important man entry to the path of souls.

The other possibility is that the man in Burial 57, like the other people in the first lobe, was chosen from the living to take a predetermined place in the sacred landscape of Mound C. His relative youth may argue for this perspective. If this is the case, it is likely that his place and purpose were determined by sacred narratives and that Burial 57 and everything after it was part of an effort to reenact (relive or live) events described in those narratives. Experiencing, reliving, or reenacting events in sacred narratives is common in ritual practices around the world and among Native Americans (see Hall 1997). A reading of the Morningstar Sacrifice among the Pawnee (Hall 1997:95–101; Dorsey 1969) provides a concrete example, as does the creation of the House of Mysteries of the Osage (Bailey 1995).

Perhaps the entire purpose of Burial 57 and everything that came after it was to recast or transform Mound C into a sacred center. As I argued above, not just any sacred center was created—it was *the* sacred center of the Etowah polity. Maybe that center served the needs of some of the powerful at Etowah or maybe it was created to serve the needs of the entire populace of the Etowah polity. This reworking of the Etowah landscape during the Late Wilbanks phase was not limited to Mound C. As noted above, the residential zone east of Mound A was transformed into a grand open plaza during the Late Wilbanks phase and the site itself was transformed from an open space to one bounded by a ditch and palisade complex. For some reason, efforts were made to transform many parts of Etowah during the Late Wilbanks phase, and the restructuring Mound C was only one part of a broader effort.

Concluding Comments

The fact that multiple groups of people were buried in the final mortuary effort at Mound C is something that we have known for a long time. As we explore the demography of those groups and the artifacts they contained, it becomes clear that those groups were similarly constituted and used many of the same kinds of symbols, suggesting that they represent (roughly) socially equivalent groups such as corporate kin groups. However, the demographic makeup of those groups is such that they almost certainly were not created by the natural life and death cycle of small social segments. The inference I draw is that the groupings positioned around the periphery of the Late Wilbanks stages of Mound C were placed there as part of an effort by the living to create a sacred space through which other realms and powers could be accessed. The nature of the burials in the two lobes appended to the north side of Mound C leaves me with the same impression.

Following Larson, the initiation of that effort to create a sacred space came with the interment of Burial 57 and associated graves under the first lobe. It is unclear to me whether the death of the man placed in Burial 57 was natural and therefore the trigger for what came next or whether his death was caused as part of the process of creating a sacred space. In either case, the evidence seems to support the inference that the Late Wilbanks phase burials and construction stages of Mound C were manipulated by the living. Perhaps the goal was to meet the needs of the dead. However, it is apparent that a larger part of Etowah was transformed in some important way during the Late Wilbanks phase. This suggests a broader effort on the part of people—possibly some elite segment—to transform the sacred landscape of Etowah. Rather than reflecting simply social status, the placement of the dead in Mound C was part of that effort to restructure space and the sacred at Etowah.

5

Social and Spatial Dimensions of Moundville Mortuary Practices

GREGORY D. WILSON, VINCAS P. STEPONAITIS, AND KEITH P. JACOBI

Moundville has an impressive mortuary data set with a long history of related investigations. Previous mortuary studies, however, have not focused on individual burial clusters as socially and spatially relevant units of analysis. Here we address this issue by documenting and interpreting the size, arrangement, and composition of selected Mississippian cemeteries at Moundville. These cemeteries were uncovered during the 1939 and 1940 excavations of the Moundville Roadway. Our analysis reveals that these cemeteries exhibit considerable internal variation in terms of age, sex, and mortuary treatment. Based on their composition, small size, strategic location, and duration, we argue that small corporate kin groups used these cemeteries to assert social and spatial claims within the Moundville polity.

Archaeological investigations have revealed that Mississippian mortuary practices were not uniform across the southeastern and midwestern United States (Brown 2006b; Conrad 1993; Emerson, Hargrave, and Hedman 2003; Goldstein 1980; Fisher-Carroll and Mainfort 2000; Peebles 1974; Sullivan and Rodning 2001). It has been clearly demonstrated that the intricacies of mortuary ritual varied along the dimensions of social status, gender, age, and regional tradition. This variability has often been used to draw conclusions about the social identity of the deceased (e.g., Binford 1971; Goldstein 1980; Peebles and Kus 1977; Saxe 1970). Scholars have only recently begun to investigate Mississippian mortuaries as important sites for the living as well as the dead. Central to this perspective is the point that mortuary ritualism commonly embodies socially relevant statements and negotiations that mourners and other surviving community members make about the current and future state of affairs (e.g., Kuijt 2000; Metcalf and Huntington 1991; Parker Pearson 1999). Accordingly, the archaeological signatures of mortuary practices not only reflect the status of the deceased but were also shaped by the social aspirations of the living (see Brown 1995; Marcoux, this volume).

By their very nature, sites of Mississippian mortuary ritual were situated at an important nexus between the living and the dead, between this world and the next, and between the past, present, and future. Indeed, the social meaning embodied by Mississippian cemeteries often appears to have been negotiated relative to the occupational history of the landscapes in which they were situated (Boudreaux 2007a; Rodning 2005; Wilson 2008). Mississippian groups who built mortuaries within the spatial boundaries of towns and villages did so in reference to mounds, plazas, domestic structures, and other places actual or remembered. Mississippian landscapes deeply sedimented with a history of past occupations would have contained many important sites of memory, the social relevance of which could have been appropriated, modified, or contested through the performance of and association with mortuary ceremonialism (Joyce 2003; Meskell 2004; Nora 1989). It is with these concepts in mind that we turn our discussion to the social and spatial dimensions of Moundville mortuary practice.

Moundville Community Organization

The Moundville site, located in the Black Warrior River valley of west-central Alabama, was the political and ceremonial capital of one of the largest and most complex Mississippian polities in the southeastern United States (Figure 5.1). Moundville's highly organized community plan has long been the subject of archaeological attention and analysis (Knight 1998; Peebles 1971, 1978, 1983). The Moundville site encompasses 75 hectares and consists of 32 mounds, mostly grouped in pairs around a rectangular plaza (Knight and Steponaitis 1998: 3). The largest mounds are located on the northern edge of the plaza and become increasingly smaller going either clockwise or counterclockwise around the plaza to the south. Knight (1998) has interpreted this community plan as a sociogram, "an architectural depiction of a social order based on ranked clans." According to this model the Moundville community was segmented into a variety of different clan precincts, the ranked position of which was represented in the size and arrangement of paired earthen mounds around the central plaza. The largest earthen mounds on the northern portion of the plaza were associated with the highest-ranking clans, while smaller mounds to the south were associated with lower-ranking clans.

Wilson's (2005, 2008) recent analysis of the 1939 and 1940 Moundville Roadway excavations has revealed that the Mississippian inhabitants of the Black Warrior River valley built and rebuilt the Moundville sociogram in a number of different ways and on a number of different scales over the course of approximately three centuries. In addition to demarcating clan precincts

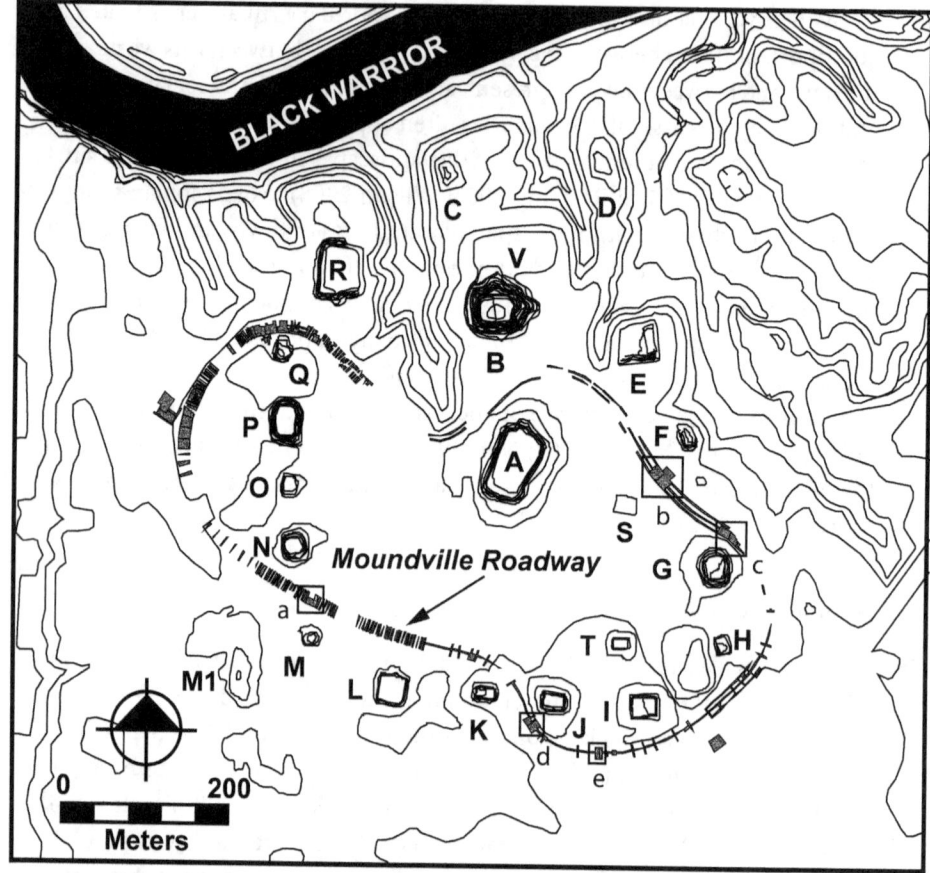

Figure 5.1. The Moundville Site Featuring the 1939 and 1940 Roadway Excavations. Uppercase letters designate the mounds; lowercase letters correspond to the cemeteries illustrated in Figure 5.2.

through mound construction, early Mississippian groups inscribed their sub-clan lineage identities onto the community by creating and maintaining the same small-scale and rigidly organized residential areas throughout Moundville's nucleated early Mississippian occupation (Wilson 2008; Wilson et al. 2006).

Some time in the final decades of the thirteenth century, Moundville ceased to be used as a nucleated residential center and was transformed into a necropolis for the relocated kin groups living in the rural countryside of the Black Warrior River valley (Knight and Steponaitis 1998; Steponaitis 1998). During the fourteenth and fifteenth centuries the dead were interred in a number of different spatial and social contexts throughout the site. We argue that important insights into these late Mississippian mortuary activities can be gained by relating them to the use of community space during Moundville's early Mississippian era of nucleated residential occupation.

The Moundville Roadway Mortuary Dataset

The mortuary data set for this investigation consists of the 265 burials uncovered by the Alabama Museum of Natural History's excavation of the Moundville Roadway. The Roadway excavations were conducted in 1939 and 1940 within a winding corridor, 50 feet wide and 1.5 miles long, that was to be disturbed by the construction of a road that now encircles portions of the plaza and areas east, west, and south of the mounds (Figure 5.1; see Peebles 1979). We conduct our analysis of this data set on two scales. First, we examine the general spatial distribution and arrangement of burials within the entire Moundville Roadway. We also consider demographic variability among these burials in relation to the distribution of artifacts. Next we focus on one particular Roadway cemetery for the purpose of providing more detailed observations.

A visual inspection of the Moundville Roadway reveals that most burials in the Moundville Roadway are arranged in small rectilinear cemeteries that overlap spatially with small groups of early Mississippian houses (Figure 5.2). Very few burials are located outside the spatial boundaries of these residential groups. The houses in these groups date to the Moundville I phase. Most of the Roadway burials, however, postdate these houses. Only one of the 34 Roadway burials analyzed by Steponaitis (1983, 1998) in his seriation of Moundville mortuary vessels positively dates to the late Moundville I or early Moundville II phase. Moreover, Wilson's (2005, 2008) recent architectural analysis has revealed that burials commonly superimpose the single-post or wall-trench foundations of early Mississippian buildings in the Moundville Roadway. These findings correspond with the sitewide pattern Steponaitis (1998: 37) identified: "Only about 7 percent of the burials were interred during Moundville I [A.D. 1120–1260], 38 percent during Moundville II [A.D. 1260–1400], 53 percent during Moundville III [A.D. 1400–1520], and less than 2 percent during Moundville IV [A.D. 1520–1650]" (Figure 5.3).

It is important to note that after A.D. 1300, when the majority of these burials were interred, most people in the Black Warrior River valley were no longer living at the Moundville site (Steponaitis 1998). Thus, when family members died it would have been necessary to properly prepare and transport their corpses to Moundville from the countryside. Family members and extended kin would also have had to have been notified and subsequently

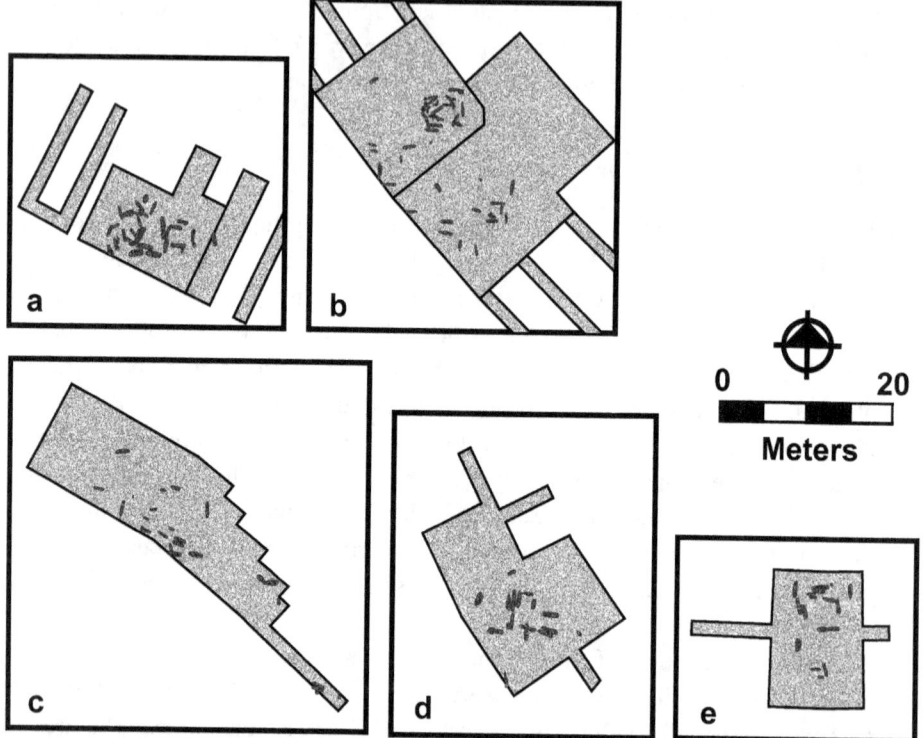

Figure 5.2. Selected Mississippian Cemeteries from the Moundville Roadway Excavations. Roadway blocks 15+00 to 15+50 (a); Roadway blocks 48+00 to 48+50 (b); Roadway blocks 43+50 to 44+50 (c); Roadway blocks 26+50 to 27+00 (d); Roadway blocks 30+00 to 30+50 (e).

would have had to have made the journey to Moundville to attend the funerary events. There may have been situations where ceremonial or logistical obstacles prevented the immediate interment of deceased relatives at Moundville. If someone died at a great distance from the site or during a season that hindered travel, family members may have opted to temporarily inter the deceased nearby with plans to eventually move the remains to Moundville for final burial.

Such considerations may explain the diversity of mortuary treatments represented among the Roadway burials. The vast majority of burials in the Roadway are extended and were probably interred shortly after the time of death. Also present in each cemetery, however, are a small number of bundle burials and individual skull burials. These secondary burials may represent individuals who were initially interred elsewhere in the valley or beyond and were later moved to Moundville for final burial (cf. Hutchinson and Aragon 2002).

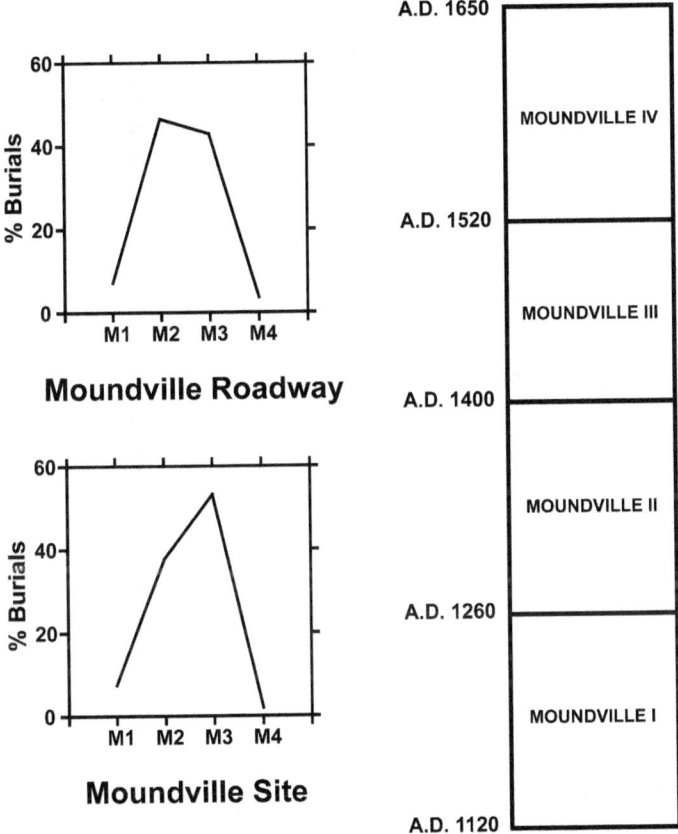

Figure 5.3. Phase-Based Chronology for the Black Warrior Valley Featuring Diachronic Changes in the Frequency of Burials for the Moundville Roadway Excavations and the Entire Moundville Site

We gathered basic data from five Roadway burial clusters to provide a general overview of their size, arrangement, and composition. These cemeteries, marked a through e in Figure 5.2, are located in widely separated portions of the Moundville Roadway (Table 5.1). Each of the five cemeteries includes a tightly arranged rectilinear cluster of burials that forms the core of the mortuary. These clusters range in size from 23 to 59 m². In each cemetery, burials are arranged in clusters around central open spaces. Around the perimeter of these tightly arranged burial clusters is a more dispersed and amorphous scattering of associated burials. The number of individuals within each cemetery varies between 25 and 57. This variation is difficult to evaluate as it is strongly influenced by the size of the area excavated around the central portions of each

Table 5.1. Inventory of Age and Sex Data for the Moundville Roadway Burials

Burial ID	Age	Sex	Phase	Roadway Excavation Block
2648	20–24	F	—	70+15
2651	3–6	—	—	70+65
2652	16–20	—	—	70+65
2653	30–35	—	—	70+65
2657	35–39	F	—	71+11
2658	1–4	—	—	70+75
2660	35–39	F	—	71+65
2661	35–39	F	—	71+65
2662	16–18	M	—	71+65
2663	25–29	F	—	71+65
2664	1–4	—	MIII	71+70
2665	1–4	—	MIII	71+70
2666	1–4	—	—	71+80
2667	30–34	F	—	71+65
2668	15–19	M	—	71+90
2671	1–4	—	—	71+75
2672	25–29	—	—	1+00
2673	1–4	—	MII–III	1+00
2677	5–9	—	—	0+95
2679	15–19	—	—	0+95
2680	15–19	—	—	71+75
2681	30–34	M	—	71+75
2683	5–9	—	—	70+15
2685	20–24	—	—	70+05
2686	20–24	—	—	71+85
2687	35–39	M	MII	3+40
2688	10–14	—	—	3+40
2690	10–14	—	—	3+40
2691	25–34	—	—	3+40
2695	25–34	—	—	4+10
2698	45–54	F	—	4+25
2700	30–34	—	—	5+00
2703	40–44	F	—	5+10
2726	25–29	M	MII–III	15+30
2730	30–35	—	—	15+25
2735	40–44	M	—	15+20
2802	30–34	M	—	30+45
2804	30–34	M	—	30+45
2807	20–24	—	—	30+45
2825	30–34	F	—	43+60
2826	40–44	F	—	44+00
2827	30–32	F	—	44+00
2828	40–44	F	—	43+90
2829	30–34	F	—	44+25
2833	25–34	—	—	44+35
2834	30–34	F	—	44+35

continued

2835	15–19	M	—		43+60
2836	30–34	M	—		44+40
2838	35–39	M	—		44+50
2845	20–24	—	—		44+75
2847	25–35	M	—		48+15
2848	30–34	M	—		48+25
2851	50 plus	F	—		48+15
2856	30–34	M	—		48+25
2857	10–14	—	MII–III		48+30
2858	50 plus	F	—		48+25
2859	30–34	M	MII		48+25
2860	45–49	M	—		48+40
2862	50 plus	M	—		off Roadway
2863	30–34	F	—		off Roadway
2864	45–49	F	—		48+50
2865	45–49	F	—		48+60
2866	40–44	M	—		48+60
2868	40–44	—	—		48+60
2869	1–4	—	—		48+55
2870	40–44	M	—		48+55
2872	30–34	F	—		48+55
2873	35–39	F	—		48+55
2874	30–34	M	—		48+60
2875	25–29	F	—		48+60
2876	<1	—	—		48+60
2877	5–9	—	—		48+60
2882	30–34	M	MII		48+60
2883	35–39	F	—		48+60
2884	50 plus	M	MI		48+65
2887	25–29	M	—		48+60
2889	<1	—	—		48+65
2892	10–11	—	—		48+65
2893	1–4	—	—		48+65
2894	40–44	F	—		48+70
2895	30–34	M	—		48+70
2896	24–30	—	—		48+65
2898	35–39	F	—		48+70

cemetery. Nevertheless, it is worth drawing the obvious comparison between these Roadway cemeteries and Mississippian cemeteries such as those at the Kellogg and 1GR2 sites in the Tombigbee River valley. Blitz (1993: 62–68) has interpreted these Tombigbee valley cemeteries as representing small social groups. They are similar in size to the Moundville Roadway cemeteries and include comparable numbers of individuals.

Figure 5.4 illustrates the composition of these Moundville Roadway cemeteries. The age and sex data displayed in this figure and in Table 5.1 are based

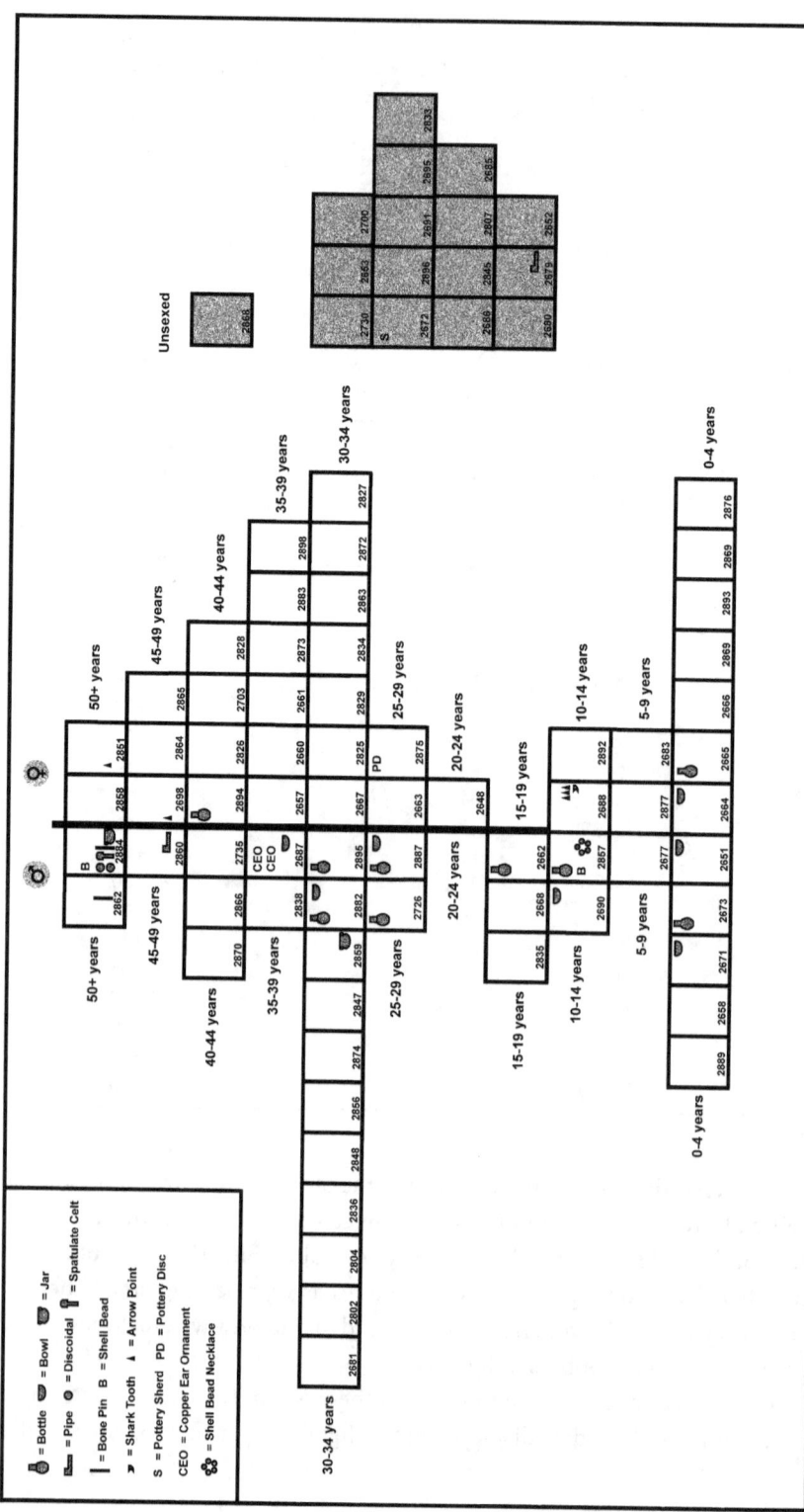

Figure 5.4. Sheratt Diagram for the Roadway Excavations at the Moundville Site. Each block represents an individual burial, with males on the left of the central axis, females on the right, and age categories arranged vertically. Artifacts associated with each burial are indicated by symbols.

on analyses previously conducted by Powell (1988) and more recently by Jacobi. Age and sex information are available for 83 of the Roadway burials (Table 5.1). An examination of these data reveals several important patterns. First, there is a high infant mortality rate (15 percent for the 0 to 5 age group) with an ensuing decline in childhood mortality. Second, the percentages of male and female mortality in other age categories are roughly comparable. Finally, both males and female exhibit a peak in mortality between 30 and 35 years of age. These demographic data indicate a mortality profile that is comparable to that of other Mississippian populations (Bridges et al. 2000; Goldstein 1980; Sullivan 2006). Moreover, this demographic profile, with all age and sex groups represented, is consistent with the use of these cemeteries by discrete kin groups (see Howell and Kintigh 1996).

Burial Goods and Status

Examination of burial goods provides insight into status differences among the individuals uncovered in the Moundville Roadway excavations (Figure 5.4). Our approach to the issue of status is based on several expectations. First, we assume that individuals interred with more artifacts were of higher status than individuals interred with fewer artifacts (see Bennett 1984: 39; Champion 1982: 70). We presume that a system of achieved status can be discerned on the basis of a mortuary program characterized by a greater number and combination of artifacts interred with older individuals than with younger individuals, particularly adolescents or young adults (Binford 1971; Braun 1979). A system of achieved status may also be represented in sex-based differences in burial goods. A system of ascribed status, in contrast, is represented in a mortuary program in which grave goods cut-across categories of age and sex (Peebles 1974).

Our analysis revealed that most individuals (n = 196) in the Moundville Roadway were buried with nothing. Moreover, an inverse relationship exists between the "richness" of a grave (i.e., the number of artifacts it contains) and the number of graves that exhibit this richness (Figure 5.5). This pattern is consistent with what might be expected if there were hierarchical differences among the individuals buried in the Moundville Roadway. Even so, based on the differential distribution of mortuary artifacts by age and sex, it appears that social status was achieved rather than ascribed among the social groups that comprised the Roadway cemeteries (Figure 5.4). Only four females were interred with artifacts, and these four were interred with a single artifact each. Burial Rw 2875 was associated with a pottery disc, burial Rw 2894 was associated with a ceramic water bottle, and burials Rw 2698 and Rw 2851 were

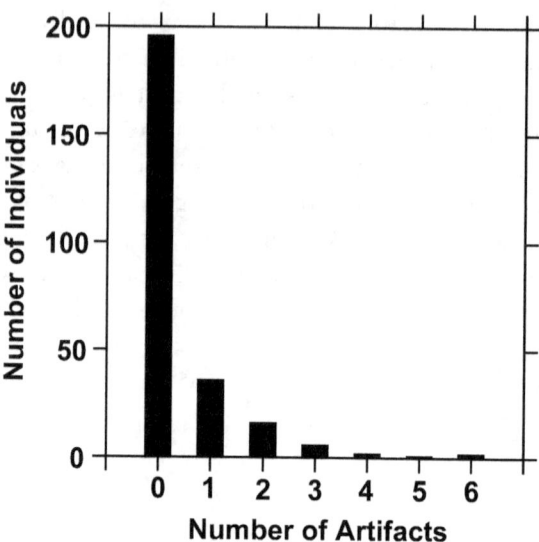

Figure 5.5. Number of Artifacts per Individual Burial for the Roadway Excavations at the Moundville Site

associated with a chert arrow point each. A greater number of adult men (n = 11) were buried with artifacts than adult women (n = 4). Adult men were also buried with a greater number and variety of artifacts than adult women. One male (Rw 2884) buried with six items deserves special attention. This man, over 50 years of age, was interred with a Carthage Incised, *var. Summerville* jar next to his right foot, a bone hairpin and shell bead behind his head, two stone discoidals on either side of his pelvis, and a long-stemmed, greenstone spatulate celt underneath his thighs (Figure 5.6). Spatulate celts and other forms of ceremonial weaponry have been interpreted as markers of elevated status in Mississippian societies (Dye 2004; Wilson 2001). In addition, the presence of ceremonial items such as the two chunky gaming stones suggest that this man held a position of elevated status relative to other men and women in the Moundville Roadway cemeteries (cf. DeBoer 1993). As will be elaborated below, it is also noteworthy that this is the only Roadway burial that positively dates to the early Mississippian late Moundville I or early Moundville II phase.

While a comprehensive discussion of the different kinds of Moundville cemeteries is beyond the scope of this essay, it is worth noting that that these small off-mound cemeteries differ considerably from mound cemeteries in the number and variety of artifacts associated with individual burials. As Peebles (1974) noted, the majority of burials Moore (1905, 1907) uncovered in

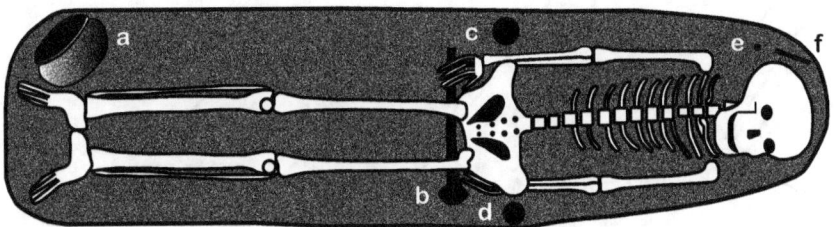

Figure 5.6. Burial RW 2884, Man over 50 years Old Located in the Center of a Cemetery in Moundville Roadway Block 48+65. Carthage Incised *var. Summerville* jar (a); greenstone spatulate celt (b); stone discoidal (c); stone discoidal (d); marine shell bead (e); bone hairpin (f).

his excavations at Mound C were interred with multiple artifacts such as copper ornaments, shell beads, and freshwater pearls. Thus, it appears that both achieved and ascribed dimensions of social status were expressed through mortuary practices at Moundville. It is likely, however, that both ascribed and achieved statuses were intertwined rather than separate domains of authority and ranking in late prehistoric west-central Alabama.

A Closer Look at a Moundville Cemetery

We now turn our attention to Roadway excavation blocks 48+00 to 48+50 to provide a more detailed analysis of an individual cemetery. This portion of the Moundville Roadway consists of a tight cluster of early Mississippian domestic structures superimposed by a cemetery that primarily dates to the Moundville II and III phases (Figure 5.7). This cemetery consists of 57 burials, 36 of which are located in a small rectilinear cluster. The other 21 burials are dispersed immediately to the south. Like the Roadway population as a whole, the demographics of this small cemetery are characterized by a roughly equal number of men and women and a wide range of ages, a pattern that is consistent with its use by an individual kin group (Table 5.1; Howell and Kintigh 1996).

Six of the 57 burials in this cemetery could be dated based on Steponaitis's (1983) seriation of mortuary vessels. Of these, one positively dates to the late Moundville I to early Moundville II phase, three to the Moundville II phase, and two to the Moundville III phase. Thirteen additional burials postdate the late Moundville I phase based on their superimposition of late Moundville I features. Thus, this cemetery has a long history of use. At least one individual (Rw 2884) was buried in this location during or perhaps immediately after Moundville's early Mississippian occupation, a male over 50 years of age

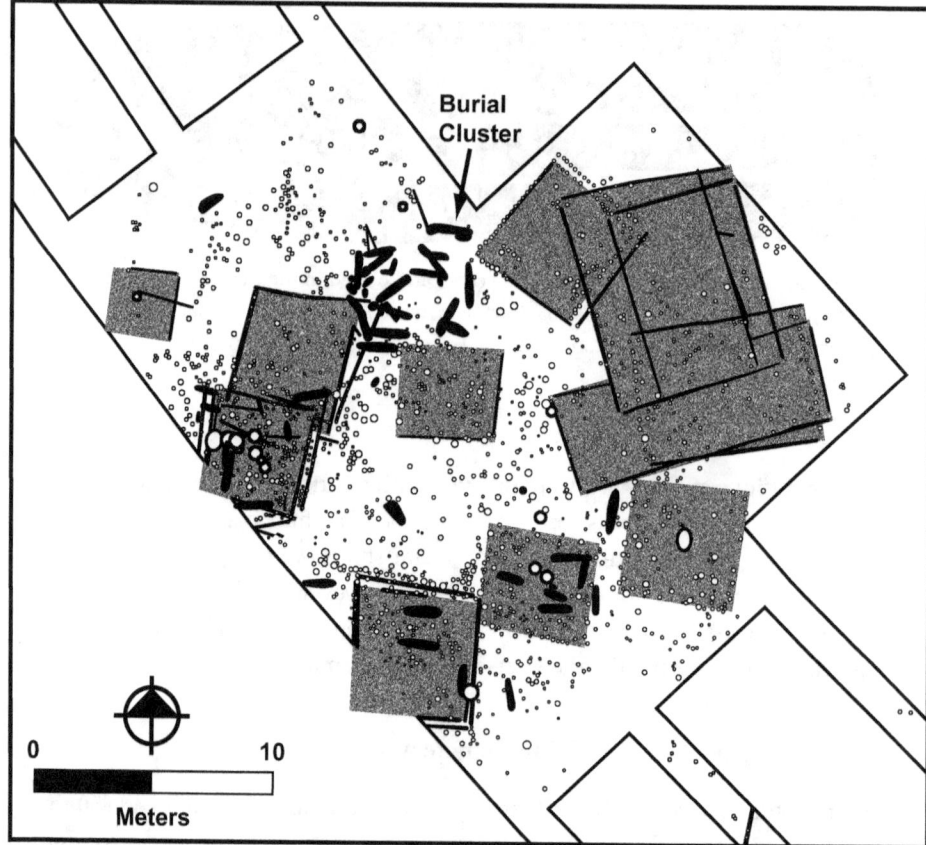

Figure 5.7. Moundville II–III cemetery superimposing Moundville I residential group (Roadway blocks 48+00 to 40+00). Moundville II–III Cemetery Superimposing Moundville I Residential Group (Roadway blocks 48+00 to 49+00)

(mentioned previously) who was interred with artifacts of ritual and political importance (Figure 5.6). He was buried in a location that later became the center of this tightly organized cemetery. If we are correct in interpreting these cemeteries as representing small kin groups, then for close to two centuries a Mississippian kin group literally built and expanded this cemetery around the grave of a prominent ancestor. Moreover, they did so in an area that had been previously used and carefully maintained as the corporate residential space by their early Mississippian ancestors.

The frequency with which burials were superpositioned in the central portion of this cemetery also points to its long history of use (Figure 5.8). In several cases it appears that when an older burial was encountered while digging a new grave, the older bones were pushed to the side to make room for the

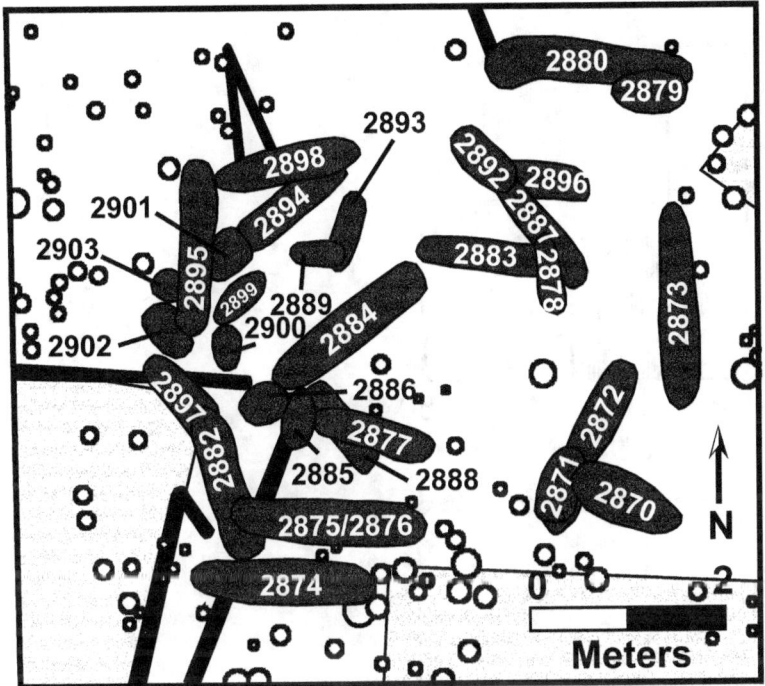

Figure 5.8. Detail of the Moundville II–III cemetery shown in Figure 5.7 (Roadway blocks 48+00 to 48+50).

new interment. Indeed, Jacobi's recent analysis of the Roadway burials identified a number of incomplete skeletons mixed in with complete skeletons. The presence of many of these fragmentary individuals may be the result of this mortuary practice.

Discussion and Conclusion

It is not surprising that specific Mississippian kin groups at Moundville used spatially discrete cemeteries to bury their dead. Drawing on global ethnographic data, Goldstein (1980) and Saxe (1970) have demonstrated that agricultural societies with lineal corporate rights over the use and inheritance of land often have cemeteries that are exclusively used by specific kin groups (see also Howell and Kintigh 1996; Meggitt 1965: 131; Morris 1991). Both scholars argue that these exclusive mortuary arrangements are part of broader strategies by which individuals seek to affirm their membership in a descent group and the land-inheritance rights that come with it. The heritability of social and economic resources no doubt helped inspire the initial construction of

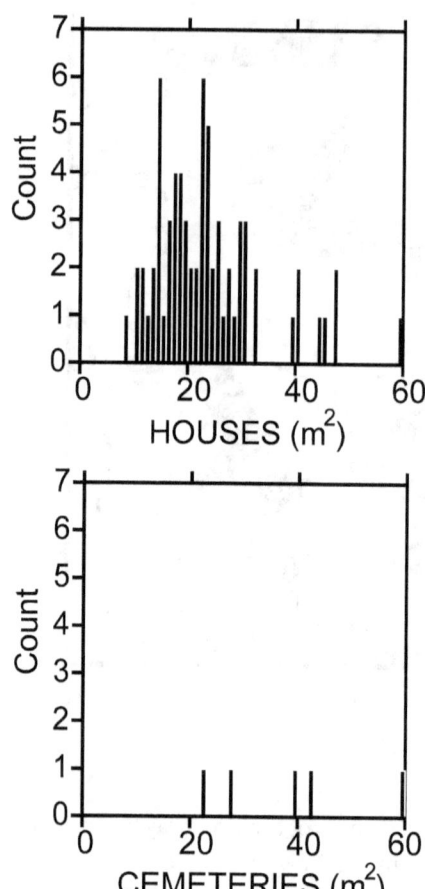

Figure 5.9. Spatial Comparison of Mississippian Structure Floor Areas to Burial Clusters in the Moundville Roadway

Moundville's mound and plaza complex and the clan-based political and ceremonial order it embodied. It is also important to note that the decades bracketing the construction of this mound and plaza complex correspond with Moundville's political consolidation of the region and the intensification of agricultural production (Knight and Steponaitis 1998; Scarry 1986, 1995).

The length of time these kin groups used their cemeteries, thereby inscribing their corporate identities onto the Moundville sociogram, is intriguing. Our analysis of the cemetery in roadway blocks 48+00 to 48+50 revealed a small mortuary complex that spanned some two centuries. Moreover, it is quite clear that these spatially discrete cemeteries were intentionally placed in the exact areas previously occupied by equally discrete residential groups (Wilson 2008). It follows that part of the broader meaning and purpose of these small cemeteries was to establish social and spatial continuity with ancestral residential space. Indeed, some clues in the organization of these cemeteries indicate that their spatial arrangements intentionally referenced this early Mississippian residential past. For example, the rectilinear arrangement of most burials in these cemeteries corresponds to the dimensions of early Mississippian houses at Moundville (Figure 5.9; Wilson 2005). Thus, it is not unreasonable to speculate that these cemeteries served as a metaphor for a house that embodied kin-group identity while maintaining continuity with the residential origin and history of kin groups at Moundville.

Mississippian clan and subclan groups maintained their coherence throughout much of Moundville's occupation; this is demonstrated in how they spatially delimited their corporate kin identities at Moundville. As a regional Mississippian polity, Moundville went through considerable political and economic change during this lengthy period. Creating and recreating the Moundville sociogram—in different ways and on different scales—provided kin groups a means of asserting their corporate identities and the rights, privileges, and social histories that came with them.

Acknowledgments

We wish to thank Jon Blitz, Eugene Futato, Dale Hutchinson, Jim Knight, Jon Marcoux, and Amber VanDerwarker for their help and advice in preparing this essay.

6

Aztalan Mortuary Practices Revisited

LYNNE G. GOLDSTEIN

The Aztalan site (47JE1) sits on the banks of the Crawfish River in Jefferson County, Wisconsin, between the modern cities of Milwaukee and Madison (see Figure 6.1). The site has been protected as a state park for more than 50 years. While several occupations have been discovered at this multicomponent site, Aztalan is best known for its Late Woodland and Middle Mississippian components that range from A.D. 800 to A.D. 1200. Grit-tempered collared wares represent the majority of the Late Woodland occupation, and shell-tempered ceramics indicate the Middle Mississippian occupation. Prominent architectural features such as a substantial stockade and platform mounds are believed to date to the Mississippian Period (Barrett 1933; Birmingham and Goldstein 2005; Goldstein and Freeman 1997; Richards 1992).

The first published description of Aztalan appeared in 1837 (Hyer 1837). The first excavations at Aztalan took place in 1838 and were carried out by W. T. Sterling in an attempt to ascertain the nature of the "ruins" of the stockade (Sterling 1920). Sustained investigations began in 1850 with the work of Increase A. Lapham, Wisconsin's prominent antiquarian. His work consisted of some limited exploratory excavations as well as a detailed mapping of the site (Figure 6.2; Lapham 1855). The first modern excavation came early in the twentieth century with the work of Samuel A. Barrett of the Milwaukee Public Museum. This research culminated in the publication of *Ancient Aztalan* (Barrett 1933), a seminal work that is the most complete description of the site and has had a lasting effect on interpretations of the site. In the 1950s and 1960s, a variety of excavations were related to the development of the site as a state park, some of which were done in the context of reconstructing a portion of the stockade and two of the platform mounds. Much of this work was conducted under the auspices of the Wisconsin Archeological Survey in the 1950s and later under the direction of Joan E. Freeman, then state archaeologist. Beginning in 1976, the University of Wisconsin-Milwaukee, under Lynne Goldstein's direction, initiated a sustained research effort directed at the site

Figure 6.1. Location of the Aztalan Site in the State of Wisconsin

and its regional context (Goldstein and Freeman 1997; Goldstein 1997; Richards 1992), and this research tradition has continued under Goldstein's direction at Michigan State University (Goldstein and Gaff 2002). A number of other researchers have conducted specialized excavations and analyses at the site, but these projects have generally been limited in extent and duration.

This long history of research at Aztalan, while of immense importance, has inadvertently had a deleterious effect on the generation of new knowledge about the site for two primary reasons. Older interpretations often haunt our current understanding and perceptions of the site by permeating the process of knowledge production. Particular views of the site, in part generated and sustained by the prominence of and fascination with the Aztalan site, have long structured research design. The very name of the site itself, Aztalan, encapsulates this notion. Nathaniel Hyer, who reported the site in 1837, named it on the mistaken belief that it was the ancestral home of the Aztecs. Hyer based his assessment on his reading of Alexander von Humboldt's travel narratives about the Aztecs and their ancestral home, Aztlan. Despite Hyer's erroneous judgment, the name, Aztalan (which in itself was incorrect) persists today (cf. Hall 1986).

Another reason that the long history of research at the site has had a deleterious effect on knowledge generation is less obvious. For many years, each new researcher at Aztalan accepted a number of the interpretations of previous re-

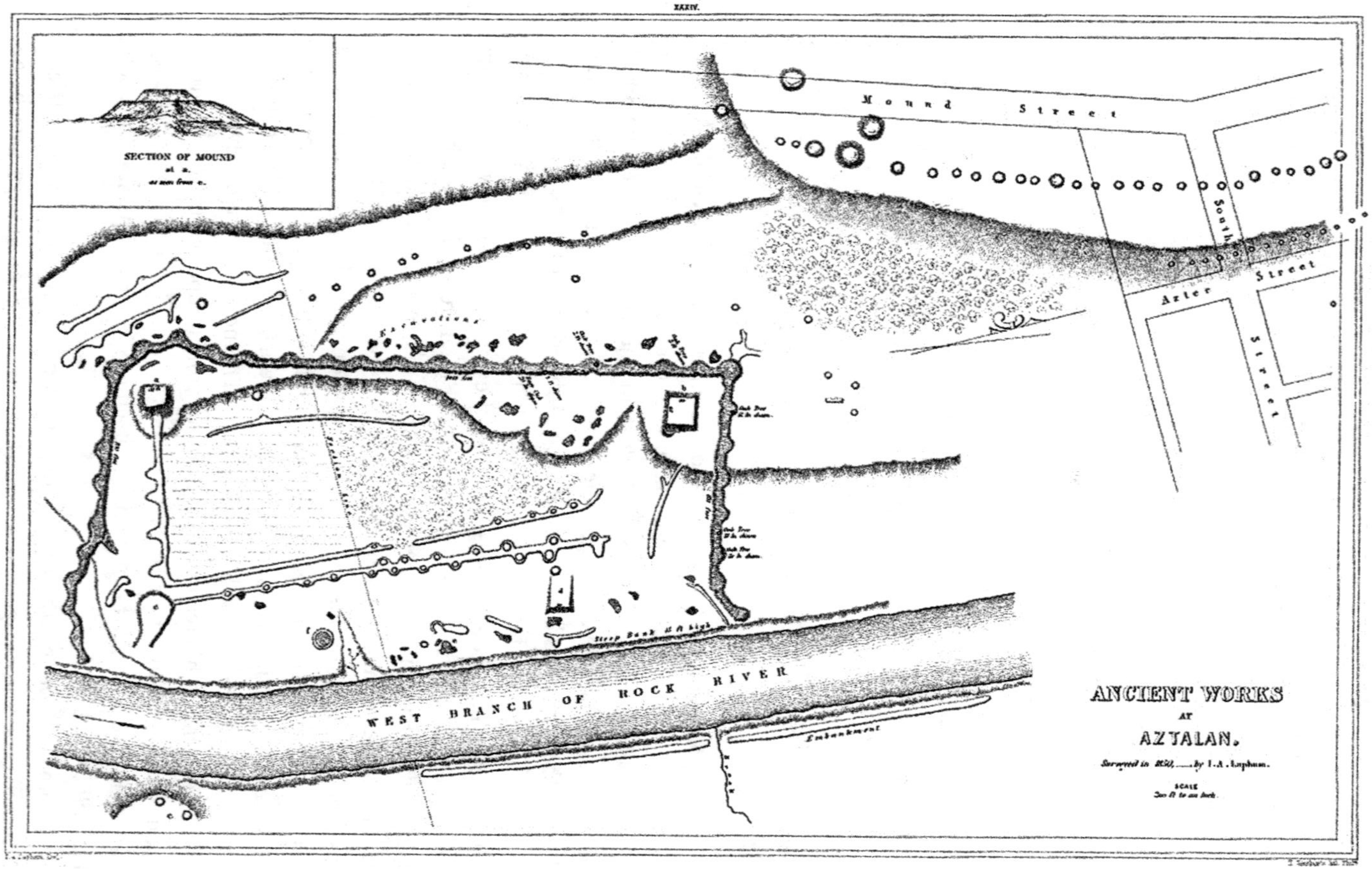

Figure 6.2. Increase A. Lapham's 1855 Detailed Map of the Aztalan Site. From Lapham 1855: Plate 34.

searchers, but individuals rarely examined the artifacts and other information excavated by those archaeologists. Barrett excavated more area of the site than anyone else, and his collections are readily accessible at the Milwaukee Public Museum, yet because those artifacts were excavated in the early 1900s, few archaeologists gave them more than a cursory examination until the 1980s. Researchers focused on their own investigations and findings and did not integrate what they found into a larger picture.

One long-standing interpretation about Aztalan involves the idea that the inhabitants of the site regularly practiced cannibalism. Excavations by Barrett (1933) in the early twentieth century produced quantities of scattered human bone in unusual contexts such as hearths and pits, suggesting the bones were treated as trash or food waste. Despite the relatively low quantity of remains given the large volume of excavation, Barrett (1933) concluded that these bones recovered in a domestic context constituted evidence for cannibalism. He was convinced of these findings because of the context and because the bones were often broken. Given what little was known about Mississippian societies at the time and what little was known about the range of mortuary practices in particular, Barrett's conclusion was logical. Since that time, however, we have learned much about the range of Late Woodland and Mississippian mortuary practices, including the importance in some contexts of extensive processing and placement of remains. However, although we have learned much since 1933, few have reexamined this material, questioned Barrett's conclusions, or suggested that there might be alternative interpretations. Indeed, until 1991, the Wisconsin Historical Marker at Aztalan included the phrase "and their cannibalism made them unsatisfactory neighbors."

In 1986, Goldstein and Sullivan presented a paper at the Society for American Archaeology Annual Meetings that systematically examined Barrett's conclusions. They proposed that the remains might also be the signature of a set of mortuary practices. The paper did not necessarily discount the possibility of cannibalism, but it suggested an alternate scenario rooted in archaeological data from other sites and ethnohistoric analogies (Goldstein and Sullivan 1986). While the debate about cannibalism remains unresolved to the satisfaction of some archaeologists, the phenomena of scattered human remains is no longer conceptualized as necessarily representing a people's subsistence base; now it is seen as likely or more likely the residue of mortuary ritual. Anderson (1994) conducted a more detailed analysis of the human bone, but the question of the process that resulted in the fragmented remains is still unresolved. The issue is not whether or not Barrett was correct but rather that all interpretations must be reexamined and reanalyzed given new data at Aztalan and new work at other sites.

Among its other qualities, Aztalan is unusual in terms of its apparent mortuary ritual. No cemetery has been documented at Aztalan, although human remains have been found in one of three sets of contexts on the site proper:

1. Eleven adult individuals were recovered from what was originally described as a "crematorium" on the second stage of the northwest pyramidal mound (Rowe 1958b). The word "crematorium" is misleading, however. The feature consisted of a wooden structure with plastered walls and a covered floor into which the remains of the 11 individuals and associated offerings were placed. This structure subsequently burned. Ten of the individuals were extended and may or may not have been placed in the structure as primary interments. The eleventh individual was a bundle reburial, clearly the result of secondary treatment. Because of the nature of the structure, the terms "charnel house" or "mortuary house" seem more appropriate than "crematorium." Although the burning may have been deliberate, the fact that a separate mortuary house existed must be stressed . This was much more than a crematory. Because the structure burned, the bones were very fragile; Anderson (1994) was able to identify three males and three females but was unable to identify the sex of five individuals.
2. Primary inhumations are limited in number and usually consist of a flexed or partially flexed individual placed in a burial pit with few or no grave goods. These primary burials are often located at or near major structural features such as stockade walls or platform mounds. Occasionally primary inhumations include one or more bones (often long bones) of a second individual.
3. The third mortuary context includes scattered pieces of human bone recovered from refuse pits, storage pits, so-called firepits, or general habitation debris. Some of these bones exhibit cutmarks, but these bones are almost never burned.

As noted above, Barrett's original interpretation of the scattered human bone at the site has formed the basis of all subsequent interpretations of the Aztalan mortuary ritual:

> Revolutionary as this idea may seem, we are forced to suggest that the evidence points to the probability that human flesh was here used as a regular article of diet. . . . In no instance was evidence found that these human remnants of the feast or of the daily meal . . . were treated in any degree differently from those of any other part of the aboriginal menu. (Barrett 1933: 361)

After Barrett's interpretations were published, the idea of cannibalism at Aztalan was not seriously questioned and research was oriented toward determining details of the interpretation. However, Barrett was not the first to suggest cannibalism at Aztalan. The Rev. A. N. Somers conducted excavations at Aztalan in 1888 with his church Sunday school class. They excavated what he termed a "communal refuse-heap" (Somers 1892). Somers claimed that 40 percent of the almost 2,000 bones he recovered were human and had cutmarks around the joints. These bones had been "mixed" with those of animals. The location of the materials Somers excavated is unknown.

A good example of the prevalent attitude toward the interpretation and analysis of cannibalism at Aztalan is found in an introduction to an M.A. thesis on the Aztalan human bone:

> The argument of whether or not it (cannibalism) existed or whether or not it was of a ceremonial nature is not dealt with since this has been treated at length by Barrett. . . . [Instead, the question is] who was eaten by the Aztalan inhabitants? Did they generally eat only members of the surrounding tribes whom they had captured in warfare, or did they 'prefer' members of their own community? . . . What was the sex of the victims? . . . A supplementary problem would be to determine what parts of the human body were generally eaten. (Holcomb 1952: 2)

In her more recent reanalysis of the human bone at Aztalan, Anderson (1994) found that the scattered human bone had an average minimum number of individuals (MNI) of 56 (depending how one calculated it) and that males were more numerous when sex could be determined (69 percent). However, sex cannot be determined for a majority of these scattered remains. The majority of the scattered bones are from adults (92 percent).

Anderson's analysis of the cutmarks on the scattered bone demonstrated that most of the marks are located on the ends of long bones. She found no significance in the distribution of postmortem cutmarks on the cranium.

Anderson also examined 17 inhumations that are likely contemporary with the scattered human bone. Most (n = 15) are adults, including the so-called Princess Burial from a conical mound at the very northern end of the site (outside the palisade walls) and the individuals from the northwest pyramidal mound charnel house. Nine of the 17 were not affected by burning (this is interesting, since there were 11 in the burned charnel structure). Seven are young adult females. No cutmarks were found on any of these individuals, but many of the bones in the charnel house were severely burned.

Anderson counted a total of 73 individuals, including the scattered fragments and primary inhumations. This is far fewer than one would expect for any projected population size for Aztalan. Richards (1992: 118) estimates a population of 150 to 538, guessing 350 to be a reasonable number. Whatever the number, this population of 73 is too small and too skewed to be representative of the whole. Clearly a number of people and segments of the population are missing. Since Anderson's analysis, some additional human bone has been discovered. It is discussed below, but it does not significantly change this biased distribution.

The spatial patterning of human bone at Aztalan is not random. The few primary interments are located in small clusters within the habitation precinct or along palisade walls. The scattered human bone is almost exclusively located within the inner palisade—that is, within the habitation precinct—but tends to be clustered along the inner palisade walls. Barrett notes two kinds of contexts for human bones found in features: standard refuse pits or firepits—refuse pits with quantities of ash and "Aztalan brick." These firepit features with bone are rare, however, and tend to be located at the corners of the habitation precinct.

Reconsidering Landscape and Structures

Archaeologists increasingly view landscapes as dynamic entities that are constantly being constructed, deconstructed, negotiated, and rebuilt. The landscape is "always artificial, always synthetic, always subject to sudden or unpredictable change" (Jackson 1984: 8). People regularly alter the landscape to accommodate changes in the political and social order (Alcock 1993: 7). Human behavior does not simply happen in vacuous space. Behavior has its own spatial forms, and these spatial forms "imprint upon the landscape in a variety of ways including architecture" (Hillier 1996: 29). However, the structure of space is not merely determined by the social processes that occur there. Spatial forms act as active participants in affecting cultural change, and the arrangement of space can likewise structure and control human activity (Alcock 1993: 7). Landscapes act to structure social action, and at the same time they are structured by social action.

For Mississippian societies, perhaps the most obvious of such forms are the mound and the palisade. A variety of authors have discussed the reasons people built mounds, much of them related to power, the maintenance of power, and who decides what is built where and how. Recently, Brown (2003, 2006a) has questioned these approaches, using Cahokia's Mound 72 beaded burial to demonstrate that instead of interpreting this individual as a member of the high-status elite, it can, using Wolf's (1999) notion of structural power, be viewed as part of a collective undertaking of a dramatic performance of an important myth. In other words, it may not *always* be about power and control or it may not be about *only* power and control.

The landscape is an ordered assemblage of objects through which complex messages are communicated, reproduced, and experienced within a cultural system, and we need to consider how landscapes signify meanings across a site. An important aspect of landscapes is their experiential nature. Landscapes are perceived and imbued with meaning based on how people experience the world around them. In a notable example, Bradley (1998) emphasizes that neolithic monuments developed out of the daily routines of people who were living in an environment that was familiar and steeped in symbolism.

Gourgeon (2006: 189—90) notes a particularly interesting pattern for the Coosa area. House form itself did not vary between elites and commoners, but the size of the houses and items within the houses did. In other words, differences were masked in household contexts. The group was likewise enforced through the terms of ritual spaces and symbols. A corporate strategy seemed to be highlighted within the village, suggesting an integrated society and perhaps a network strategy that operated at a regional level.

Similarly, landscapes can be regarded as the materialization of memory by providing a place for social and individual histories (Knapp and Ashmore 1999: 13). The sensual experience of landscapes is an important element of how they act as memory. All five senses can serve as mnemonic devices to trigger memories (Tuan 1977). Even a smell or particular sounds can activate people's memories. In the field of urban planning and design, Dolores Hayden has shown how memory and place are intrinsically tied together (Hayden 1995). The elements of a social history of space connect people's lives and livelihoods to the landscape as it changes over time. Space is culturally constructed to provoke certain responses from people and tie their actions to the past (Hayden 1995).

It therefore makes sense that myth plays an important and active role in the power of landscape as memory (Cosgrove 1993: 282) and that myths give a power to the surrounding landscape in which people live their everyday lives. Landscape myths and memories have been tied to the "ferocious enchantment" of national identities through modern territorial feuds (Schama 1995: 15). Brown's (2006a) analysis is again an example of the role of myth in the power of landscape as memory.

Sullivan's (2006) analysis of Dallas phase sites makes a critical point about memory, social histories, and the past. Archaeologists have made the assumption that women had little political power because they were not well represented in mounds but did not consider the potential meaning of the house burials of the women in the Dallas phase. Sullivan's (2006) careful analysis has demonstrated a kind of spatial complementarity operating within the sites she examined, going beyond the simple limits of the mounds themselves. The houses were indeed part of the burial accompaniment.

Certain places in the landscape help create and express social identity. Bradley (1993: 26) suggests that these places on the landscape may act as markers to draw attention to socially significant features, such as visually prominent landmarks, locations of important ecological niches, or places where important (possibly mythic) past events transpired. These places are often given form through some material manifestation such as rock painting or mound building. No matter what form these manifestations take, they signify identity by literally marking the landscape.

Landscapes can be active participants in the ordering of cultural relations. As discussed above, landscapes are not merely determined by the social actions that take place across them; they also can shape and determine social relations by allowing or restricting access to certain areas, by making things visible or hiding them from view, or by directing the flow of people and/or ideas. Relationships of power and influence come to the forefront when one views the landscape as an ideologically manipulated arena. This approach emphasizes the social contradictions and conflicts played out in the known landscape, which may emerge in power relationships. Alcock shows how the Roman landscape in Greece continued to be vital and dynamic, responding in a variety of ways to imperial Roman control (Alcock 1993). On a more intimate scale, Leone studied the landscaped garden of a colonial house in Annapolis, Maryland, where the garden acted to naturalize arbitrary relations of power (Leone 1984). Landscape as an arena for power relationships requires that the actors in a landscape have a political awareness of their environment.

Kelly (2006) uses ethnographic, oral history, and archaeological data of different types and from multiple scales to demonstrate how the production of craft items associated with the elite in Mississippian society was organized. Most relevant here is the spatial separation of this production and the way that production was the result of cooperation by different groups operating through different rituals on different scales, all of which was in some way controlled by the religious elite.

In her analysis of Mississippian in northwestern Florida, Payne (2006) employs ethnographic analogy and analysis of the landscape to outline how space and other items are used to map position and relationships, noting that at smaller sites, some kinds of relationships are absent. For example, she argues (2006: 105) that divine support for authority comes with increasing chiefdom or site size. She suggests that deliberate and explicit use of space, large mounds, wealthy burials, and Southeastern Ceremonial Complex artifacts emphasize kinship and divine support to legitimate power.

Landscapes are also arenas of transformation, necessarily embodying multiple time periods, and as such have the potential to demonstrate both continuity and transformation (Knapp and Ashmore 1999: 18). Even after monuments have passed out of active use, they are still part of an active landscape, and their meaning is transformed as those places are encountered and reused by new people (Bradley 1993, 1998). Landscapes can be transformed by numerous factors and can take many different forms. Monuments can be destroyed, effectively destroying the symbolic markings of the landscape, after a conquest by neighboring people. Or the neglect of monuments can signify as profound a cultural change as conquest by signaling a fundamental change in the perception of the landscape (Knapp and Ashmore 1999: 19).

Schroeder's (2006) work on the Jonathan Creek site and her examination of Mississippian palisades is an excellent example of the study of landscapes as arenas of continuity and transformation. One of the most notable features of many large Mississippian settlements is a substantial bastioned stockade. While it is convenient to talk about such walls as being for defense and controlling external relationships, such a view ignores those who lived within that setting. As Schroeder (2006: 117) notes: "Walls served additional social, political, ideological, and symbolic agendas, which at certain times may have overshadowed the defensive functions of these structures." She further comments that there are often changes over time to these walls and that these changes have implications for the chiefly authority and the responses by the community. Using modifications in the palisade, she outlines a series of changes in orientation and perspective for the people of Jonathan Creek over time.

Aztalan's Landscape and Structures

One of the main aspects of my most recent research at Aztalan was the development of a coordinated database for understanding site structure that took Aztalan's landscape into account. We also examined areas outside the palisaded portion of the site (Figure 6.3). Since Aztalan was first explored by early antiquarians, research at the site has focused on the area within the palisaded village (Barrett 1933; Richards 1992; Goldstein 1999). Nearly all excavations took place inside the walls, and a great deal of the excavation work focused on revealing the nature of the stockade. The few excavations outside the palisade that were not related to mounds were conducted because new construction of parking lots and other park features were going to disturb these areas.

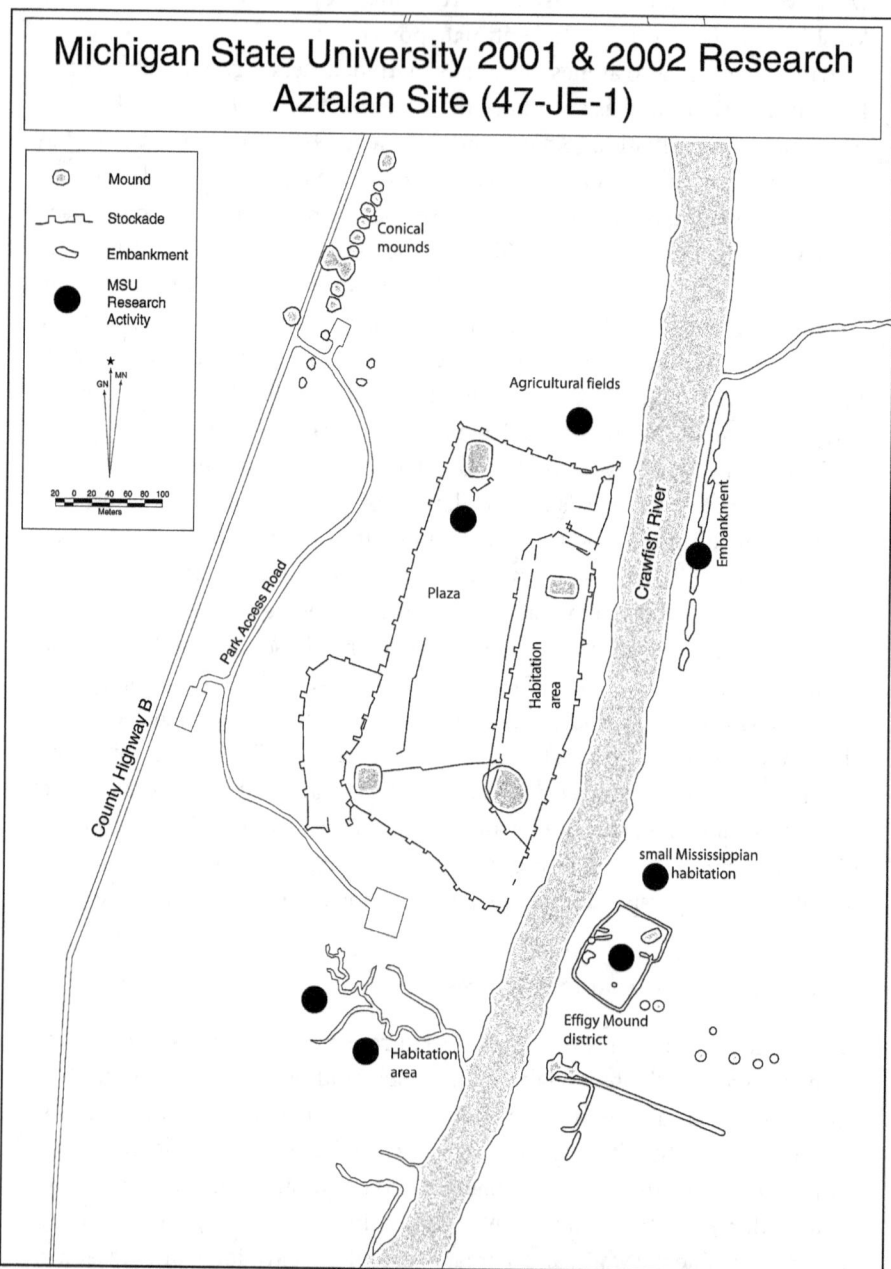

Figure 6.3. An Outline Map of General Activity Areas at Aztalan Indicating Michigan State University's 2000 and 2001 Research Activity Locations

Excavations and coring north of the stockade (see Figure 6.3) were intended to provide evidence of agricultural fields noted on an early map of the site (Goldstein and Freeman 1997). To the contrary, these widely spaced excavations contained several features and general refuse, including a portion of a human mandible. In addition to extending our knowledge of the distribution of scattered human bone, these excavations also suggest that modern agriculture has not destroyed everything in this area. Most interestingly, however, there was evidence of prehistoric removal of a significant portion of the A Horizon soil, presumably for building the nearby platform mounds. Further investigation may result in the discovery of remnants of the agricultural fields seen by early European visitors to the site, but to date we have not been able to identify evidence of these fields.

Excavations also took place on the eastern bank of the Crawfish River, opposite the main village (Figure 6.3). Barrett (1933) reported finding evidence of occupations related to Aztalan across the river, including the remnants of a rectangular enclosure. In the late 1970s, work by Goldstein (1979) documented that most of the materials found on the east bank were Effigy Mound in association, including one large effigy mound that Barrett had noted earlier. Recent coring and limited excavations suggest that it is possible that what Barrett identified as an enclosure may actually be a set of effigy mounds that had eroded, but our 2001 excavations also demonstrated that there was a small confined Mississippian occupation on the east bank of the river as well, to the north of Barrett's enclosure.

We also excavated in the plaza area of the site just south of the northwest platform mound to explore oval-shaped features that became visible only after this area was mowed following a drought. A total of 70 ovals were observed in what appeared to be a series of rows. This locale has shown up as notably distinct in many different contexts, such as aerial photographs and even on Lapham's 1855 map (see Figure 6.1), which indicates pits and disturbances in the same vicinity. Excavation of a trench to cross-section a set of these pits revealed 14 large deep storage pits that were prehistorically excavated into a sand and gravel surface (Figure 6.4).

As surprising as the size and depth and regularity of the pits was the fact that they were excavated into bedded gravels. Because gravel does not have a great deal of strength or structure to hold vertical walls, the storage pits probably had to be lined with a fine-grained material. There is evidence of fine sediment lining the pits (see Figure 6.4); clays would have been practical liners due to their ability to prevent moisture seepage.

Of interest are the facts that the A Horizon is missing from the general area of the oval features and the landform was greatly altered. In fact, it ap-

Figure 6.4. Cross-Sections of Two of the Large Pits in the Sculptuary Area

Figure 6.5. The Sculptuary as Seen from the Ground. Each person is standing on a rise in elevation or tier, and the person on the right is on the highest point of the sculpted feature. Photo taken looking south.

pears that the landform was deliberately sculpted into a tiered mound-like structure that was incorporated into the side of the hill. The sculpted tiers or terraces face east toward the Crawfish River. To the west, the sculpted tiers merge with the landform. There are at least three distinct tiers to the feature, each one separated by an elevation of approximately 1.5 meters (Figure 6.5). These horizons were removed some time in prehistory—probably during the construction and sculpting of the feature within which the pits are found and possibly also during the construction of the northwest platform mound.

Each of the three tiers of the sculpted surface served a slightly different function:

1. The westernmost or highest tier or terrace had pits with the most structure and included the largest quantity of scattered human remains. These features were generally filled with fine-grained sediments, did not appear to have been left open for long periods, and had few artifacts or debris. The debris recovered included a pipestone earspool (sourced to what is now Pipestone National Monument in Minnesota), shell beads, a few projectile points, and several Mississippian rimsherds.
2. Pits in the middle terrace or tier appear to be more stratified and may have been left open for periods of time. There are very few artifacts or

debris in these pits, and they may have been used for community food storage, processing, or dumping. Some have evidence of corn and wild rice.
3. The topographically lowest tier had the most variability in feature shape but also includes large features with few artifacts and debris. Exceptions to this pattern were located at the edge of or just off the edge of the sculpted surface. A burial of a partially disarticulated individual was found in a pit at the eastern end of the surface. The articulated bones include a femur, a fibula, a tibia, a metatarsal, the pelvis, the sacrum, and some vertebrae. The disarticulated bones were a rib, some additional metatarsals, one vertebra, pelvis fragments, and some tarsal bones. What was unusual about the burial was that a femur from a much larger individual had been placed on top of the remains of the smaller individual; the femur of the larger individual had been deliberately cut.

This portion of the site was carefully planned. The spatial arrangement of the pits is significant and is tied to both the terracing and the northwest platform mound (Figure 6.6). Given that the tiered feature was sculpted and also was a place for processing human remains, we have termed it a "sculptuary."

Barrett (1933) assumed that because human bone was found cracked and in refuse pits, the only possible explanation was cannibalism. He then focused his attentions on determining the particular variety of cannibalism practiced. His conclusion was based on the fact that the bone was widely scattered. He also assumed that because there was a considerable amount of bone, the cannibalism could not be considered part of a ritual practice.

Barrett's interpretation of the presence of cannibalism was done at a time when our understandings of the variability of mortuary ritual were limited; this was especially true of our knowledge at the time of Late Woodland/Mississippian mortuary ritual. Also, at the time Barrett was writing, descriptions and reports of cannibalism in the ethnographic literature were limited and not well understood. Barrett's argument that the evidence at Aztalan could not be evidence of ritual cannibalism did not consider temporal depth. The dispersal of a large number of bones could actually be evidence of an aspect of ritual cannibalism—that is, everyone participates. Anderson (1994) finds that the scattered bone at Aztalan compares well with Turner's and White's criteria for cannibalism on some measures but not on others. In particular, all of the cutmarks are on the ends of long bones and few of the scattered bones are burned.

Given the context of the times, it is not surprising that Barrett ignored the complex interrelationships between disposal and death; like many others, he

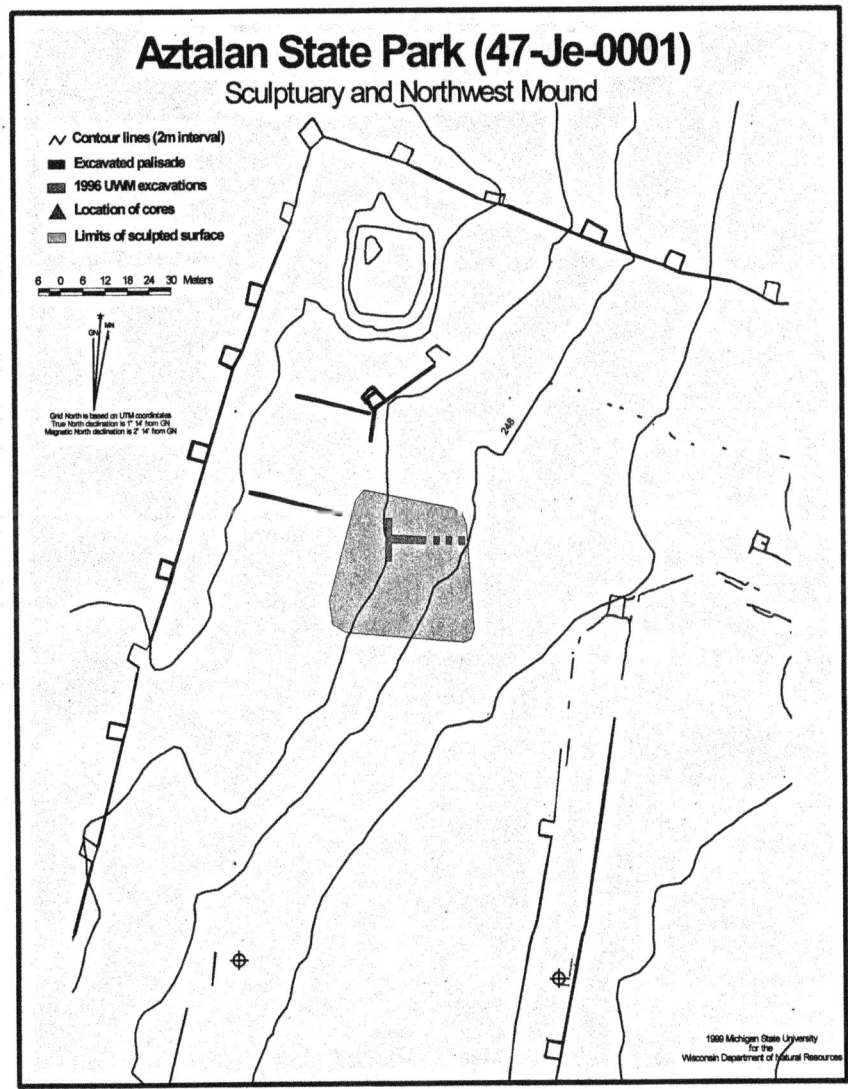

Figure 6.6. Map of the Sculptuary Location, Outline of the Feature, and Michigan State University Excavations in Relation to the Northwest Platform Mound.

assumed that disposal is a direct consequence of death, specifically death in the immediate vicinity. Archaeologists who followed Barrett never reexamined Barrett's conclusions with respect to his assumptions—they accepted Barrett's original conclusions and moved forward from there. Given this overall context and the discussion of leadership, symbols, and space earlier, it is appropriate to reexamine the mortuary ritual as represented at Aztalan.

First, the scattered bone is represented almost exclusively by long bones. Where are the bones of the torso and other bones? This differential pattern of bone distribution does not seem to be the result of collecting bias because there are many other items of varying sizes and shapes.. Differential preservation cannot explain the selective distribution of bones. Therefore, we infer that these bones (pelvis, vertebrae, ribs, etc.) must be somewhere else. Unfortunately, there is no evidence (from any of the Aztalan excavations) to suggest that they are elsewhere at the site. Although the negative inference is proper here, we cannot say that the torso bones were never at the site or that the bones were at the site but were removed. We simply don't know.

At least three methods of disposal are represented at Aztalan: 1) primary interments; 2) disposal in the charnel house that is likely a combination of primary and secondary interment; and 3) bone scattering, which represents secondary disposal or extensive mortuary processing. The differential spatial patterning of these disposal methods provides additional evidence of the distinctive nature of each method (Figure 6.7):

1. The charnel house (or "crematorium" à la Rowe 1958b) location at the summit of the Northwest platform mound is the only such structure documented for the site.
2. The primary interments so far discovered tend to occur in small clusters and are confined to either the habitation precinct and/or the palisade structure.
3. In sharp contrast, the scattered bone is not everywhere—it is limited to the area within the inner stockade or is specifically associated with major structures such as sculpted features. The class of scattered bone may have an additional or secondary patterning within it: some bones are associated with firepits, which are clustered at the edges and corners of the inner stockade structure. Firepits are relatively rare at this site; the three sets associated with scattered human remains are located just east of the gravel knoll that may have been used as a southeast mound; just north and slightly east of the northeast platform mound; and at the northwest corner of the inner palisade and east of the sculptuary. At each of these locations, at least one articulated individual is in the immediate vicinity (see Figure 6.7).

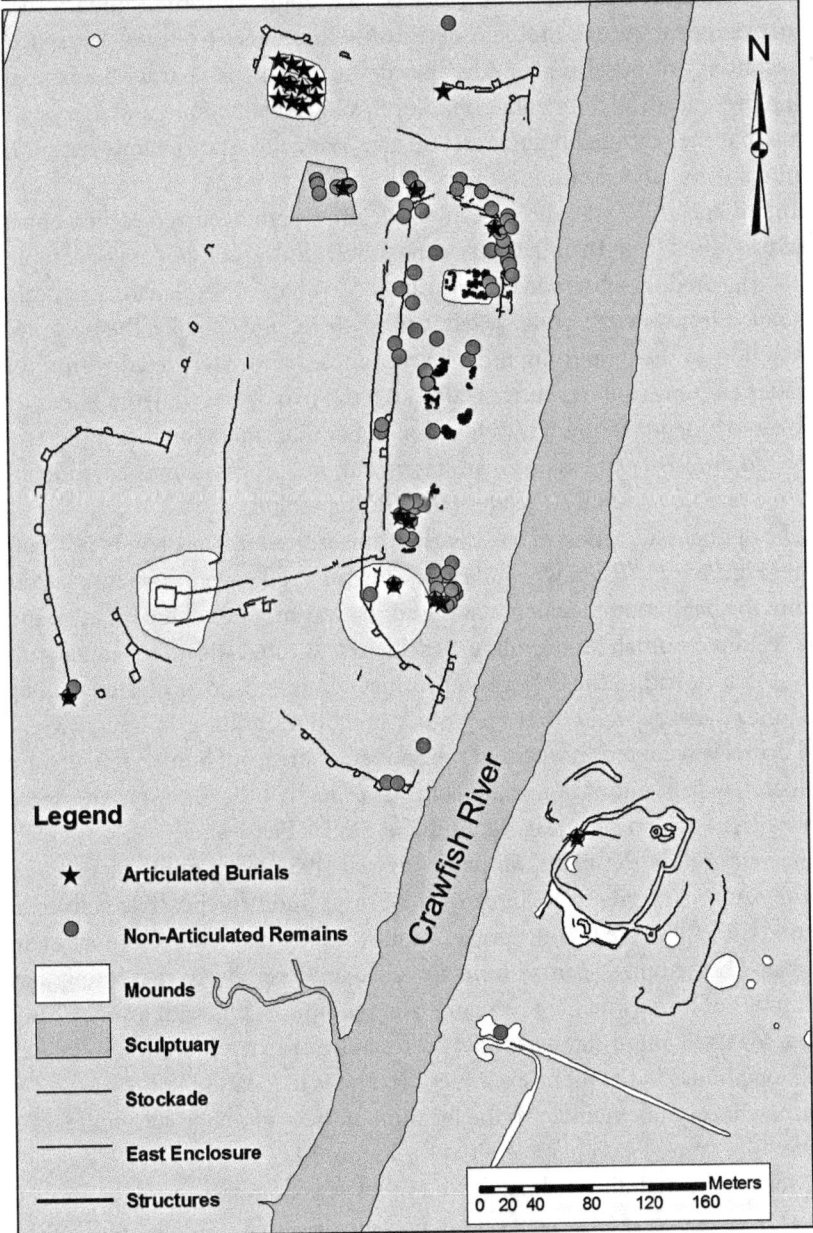

Figure 6.7. Location of Articulated Burials, Nonarticulated Human Remains, and Structures at the Aztalan Site.

Secondary disposal of the dead is common within Mississippian societies, and at Aztalan there is evidence for such treatment—the bundle burial in the charnel house and the scattered bone. However, although both are secondary, they clearly demonstrate the problem of drawing inferences from the "presence" of secondary disposal per se. The bundle burial in the charnel house may well represent social differentiation or even status distinctions, and one might argue that the scattered bone represents an "opposite" status. However, more significant for understanding the organization of Aztalan is the point that neither disposal was the direct result of death. Death occurred earlier, bones were processed later. In both cases, some other cultural component or components triggered the observed disposal activity. Whatever explanatory hypothesis one espouses concerning status, cannibalism, and the like, the observed distinction in the patterning must be recognized and interpreted within the broader cultural context. Further, although the two disposal methods cannot be treated independently, it is well to remember that similar cultural processes may find different expression and different cultural processes may have identical recoverable material correlates (cf. Goldstein 2000).

The spatial patterning of the distribution of the human bone is not random (Figure 6.7). The few primary interments are located in small clusters within the habitation precinct or at the edges near mounds and palisade walls. The scattered human bone is almost exclusively located within the inner palisade—that is, within the habitation precinct—but tends to be clustered along the inner palisade walls. They are not located on mounds or in houses. General debris is scattered throughout the habitation area, but human remains are deliberately kept out of houses, in contrast to many other cultures and some other Mississippian sites (e.g., Moundville, Dallas Phase sites).

Barrett and, in the 1950s, Moreau Maxwell (1952) each found pits similar to the sculptuary pits in the area of the gravel knoll (or possible southeast mound); it is possible that the gravel knoll is analogous to the sculptuary and may also be sculpted. It may have an A Horizon removed; it certainly has groupings of burials that are similar to the sculptuary, pits with artifacts, and so on. Maxwell found clay earspools, corn, shell beads, copper, and several human long bones in the pit he excavated. The pit is in location in the site that is a somewhat complementary to the location of the sculptuary (see Figure 6.7). Barrett illustrates a comparable pit as his Figure 34.

Mortuary variability and patterning in a site encompass more than social statuses or economic elements. Our present-day views about cannibalism have dramatically colored our interpretations about Aztalan in the past. For a variety of reasons, past interpretations have largely ignored the use and construction of space and ideas and the importance of collective memory and site planning.

As Hendon has noted, "Places, like people and objects, also incarnate, fix, and reiterate social memory. By creating and modifying a landscape of natural and built forms, groups construct a setting that gives concrete, permanent expression to relationships and identities" (2000, 50). At Aztalan, it is time to tell a more complete, a more complex, and perhaps a more compelling story.

Aztalan Mortuary Rituals

Coordinating the mortuary data for Aztalan remains somewhat of a problem since only a portion of the ritual and the population are represented at the site; we do not know what happened to most people at death. Further, due to the variability in preservation, it is difficult to say much about gender relationships and contexts. Nonetheless, we have significantly more and better integrated information than existed previously.

The substantial stockade structure at Aztalan may have originally been built for defensive purposes, but it was modified over the course of its existence and internal palisades were added at least once and possibly more than once. It seems less certain that the internal palisades, which were less massive than the external palisade but did include bastions, were strictly for defensive purposes. The internal walls may well have had a social, ideological, or political purpose or they may have divided activities for other reasons. From a mortuary perspective, what is most interesting is the fact that a majority of the individual articulated burials recovered were placed along palisade walls or at or near a corner of an internal or external palisade wall. Locating the articulated burials in this deliberate pattern may have reinforced memory within the community or within a particular segment or group. This mortuary treatment was not available to all.

The inner palisade walled off a habitation area, but it was also an ideologically manipulated arena. When a person died, their remains were processed in one of several places, depending on who they were and what group they were affiliated with. Some were processed through a charnel structure like the one on the northwest platform mound. Others were processed through a series of pits on the sculpted surface (the sculptuary); movement of the bones through those pits was related to the distribution and storage of certain foodstuffs, the movement of specialized craft items, and other rituals. It is likely that an analogous and complementary process took place at the opposite end of the site where there is a gravel knoll today.

When the bones of an individual had been processed, they were placed in a refuse pit or otherwise discarded, but they were never placed inside a house where people lived. The rules for proper disposal of human bones were strict. In addition no human bone was found in the plaza area of the site, except within the sculptuary. To date, the only location where human bones have been found outside the palisade walls is north of the palisade, where we found another A Horizon removed (this is where we found the single mandible); in the northernmost conical mound at a significant distance from the rest of the site (the so-called Princess Burial, Barrett 1933); and on the east side of the river in association with the possibly earlier rectangular structure (Barrett 1933).

The association of the rare firepits with unarticulated human bone and articulated burials that appear in the corners of the interior palisade may represent an opening or closing offering of some kind. A similar sort of distinctive feature closed the Schild mortuary sequence (Goldstein 1980). It is not clear that these features opened or closed the sequence at Aztalan, but their location, consistency, and symbolism are evidence of their importance.

Conclusions and Comparisons

It is beyond the scope of this essay to provide a detailed comparison of Aztalan mortuary ritual with all other Mississippian mortuary sites or features. That could be an important and useful project, but in addition to the time involved in such a project, at Aztalan, as at many other Mississippian sites, only a portion of the total range of mortuary practices have been discovered. Nonetheless, some general trends and patterns are apparent as well as key Mississippian elements that appear at many sites.

In his 2003 overview of Mississippian chiefdoms, Cobb notes that "elaborate burials associated with many Mississippian sites, in conjunction with earthworks, have served as some of our richest sources of inspiration about the structure of complexity" (2003: 72). Focusing primarily on artifacts, Cobb discusses status distinctions and prestige-goods economies, noting that these models have been critiqued in recent years (2003: 73). While few question the role of power at some level in Mississippian societies, mortuary research today is far more multidimensional in scope and looks beyond mounds and elites. It is in this context that we can place the mortuary ritual that is represented at Aztalan.

As I noted in my analysis of the Moss and Schild sites in the lower Illinois River valley (Goldstein 1980), organizational principles are apparent at a number of Mississippian sites of varying size and complexity. This does not necessarily mean that exactly the same things were happening in each place but rather that the same kind of organization seems to be operating. This insight relates to group structure and the importance of the group over the individual at times. The elements outlined (ordered from least to most complex) include (Goldstein 1980: 137):

1. *Row structure only*, found in small cemeteries, with the rows representing families or extended kin.
2. *Charnel-row structure*, a combination of rows with a charnel area that emphasizes the charnel area. The idea here is that this kind of cemetery or burial area represents either a large community or more than one community.
3. *Charnel-row structure/accretional mound*, which may represent one or more community or group in control over several generations.
4. *All of the above* can occur at centers or large sites, reflecting more people and more distinctions between people.

The other point Goldstein made about these categories was that taken in order, there was "an increase in the amount of handling or processing of the body (with more secondary and bundle burials represented at each stage)" (Goldstein 1980: 137). Various researchers since 1980 have elaborated on this theme, demonstrating more complexity than I originally outlined in Mississippian mortuary practices. In particular, work such as Sullivan's (2006) reminds us that gender may cut across some of the spatial differences that are apparent and that our excavation biases may lead us to faulty interpretations.

Spatial symmetry is often a part of Mississippian mortuary practices. The mortuary site was planned and ritual was played out carefully in space. As noted earlier, ritual fixes memory, especially when it occurs in a special place. The placement of human bone across a Mississippian site is not random, and archaeologists should examine both the distribution of human bone across the site and the distribution of human bone vis-à-vis the human-created features on the site. The placement of the sculptuary at one corner of the site and the "gravel knoll," which is similar in structure to the sculptuary and contains similar remains (and which may well also be a sculpted surface), at the opposite corner is unlikely to be a coincidence.

Aztalan fits well as a Mississippian mortuary site. It features the use of the row structure, both in the charnel house at the top of the northwest platform mound and in the sculptuary area and in the area where a few primary burials are found together. The charnel-row structure is evident in the northwest mound, within which the individuals are laid out in a row. This is not always the case in a charnel structure, but it was important here. While there is no evidence of accretional mounds, there is evidence of sculpted surfaces. I am not necessarily arguing that sculpted surfaces are the equivalent of accretional mounds, but both contain structured and patterned evidence of human remains and mortuary behavior over time.

What we do not have at Aztalan is knowledge of where most people are buried; we do not know what happened when most people died. We have evidence of some leaders of the group and evidence of individuals whose death or burial served as markers in some way. The placement of their graves marked spots in the stockade or inner stockade. Other individuals were part of a ritual in which their bodies went through several stages of processing. None of these acts were unusual for Mississippian sites, but the particular ways that the people at Aztalan conducted the rituals may have differed from some other sites. At some other Mississippian sites individuals are buried in houses, but not here. At some other Mississippian sites there are clear burial areas, but we have not found such areas here, and so on. The basic structure of the mortuary ritual, however, is the same.

One feature found at Aztalan and not noted elsewhere (to our knowledge) is the sculptuary, or sculpted surface. This does not mean that such features do not exist elsewhere. These surfaces are difficult to detect and analyze. Most large Mississippian sites were plowed extensively and deeply long before major archaeological research was conducted because these sites are on located on prime agricultural land. It is possible that evidence of such surfaces has been destroyed. We were able to determine the existence of the surface at Aztalan because of the unique setting in which it exists and a happy series of accidents, but note that it too had been ignored by archaeologists for well over 100 years.

This exercise in the analysis of Aztalan mortuary practices has demonstrated the importance of reexamining both past assumptions and the physical data. It has also provided a potentially different framework for the interpretation of mortuary remains. Providing a theoretical framework for the spatial organization of the site and for the concept of secondary disposal independent of a particular death shifts the focus of possible explanation to include a much wider and better-defined sphere. It also allows us to place Aztalan more solidly into Mississippian mortuary practices instead of simply considering it an outlier.

7

Mississippian Dimensions of a Fort Ancient Mortuary Program

The Development of Authority and Spatial Grammar at SunWatch Village

ROBERT A. COOK

Interregional studies have long been hampered by essentialist categories, which are attributable in archaeology to cultural-historical frameworks designed for other purposes (Dunnell 1971; Essenpreis 1978; Hart and Brumbach 2003; Pauketat 2001b; Lyman and O'Brien 1998). Several researchers of Fort Ancient evolution have concluded that Mississippian migrations and interactions stimulated Fort Ancient development (Cowan 1987; Essenpreis 1978; Griffin 1943; Prufer and Shane 1970), while others have denied any significant outside influence on the development of the Fort Ancient way of life (Henderson 1998; Pollack and Henderson 1992, 2000). This view regards the influence at any point to be relatively insignificant due to the absence of a clearly identifiable elite and hierarchical settlement pattern in Fort Ancient cases (Griffin 1992). But as is discussed and demonstrated in this volume and elsewhere, we can no longer assume that a clearly identifiable elite and a hierarchical settlement pattern were universal characteristics of Mississippian societies.

Mississippian and Fort Ancient communities also are commonly described as chiefdoms and tribes, respectively, the outcomes of different evolutionary pathways. The limitations of the chiefdom model (and by implication the tribe) for revealing the diversity inherent in late prehistoric societies of eastern North America also are now apparent. There are a number of exceptions to the chiefdom model (Boudreaux 2007a; Cobb 2003; Goldstein 1991; Hammerstedt 2005; Sullivan 1995). Some have sought to understand the exceptions as various points on the pathway to complexity in relation to environmental variations (e.g., Clay 1976), while others have suggested more recently that we abandon the chiefdom concept altogether (e.g., Pauketat 2007).

I suggest that classifying Fort Ancient and Mississippian sites into distinctive social types and overemphasizing regional differences between then has limited our ability to discern the evolutionary consequences of interactions between them. While social typologies can be useful for other ends, they are not useful for examining culture change, particularly with respect to interregional interaction (Pauketat 2001b, 2007; Yoffee 1993, 2005). A nontypological approach is better suited for this purpose, as it facilitates the examination of a broader spectrum of possible outcomes. A particular focus on subsystems such as leadership development and kin-group structures has proven particularly useful in this regard (Crumley 1979, 1995; Upham 1990), as have examinations of resistance (Alt 2001; Pauketat 2001b).

Theories that deny significant Mississippian influence on Fort Ancient societies largely derive from an acculturative framework: the assumption is that because there are few Mississippian artifacts in Fort Ancient villages (pottery in particular), the contribution must have been minimal. This essay argues that we need to pay closer attention to the Mississippian artifacts that are present as well as to the spatial relationships of architectural remains in Fort Ancient sites. This orientation follows recent theoretical developments that recognize peripheries as being critical areas for examining culture change (Rice 1998; Stein 2002). Instead of lamenting the "noise" these artifacts and relationships bring to a "pure" Fort Ancient culture, we must closely examine such items in a theoretical context that includes the possibility of creolization (Lightfoot and Martinez 1995; see also Pauketat 2001b).

The boundaries between Fort Ancient residents and neighboring Mississippians are not clear and may be better characterized as a gradation of one group into another (Figure 7.1). Fort Ancient and Mississippian sites are, however, generally located in distinct environmental zones, which is arguably the main evidence for theories that draw an ethnic distinction between them (Wheelersburg 1992). Mississippians are typically located along major rivers with soils that are well suited for intensive agriculture (Smith 1978), whereas Fort Ancient settlements are located in less productive areas. This environmental distinction appears to have had consequences for maize dependency, which was generally lower for Fort Ancient groups than for neighboring Mississippian societies (Schurr and Schoeninger 1995). With this distinction in mind, it has been suggested that Fort Ancient and Mississippian may be symbiotically related ethnic groups that inhabited different econiches (Wheelersburg 1992; see also Barth 1969), although the spatial boundaries for such groups remain open for question.

In setting up a theoretical context to examine the problem, I have expanded Renfrew's (1986) version of peer polity interaction into what I call the pe-

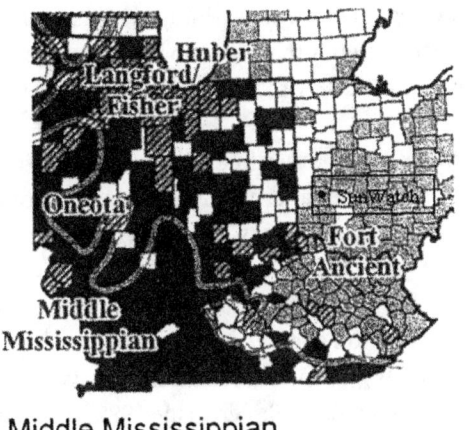

Figure 7.1. Study region for the SunWatch Site. Adapted from Schroeder 2004b: Figures 3 and 4; produced with assistance from William Kennedy.

riphery peer model (Cook 2008). The difference is in what is considered to constitute peers. The most extreme versions of Mississippian and Fort Ancient societies were composed of different types of polities, no matter what labels are applied. However, there are many shades in between that we must closely consider before investigating the establishment of authority positions and site grammar. I suggest that even in complex Mississippian cases, the most logical place to begin is in villages because these are the types of sites in closest proximity to Fort Ancient settlements.

Several recent studies suggest a relatively low level of complexity for Mississippian chiefdoms (Milner 1998; Muller 1997). Drawing on this theory, I argue that mound centers would have had little control over villages and other lower-order settlements in the hierarchy. This relationship would place them on a fairly equal footing with their non-Mississippian neighbors, creating a situation for peer-level interactions. These circumstances are particularly germane in the later stages of Mississippian development in the region, where sites are typically nonmounded villages (Cobb and Butler 2002; Pollack 2004). At this time, there was also a notable abandonment of the region bordering Fort Ancient to the west, which became the so-called Vacant Quarter in the fifteenth century (Cobb and Butler 2002; Williams 1990). Based on this logic, I suggest that Mississippian—Fort Ancient interactions were generally those among equals, regardless of whether we are dealing with "simple" or "complex" cases. But Mississippian societies that surround the Fort Ancient region are less complex (for a general summary of key sites, see Hammerstedt 2005a: Chapter 9).

Peers that co-evolve emulate each other in a variety of ways. In this essay, I investigate similarities in site layout and prestige goods, both of which are key expectations in a peer polity evolutionary scenario (Renfrew 1986). Some interregional theories more generally hold that network participants use a symbolic vocabulary referred to as "diacritics" or an "international style" that crosses cultural boundaries (Blanton et al. 1996; Schortman and Urban 1987). Traffic in prestige goods has long been implicated in the evolution of Mississippian societies (e.g., Brown et al. 1990; Peregrine 1992), but surprisingly little attention has been given to the context of such items in Fort Ancient contexts.

Mississippian Mortuary Variability

As this volume demonstrates, there is considerable temporal and spatial variation in Mississippian mortuary practices. A commonly mentioned aspect of Mississippian mortuary domains is that they were hierarchically structured. Evidence of social ranking is restricted to mound centers, where a particular segment of the population is interred in mounds accompanied by exotic artifacts. For example, Brown (1971: 2) noted two points of commonality in his comparison of Moundville, Etowah, and Spiro: (1) high-status individuals were interred in or near platform mounds; and (2) high-status individuals were usually buried with supralocal status accoutrements (see Brown and King this volume for new thoughts on interpretations of individuals in the Spiro and Etowah mounds).

A wide variety of exotics have been noted as status symbols. Supralocal symbols, defined as nonutilitarian artifacts recognized over a wide geographic area, are often important for identifying the highest-ranking members of a polity. Most notable is the restriction of these types of items to predominantly adult male burials. Seashells, especially lightning whelk, were one of the most important, and it has been suggested that these materials and the items fashioned from them defined positions of authority (Brown 1981a). Triangular symbol "badges," large axes and blades, and some pottery types have also been noted as status markers (see below and Fisher-Carroll and Mainfort 2000). Craft production and in some cases craft specialization is often associated with leaders. I recognize that some of these characteristics are not strictly Mississippian, but the general indicators of leadership and resource intensification take on such a connection when found with much clearer Mississippian attributes.

In contrast to the general pattern of a mound center, villages and smaller sites have produced mortuary assemblages that are more consistent with egalitarian societies, although they were sometimes still part of hierarchical settlement systems (Goldstein 1980; Hally 2004; Milner 1984). For example, Coosa mound centers contain indicators of elite status that are absent in smaller sites such as the King village (Hally 2004, 2008). The mortuary pattern of "outlying" cemeteries near Cahokia evidences less of a similar distinction, where marine-shell cups accompany the local elites (Milner 1984). Key solar alignments have been linked with leaders' residences in Mississippian centers (e.g., Cahokia), which may signify one way that an elite maintained power (Smith 1992). Row patterning in burials has been noted as a Mississippian characteristic in some areas, especially in the Midwest (Goldstein 1980).

The SunWatch Village Case Study

Mississippian dimensions of Fort Ancient mortuary practices are examined below at the SunWatch site, which is located in Dayton, Ohio (Heilman et al. 1988). The site was chosen for the simple reason that it has been extensively excavated, contains a clearly Mississippian-style feature (a wall-trench house) and artifacts (negative-painted pottery, shell-tempered pottery, discoidals), and was occupied during the "crest" of neighboring Mississippian developments (between A.D. 1100 and 1500) (Griffin 1985). Moreover, a recent examination of the formation history of the site provides a diachronic context in which to examine the mortuary program (Cook 2007). This examination allows us to inspect the relationship between Mississippian characteristics and the emergence of power within a defined social group.

Row patterning is evident in burial groups throughout the village, particularly near the wall-trench house and in burial groups in the western portion of the site, each of which can be associated with key solar alignments and structures (Figure 7.2) (Heilman and Hoefer 1981). Two structures in the western part of the site are noteworthy, one constructed from eastern red cedar (Wagner 1988), a wood commonly used in Mississippian ritual contexts, and another recognized only after an intensive plotting of all postholes (see Cook 2008: Figure 5.5). This structure's orientation to the winter solstice and its location alongside an important burial row hint at a mortuary connection (see Birmingham and Goldstein 2005: Figure 4.20b; and Kay and Sabo 2006), although we will not know whether it also served a charnel function without further investigation. Of particular interest is the fact that the two

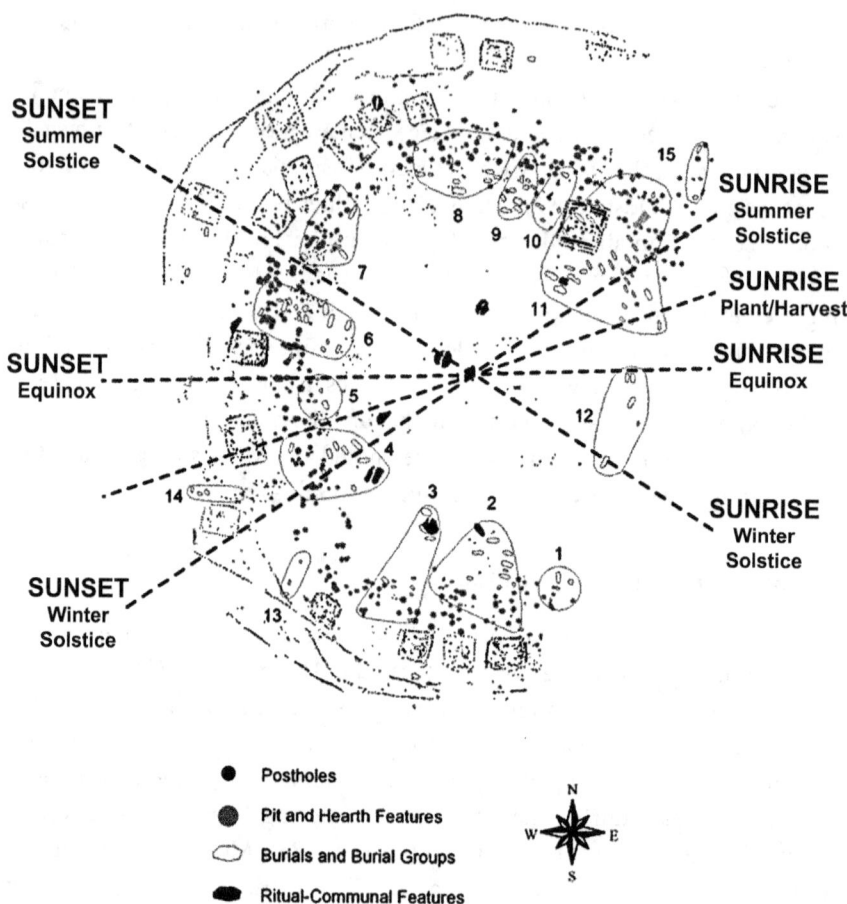

Figure 7.2. SunWatch Site Map Highlighting Burial Group Locations and Solar Alignments

burial groups (Burial Groups 6 and 11; see Figure 7.2) nearest to the unique structures (west and wall trench) contain more occurrences of stone-covered graves than do most other groups (each has 83 percent; see Cook 2004: Table 10), and Burial Group 6 is composed exclusively of males and children.

Mortuary ranking was statistically examined with cluster analysis of 21 artifact types that were present in more than one burial using Ward's Method (see O'Shea 1984) using SPSS v. 11. A variety of cluster solutions were explored, but the five-cluster solution produced the clearest distinctions (Table 7.1). Clusters 1, 2, and 3 are composed of children, females, and males of all ages. Cluster 4 is composed of a relatively equal proportion of males and children. The males are between the ages of 25 and 44 and the children were less than four years

Table 7.1. Cluster Analysis Results of SunWatch Burials

Cluster	N	Associated with Artifacts	Extended	Males	Females	Children	Indeterminate
5	1	100%	100%	100%	0%	0%	0%
4	11	100%	55%	46%	0%	54%	0%
3	23	83%	61%	17%	26%	57%	0%
2	10	80%	80%	10%	30%	40%	20%
1	136	6%	39%	23%	18%	56%	3%

Source: See Cook 2008: 114–120 for more details.

old (most were less than one). Cluster 5 contains one body, that of a 35—year-old male. Cluster 1 contains the most members but the lowest percentage of artifacts. It also contains the only occurrences of discoidals, along with pottery and two wolf jaws. Cluster 2 contains all the occurrences of shell barrel beads and a relatively large proportion of shell disc beads. Cluster 3 contains all occurrences of burned corn and a relatively large proportion of *Marginella* shells and hammerstones, along with pottery and a wolf jaw. Cluster 4 contains all occurrences of triangular shell pendants and shell discs with one exception, that occurs in Cluster 5. One grave contains a fragment of a whelk shell. A relatively large proportion of *Marginella* shells are also associated with this cluster (see Cook 2008: Table 5.1 for more details).

The grave goods for the individual that constitutes Cluster 5 include shell discs and the only complete whelk shell, which was drilled and worn as a pendant (Figure 7.3). I interpret Clusters 4 and 5 as being of different status than

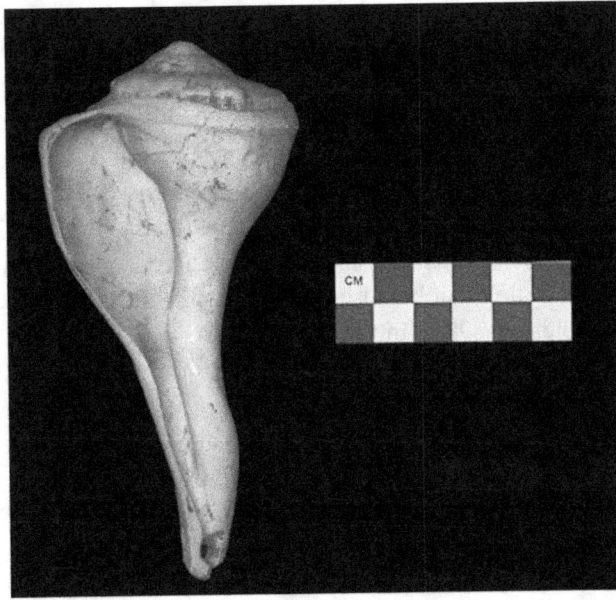

Figure 7.3. Photo of the Complete Whelk Shell from SunWatch. Photograph by author.

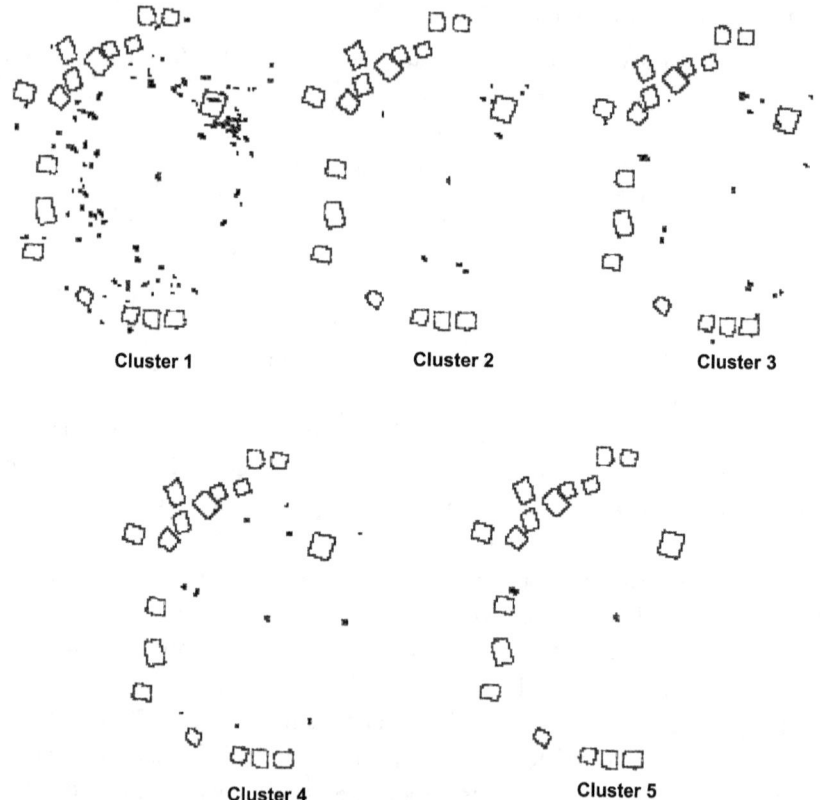

Figure 7.4. SunWatch Burial Cluster Locations.

the other clusters based on the fact that they contain only males and children and the only occurrences of a supralocal artifact type (whelk shells). The individual in Cluster 5 appears to be the village leader who was associated with the burials in Cluster 4 in that they had also been interred with shell discs. Some level of ascriptive status is implicated in the association of certain shell artifacts with children, a finding that has also been noted in rural Mississippian cemeteries (e.g., Goldstein 1980). In the absence of supralocal symbols and a more representative sex and age composition, I consider Clusters 1, 2, and 3 to be of a different status than Clusters 4 and 5.

Cluster 2 is clearly associated with the wall-trench house (Figure 7.4). A Mississippian connection is strengthened by the fact that burials in this cluster contain a high proportion of shell disc beads and stone grave covers (see Cook 2008). No burials in this cluster are located inside this house, possibly because it was occupied at the time of these interments. It is interesting that the Cluster

2 burials in the southern part of the site are adults, while individuals located near the wall-trench house are mostly children 15 years old or younger. The southern group of Cluster 2 burials includes two younger females—19 and 26 years old—both of which are extended and covered with stone slabs. The other Cluster 2 burial in this part of the site is a male of 45 to 49 years who is also covered with stone slabs. The two relatively young females in the southern part of the site associated with this cluster are intriguing, perhaps revealing marriage alliances between "newcomers" and "locals," although this interpretation goes beyond available data. Cluster 3 burials are concentrated in key burial rows in four different parts of the site. Cluster 4 burials are more common in the northern half of the village, and the Cluster 5 burial is located close to an unusual red-cedar house, which is associated with the highest concentration of shell-tempered pottery (Cook and Fargher 2007, 2008).

The two individuals with the most diverse sets of artifacts—a proxy measure of the broadest range of statuses—are positioned in the western and southern parts of the village. They are also both extended adult males with stone grave covers. The 35—year-old in the west is the only individual associated with a drilled whelk-shell pendant, which is similar to those depicted on engravings on Mississippian whelk shell pendants (e.g., Phillips and Brown 1978). He was also accompanied by shell discs, bone pins, a fish-teeth "mosaic" atop the head, a hammerstone, a bone awl, projectile points, and a lithic perform. The 41—year-old in the south is also associated with shell discs, shell disc bead bracelets, an antler flaker, bone pins, bone awls, red ochre, and a platform pipe.

Based on the location of the two individuals with the most diverse artifact sets, one could conclude that there is a relationship between the southern and western parts of the site with respect to village-level leadership. Other dimensions further support such a connection. Whelk shells were present only in burials located in the western and southern parts of the village. The whelk shell (complete) located in the west is with the Cluster 5 individual. The only other occurrence of a whelk shell (fragment) was with a multiple burial that included a child and two infants. One of the nonornamental artifact types associated with the highest-status individual was a hammerstone. This artifact type occurred close to pits with flaking tools and concentrations of lithic debitage (Figure 7.5). Cumulatively, these data support a close relationship between the southern and western parts of the village in terms of leadership and tool making. Based on this evidence, I suggest that male village-level leadership developed in tandem with craft production and long-distance exchange.

The final part of the analysis involved assessing whether leadership emerged toward the end of the village occupation in tandem with the appearance of

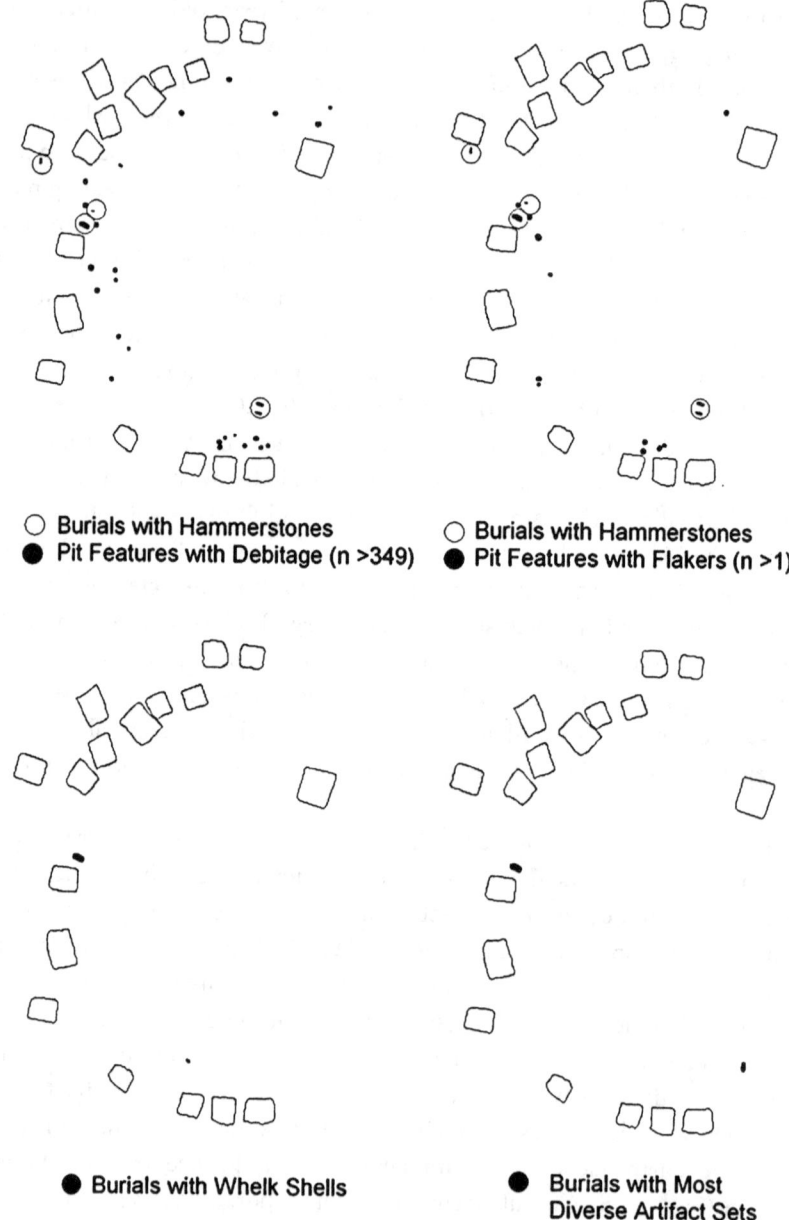

Figure 7.5. Mortuary and Lithic Production Relationships Between the South and West Portions of SunWatch.

the Mississippian-style wall-trench house. General theoretical expectations hold that the emergence of leaders should occur over time, particularly with respect to administering a growing local population (e.g., Johnson 1982) and the development of long-distance exchange relationships (e.g., Peregrine 1992; Blanton et al. 1996; Douglas 1967; Renfrew 1986; Helms 1988, 1993). I reasoned that the best method for assessing this timing was directly dating individual burials. I submitted collagen samples from rib fragments of the two individuals of highest status for AMS dating. The results indicated that the remains were indeed from late in the village occupation; the 2—sigma calibrated date ranges were A.D. 1407—1513 ($p = 0.96$) and A.D. 1394—1475 ($p = 0.98$) (see Cook 2008 for more details). This finding is consistent with theoretical expectations and fits well with the last uses of the site, including the appearance of the Mississippian-style house (Cook 2007).

A marked increase in the population of SunWatch occurred in tandem with the construction of the wall-trench and red-cedar houses. I suggest that the red-cedar house was used in part as the residence of a village leader. The localization of Mississippian-style negative-painted and shell-tempered pottery in contexts linking the village leader to the wall-trench area warrants a specific Mississippian connection with the emergence of political power at SunWatch. However, the leader is intimately connected to the southern portion of the site in a variety of ways, supporting the hypothesis that a local leader legitimized power through connections with Mississippians. More research is needed to further address this issue.

Discussion

The SunWatch site presents several similarities with and a few distinctions from patterns observed in Mississippian villages. In some respects, the Fort Ancient mortuary patterns appear more similar to those toward the south (e.g., the Middle Cumberland area) than to Mississippian communities to the west (e.g., the Angel Phase). The Middle Cumberland region is known for its use of stone in grave construction (I. Brown 1981). Usually Fort Ancient peoples employed stone only for grave covers (though there are several examples of Fort Ancient box graves), whereas in Middle Cumberland contexts the entire grave typically forms such a stone box. At SunWatch, stone slabs appear in greater numbers in Burial Groups 6 and 11 and in Burial Cluster 2, which includes several individuals on the perimeter of the wall-trench house. These spaces are all associated with the later occupation of the site, along with other Mississippian diagnostics and shell-tempered pottery (Cook 2007; Cook and Fargher 2007, 2008).

SunWatch males were buried with many more artifacts than were females (Cook 2008). A group of adult males and children were buried near a unique structure (both of these findings are similar to the King site; Hally 2004, 2008). Higher-status Mississippian males often are accompanied by exotic marine shell, as is the case at SunWatch. There is a connection between adult male status and stone tool-making implements at SunWatch, which is common in lower-order Mississippian cemeteries and villages. Intensified craft production is often stimulated by leaders who use the products for intersocietal exchange (Robertson 1980). While a case may be made for a relationship between craft production and leadership at SunWatch, the site does not include clear evidence of the craft specialization that is associated with some Mississippian settlements (Nass and Yerkes 1995; Yerkes 1983, 1989), although the issue of craft specialization in Mississippian settlements remains a matter of some debate (see Milner 1998; Muller 1997).

There are two notable differences between Mississippian and SunWatch mortuary practices. First, pottery is present with only two burials at SunWatch, while this artifact type is a common funerary accompaniment in many Mississippian burials (although it became much more common in Late Fort Ancient burials; Drooker 1997). Second, only children were buried with discoidals at SunWatch, which does not fit some Mississippian examples where this item is associated with adult males who may have excelled in the game of chunky (Hally 2004, 2008).

It is difficult to recognize the differences between SunWatch and Mississippian villages of comparable size (Figure 7.6). A Fort Ancient villager would have felt quite at home in a Mississippian village and vice versa. In other words, the similarity between some Mississippian and Fort Ancient villages is reflected in several dimensions of site grammar, most notable of which are plaza posts (Table 7.2). I suggest that a theoretical model that best accounts for these findings is that Fort Ancient villages formed in periphery peer relations with Mississippian villages—either in hierarchical systems or in those of lesser complexity—followed by peer interactions with other Fort Ancient villages. The end result was a system of ranked corporate groups consistent with Mississippian social organization (see Knight 1990). Of course, movement of Mississippians into Fort Ancient villages can also be linked to the ripple effects of migration that emanated from major Mississippian centers (Anderson 1997; Pauketat 2007). The possible connections with Middle Cumberland Mississippian populations are particularly intriguing given the fact that groups dispersed in that region in the fifteenth century (Cobb and

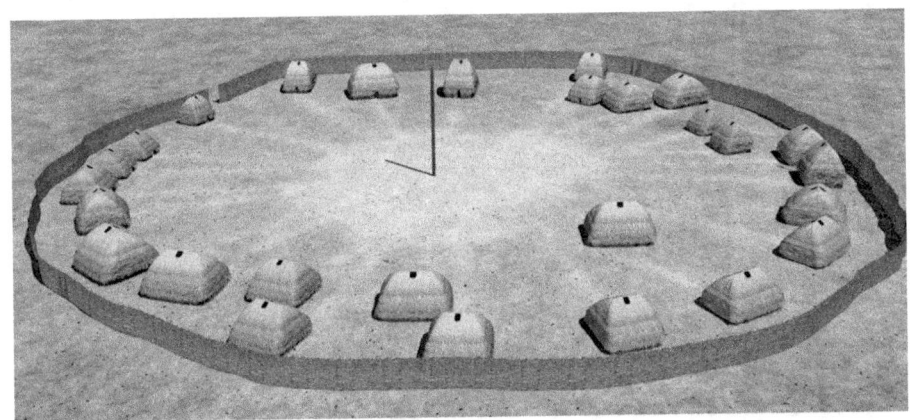

Figure 7.6. Reconstructions of SunWatch (top) and a Mississippian Village (bottom). King site painting by Kenneth Townsend, courtesy of the National Park Service; SunWatch rendering by Jeff Door and Robert Cook.

Butler 2002) and the similar time frame for the appearance of Mississippian-like characteristics at SunWatch.

SunWatch could be considered equivalent to the lower end of the range of Mississippian social complexities, but this interpretation does not mean that Fort Ancient is simply a watered-down version of "big city" Mississippians. I suggest that the development of both was simultaneous, which is a basic tenet of peer interaction theories (Renfrew 1986). Using a coevolutionary frame of reference, with the village as the point of comparison, aids greatly in examining the nature of this process (Cook 2008).

Table 7.2. Characteristics of Site Planning and Architecture for a Selection of Mississippian Villages and Fort Ancient Villages in Southwest Ohio

	Mounds	Plaza Posts	Architecture		Burials	
			Trench	Post	Rows[a]	Stone
Mississippian						
Annis (Green River)	X	—	X	X	—	—
Arnold (Cumberland)	—	—	X	—	X	X
Averbuch (Cumberland)	—	—	X	—	X	X
Bridges (Illinois)	—	X	X	—	—	—
Ganier (Cumberland)	—	—	—	—	X	X
King (Coosa)	—	X	X	X	—	X
Ledford Island (Mouse Creek)	—	X	X	X	X	—
Southwind (Angel)	—	X	X	X	—	—
Fort Ancient						
Anderson	—	—	—	—	X	X
Madisonville	—	X	X	—	X	X
Schomaker	—	—	X	X	—	—
Stateline	X	—	X	X	X	X
SunWatch	—	X	X	X	X	X
Taylor	X	—	—	—	—	X
Turpin	X	—	X	X	—	X

Note: [a]Row patterns are generally restricted to plaza burials.

SunWatch is not unique, as wall-trench houses in other Fort Ancient sites have been dated to similar points in time (around A.D. 1400; e.g., Cowan et al. 1990; Henderson 1992). After this date, Fort Ancient communities became larger, socially more complex, and more firmly drawn into long-distance exchange networks during the Madisonville horizon (Drooker 1997). Mississippian interactions increased greatly during this time (Pollack et al. 2002). I suggest that the emergence of incipient ranking in Middle Fort Ancient villages occurred in relation to increased Mississippian interactions and possibly in relation to in-migrations from the Vacant Quarter region, including the Middle Cumberland area (Cobb and Butler 2002; Williams 1990). These events seem to have spurred a "little bang" in the middle Ohio River valley that occurred around A.D. 1400. But this political and ideological process likely began earlier in time. The Turpin and State Line sites contain numerous Mississippian diagnostics and appear to be relatively early (Oehler 1973; Vickery et al. 2000), but we sorely need dates from their wall-trench houses and a better understanding of their site structures.

At this point, all signs suggest that a co-evolutionary process led to the development of Fort Ancient and Mississippian villages. At about A.D. 1400 much of the Mississippian world became more like Fort Ancient in the shift to less complex social systems (e.g., Pollack 2004). The growth of Fort Ancient villages as exemplified by SunWatch happened within a context of general decentralization of Mississippian mound centers and out-migrations (Cobb and Butler 2002; Williams 1990), a period of "communalization" of elite symbols throughout much of the southeast (Knight 1997).

In some respects, Fort Ancient can be seen to "resist" Mississippianization in that shell-tempered pottery was not common there until relatively late and wall-trench houses were a rare occurrence throughout the period (see Alt 2001). However, this study has shown that when a village leader developed at SunWatch, he did so along with a set of Mississippian characteristics that operated in a significant fashion. Shell-tempered pottery and wall-trench houses co-developed with a village leader who was accompanied by a Mississippian supralocal symbol of authority (Cook and Fargher 2007, 2008). Based on these findings, I suggest that we cannot afford to overlook the "noise" of Mississippian items in Fort Ancient villages. The combination of general processes (village growth and leadership development) and particular historical connections (contact with Mississippians) is an apt illustration of a changing tradition in archaeological theory (Pauketat 2001b).

Acknowledgements

This essay was considerably improved by comments from Lynne Sullivan and Bob Mainfort. Heartfelt thanks for these efforts as well as for the invitation to participate in the Southeastern Archaeological Conference symposium from which this paper grew. Discussions with several participants after the session considerably improved my thinking. In particular, I would like to acknowledge Scott Hammerstedt, Chris Rodning, and Greg Wilson. The section on cluster analysis is based closely on a recent publication (Cook 2008) entitled *SunWatch: Fort Ancient Development in the Mississippian World*, particularly pp. 114—123. I thank the University of Alabama Press for allowing me to use these sections for this essay.

8

Temporal Changes in Mortuary Behavior

Evidence from the Middle and Upper Nodena Sites, Arkansas

ROBERT C. MAINFORT JR. AND RITA FISHER-CARROLL

Funerary rites are, of course, one sort of ritual. A key characteristic of rituals is that they are performed repeatedly within a time-honored structure. The performance of rituals as prescribed by tradition essentially constitutes an acknowledgment of the authority of the respected ancestors who passed down the rituals to their descendants (Geertz 1966; Lewis 1979; Rappaport 1979). Thus, rituals, including mortuary rites, have an element of unchanging timelessness about them. They invoke from the distant past ("so it has always been") to the future ("so it always shall be").

Certain aspects of mortuary ritual do, however, change over time (Cannon 1989; Mainfort 1979). For example, O'Shea (1984) has documented fairly dramatic changes in mortuary practices (more particularly, interment) among Native American groups on the Plains during the eighteenth and nineteenth centuries, a period of dramatic social and political changes in the region.

Few studies of prehistoric mortuary practices have explicitly investigated nuanced temporal changes in prehistoric mortuary practices within a region. Examples include research by Chapman (2005), Kerber (1986), O'Shea (1995), Rakita (2001), and Tainter (1977); all encompass spans of roughly 500 to 1,000 years. Charles (1995) looks at the *longue durée* of roughly 10,000 years on the lower Illinois River valley. In the Classical world, Morris (1987) demonstrates how changes in burial rites reflect social and political processes that led to the formation of the Greek city-state.

Our region of interest is the central Mississippi valley (Morse and Morse 1983), more specifically late-period mortuary populations therein, that are roughly contemporary and probably date between about A.D. 1350 and 1550 (Fisher-Carroll 2001a; Mainfort 2001). There are few radiocarbon dates, and none directly date human burials. The few proposed temporal markers that may be characteristic of the Soto era (circa A.D. 1540) occur infrequently in

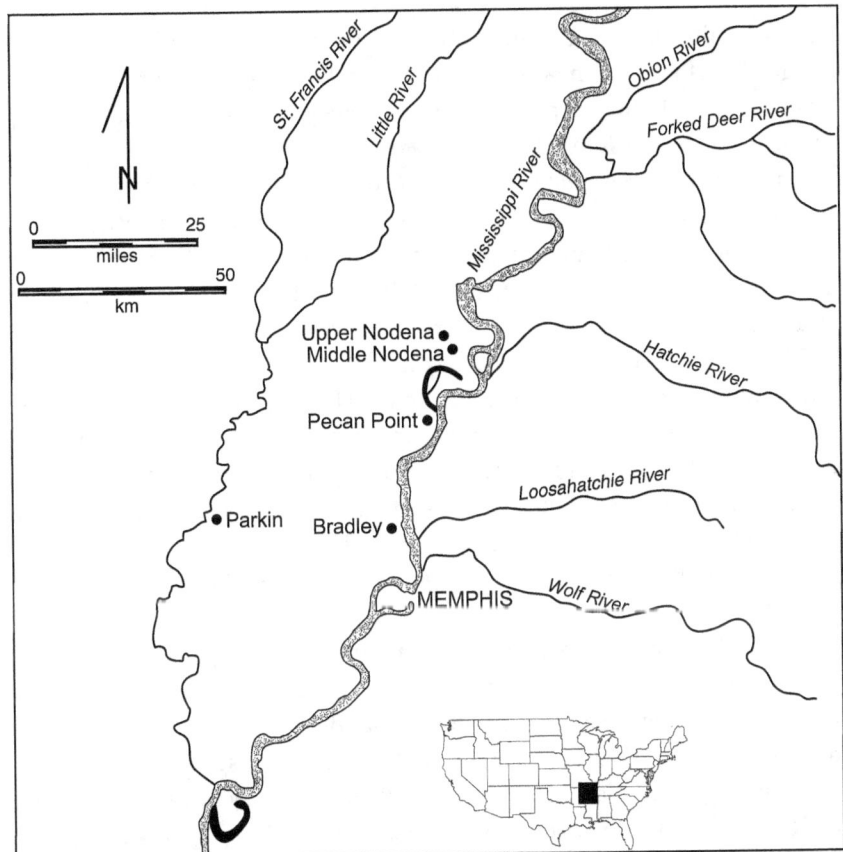

Figure 8.1. Location of the Middle and Upper Nodena and Nearby Sites

funerary object assemblages (Mainfort 2001; Williams 1980). Some attributes of ceramic vessel rims appear to have temporal importance, but these also vary geographically (Mainfort 2003). In short, there is at present little basis for inferring temporal relationships between late-period sites in the region, much less for seriating graves within individual sites.

In this essay, we are concerned with identifying changes in mortuary practices that probably occurred within a few generations at two late-period sites in northeast Arkansas, Middle Nodena and Upper Nodena. The latter has been the subject of two monographs (Fisher-Carroll 2001b; Morse 1989; Fisher-Carroll and Mainfort 2000), but very little has been published about Middle Nodena (Durham 1989; Finger 1989).

Both sites are located on a relict levee or point bar of the Mississippi River about 8 km northeast of Wilson in Mississippi County, Arkansas (Figure 8.1). The soils along this low ridge are among those most productive for modern agriculture (Fisher-Carroll 2001b: 33), and the slightly raised elevation was less susceptible to seasonal inundation than the surrounding land. A slough about 400 m to the east marks a former channel of the river. A fairly large shallow lake, now drained, was located immediately west of the sites, providing residents ready access to fish and waterfowl.

The sites take their names from the Nodena Plantation, which was owned for many years by the family of Dr. James K. Hampson, a physician who was one of the best-known avocational archaeologists in the Midsouth. He amassed a sizable collection during his life and kept some records of his finds (Hampson n.d.a; Mainfort 2005; Morse 1989; Williams 1957).

The larger site, Upper Nodena, encompasses about 6.7 ha and is one of the largest of more than 60 sites assigned to the Nodena phase construct (Morse 1989, 1990). Hampson (1989: 9) recalled seeing two rectangular substructural mounds and 12 to 15 smaller mounds when the site was first cleared, but only the two largest mounds appear on his site map (Morse 1989: 98). Morse has suggested the presence of an encircling ditch or palisade (Morse 1989: 101, 1990: 73), but this has not confirmed (see Morse 1989: 101; Tuttle et al. 2002: 24–29).

The Middle Nodena site is located 2 km southeast of Upper Nodena, within the middle portion of the Nodena plantation (Upper Nodena being the most northerly). With an area of roughly 3.3 ha, Middle Nodena falls within the second tier of Morse's (1989: 103–105) proposed Nodena phase settlement pattern. A composite of the Alabama Museum of Natural History maps dating to 1932 locates excavated human burials within an area measuring approximately 630 feet by 200 feet; the resulting map is too large to reproduce here.

According to Dr. Hampson (1989: 9):

> On March 17, 1897, the levee broke at Middle Nodena. When the river returned to its banks about the first of May it had washed away from 2 to 3 feet of Congress Ridge, exposing an aboriginal burial ground about 1¼ miles south of the mounds [i.e., south of the Upper Nodena site].... We believe that these two sites [Upper Nodena and Middle Nodena] are in fact only one, that they were occupied by the same people at the same time, and that they can be connected by isolated groups of burials. We have, in fact, found two such groups, one of 30 graves, the other of 5. While there is no sign of any mound at Middle Nodena, it does not mean that there were none there originally. The site had been in cultivation for over 50 years when I first knew it and what mounds the plow had failed to obliterate the overflow completed.

Hampson's comment about the possibility of mounds at Middle Nodena is important. Between 1907 and 1927 the largest mound at Upper Nodena was reduced to "little more than half" its former size (Hampson 1989: 10). Fifty years of cultivation coupled with flooding could indeed have obliterated all evidence of mounds at Middle Nodena by 1897; it is unlikely that we will ever know. No modern excavations have been conducted at Middle Nodena, so the actual nature of deposits at the site remains unknown, save for the presence of human burials and Hampson's mention of a "kitchen midden 4 by 10 feet and 7 feet deep" (1989: 15).

Researchers have long felt that the two sites represent the archaeological remains of a single sociopolitical group and that Middle Nodena postdates Upper Nodena (Mainfort 2001: 187; Morse 1973: 2, 1989: 2, 1990: 77; S. Williams 1999: 13; cf. S. Williams 1980: 105). Several recent studies confirm similarities in material culture but raise questions about the basis for the assumed temporal sequence (Mainfort et al. 2007; Tavaszi 2004). Two sets of AMS radiocarbon dates from Upper Nodena confirm habitation within the expected range of A.D. 1400–1550 (Mainfort et al. 2007: 30–31). There are no radiocarbon dates for Middle Nodena. The relative ages of the sites probably could not be resolved through radiometric dating, given typical standard deviations of AMS dates (roughly 50 years). Moreover, the limited sample of human remains and the marked underrepresentation of subadults at both sites militate against estimating length of use based on demographics. We propose to examine the issue of relative ages of the sites based upon mortuary data (including funerary objects). As we demonstrate below, there are some striking differences between the two sites.

History of Excavations

In 1932, Dr. Hampson invited the University of Arkansas Museum (hereinafter Arkansas) and the Alabama Museum of Natural History (hereinafter Alabama) to excavate at the Upper and Middle Nodena sites. Although far below modern standards, both the excavation techniques and the records kept by representatives of both institutions certainly were acceptable, if not fairly good, by the standards of the time. As in our earlier study of Upper Nodena (Fisher-Carroll 2001b; Fisher-Carroll and Mainfort 2000), the prefix "A" denotes burials excavated by the Alabama crew, while burials excavated by the Arkansas crew do not have a prefix.

The goal of both institutions was to collect high-quality relics, particularly complete ceramic vessels. Accordingly, the excavation strategy was simply to locate human burials via probing. There was no effort to excavate within gridded units, and very little artifactual material other than funerary objects was saved. A paucity of bioarchaeological data constrains this and any study utilizing late-period mortuary data from the central Mississippi valley (Fisher-Carroll 2001a, 2001b). Most human remains were left in the ground. For example, of the over 900 burials excavated by Alabama and Arkansas at Upper Nodena, the field crews collected skeletal remains from only 134 individuals (cf. Powell 1990: 101). Crania and postcranial elements with unusual morphology or pathological lesions were favored for collection by the excavators (Fisher-Carroll 2001b). For most interments, only gross age assessments (adult/subadult) are available, and the sex of most individuals is unknown. Rather than bemoan that which is lost, we have chosen to focus on detecting and explaining variation using the available data.

The Alabama field crew excavated 616 human burials at Upper Nodena, including about 350 located within a relatively small area designated Mound C (Fisher-Carroll 2001b; Mainfort et al. 2006). The Mound C locality is the only recorded example of a formal burial area at late-period sites in northeast Arkansas and southeast Missouri. Most interments were placed throughout habitation areas. The Arkansas crew excavated 352 burials from areas south of the Alabama excavations. The Alabama and Arkansas excavators produced brief descriptions of all burials as well as plane table maps showing the locations of the excavated burials. There are 893 burials with fairly good documentation, and our discussion below is based primarily on these. The mortuary population from Upper Nodena is by far the largest in our regional database (Fisher-Carroll 2001a: 36). Fisher-Carroll (2001b) provides a comprehensive summary of the 1932 excavations as well as a detailed analysis of the mortuary data.

Dr. Hampson excavated over 800 human burials at Upper Nodena (Hampson 1989: 15), and although he kept some records of his excavations, few of these survive (Fisher-Carroll 2001b: 40–41; Mainfort 2003, 2005). The only modern professional excavations at Upper Nodena were conducted in 1973 by Dan Morse of the Arkansas Archeological Survey (Mainfort 2003; Mainfort et al. 2007).

Prior to working at Upper Nodena, the Alabama crew excavated 182 human burials at Middle Nodena (Durham 1989: 24; also based on examination of burial cards) and produced four plane table maps of their excavations, showing burial locations and approximate burial orientations. The Arkansas crew excavated 73 burials at Middle Nodena. Durham (1989: 24) recalled that "the burials were recorded and mapped with plane table, alidade, and chain." Unfortunately, the field maps are not curated by the University of Arkansas Museum, nor were they present in the mid-1950s (Stephen Williams, personal communication, 2003). We suspect that the burials excavated by the Arkansas crew were located within the limits of the maps produced by the Alabama crew, but this is conjectural. As with Upper Nodena, the Arkansas burial cards include drawings, but those prepared by the Alabama crew do not.

Between 1932 and 1941, Dr. Hampson excavated 452 graves at Middle Nodena (Hampson 1989); he also excavated an unknown (but small) number around 1900. Only two of Hampson's burial cards for Middle Nodena are preserved, and if he ever produced maps showing burial locations at the site, they do not survive. The relatively small number of objects from Middle Nodena listed in Hampson's catalog of his collection is incommensurate with the number of reported graves.

Associated records are available for 257 burials from Middle Nodena (not counting N-1 and counting both individuals in grave A179). In the discussion that follows, we have not included the interments represented by Hampson's two surviving burial cards, making our total sample 255 graves. Among late-period sites in the study area, this total is exceeded only at Upper Nodena, Hazel, Banks, Pecan Point, and Bradley (Fisher-Carroll 2001a: 36).

The limitations of the 1932 field records and the selective retention of human remains have been discussed at length by Fisher-Carroll (2001b). Although the field assessments of sex are questionable, we used the field records of skeletal length to distinguish between adults and subadults (a term used to include all nonadults) using Powell's (1989, 1990) estimates of adult stature as a baseline. Among the 893 Upper Nodena burials used here, there are 789 adults and 104 subadults. Of the individuals for whom Powell (1989) was able to determine sex, there are 65 females and 42 males. For Middle Nodena, the combined mortuary population includes 219 adults and 34 subadults; no data are available for two individuals. Among the extant adult remains, Powell (1989) identified 18 males and 12 females. At both sites, subadults are markedly underrepresented, as is often the case in archaeological mortuary populations in eastern North America (Konigsberg 1985). The small number of individuals who could be sexed and the very small number of subadults largely precludes analysis of mortuary variation based on gender.

Before proceeding further, we will note that in our publications concerning mortuary patterning at Upper Nodena (Fisher-Carroll 2001b; Fisher-Carroll and Mainfort 2000), our focus was on demonstrating that the degree of social differentiation inferred for Moundville (Peebles 1971; Peebles and Kus 1977) did not exist at Upper Nodena. This was dictated by previous interpretations of late-period societies in the study area as markedly hierarchical (e.g., P. Morse 1981; Morse and Morse 1983). We will not pursue this line of inquiry here, other than to note that our conclusions regarding Upper Nodena apply even more strongly to Middle Nodena, for reasons that should be evident in the discussion that follows.

General Comparisons between the Sites

Hampson's report of severe erosion at Middle Nodena during the 1897 flood suggests that during the 1932 excavations, burial depth below the surface should be shallower at that site than at Upper Nodena. This is indeed the case; the mean depth of burials at Upper Nodena were about 18 inches greater than at Middle Nodena (Table 8.1). Without Hampson's historical account, it would have been quite reasonable to attribute this difference to cultural factors.

At both Upper Nodena and Middle Nodena, an overwhelming majority of individuals were interred in a supine extended position. In fact, the percentages of nonnormative burial positions are virtually identical for the two sites—5.5 and 5.1 percent, respectively (see Fisher-Carroll and Mainfort 2000: 110). No nonnormative interment modes appear to be unique to either site; partially flexed, prone, and skull burials occur at both sites, as do some supine extended individuals with their ankles crossed. Nonnormative interment modes are not linked with the presence or absence of funerary objects.

As in our earlier study (Fisher-Carroll and Mainfort 2000), we collapsed the data on burial orientation into 40–degree increments (0–39 degrees, 40–79 degrees, etc.). The relatively primitive recording techniques used during excavation make it unlikely that the exact orientation of each burial was precisely illustrated. Moreover, orientations of burials excavated by the Alabama crew could be obtained only from the field maps. Given the small scale of these, it is likely that the orientations are shown even less precisely on the maps than on the burial cards. The concentration of overlapping individuals in Mound C made assessment of orientation impossible in many instances. Note that the figures for Upper Nodena differ from those presented in our earlier work

Table 8.1. Burial Depths

Depth (inches)	Middle Nodena	Upper Nodena
0–6	5.9% (15)	4.3% (29)
6–12	5.9% (15)	3.1% (21)
12–18	20.4% (52)	7.6% (51)
18–24	26.3% (67)	17.7% (119)
24–30	16.9% (43)	16.9% (114)
30–36	12.2% (31)	18.0% (121)
36–42	7.8% (20)	16.3% (110)
42–48	3.9% (10)	11.7% (79)
48–54	0.4% (1)	3.0% (20)
54–60	0.4% (1)	1.6% (11)
Total burials	255	673
Mean depths	12.8	30.9

Table 8.2. Burial Orientations

Degrees	Middle Nodena (N = 238)	Upper Nodena Nonmound (N = 542)	Upper Nodena Mound C (N = 205)
0–40	14 (5.9%)	66 (12.2%)	8 (3.9%)
40–80	15 (6.3%)	57 (10.5%)	26 (12.7%)
80–120	18 (7.6%)	61 (11.3%)	36 (17.6%)
120–160	23 (9.7%)	87 (16.1%)	45 (21.9%)
160–200	15 (6.3%)	40 (7.4%)	14 (6.8%)
200–240	34 (14.3%)	89 (16.4%)	32 (15.6%)
240–280	27 (11.3%)	34 (6.3%)	20 (9.8%)
280–320	68 (28.6%)	61 (11.3%)	11 (5.4%)
320–360	24 (10.1%)	47 (8.7%)	13 (6.3%)
Mean	214	166	159

(Fisher-Carroll 2001b; Fisher-Carroll and Mainfort 2000); we now have better copies of the Alabama maps, which allowed us to determine orientation for more burials.

In Table 8.2, burials at Upper Nodena are divided into those from Mound C and those located elsewhere within the site. The difference in the mean orientation between Middle and Upper Nodena is statistically significant ($t = 2.13$ using the non–Mound C burials from Upper Nodena), largely due to the high percentage (over 25 percent) of burials in the 280–320 degree interval at Middle Nodena. Even allowing for imprecise field measurement and recording, this difference is impressive. The 120–160 degree interval (the complement of 280–320) is fairly common at Upper Nodena. These contrasts are intriguing, but burial orientation is not linked to differences in associated funerary objects or their placement within individual graves.

Ceramic Vessels and Their Locations

The mortuary population at Middle Nodena differs dramatically from that at Upper Nodena with respect to the percentage of individuals with associated funerary objects. In the burial sample from Middle Nodena, 90 percent (N = 229/255) of the interred individuals were accompanied by one or more preserved funerary objects. At Upper Nodena, the percentage of interments with funerary objects is 56 percent (N = 500/893) (cf. Fisher-Carroll 2001a: 42). This contrast between two sites of roughly the same age (perhaps even partially contemporary) located only a few kilometers apart is extraordinary. Could the difference be a product of sampling problems with the smaller burial population from Middle Nodena?

As mentioned earlier, Dr. Hampson excavated about 450 human burials at Middle Nodena. All but two of the associated records are lost, but Hampson's (1989) historical narrative provides information that can be used to address the issue of sampling error. Among the Middle Nodena burials for which Hampson gave summary counts of associated artifacts (only pottery in most instances), there are 195 individuals and 249 pottery vessels. The totals for March 1933 are 46 graves and 84 vessels; for December 1933, 62 graves and 51 vessels; for March and April 1934, 44 graves and 92 vessels; for winter 1936, 43 burials and 22 pottery vessels. Among these 195 graves, only 32 (excavated in December 1933 and winter 1936) definitely lacked an associated ceramic vessel. Combining these figures, a maximum of 84 percent (N = 163) of the interments were accompanied by at least one vessel; the actual number is likely to be smaller because many graves included more than a single vessel. Hampson's summary counts, however, are limited almost exclusively to pottery vessels; including other types of artifacts might increase the number of graves at Middle Nodena with at least one funerary object. At the very least, Hampson's data, limited though they are, provide confirmation that at Middle Nodena funerary objects occur in a much higher percentage of graves than at Upper Nodena.

Not surprisingly, the mean number of pottery vessels per individual at the two sites reflects this difference. At Upper Nodena, 647 vessels were recorded with 893 well-documented individuals for a ratio of about 0.7 vessels per burial. Middle Nodena, with 441 ceramic vessels associated with a mortuary population of only 255 individuals, has a mean of 1.7 vessels per burial. Again, Dr. Hampson's tabulations of burials and ceramic vessels provide additional data. Combining Hampson's figures with the Alabama and Arkansas data produces totals of 690 vessels with 450 burials for a ratio of 1.5 vessels per burial at Middle Nodena.

Perhaps even more striking are the percentages of burials accompanied by more than one ceramic vessel (Table 8.3). At Upper Nodena, 19.7 percent of the recorded burials were accompanied by more than one ceramic vessel versus 63.8 percent at Middle Nodena (Fisher-Carroll 2001a: 42). Fisher-Carroll (2001a: 43) has suggested that one temporal trend among late-period burials in our study area was an increase in the number of vessels per burial.

Middle and Upper Nodena also differ with respect to the locations of ceramic vessels within individual graves. The Arkansas and Alabama crews recorded the locations of 398 of the 441 mortuary vessels they excavated at Middle Nodena. At Upper Nodena, the excavators recorded the locations of 609 of the 647 vessels used as funerary objects.

Table 8.3. Number of Pottery Vessels per Grave

n	Middle Nodena	Pecan Point	Upper Nodena
0	25 (9.8%)	64 (17%)	448 (50%)
1	71 (29.4%)	95 (28%)	269 (30%)
2	133 (52.2%)	142 (41%)	149 (17%)
3	14 (5.5%)	35 (10%)	21 (2%)
4+	12 (4.7%)	13 (4%)	6 (1%)

Archaeologists and pothunters have long known that at late-period sites in northeast Arkansas pottery vessels often were placed near the head of the deceased (e.g., Griffin 1952: 232; D. Morse 1989: 102; Thomas 1894: 221), though this has never been demonstrated formally. At Upper Nodena, 62 percent (N = 375) of the mortuary ceramic vessels were located adjacent to the head. In contrast, only 41 percent (N = 163) of the Middle Nodena vessels occurred by the head. Given this much lower frequency, one might expect a correspondingly higher frequency of pottery at another location around the body, but this is not the case (Table 8.4). Rather, at Middle Nodena, vessels occur a bit more frequently in a number of locations compared to the location of vessels at Upper Nodena. Parenthetically, it is curious that at both sites roughly the same numbers of vessels were located at the left and right arms (20 at Upper Nodena, 25 at Middle Nodena).

As shown in Table 8.5, the percentages of basic vessel forms in the Middle Nodena mortuary ceramic assemblage differ from those recorded at Upper Nodena, but the differences are not dramatic. Although few compound vessels were excavated at either site, their greater frequency (numerically and percentage-wise) at Middle Nodena (N = 11; 2.5 percent) may be noteworthy because this vessel form is considered characteristic of very late sites (after

Table 8.4. Selected Locations of Ceramic Vessels at Upper Nodena and Middle Nodena

Location	Upper Nodena	Middle Nodena
Skull area (excluding chin)	395 (62%)	163 (41%)
Left shoulder	47 (7.7%)	38 (9.5%)
Left arm	20 (3.3%)	25 (6.3%)
Right shoulder	65 (10.7%)	53 (13.3%)
Right arm	20 (3.3%)	25 (6.3%)
Legs	10 (1.6%)	20 (5.0%)
Hips/pelvis	9 (1.5%)	21 (5.3%)
Feet	14 (2.3%)	7 (1.8%)

Table 8.5. Frequency of Vessel Forms at Middle Nodena and Upper Nodena (data from the Alabama and Arkansas excavations)

	Bottles	Bowls	Jars	Compound	Unknown	N
Middle Nodena	182 (41.3%)	202 (45.8%)	38 (8.6%)	11 (2.5%)	8	441
Upper Nodena	325 (50.2%)	213 (33.0%)	91 (14.1%)	9 (1.4%)	3	647
Pecan Point	230 (42.0%)	242 (44.2%)	52 (9.5%)	5 (0.9%)	19	548

A.D. 1541) in the study area (Mainfort 2001; Williams 1980). Thus, the higher frequency of compound vessels at Middle Nodena might lend a small measure of support to the interpretation that the site postdates Upper Nodena (N = 9; 1.4 percent).

Another contrast is the frequency of effigy vessels at the two sites. At Middle Nodena, there are 46 effigy vessels, representing 10.4 percent of the total number of mortuary vessels, while effigy vessels comprise 19.1 percent (N = 124) of the Upper Nodena ceramic vessel assemblage (cf. Fisher-Carroll 2001b: 73; we have since obtained additional data about the vessels excavated by the Alabama crew). Red and white painted vessels (Nodena Red and White) are poorly represented at both sites, with five examples at Middle Nodena and nine at Upper Nodena.

Contrasts Involving Other Classes of Artifacts

Of the late-period sites in the central Mississippi valley for which a fairly large number of human burials has been recorded, Middle Nodena has both the highest frequency (N = 12; 4.7 percent of burials) and greatest number (N = 17) of stone discoidals (cf. Fisher-Carroll 2001a: 55; the figures presented here are based on a reexamination of collections and field records). In five instances, two discoidals were found with a single individual (Table 8.6). Discoidals were found with six and adults and six children. Only one Middle Nodena burial excavated by the Arkansas crew had an associated discoidal; this may reflect spatial differentiation between the areas excavated by the two crews. With only one exception (A24), a bottle accompanied each individual with a stone discoidal. In four instances at Middle Nodena, a discoidal was placed within a ceramic vessel that accompanied the deceased; there are no examples of this at Upper Nodena.

At Upper Nodena, 14 discoidals were distributed among only 1.1 percent (N = 10) of the burial population (Table 8.7). Stone discoidals accompanied five adults and five children (two of whom were infants). Multiple discoidals were found with three individuals, and half of a discoidal was located between

Table 8.6. Middle Nodena Burials with Stone Discoidals

Burial	Location	Age/Sex	Other Funerary Artifacts
A16	?	child	plain bottle
A24 (2)[a]	chest, feet	child	plain jar, limestone pendant
A31 (2)	"hips"[b]	child	effigy bottle, 2 plain bowls
A67 (2)	left of skull	adult	plain bottle, fish-effigy bowl (discoidal in bowl)
A75 (2)	right hip	child	plain bottle, plain bowl, 2 plain jars, ochre
A77	left knee	adult	plain bottle, plain bowl
A84 (2)	right hip	child	plain bottle, plain bowl
A106	right of skull	adult	plain bowl (discoidal in bowl), plain jar
A120	left elbow	male	plain bottle
A143	skull (in bowl)	adult	plain bottle, plain bowl (discoidal in bowl), shell bead
A147	left of skull (in jar)	child	bottle with appliqué ogee, miniature jar, effigy jar (discoidal in jar), hammerstone, ceramic discoidal
20	?	adult	plain bottle, 2 plain bowls, bird-effigy bowl

Note: [a]Occurrences of multiple objects are noted in parentheses next to the burial numbers.
[b]Quotation from burial card prepared by excavator.

the feet of burial A293. Bottles co-occurred with a discoidal in six graves; two individuals with a discoidal lacked other funerary objects. Given the marked underrepresentation of subadults at both sites, it is notable that half of the individuals with stone discoidals were children (see Fisher-Carroll 2001b: 86; Fisher-Carroll and Mainfort 2000: 115). This likely reflects continuity in burial practices between the sites.

Table 8.7. Upper Nodena Burials with Stone Discoidals

Burial	Location	Age	Other Funerary Objects
71	left shoulder, in pot	child	zoomorphic effigy bowl, plain jar, bone dice, bone needle, ceramic disc
110 (3)[a]	left shoulder	infant	plain bottle, shell bead necklace
193	left shoulder	adult	none (lower skeleton missing)
A188	right shoulder	child	plain bowl, untyped incised jar (cf. Ranch Incised)
A293 (1/2)	between feet	adult	none
A301 (2)	right hand, ?	infant	plain bottle, plain bowl
A302	feet	adult	bottle with 3 human faces, shell beads, 16 Nodena points, lithic preform, catlinite disc pipe, bone awl
A532	left hand	child	plain bottle, bone "dice"
A554 (2)	right hand, right elbow	adult	2 plain bottles, effigy bowl, quartz crystal
A630	right of skull	adult	2 plain bottles, plain bowl

Note: [a]Occurrences of multiple objects are noted in parentheses next to the burial numbers.

Table 8.8. Middle Nodena Burials with Shell Earplugs

Burial	Age/Sex	Other Funerary Objects
57	old male	plain bottle, plain bowl, mussel shell
61	adult	incised jar with 4 lobes

Table 8.9. Upper Nodena Burials with Shell Earplugs

Burial	Age/Sex	Other Funerary Objects
16	female	zoomorphic bottle, "paint"
209 (1)	old female	plain bottle, zoomorphic bottle, clay discoidal, stone discoidal, shell bead necklace and bracelets
A325	old female	plain bottle, plain bowl
A337	female	plain bottle
A745	adult	2 plain bottles, plain bowl, shell bead bracelets

The paucity of shell beads at Middle Nodena relative to Upper Nodena is striking. Only two shell beads were recorded during the 1932 excavations at the former site—a single specimen each with burials A49 (a subadult with no other funerary objects) and A143 (an adult who was also accompanied by a plain bowl and a plain bottle). Not only were shell beads interred with fewer individuals at Middle Nodena (2/255 burials; 0.8 percent) than at Upper Nodena (14/893 burials; 1.6 percent) but also there were fewer beads with these individuals than with individuals at Upper Nodena. At Upper Nodena (Fisher-Carroll 2001b: 83–84), the Alabama and Arkansas crews recorded six shell bead bracelets and four shell bead necklaces, and Burial A694 was covered with beads "from ankles to skull," according to the burial card.

Both burials at Middle Nodena with shell earplugs were excavated by the Arkansas crew (Table 8.8). Two earplugs of the "pin" style accompanied Burial 57 (an old male), one on each side of the skull; also found with this individual were a plain bottle, a plain bowl, and a mussel shell. A single shell earplug of the mushroom-shaped style was found near the top of the skull with Burial 61 (an adult); an incised jar with four lobes was the only other funerary object with this individual. (Table 8.8 near here}

Shell earplugs also occur infrequently at Upper Nodena (5/893 burials; Fisher-Carroll 2001b: 85). At Upper Nodena, all five individuals with shell earplugs were adults and the four that have been sexed are all women (Table 8.9). As at Middle Nodena, each of the five burials was accompanied by a bottle—another seeming instance of mortuary continuity between the sites.

Table 8.10. Middle Nodena Burials with Pipes

Burial	Material	Location	Age/Sex	Other Funerary Objects
A114	clay	right hip	adult male	decorated bottle, plain bowl
A178	unknown	left hip	adult	plain bottle, plain bowl

Table 8.11. Upper Nodena Burials with Pipes

Burial	Material	Location	Age	Other Funerary Objects
A223	unknown stone	?	adult	plain bottle, plain bowl
A302	catlinite	right chin	adult	bottle with 3 human faces, shell beads, 16 Nodena points, lithic preform, stone discoidal, bone awl
A543	clay	left shoulder	adult	none
A713	clay	left hand	adult	none

Few smoking pipes were placed with the dead at either site (Tables 8.10 and 8.11). Pipes accompanied two burials at Middle Nodena, both of whom were adults, and in both instances, the pipe was found at the hips. All four pipes from Upper Nodena occurred with adults, but none of the three pipes for which location is known was found at the hips (Fisher-Carroll 2001b: 87).

Several other contrasts in the funerary object assemblages from the two sites merit comment. The most noteworthy of these is the placement of four spatulate celts with burials at Upper Nodena; a fragment of a fifth was not found with a burial (Gall et al. 2002; Mainfort et al. 2006). Neither the university excavators nor Dr. Hampson found any at Middle Nodena, and the large number of spatulate celts at Upper Nodena is unique among sites in our regional database (Mainfort et al. 2006). One spatulate celt from Upper Nodena was crafted from Alabama greenstone, and several fragmentary artifacts of the same material were found in nonburial contexts there (Gall et al. 2002); no greenstone is present in the collections from Middle Nodena.

There are four documented occurrences of astragalus dice with burials at Upper Nodena, but none are reported at Middle Nodena. Copper artifacts are reported with two burials at Middle Nodena. At the "left rear" of the skull of Burial A66, the Alabama crew found a "copper ring 1" in diameter" (NOD 123), and in 1902, Dr. Hampson found nine copper beads in a grave at Middle Nodena (Hampson n.d.b, MN 371–379). The Alabama excavators also found a "copper coated bead" (NOD 331) at Middle Nodena that was not associated

Table 8.12. Burial Diversity Scores for Middle Nodena and Upper Nodena

Score	Middle Nodena	Upper Nodena
0	21 (8.2%)	393 (44.0%)
1	65 (25.5%)	280 (31.4%)
2	124 (46.7%)	170 (19.0%)
3	31 (12.2%)	32 (3.6%)
4	6 (2.4%)	8 (0.9%)
5	5 (2.0%)	3 (0.3%)
6	2 (0.8%)	4 (0.4%)
7	0 (0.0%)	2 (0.2%)
8	1 (0.4%)	1 (0.1%)

with a human burial. No copper objects have been recorded at Upper Nodena (Fisher-Carroll 2001b).

Burial Diversity Scores

As in our earlier study, we have computed a diversity score for each burial at the sites. Diversity scores reflect the number of different artifact classes used as funerary objects, not simply the number of objects. The artifact classes we used to compute artifact diversity scores included plain bowl, plain bottle, painted bottle, other bottle, plain jar, decorated jar, compound vessel, kneeling human-effigy vessel, other human-effigy vessel, triune/triune-like vessel, fish-effigy vessel, bird-effigy vessel, frog-effigy vessel, other zoomorphic vessel, spatulate axe, greenstone celt, other celt/axe, stone discoidal, clay disc/discoidal, shell bead necklace, shell bead bracelet, large quantity of shell beads (e.g., covering the body), other shell beads (over pelvis, etc.), shell earplug, stone pipe, ceramic pipe, shell mask gorget, shell spoon bone tool, astragalus "dice," stone point, and other stone tool. In computing diversity scores, we also counted some additional unique or rare items; see Fisher-Carroll (2001b) for some examples.

From the earlier discussion of ceramic vessels, it should be evident that burial diversity scores are higher at Middle Nodena than at Upper Nodena. Table 8.12 provides confirmation. The far greater percentage of burials at Upper Nodena without any preserved funerary objects is particularly noteworthy, but the higher percentages of burials with diversity scores of 2 or 3 at Middle Nodena provide further evidence of striking differences between the sites.

Concluding Remarks

Middle Nodena and Upper Nodena are roughly contemporary (ca. A.D. 1400–1550) sites that are separated by only a few kilometers. We have evaluated the long-held assumption that Middle Nodena postdates Upper Nodena using a class of data not exploited by earlier researchers, namely human mortuary data. The relative ages of the sites probably could not be resolved through radiometric dating, given typical standard deviations of AMS dates.

From Upper Nodena there are 893 burials with fairly good documentation; this is by far the largest mortuary population from a single late-period site in the central Mississippi valley. With 255 well-documented human burials, Middle Nodena has the sixth largest mortuary sample (Fisher-Carroll 2001a: 36).

At both sites, nearly all individuals were interred in a supine extended position; this is characteristic of late-period sites throughout the central Mississippi valley (Fisher-Carroll 2001a: 38–39). There are statistically significant differences between the sites with respect to the angle of burial orientation. We will not speculate about what this may mean, but time of burial is a reasonable (though not provable) possibility (Holland 1991; Mainfort 1996).

There are a number of contrasts, some pronounced, between the burial populations at Middle and Upper Nodena with regard to funerary objects. Perhaps the most noteworthy of these is the percentage of individuals accompanied by one or more preserved funerary objects—92 percent at Middle Nodena versus 56 percent at Upper Nodena. Pottery vessels are by far the most numerous class of funerary objects at both sites, and it follows from the preceding figures that the mean number of pottery vessels per individual at the two sites would differ significantly. At Upper Nodena this is about 0.7 vessels per burial, which is less than half the number at Middle Nodena (1.5 vessels). These figures are mirrored by the percentages of burials accompanied by more than one ceramic vessel—19.7 percent at Upper Nodena but 63.8 percent at Middle Nodena. These differences also are reflected in burial diversity scores.

The sites also differ in the location of ceramic vessels within individual graves. At Upper Nodena, 62 percent of the mortuary ceramic vessels were located adjacent to the head; only 41 percent of the Middle Nodena vessels occurred by the head. Other differences include numerically smaller artifact classes, including stone discoidals, shell beads, spatulate celts, and copper objects; all these examples may be considered socially valued goods.

That the mortuary data from Middle and Upper Nodena reveal some pronounced differences between the sites is beyond dispute. There remains the question of what factor(s) may account for these differences. The overwhelming similarities in material culture between the sites provide no compelling reason to attribute the differences to ethnicity or group identity (but see Jones 1997). These similarities and the close proximity of the sites caused earlier researchers to suggest that Upper and Middle Nodena represent sequent occupations by the same social group. Contrasts in mortuary behavior between the sites lead us to the same conclusion.

9

The Materialization of Status and Social Structure at Koger's Island Cemetery, Alabama

JON BERNARD MARCOUX

The explanatory frameworks used to interpret the mortuary practices of Mississippian societies have undergone a significant amount of change within the last 35 years. Early mortuary studies of these societies relied heavily on the socio-evolutionary typologies of the late 1960s and early 1970s (Fried 1967; Service 1962) and the related notion of a cross-culturally valid social type known as a "ranked" society (e.g., Binford 1971; Brown 1971; Goldstein 1980, 1981; Peebles 1971, 1974). The authors of these works developed their interpretations around this notion using the Binford-Saxe mortuary program, a theoretical construct that considered mortuary events to be expressions of the social persona of the deceased individual and his/her inherited place in the rigid and hierarchical social order of a ranked society.

While the authors of more recent studies continue to use the Binford-Saxe program to derive information about Mississippian social structure, they have largely moved away from interpretations that are cast in the language of social evolution. These authors consider mortuary practices within the social contexts of particular native southeastern societies (e.g., Eastman 2001; Rodning 1996, 2001; Sullivan 2001). Consequently, their attempts to understand the social context of mortuary practices rely more upon ethnohistoric accounts of southeastern Indian societies than upon ethnographic analogies to Polynesian groups and other societies exhibiting a similar level of social complexity.

This essay addresses the current shift in explanatory frameworks by offering an alternative interpretation of the mortuary practices materialized at the Koger's Island site, a Mississippian cemetery located in the middle Tennessee River Valley of northern Alabama (Figures 9.1 and 9.2). I contrast my interpretation with that of Christopher Peebles (1971), who structured his analysis of the Koger's Island cemetery around the Binford-Saxe mortuary program and the socioevolutionary concept of the ranked society.

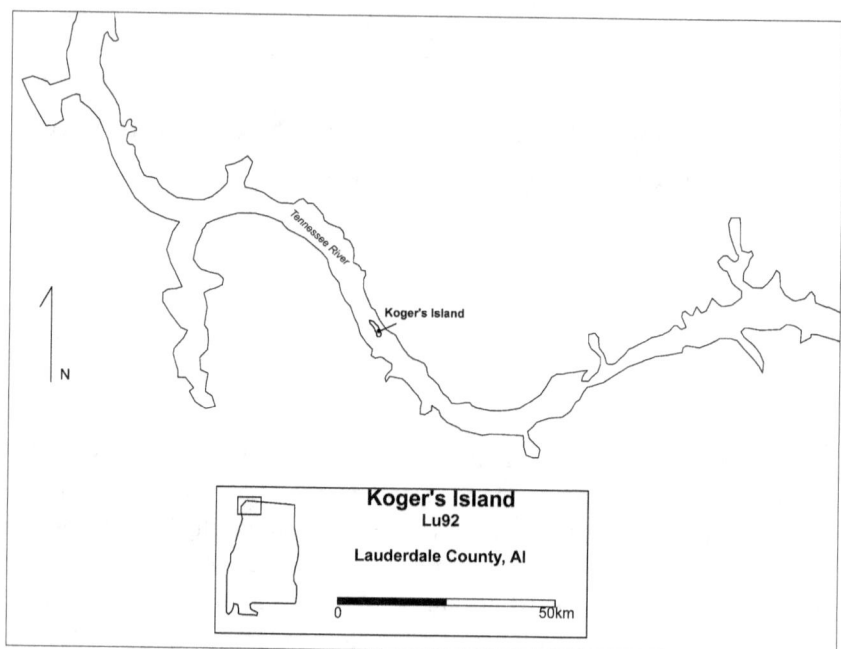

Figure 9.1. Areal Map Showing the Location of the Koger's Island Cemetery.

Like Peebles, I test the relationship between social structure and mortuary practices by using a Binford-Saxe–type analysis that focuses on burial types, variability in the distribution of artifacts, and the spatial arrangement of graves within the Koger's Island cemetery. However, instead of testing a socio-evolutionary model of social structure, as Peebles did, I use the burial data to test the applicability of ethnohistorically derived models of dual social structure such as those Knight (1990, 1997) and Hudson (1976) have posited. These models have become more popular in recent years and describe a somewhat different form of social structure than a ranked society. First, Knight and Hudson argue that hierarchical status in these models was achieved through an individual's age and exploits instead of being strictly inherited. Furthermore, members of such societies reckoned relationships among members of dually organized societies differently than in ranked societies, where descent and status were so intertwined. These models predict archaeological materializations of social structure (e.g., spatial organization of cemeteries, settlement layout) that are not weighed so heavily toward differences in hierarchical status.

Given the patterns I identify through individual-level and spatial analyses, I conclude that while the hierarchical status of individuals was materialized in

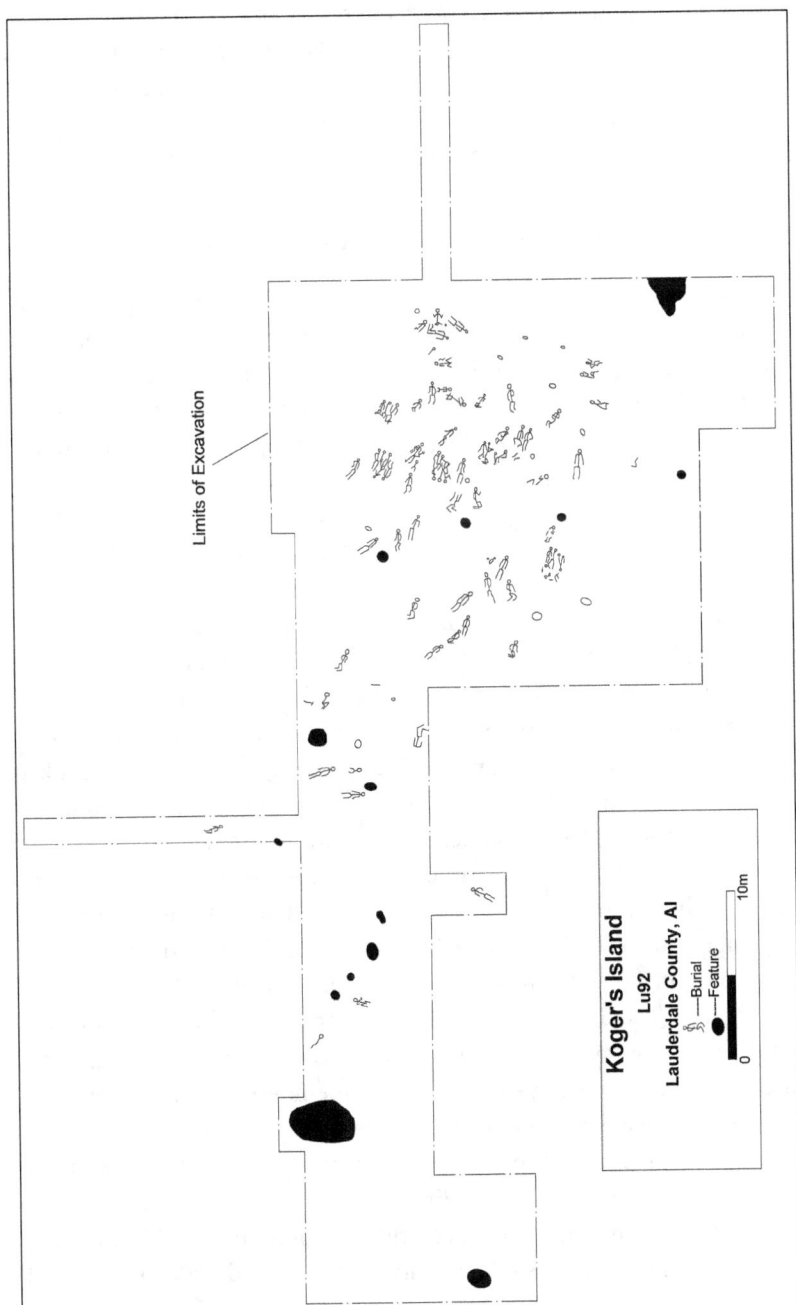

Figure 9.2. Plan Map Depicting the Excavated Burials and Features at the Koger's Island Cemetery. Adapted from Webb and DeJarnette 1942: Figure 70.

some of the mortuary events, it appears to have been based on achievement rather than inheritance. Furthermore, I argue that status was not the sole organizing principle of the cemetery. Instead, I hold that the spatial distribution of interments and funerary objects indicates that the mortuary practices of the local community were more likely structured by a form of dual social structure in that these practices marked either the membership of the deceased in one of two corporate kin groups or their status as an "outsider."

Mississippian Mortuary Analysis and Socio-Evolutionary Typologies

Together with Arthur Saxe (1970), Lewis Binford (1971) developed the body of middle-range theory known as the Binford-Saxe mortuary program. The foundation of their program rested upon the belief that mortuary practices were dictated by two symbolic referents to the deceased individual: the social persona of the deceased and the size of the group that had "duty-status" relationships with the deceased. Both researchers noted that the identity constructed for the deceased by his or her mourners likely reflected the status position enjoyed by that individual (Binford 1971: 25, 39; Saxe 1970: 6). Furthermore, they held that the differences between the burial treatments of individuals likely reflected the degree of social complexity exhibited by a society. Fried's (1960, 1967) socio-evolutionary stages (i.e., egalitarian, ranked, stratified, state) provided the scale upon which Binford measured complexity.

Because Fried's (1967: 109) definition of ranked societies forms the basis of many subsequent works, it bears some discussion. Fried held that ranked societies were social units "in which positions of valued status are somehow limited so that not all those of sufficient talent to occupy such statuses actually achieve them" (1967: 126). He argued that access to the limited positions of prestige in this type of society was largely controlled by descent. Combined with a principle of seniority (i.e., birth order), rank based on descent from a common founding ancestor resulted in what Kirchoff (1959: 260–270) called a "conical clan." The apical position of a ranked society, what we may call the "chief," was reserved for the person who was most closely related to the mythical founder. The relative statuses of all members of society were then determined by genealogical distance from the chief.

The seminal papers published in *Approaches to the Social Dimensions of Mortuary Practices* reflect how the Binford-Saxe program and socio-evolutionary typological thinking influenced the interpretations of Mississippian social structure that dominated the literature of 1970s and 1980s (Brown 1971; Larson 1971; Peebles 1971). Among this group of archaeologists, Peebles's oft-cited mortuary analysis of Moundville burials and less-often-cited work with

Koger's Island burials largely cemented the view that Mississippian communities in Alabama were ranked societies (Peebles 1971, 1974).

In his dissertation, Peebles (1974) tested this model of social structure with burial data from Moundville. In an innovative attempt to create testable and empirical bridging arguments that linked ethnohistoric records to archaeological data, he proposed two analytical dimensions that could be used to test the existence of rank-based distinctions in the Moundville burial population: the *superordinate* and the *subordinate* dimensions. These basically reflected two independent hierarchically ranked groups that could be thought of as elite and commoner groups. The superordinate dimension was determined at least in part by inheritance and the subordinate dimension was determined by age, sex, and achievement. His model set forth the expectation that burials from the ascriptive (superordinate) dimension were represented by a higher cost of burial facility and funerary objects; funerary objects that were symbolic items of rank and office; and burials of children who exhibited the previous two qualities and who presumably belonged to the ascriptive dimension by virtue of inherited rank. On the other hand, burials belonging to the achieved (subordinate) dimension were represented by burial facilities and funerary objects that cost less than burials of individuals in the superordinate group; common domestic artifacts; and variation in the mortuary treatment that reflected age and sex. He further argued that these two dimensions would be expressed spatially in the form of mound and nonmound burials.

Based on the results of a cluster analysis of funerary objects interred with Moundville burials, Peebles (1974) concluded that Moundville was indeed a ranked society in Fried's sense of the term. He argued that hierarchical status in Moundville society was arranged in a pyramidal fashion with the chief at the apex, that high status was most likely inherited from one generation to the next, and that this pyramidal or conical social hierarchy was expressed in mortuary practices through restricted access to certain funerary objects and burial location (i.e., mound versus cemetery) that cut across age and sex groups.

Peebles (1971) also investigated the relationship between cemetery organization and social rank at the Koger's Island site by looking at the distribution of certain status-related artifacts that he called local symbols (e.g., hawk-sternum rattles) and supralocal symbols of high rank (e.g., iconographic artifacts). His argument that the cemetery was organized into five rows of burials was based on the distribution of these local and supralocal symbols. Whereas what he called "technomic" funerary objects (i.e., bone awls and pins, utilitarian ceramics, and projectile points) were not clustered in any rows, the symbolic artifacts were clustered with a few burials in the second and fifth rows of the cemetery (Peebles 1971: 73). Consequently, he posited that the high-status individuals interred in these two rows were spatially segregated from the rest of the burials in the cemetery. Peebles (1971: 87) concluded that like Moundville, Koger's Island was a ranked society whose members expressed status distinctions in mortuary practices through the restricted distribution of supralocal symbols in graves and through the structured use of mortuary space.

An Alternative View of Mississippian Social Organization: The Ethnohistoric Perspective

Knight (1990, 1997) has questioned the use of evolutionary social types in interpreting Mississippian social structure. His critique is based on the lack of comparability between the form of structure associated with ranked societies, namely the conical clan, and the structure described in ethnohistoric and ethnographic literature pertaining to historic North American Indian groups. To Knight (1997: 8), the conical clan describes a very specific form of social structure where every member of society occupies a unique social position based upon their genealogical distance from the chief. Because of the importance of genealogical distance in determining one's social rank, societies with a conical clan structure place a great deal of emphasis on descent reckoning and possess extensive genealogical knowledge that extends back multiple generations. Knight (1990: 5) argues, as did Paul Kirchoff (1959), the originator of the conical clan concept, that no historic Indian group in the Eastern Woodlands exhibited this form of social structure.

According to Knight (1990: 5), Eastern North American Indian societies were organized into exogamous clans that were based upon matri- or patrifiliation to an individual's parents rather than to distant ancestors. Furthermore, because genealogies in these societies were most often limited to the identification of close kin, they demonstrated very limited generational depth and were reckoned bilaterally. Knight (1990: 6) states that unlike the conical clans of ranked societies, the clans of Eastern North American Indian were not internally ranked according to a strict notion of birthright. Instead, those occupying positions of status and prestige within the clan were elected by clan members on the basis of age, ability, and achievement. Ranking did exist in these societies, but it occurred among clans rather than within them.

In Knight's model such ranked clans, in turn, belonged to one of two more inclusive kin groups that exhibited the classic traits of dual social structure. Knight (1990: 6) argues that the two kin-based divisions within a society were associated with different ritual roles and diametrically opposed characters such as those associated with the red and white divisions of the Creek, Hasinai, and Natchez (Hudson 1976: 235–237; Wyckoff and Baugh 1980: 236–237). Moreover, Knight (1990: 11) argued that in societies such as the Timucua, Chickasaw, and Natchez, these two divisions were hierarchically ranked in relation to each other and that leadership positions were limited to members of the higher-ranked kin group.[1] In the following discussion I propose how to answer the question of whether mortuary practices at Koger's Island reflected a form of social structure that is closer to this model.

Testing Models of Mississippian Social Organization

In many ways, the Koger's Island site presents a particularly good context for mortuary analysis. During the winter of 1937–1938, the site was excavated as part of a federally sponsored salvage project necessitated by the construction of the Tennessee Valley Authority's (TVA) Pickwick Dam (Webb and DeJarnette 1942: 212–235). The cemetery dates to A.D. 1300–1450 based on diagnostic artifacts, appears to have been fully excavated, and does not appear to have been extensively looted.[2] Furthermore, plow disturbance at the site was limited to a depth of six inches and bone preservation was exceptional. Most of the burials (n = 76) were single interments placed in simple pits; the remainder of the burials (n = 37) were interments of multiple individuals in single pits (Table 9.1). As others have noted, the relative absence of superimposed or intrusive graves in so small an area indicates a brief period of use for the cemetery, spanning as little as 50 years (Brain and Phillips 1996: 276; Jacobi and Dye 2000; Webb and DeJarnette 1942). Finally, previous research by Bridges, Jacobi, Dye, and Powell (Bridges 1996; Bridges et al. 2000; Dye 2000; Jacobi and Dye 2000) has provided a great deal of updated osteological and artifactual information, without which my analysis would not be possible.

As one can imagine, testing models of prehistoric social structure using mortuary data presents a complicated challenge, and it depends on the (sometimes tenuous) assumption that the community materialized social structure in their mortuary practices (see Carr 1995). Following similar work conducted by Binford (1964) and O'Shea (1984), I offer the following statements in order to test a dual model of social structure using the mortuary record of Koger's Island: I hold that if group identities associated with dual social structure were materialized in the mortuary practices of the Koger's Island community, one would expect to find (1) a distribution of artifact indicators of high status structured by age and sex reflecting elevated social position based on principles of achievement as described in Knight's (1990, 1997) model rather than birthright, as in the ranked society model used by Peebles; (2) a bilateral division in the spatial organization of the cemetery; and (3) a bilateral distribution

Table 9.1. Koger's Island Burials

Burial No.	Sex	Age Class	Burial Type	Artifact Contents
1	indeterminate	0–7 yrs.	indeterminate	Mississippi Plain *var. Warrior* jar, unknown quantity of gastropod beads, awl
2	indeterminate	8–14 yrs.	indeterminate	none
3	indeterminate	8–14 yrs.	fully flexed	none
4	male	20–29 yrs.	partly flexed	2 Mississippi Plain *var. Warrior* jars, turtle carapace, hammerstone
5	female	20–29 yrs.	partly flexed	Bell Plain subglobular bottle, Moundville Engraved *var. Tuscaloosa* subglobular bottle
6	male	20–29 yrs.	extended	Bell Plain subglobular bottle, formal notched and engraved stone palette, stone projectile point, 3 turkey-bone awls, copper-clad ear disk, Moundville Incised *var. Snow's Bend* jar, yellow pigment, 8 marine columella beads, noded jar, Moundville Engraved *var. Hemphill* subglobular bottle
7	indeterminate	8–14 yrs.	extended	none
8	indeterminate	0–7 yrs.	extended	none
9	female	15–19 yrs.	indeterminate	turtle carapace
10	female	40+ yrs.	secondary	turkey-bone awl, antler projectile point, chipped-stone knife, stone projectile point
11	male	30–39 yrs.	partly flexed	3 turkey-bone awls, split-bone pin, Mississippi Plain *var. Warrior* jar, 5 hawk sterna

Burial No.	Sex	Age Class	Burial Type	Artifact Contents
12	indeterminate	8–14 yrs.	indeterminate	none
13	male	30–39 yrs.	partly flexed	none
14	female?	20–29 yrs.	extended	none
15	male	40+ yrs.	partly flexed	none
16	female	40+ yrs.	partly flexed	none
17	male	40+ yrs.	indeterminate	none
18	indeterminate	0–7 yrs.	indeterminate	none
19	indeterminate	0–7 yrs.	indeterminate	none
20	male	30–39 yrs.	partly flexed	split-bone pin (copper stained; probably associated with a copper ear disk), 3 stone projectile points, 3 turkey-bone awls, chipped-stone knife, formal notched and engraved stone palette, deer-ulna awl, 12 hawk sterna, 16 perforated raccoon(?) teeth
21	male	30–39 yrs.	extended	Mississippi Plain *var. Warrior* jar
22	male	30–39 yrs.	extended	Mississippi Plain *var. Warrior* sherd, Mississippi Plain *var. Warrior* simple bowl, 2 Mississippi Plain *var. Warrior* jars

continued

Table 9.1.—*Continued*

Burial No.	Sex	Age Class	Burial Type	Artifact Contents
23	male	30–39 yrs.	extended	3 perforated wolf teeth, 2 perforated raccoon teeth, greenstone spatulate spade, 2 split-bone pins (copper stained; probably related to copper ear disks), 2 greenstone celts, chipped-stone knife, 9 copper symbol badges (2 Cemochechobee style, 7 baton style), 2 "killed" conch cups, 1,049 marine columella beads, beaver incisor, zoomorphic effigy pipe w/tri-lobed forked eye motif, 2 polished needles, 35 hawk sterna, 9 split-bone pins, 4 copper-clad ear disks, hematite, stone projectile point, galena, 9 antler projectile points, bald eagle bone, 2 catfish spines, Barton Incised *var. unspecified* jar fragment, rodent tooth, 12 cut marine shell fragments, formal notched and engraved palette
24	female	20–29 yrs.	extended	Mississippi Plain *var. Warrior* jar
25	female	15–19 yrs.	partly flexed	Mississippi Plain *var. Warrior* subglobular bottle, deer mandible
26*a	female	30–39 yrs.	partly flexed	3 Mississippi Plain *var. Warrior* jars
27*	indeterminate	8–14 yrs.	partly flexed	2 stone projectile points
28*	indeterminate	0–7 yrs.	indeterminate	Mississippi Plain *var. Warrior* lug-and-rim effigy bowl
101*	female	30–39 yrs.	partly flexed	12 mussel shells

Burial No.	Sex	Age Class	Burial Type	Artifact Contents
102*	indeterminate	0–7 yrs.	partly flexed	none
29*	indeterminate	0–7 yrs.	extended	none
30*	female	15–19 yrs.	extended	Mississippi Plain *var. Warrior* beaded rim bowl
31*	male	40+ yrs.	extended	none
32*	male	30–39 yrs.	extended	none
33*	male	20–29 yrs.	extended	none
34*	male	30–39 yrs.	extended	none
35*	male	40+ yrs.	extended	none
36*	male	20–29 yrs.	extended	none
37*	female	40+ yrs.	extended	none
38*	male	40+ yrs.	extended	none
39*	male	30–39 yrs.	extended	none
40	male	20–29 yrs.	extended	none
40A	female	15–19 yrs.	indeterminate	none
41*	male	30–39 yrs.	partly flexed	2 stone projectile points
42*	female	30–39 yrs.	partly flexed	Moundville Incised *var. Snow's Bend* jar
43*	female	40+ yrs.	partly flexed	Moundville Incised *var. unspecified* jar, Moundville Incised *var. Moundville* jar, engraved shell gorget (Cox Mound style bird genre), 2 Mississippi Plain *var. Warrior* jars, Mississippi Plain *var. Warrior* simple bowl, 7 turtle carapaces
44	indeterminate	0–7 yrs.	indeterminate	none
45	female	40+ yrs.	partly flexed	Mississippi Plain *var. Warrior* jar, Mississippi Plain *var. Warrior* sherd
46*	female	40+ yrs.	extended	Mississippi Plain *var. Warrior* jar

continued

Table 9.1.—*Continued*

Burial No.	Sex	Age Class	Burial Type	Artifact Contents
47*	female	40+ yrs.	extended	none
48	indeterminate	indeterminate	extended	none
49	female?	8–14 yrs.	indeterminate	none
50	indeterminate	indeterminate	indeterminate	none
51	female	15–19 yrs.	indeterminate	none
52	female	40+ yrs.	fully flexed	split-bone pin
53	female	20–29 yrs.	fully flexed	none
54	female	30–39 yrs.	partly flexed	stone projectile point, Mississippi Plain *var.* Warrior jar
55	indeterminate	0–7 yrs.	indeterminate	2 stone projectile points
56	indeterminate	8–14 yrs.	extended	split-bone pin, 6 marine columella beads
57	female	30–39 yrs.	partly flexed	3 stone projectile points
58	indeterminate	0–7 yrs.	indeterminate	none
59	male	20–29 yrs.	partly flexed	greenstone celt, Mississippi Plain *var.* Warrior sherd, 3 marine columella beads Mississippi Plain *var.* Warrior jar, split -one pin
60*	male	40+ yrs.	partly flexed	329 marine shell beads
61*	male	40+ yrs.	partly flexed	2 stone projectile points, trumpeter swan wing bones
62	indeterminate	0–7 yrs.	indeterminate	none
63	indeterminate	0–7 yrs.	indeterminate	none
64	female?	30–39 yrs.	fully flexed	none
65	female	15–19 yrs.	fully flexed	Mississippi Plain *var.* Warrior jar

Burial No.	Sex	Age Class	Burial Type	Artifact Contents
66*	male	30–39 yrs.	partly flexed	2 Mississippi Plain var. Warrior subglobular bottles
66A*	indeterminate	0–7 yrs.	indeterminate	stone projectile point
67*	female	30–39 yrs.	partly flexed	Mississippi Plain var. Warrior sherd
68	indeterminate	0–7 yrs.	indeterminate	none
68A	indeterminate	0–7 yrs.	indeterminate	none
69	indeterminate	0–7 yrs.	partly flexed	gastropod beads
70	male	30–39 yrs.	extended	Mississippi Plain var. Warrior jar
71	indeterminate	0–7 yrs.	indeterminate	none
72	female	15–19 yrs.	extended	none
73	female	40+ yrs.	partly flexed	none
74	male	40+ yrs.	partly flexed	Moundville Engraved var. Tuscaloosa ovoid bottle
75	male	40+ yrs.	partly flexed	none
76	indeterminate	0–7 yrs.	partly flexed	none
77	indeterminate	0–7 yrs.	indeterminate	Mississippi Plain var. Warrior jar
78	female	20–29 yrs.	partly flexed	3 Mississippi Plain var. Warrior jars, Mississippi Plain var. Warrior lobate bottle
79	male	30–39 yrs.	extended	"killed" conch cup, Moundville Engraved var. Hemphill subglobular bottle
80	indeterminate	0–7 yrs.	extended	Mississippi Plain var. Warrior jar
80A	indeterminate	0–7 yrs.	indeterminate	none
81	female	20–29 yrs.	extended	none
81A	indeterminate	0–7 yrs.	indeterminate	none

continued

Table 9.1.—*Continued*

Burial No.	Sex	Age Class	Burial Type	Artifact Contents
82	indeterminate	0–7 yrs.	indeterminate	none
83	female	20–29 yrs.	extended	gastropod beads
84	indeterminate	0–7 yrs.	indeterminate	none
84A	male	30–39 yrs.	indeterminate	none
84B	indeterminate	0–7 yrs.	indeterminate	none
84C	indeterminate	0–7 yrs.	indeterminate	none
85	male?	30–39 yrs.	partly flexed	none
86	female	30–39 yrs.	fully flexed	none
87	indeterminate	0–7 yrs.	extended	none
88	indeterminate	indeterminate	fully flexed	none
89*	female	20–29 yrs.	extended	2 greenstone celts
90*	male	30–39 yrs.	extended	2 chipped stone knives
91*	female	40+ yrs.	extended	2 bone awls
92*	male	30–39 yrs.	extended	2 stone projectile points
93*	male	30–39 yrs.	extended	5 turkey-bone awls
94*	male	30–39 yrs.	secondary	polished needle
95*	male	30–39 yrs.	secondary	Mississippi Plain *var. Warrior* subglobular bottle
96*	indeterminate	indeterminate	secondary	Mississippi Plain *var. Warrior* jar, 32 antler projectile points
97	indeterminate	0–7 yrs.	indeterminate	none
98	indeterminate	8–14 yrs.	extended	Mississippi Plain *var. Warrior* sherd
98A	indeterminate	8–14 yrs.	indeterminate	none
99	indeterminate	0–7 yrs.	indeterminate	none
100	female?	30–39 yrs.	isolated skull	none
100A	indeterminate	0–7 yrs.	indeterminate	none
100B	indeterminate	8–14 yrs.	indeterminate	none

Note: [a] Asterisks indicate multiple burials in the same pit.

of certain burial forms, artifact types, or artifact styles possibly associated with the different characters and/or ritual roles filled by members of these two divisions.[3]

Addressing the first expectation, an admittedly rough proxy of the presence of hierarchical status differences was achieved through a number of artifact types (NAT) analysis (Champion 1982: 70; see also Fisher-Carroll and Mainfort 2000 for a Mississippian example). This is a simple graphic display of the number of different artifact categories that were included with each burial. This method was originally based upon the notion that one could "measure" the degree of hierarchical status enjoyed by a deceased individual as it was reflected in the elaborate and diverse nature of mortuary offerings. However, this notion employed a somewhat outdated and overly mechanistic view of a measurable correlation between energy expenditure and hierarchical status. Consequently, in this study NAT analysis was not used to measure hierarchical status but was used with other quantitative and qualitative analyses to explore the nature of status differences. Indeed, it was employed as a simple but clear way to demonstrate the *presence* of status differences among burials by uncovering a gap between a few individuals who were buried with many different artifact types and the majority of the burial population, which was buried with a few types of artifacts.[4]

Figure 9.3 presents the results of the NAT analysis for individual burials in the Koger's Island cemetery. The figure displays the profile one would expect if hierarchical status differences were expressed in funerary object accompaniment. The figure shows that many individuals were not interred with funerary objects (n = 35) and that a fall-off relationship exists between the number of burials and number of artifact types. Three outliers in this relationship (one of which contained 25 different categories; see Burials 6, 20, and 23 in Table 9.1) were separated from burials containing five or fewer categories of artifacts. Further examination of these three outliers revealed some interesting similarities. First, these three male burials share artifact types such as columella beads, chipped-stone knives, turkey-bone awls, hawk-sternum rattles, perforated wolf/raccoon teeth, copper-clad ear disks, and split-bone pins. Moreover, the distribution of sandstone palettes and mineral pigments throughout the entire cemetery was restricted to these individuals.

In addition to the NAT results, previous research by David Dye (2000) has supported the association of these types of items with high-status individuals. In his work with the Koger's Island dataset, Dye made an analogy between the co-occurrence of the sharp bone implements, mineral pigments, and stylized palettes in these outlier burials and the ritual bundles associated with tattooing and bloodletting practices among high-status males in historic southeastern and Plains Indian groups. Also, copper-clad ear disks and copper symbol badges, both of which occurred in these outlier burials, have long been regarded as markers of high status among Mississippian groups (e.g., Brain and Phillips 1996; Scarry 1999; Steponaitis 1991).

Constructing a Sherratt (1982: 22) diagram provided further information about the principles underlying how status might have been conferred upon individuals in life.[5] Because the Sherratt diagram displays age, sex, and artifact information, it was particularly useful in determining whether the status was inherited (i.e., ascribed) and/or whether it was based upon a combination of age, sex, and achievements (i.e., achieved). The presence of ascribed hierarchical status is often inferred when the distribution of items associated with high status consistently cuts across sex and age categories. The presence of achieved hierarchical status is commonly inferred when the distribution of high-status funerary objects is defined largely by the age and sex of individuals. Based on the NAT analysis and Dye's (2000) research, high-status items in this analysis included fineware pottery bottles, sandstone palettes, mineral pigments, copper-clad ear disks, chipped-stone disks, turkey-bone awls, hawk-sternum rattles, greenstone celts, antler projectile points, raccoon or wolf teeth, and conch-shell cups.

An inspection of the diagram indicated that hierarchical status was largely achieved in the Koger's Island community (Figure 9.4). Most high-status items were restricted to the burials of young adult and mature adult males between the ages of 20 and 40 (n = 6). Few females were buried with high-status items (n = 3) (one individual was buried with a fineware bottle; one with a turkey-bone awl, chipped-stone knife, and antler projectile points; and one with an engraved-shell gorget).[6] Only one individual in the adolescent and child age groups (< 15 years old) was buried with high-status items; this individual was buried with a split-bone pin and six columella beads. This concentration of high-status items in the burials of adult males (20–39 years old) likely indicates that the achievements of young males largely determined the prestige they enjoyed in the community or that ritual roles were limited to certain male age categories (see Braun 1979). In interpreting this pattern, one must seriously consider the role played by warfare in gaining prestige, given the findings of Bridges et al. (2000) that perimortem wounds and violent trauma were common in the Koger's Island cemetery burial population and Dye and Jacobi's (2000) argument that extra body parts were possibly interred as war trophies in some high-status Koger's Island graves.

I addressed the second and third testable statements about the expected bilateral division of mortuary space by first reevaluating Peebles's (1971) argument regarding the structured use of space in the Koger's Island cemetery.

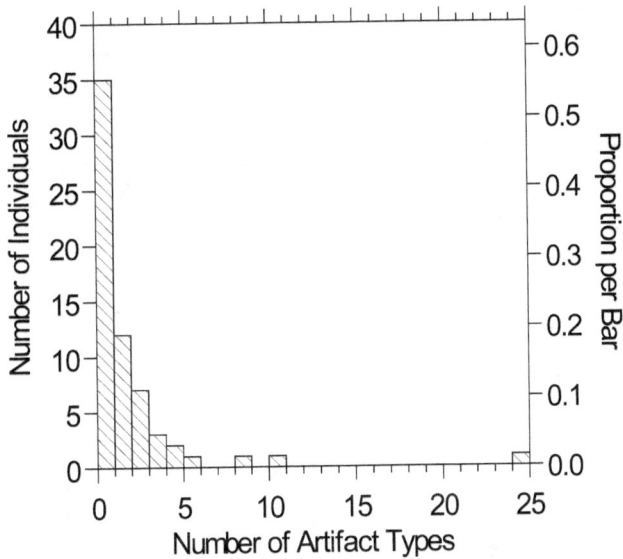

Figure 9.3. NAT Analysis at Koger's Island. Figure depicts the number of artifact types per individual burial. (Only single interments are represented in the analysis.)

When I compared Peebles's site plan, the published site map (Webb and DeJarnette 1942: Figure 70), and burial recording forms, it was difficult to see how Peebles defined his five rows. When I removed the multiple burials, represented in Figure 9.5 by tight clusters of individuals, the task of defining rows became even more difficult. Rows may have existed in the cemetery; however, I tried various row schemes and could not define any rows in such a way that additional evidence (in the form of age, sex, burial type, orientation, or artifact distributions) would support an interpretation that burials were placed in rows.

Simple visual inspection of the excavation plan suggests that the cemetery was separated into three sections (Figure 9.6). The first section was composed of 15 widely spaced burials located in the western part of the cemetery. The second section was composed of 21 burials located in the center of the cemetery. The third section was composed of the remaining 66 burials in the eastern part of the cemetery.[7]

This visually derived spatial pattern was tested by conducting a k-means cluster analysis. This is a nonhierarchical iterative clustering procedure that is particularly well suited to finding patterns in spatial distributions (Duff 1996; Kintigh and Ammerman 1982; S. J. Shennan 1997). The method begins with the analyst defining the number of clusters desired. The procedure then in-

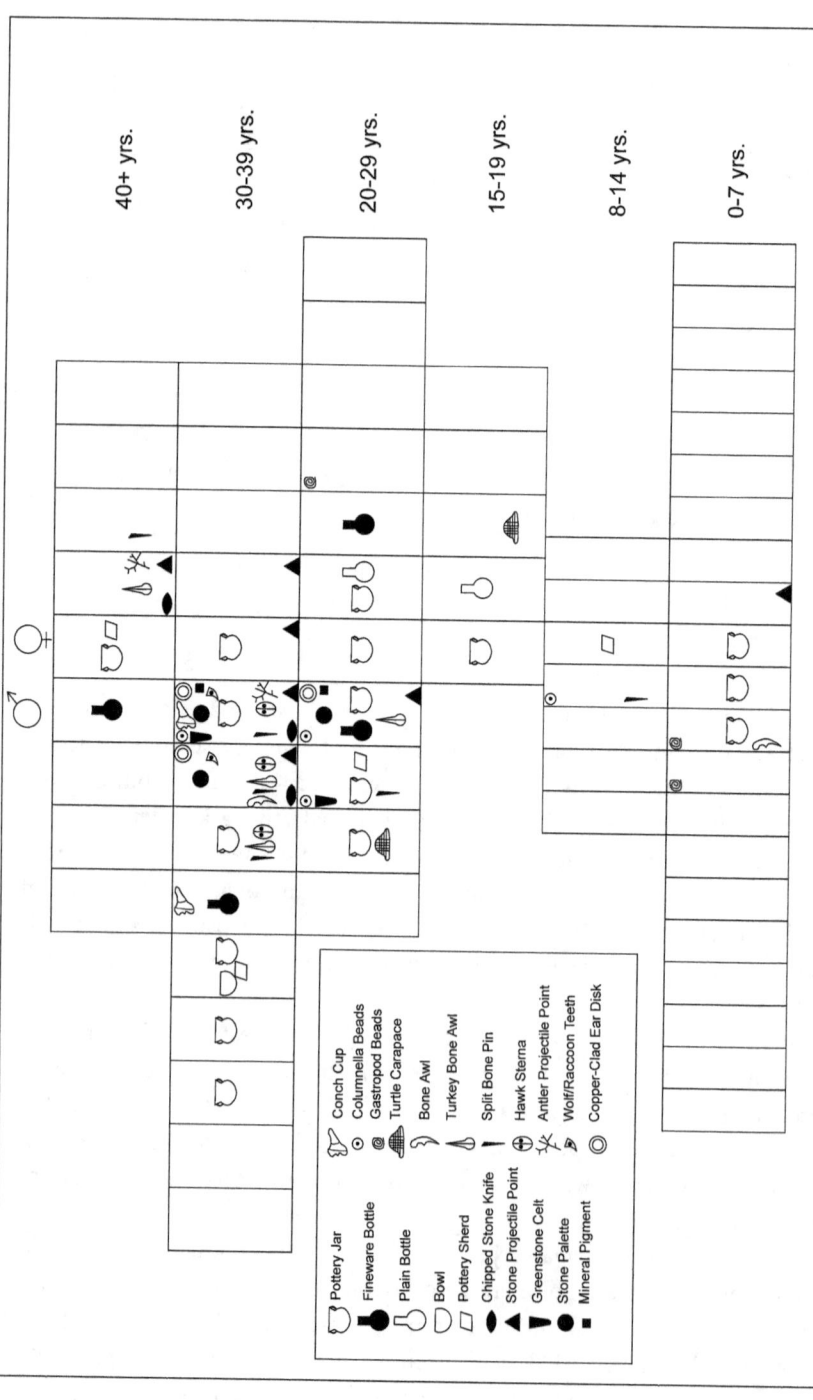

Figure 9.4. Age and Sex Distribution of Selected Artifact Types from the Koger's Island Cemetery. Individuals less than 15 years old are depicted without reference to sex. (Only single interments are included in the analysis.) Adapted from Sherrat 1982: Figure 8.2.

volves an iterative process of calculating the cluster centers and boundaries with the goal of minimizing dispersion within the clusters (measured by the midpoint of each burial in x-y space) while maximizing dispersion between clusters. When a three-cluster solution was chosen, the results of this analysis matched the cemetery sections identified through visual inspection (Figure 9.7). While three clusters obviously do not represent a strict bilateral division of mortuary space, further analyses demonstrated that this situation could be reconciled with the dual social structure model when additional lines of evidence were consulted. These analyses focused on determining whether differences existed in the distributions of age, sex, burial types, and funerary objects among the three cemetery sections. Because the evidence indicated a relatively short use-life for the cemetery, time was not considered to be a major structuring factor in the spatial layout of the cemetery.

First, there were no significant differences among the three cemetery sections with regard to age and sex. While section 2 did have relatively fewer subadults than adults, no significant differences were found among the three sections when a Chi-square statistic was calculated (the significance level was set at $p < .05$; n = 109, $\chi^2 = 2.99$, $df = 2$, $p = 0.22$; Figure 9.8).[8] The same lack of differences among the sections was found in regard to sex (n = 70, $\chi^2 = 1.36$, $df = 2$, $p = 0.50$; Figure 9.9).[9] Thus, neither age nor sex appear to have been a structuring factor in the layout of the cemetery. A lack of appreciable frequencies of the four burial modes precluded any calculation of statistical difference; however, it is interesting to note that while flexed and partly flexed burial treatments cut across all three sections, fully flexed burials occurred only in sections 1 and 3 and secondary burials occurred only in section 2 (Figure 9.10). Also, the original burial notes made particular note of four burials in which three individuals were found to be missing their heads as well as various arm and leg parts and the fourth was represented only by a skull. While Bridges et al. (2000) found evidence of trauma in all three cemetery sections, the burials of this particularly gruesome type were all located in section 1.

Funerary object distributions offered the most informative method of comparison among the three cemetery sections. A simple comparison of the presence and absence of funerary objects in the three sections demonstrated that fewer than 10 percent of the burials in section 1 were associated with funerary objects, roughly 55 percent of the burials in section 3 were associated with funerary objects, and roughly 90 percent of the burials in section 2 were associated with funerary objects (Figure 9.11). Using a Chi-square test, these differences were found to be statistically significant (n = 113, $\chi^2 = 22.98$, $df = 2$, $p < 0.001$). Group size was not a significant factor in this pattern, as sections 1 and 2 contained about the same number of individuals yet completely opposite

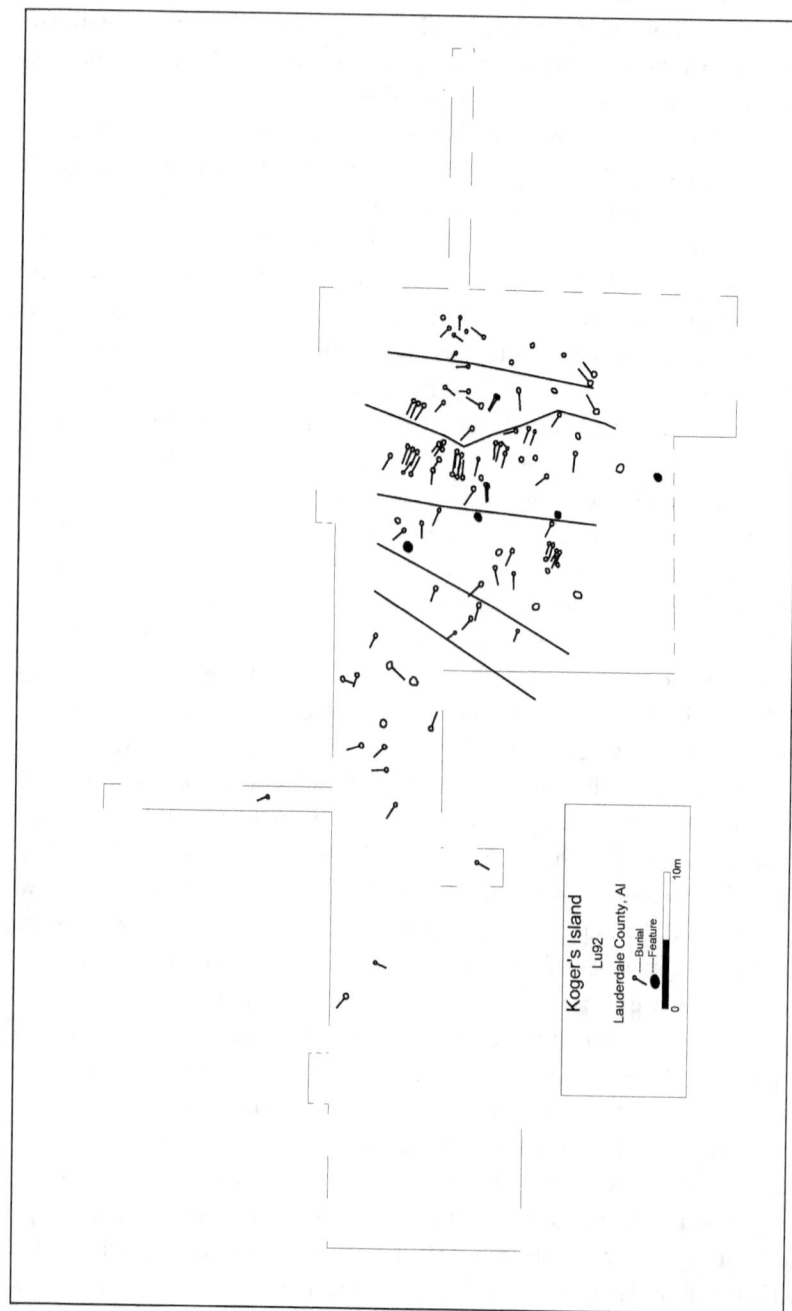

Figure 9.5. Plan Map Depicting the Cemetary Row Structure Put Forth by Peebles (1971: Figure 2).

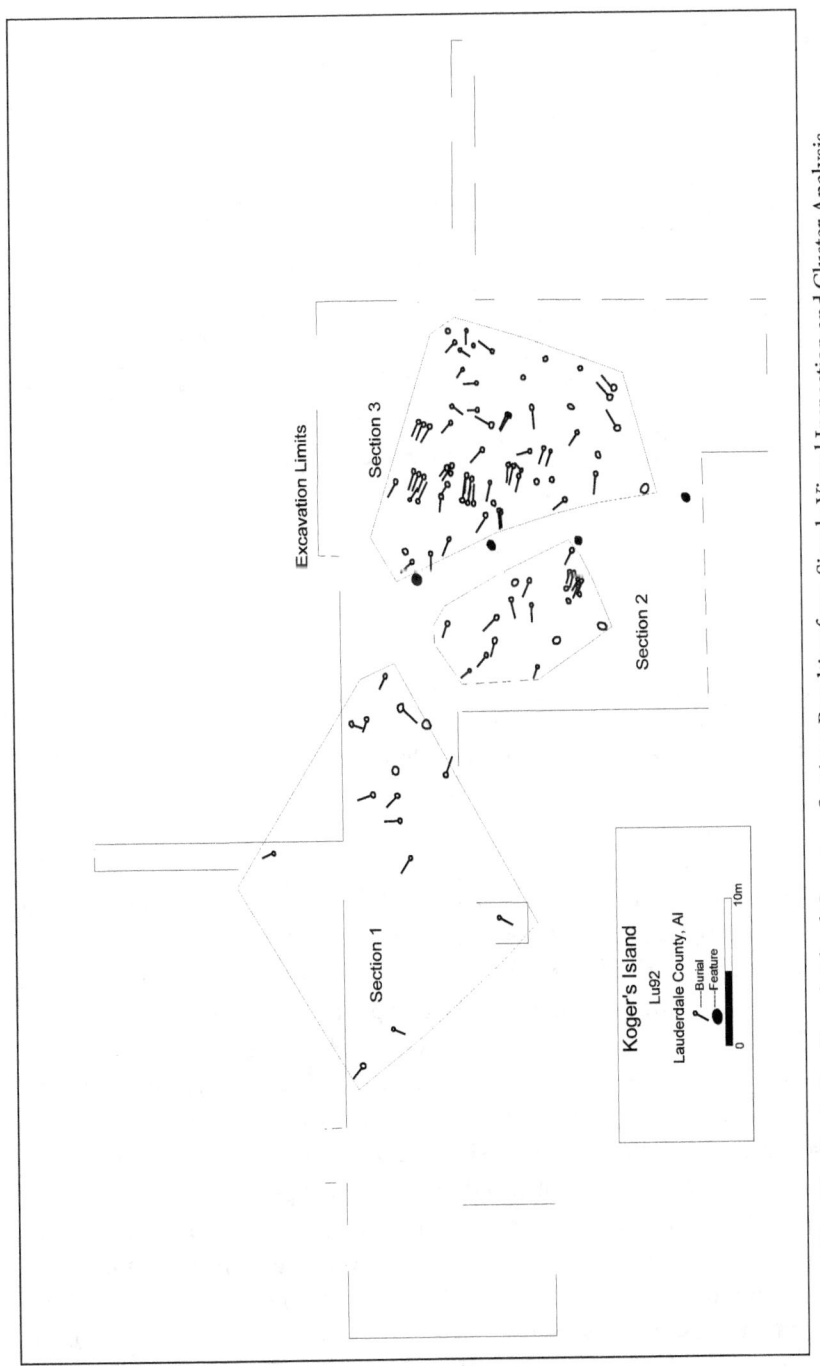

Figure 9.6. Plan Map Depicting Koger's Island Cemetery Sections Resulting from Simple Visual Inspection and Cluster Analysis. Adapted from Webb and Dejarnette 1942: Figure 70.

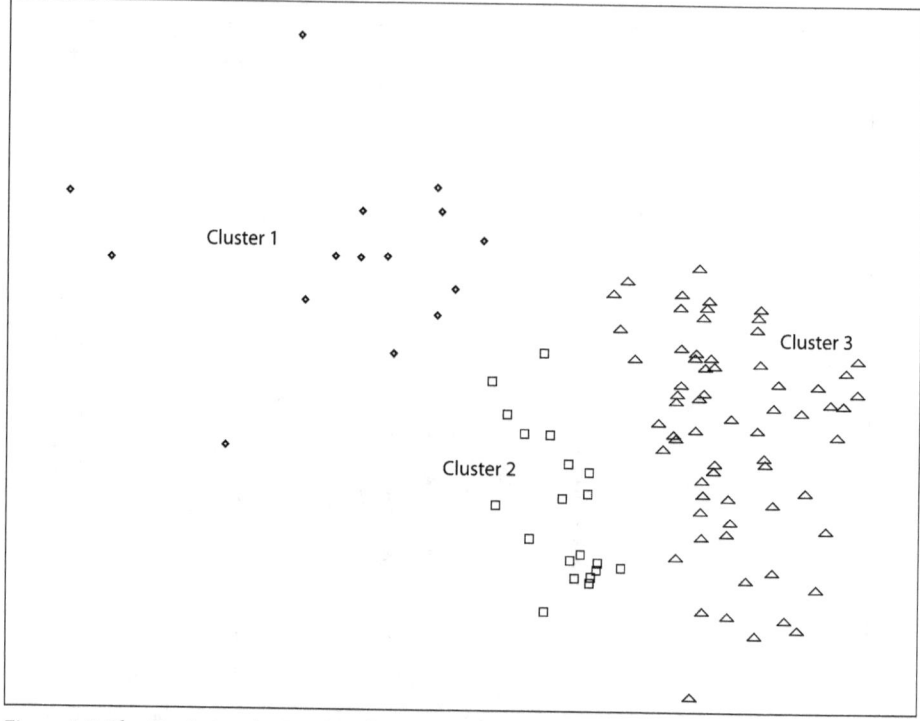

Figure 9.7. Plot Depicting the Results of a K-Means Cluster Analysis (3-Cluster Solution) Conducted on the Spatial Location of Burials at the Koger's Island Cemetery.

profiles. Also, in contrast to Peebles's (1971) findings, it appeared that burials containing high-status artifacts were not particularly isolated from the rest of the burials, as these burials occurred in both sections 2 and 3 (Figure 9.12).

The distribution of particular artifact types provided the last basis of comparison among the three cemetery sections (Table 9.2). The results of this comparison indicated that all but one of the individuals in section 1 lacked funerary objects and that the distribution of high-status items and items usually associated with daily domestic tasks cut across sections 2 and 3. The analysis also demonstrated that the distribution of certain types of artifacts was limited to either section 2 only or section 3 only. Chipped-stone knives, antler projectile points, perforated raccoon and wolf teeth, and hawk-sternum rattles occurred only in burials in section 2, while fineware pottery bottles, turtle-carapace rattles, and arcade-incised jars occurred only in section 3. These artifacts and their distributions are noteworthy because some were also identified by Dye (2000) as items associated with ritual functions.

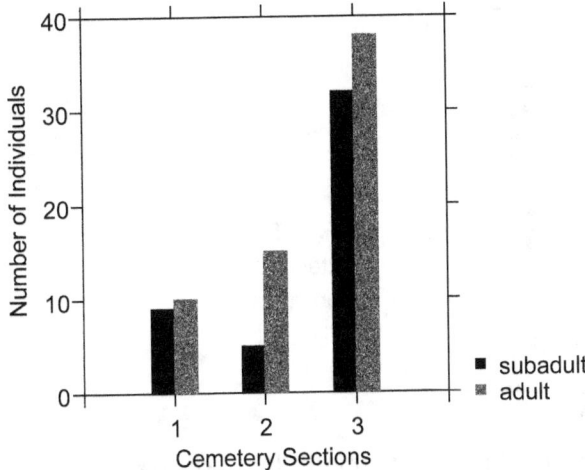

Figure 9.8. Comparison of Age-Group Frequencies in the Three Cemetery Sections at the Koger's Island Cemetery.

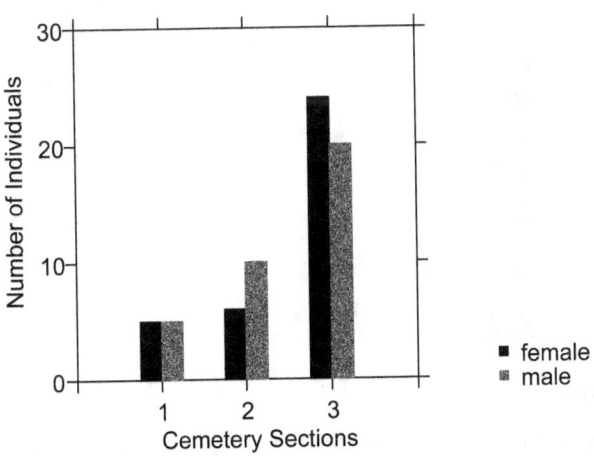

Figure 9.9. Comparison of Sex Frequencies in the Three Cemetery Sections at the Koger's Island Cemetery.

Conclusion

While my analyses affirmed the first testable statement regarding the achieved nature of high status within the Koger's Island community, we are left with a tripartite spatial division of burial locations and artifact distributions when our expectations called for a bilateral division. In order to reconcile this apparent tripartite spatial division with a dual model of social structure, I offer the following interpretation of the patterns identified above: sections 2 and 3

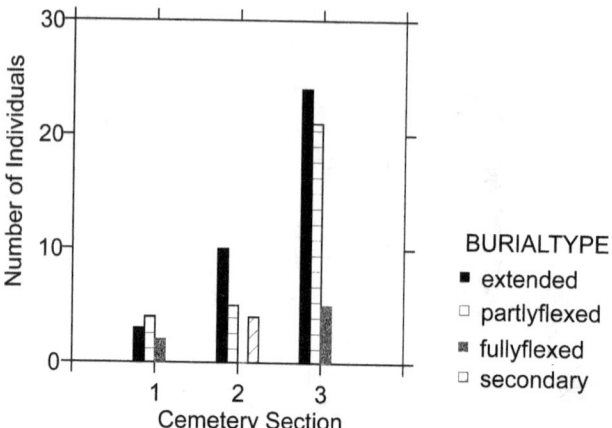

Figure 9.10. Comparison of Burial Type Frequencies in the Three Cemetery Sections at the Koger's Island Cemetery.

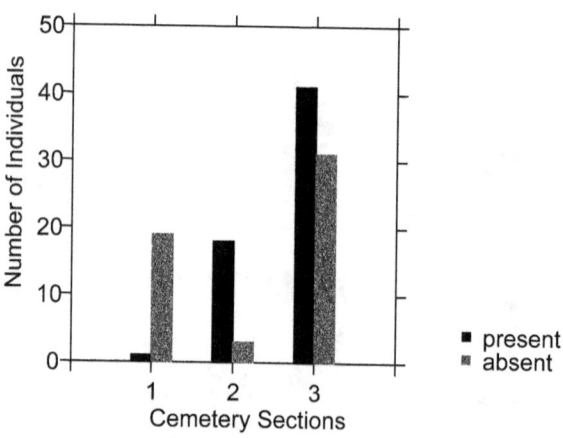

Figure 9.11. Comparison of the Presence of Funerary Objects in the Three Cemetery Sections at Koger's Island Cemetery.

of the cemetery were reserved for members of two corporate kin groups in the Koger's Island community, while section 1 may have been an area reserved for individuals who did not belong to either of these two groups.

I justify this interpretation as follows: first, the three spatial clusters did not appear to represent differences in the timing of the burials or the age or sex of the deceased. Second, sections 2 and 3 were more similar to each other than to section 1 with regard to the presence and absence of funerary objects as well as the presence of high-status burials. Certain types of items

Table 9.2. Comparison of Artifact Types Between Cemetery Sections at Koger's Island

Artifact Category	Cemetery Section		
	1	2	3
gastropod beads	1[a]	0	2
stone knives	0	4	0
antler projectile points	0	3	0
hawk sterna	0	3	0
perforated animal teeth	0	2	0
turkey-bone awls	0	4	1
plain pottery bottles	0	3	1
stone palettes	0	2	1
greenstone celts	0	2	1
copper-clad ear disks	0	2	1
bone awls	0	2	1
killed conch cups	0	1	1
pigments	0	1	1
split bone pins	0	3	3
plain pottery jars	0	7	11
stone projectile points	0	4	8
pottery bowls	0	1	3
ceramic sherds	0	1	4
columella beads	0	1	3
fineware pottery bottles	0	0	4
turtle carapaces	0	0	3
arcade incised jars	0	0	2

Note: [a]Counts represent number of burials that contain a particular type, not the quantity of that type.

were interred almost exclusively with the high-status burials in sections 2 and 3, however—items that arguably had ritual significance. I believe that the differences in funerary object assemblages between sections 2 and 3 could have marked separate ritual roles played by certain members of these two groups as outlined in Knight's (1990, 1997) model. Other researchers have offered similar interpretations of discrete clusterings of burials and artifact types. Steponaitis (1991), for example, cited the possible existence of dual social structure in interpreting a distinctive twofold pattern of artifact distributions in Mississippian burial mounds in the Pocahontas region of Mississippi. Goldstein (1980: 135–136) has also argued that the spatial patterning of burials at a Mississippian cemetery in the lower Illinois River valley indicated that separate kin units were interred in rows and that two larger and more inclusive burial clusters indicated corporate groups that probably represented both local and nonlocal individuals.

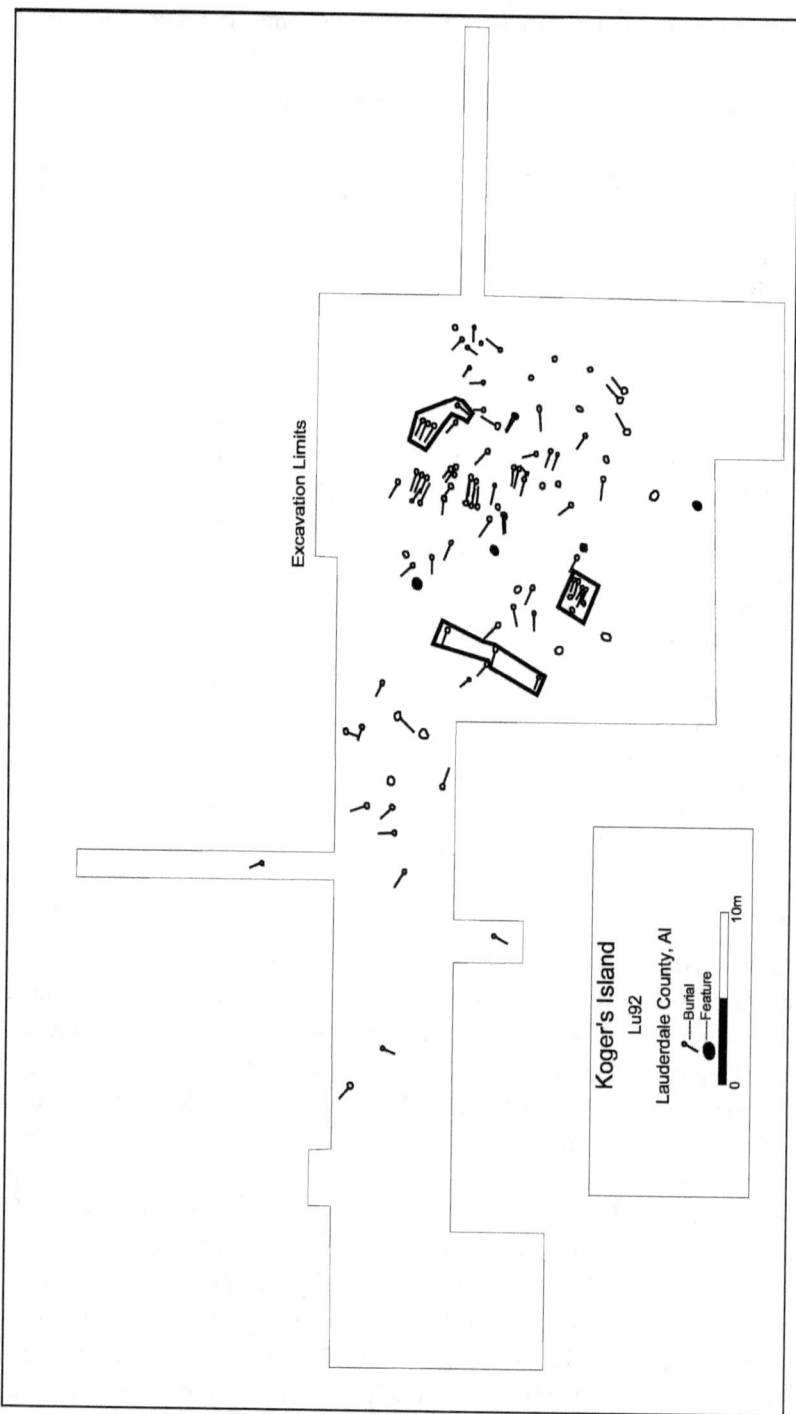

Figure 9.12. Plan Map Depicting Burials Associated with Concentrations of High-Status Items at Koger's Island Cemetery. (Burials discussed in text are outlined.)

Another implication of this study is that for the most part, the spatial structure of the Kroger's Island cemetery did not reflect the hierarchical status of deceased individuals (contra Peebles 1971). If the cemetery sections I identified did reflect the intentional practices of corporate kin groups, then the spatial distribution of high-status burials indicates that "elites" did not form an insular social group, at least not in death (Figure 9.12). Instead, it appears that elites were recruited (or more likely promoted) from within the same kin groups as folk we refer to as commoners. Indeed, if this is the case, then the location of high-status burials in kin-based cemetery sections likely reflects the intentional actions of mourners to locate the deceased individual within the collective identity of the kin group. It is perhaps an obvious conclusion to say that elites and commoners likely shared kin, but the recent research bias toward elites and their strategies has resulted in our forgetting this social fact.

On the other hand, in section 1, we find the virtual absence of funerary objects associated with burials, the presence of an isolated skull burial, and the presence of the only headless and limbless burials in the cemetery. These facts lead me to believe that this section was reserved for individuals that were somehow considered to be outside the two local kin groups. Some of these individuals may have been captives who met a violent end (Hudson 1976: 253–254), while others might have been individuals who died locally and were simply not related to members of the local community.

In conclusion, although many researchers have, in a sense, moved beyond the initial goals of the Binford-Saxe program, I believe we must heed Brown's warning that rejecting this program "is tantamount to throwing the baby out with the bathwater" (1995: 10). The solid body of middle-range theory Binford, Peebles, and others constructed still has much to offer current mortuary studies. Indeed, I believe that Mississippian mortuary practices at the Koger's Island site did in some way reflect the social persona of the deceased but through the practices of the living, as it was they who constructed the identity of the deceased. In doing so, I believe that the living also took that opportunity to construct their own identities, at least in part, by materializing in their kin-group affiliations both spatially and through the selection of funerary objects.

Acknowledgments

I would like to thank Lynne Sullivan and Robert Mainfort for the opportunity to include this essay in their wonderful volume. This essay would not have been possible without the initial efforts of David Dye, Keith Jacobi, and Pat

Bridges in working with the Koger's Island material. The analysis presented here is an extension of their work. I thank Vin Steponaitis for guiding me through this project and Brian Billman and Dale Hutchinson for reviewing a much longer version of this paper. Also, I extend my sincere appreciation to Greg Wilson, Chris Rodning, Amber VanDerwarker, Duke Beasley, and Tony Boudreaux for their insightful comments. I thank Eugene Futato for permission to inspect the artifacts from Koger's Island. These are housed in the Erskine Ramsay Archaeological Repository and are curated by The University of Alabama Museum's Office of Archaeological Research. A final note of thanks to Kim Rutherford and Marina Beasley, who helped tremendously in the data collection portion of this project. Any errors in this paper are my own.

Notes

1. For Knight, this form of social structure in historic groups would have provided a seed for the development of nascent corporate "noble" and "commoner" groups and the formation of institutional social and political inequality among members of Mississippian societies.

2. The diagnostic artifacts include Mississippi Plain jars with two and four strap handles, two Moundville Engraved var. Hemphill subglobular bottles, one Moundville Engraved var. Tuscaloosa subglobular bottle, one Moundville Engraved var. Tuscaloosa ovoid bottle with a pedestal base, Cemochechobee and baton-style copper symbol badges, and a Cox-style bird genre engraved shell gorget.

3. The distribution of high-status funerary objects among Koger's Island burials did not indicate a hierarchical relationship between two social divisions. Nevertheless, other evidence suggests that the Kroger's Island community operated within a dual social structure. While such a relationship is important to Knight's particular model of Mississippian dual structure, I nevertheless argue that the patterns I will describe provide a good case for the dual structure of the Koger's Island community.

4. I defined the artifact types included in this analysis based on material type and function; they are generally those listed in Figure 9.4. I excluded burials containing multiple individuals from this analysis because the exact association of artifacts with particular individuals could not be determined.

5. The Sherratt diagram is another simple yet effective technique for exploring status in mortuary contexts (Sherratt 1982: 22). It is another graphic representation of data that allows the analyst to display a great deal of information about the age and sex distributions of funerary objects. In this analysis the burial population is broken into age and sex categories. Age categories include children (0–7 years), adolescents (8–14 years), subadults (15–19 years), young adults (20–29 years), mature adults (30–39 years), and older adults (40+ years). Males and females are also separated within the age categories. (In this case, I did not separate the two youngest age categories by sex because it was not possible to confidently identify sex from the remains of individuals

at these ages.) Age categories in the diagram are arranged along the vertical dimension and sex is divided horizontally with males on the left side and females on the right side. Each individual interment in the cemetery is plotted in the diagram according to their age and sex along with information about any accompanying funerary objects.

6. I did not include this last burial in the figure because she was part of a multiple burial and the gorget was a unique item.

7. This total number of individuals (n = 102) is based upon the tally of burials that was used to create the original plan map of the cemetery. The total reported earlier (n = 113) is based on Bridges and Jacobi's reexamination of the osteological remains (Bridges 1996; Bridges et al. 2000: Table 3.2). The difference results from the fact that elements from multiple individuals in a single grave were originally recorded as a single individual interment. In most cases, these additional elements belonged to children or infants who were buried with a single adult or belonged to adults who may have been interred as "trophies" taken in combat.

8. Age categories used in the analysis originally included children (0–7 years), adolescents (8–14 years), subadults (15–19 years), young adults (20–29 years), mature adults (30–39 years), and older adults (40+ years). In this test, the six categories were collapsed into two groups, subadults (0–19 years) and adults (20–40+ years) in order to avoid problems with cell frequencies below the minimum associated with Chi-square tests (i.e., frequency < 5). Also, four individuals were left out of the analysis because their age could not be determined.

9. Only 70 individuals were included in this test because sex could not be confidently assigned to some adults and most subadults.

10

Pecan Point as the "Capital" of Pacaha

A Mortuary Perspective

RITA FISHER-CARROLL AND ROBERT C. MAINFORT JR.

> The famous old Pecan Point site has gone into the Mississippi River.
> (Phillips et al. 1951: 387).

Many years ago, the Pecan Point site attained near-legendary status among professional and avocational archaeologists. It is not the size of the site or its mounds (both of which are poorly documented) that made Pecan Point of such interest but rather the large collections of mortuary ceramics from the site. For instance, Holmes (1886: 125) stated that the "pretty decided focal center" of his "Middle Mississippi Province" was Pecan Point, and Phillips et al. (1951: 165) mention "classic Pecan Point head vases," of which the site has yielded several examples (Cherry 2009).

Our focus here, however, is not on ceramic artistry but on mortuary patterning, particularly with regard to intimations of social ranking and possible indicators of group identity. The data come largely from the unpublished field notes of C. B. Moore, whose excavations at Pecan Point were his most extensive in northeast Arkansas (Fisher-Carroll 2001a; Moore 1911), resulting in the documentation of 349 human burials.

The Pecan Point site was located on a prominent bend of the same name located a very short distance west of the Mississippi River in Mississippi County, Arkansas, about 15 km south of Middle and Upper Nodena (see Figure 10.1). The site takes its name from the former Pecan Point plantation, purchased in the 1870s by R. W. Friend and owned by him during the only reported excavations. The earliest known mention of the site appears in a letter written in March 1881 by Capt. Wilfred P. Hall, who collected a great deal of archaeological material (including human remains) from the region on behalf of the Davenport Academy of Sciences (Hall to Pratt, March 21, 1881, Capt. Wilfred Peter Hall Correspondence, #3442, Putnam Museum of History and Natural Science, Davenport, Iowa). In December 1881, Edward Palmer of the Smithsonian Institution excavated at Pecan Point and provided some description of

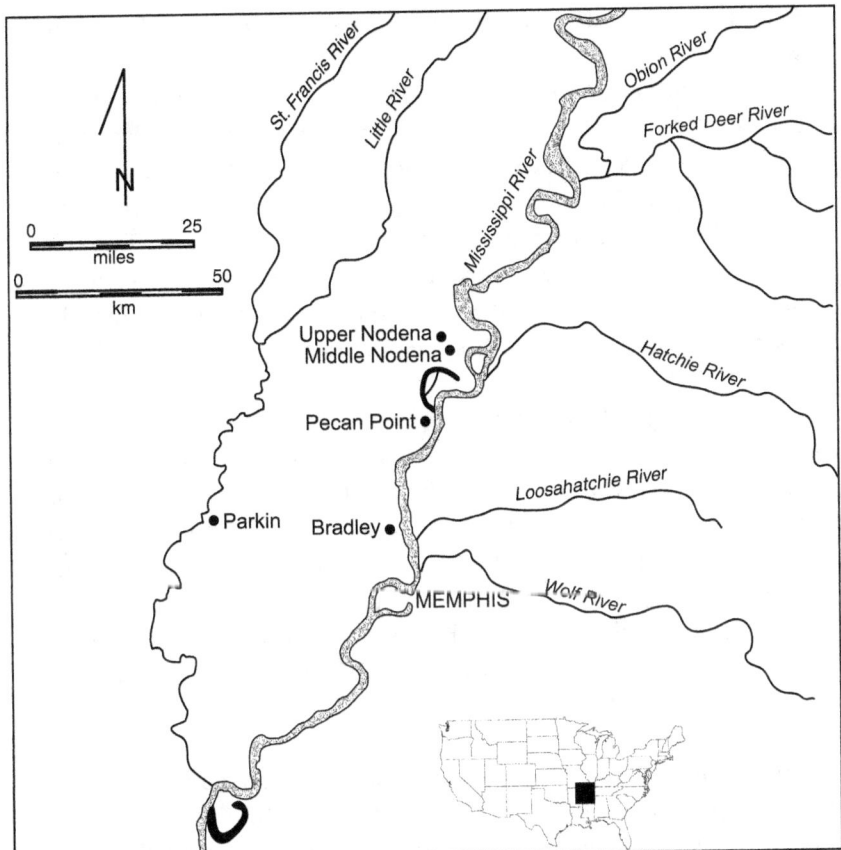

Figure 10.1. Location of Pecan Point and Nearby Sites.

the area (Jeter 1990: 131–133). Relying largely on the records of Philetus Norris (written in 1884) rather than on Palmer's correspondence, Cyrus Thomas (1894: 220–221) described the Pecan Point site in the 1890s and published a sketch map as well as a steel plate engraving of one of the headpots from the site.

Moore (1911: 447–448) published the following description of the site as it appeared roughly three decades after the excavations by Hall and Palmer:

> About one mile above the main settlement at Pecan Point, though still in its outskirts, a short distance from the river, is a mound which has been used as a cemetery in recent times. The mound, which has suffered some in shape in the lapse of years, is about 12 feet in height and is approximately square with rounded corners, its sides nearly facing the cardinal points. The basal diameter is about 110 feet; that of the summit-plateau,

50 feet, approximately. Apparently a causeway connected the mound with the level ground in former times.[1]

A short distance from this mound (which probably was domiciliary and was not dug into by us) is the northwestern corner of a large field which has been long under cultivation, and part of which, judging from the quantity of aboriginal debris scattered over the surface, must have been a dwelling-site for a considerable period in early times. This field, we were told by Mr. Friend, was where the digging previous to our own had been carried on.[2] Since then, however, that part of the field in which aboriginal burials are found has been curtailed by the building of new levees (see Figure 10.2).

Our digging at Pecan Point occupied fourteen and one-half days of eight hours each, with a force of nine men to handle the spades and four men to supervise. The work was done in the northwestern part of the field, to which reference has been made, and the area searched extended from the northwest corner of the field, a distance of 162 paces along the northern side, and had a breadth of 89 paces at the western end, where the fence meets that of the northern side at a moderately acute angle, and covered all that part of the field on which signs of aboriginal occupancy were evident.

The area of the Pecan Point site is unknown. Based on the dimensions given by Moore (1911: 447–448), the main habitation and burial area of the Pecan Point site covered about 3 acres (1.2 ha) (assuming that the length of Moore's pace was about three feet). The map and the dimensions of the mound given by Thomas (1894: 220) suggest an area of about 8 acres (3.3 ha). Finally, if the entire 15-acre field mentioned by Edward Palmer (Jeter 1990: 131–132) is accepted as the approximate site size, the area was close to that of Upper Nodena. At the very least, these figures suggest that Pecan Point was not remarkably large relative to other sites assigned to the Nodena phase (D. Morse 1989, 1990).

The accounts of Thomas and Moore suggest that as is the case throughout the study area, most (if not all) human burials were not located in a formal cemetery but occurred among habitation areas. Unfortunately, we will never know more about the size and layout of the site. Six years after his excavations at Pecan Point, Moore visited the area again and mentioned in his report for that year that the site had been washed away by the Mississippi River (Moore 1916: 494).

The 1912–1915 Mississippi River Commission (MRC) chart for Pecan Point (No. 17), which was based on a field survey that was done two years after

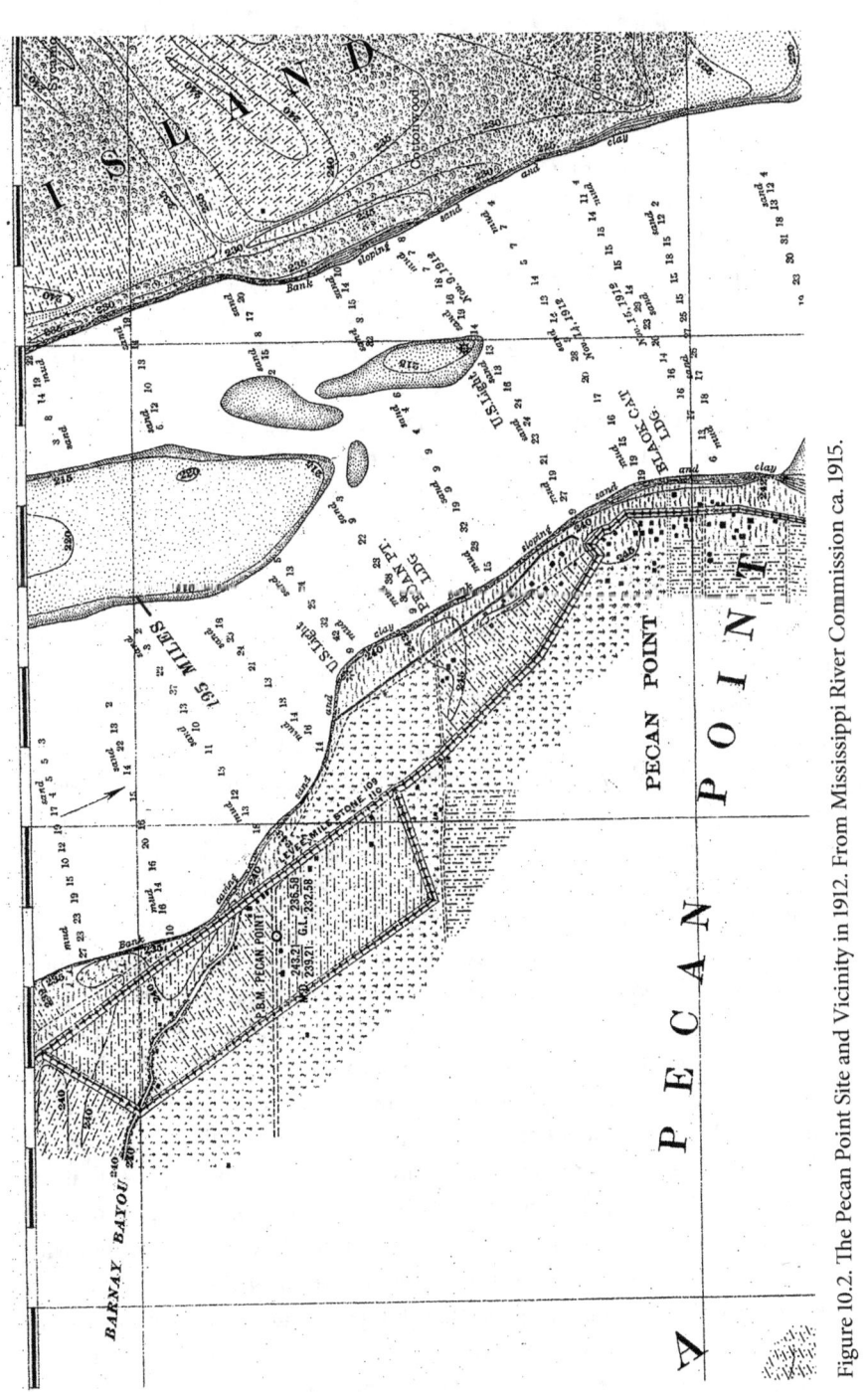

Figure 10.2. The Pecan Point Site and Vicinity in 1912. From Mississippi River Commission ca. 1915.

Moore's excavations, provides clues about the actual site location (Figure 10.3). This map shows a system of levees that had been constructed in Pecan Point bend under the authority of the St. Francis Levee Board, which was organized and authorized by the state legislature in 1893 to issue bonds and collect taxes to fund construction along the eastern front of the St. Francis Basin (Fox 1902: 16). At Pecan Point Landing, which was north of the "main settlement at Pecan Point, though still in its outskirts," the MRC map shows a mound-like feature located very near the Mississippi River with a "causeway" on the west side. Moreover, this topographic feature was situated in the "northwestern corner of a large field," and there were levees in the immediate vicinity. The possible mound does not appear on the 1939 U.S.G.S. Jericho quadrangle, which also shows that portions of the Pecan Point levees that had been extant in 1912 had been claimed by the river. It seems likely, therefore, that the Pecan Point site was located along this portion of the levee.

Analytical Background

Based in part on accounts of the Soto entrada (Clayton et al. 1993; Varner and Varner 1951), and various studies of Moundville (e.g., Peebles 1971; Peebles and Kus 1977), the late-period societies of northeast Arkansas (including those represented archaeologically by sites assigned to the Nodena phase) have been traditionally interpreted as chiefdoms (e.g., D. Morse 1990; P. Morse 1981, 1990). Our evaluation of a very large set of mortuary data from Upper Nodena (Fisher-Carroll and Mainfort 2000; Fisher-Carroll 2001b; Mainfort and Fisher-Carroll this volume) revealed little evidence of marked social differentiation, one of the key characteristics of chiefly societies. Pecan Point has been accorded a more prominent role in the inferred Nodena phase site hierarchy (D. Morse 1989, 1990), including the suggestion that the site may "have served as the capital of the Nodena phase" (Morse and Morse 1996: 132; see also P. Morse 1981: 68; Morse and Morse 1983: 311; and Phillips et al. 1951: 387). If this interpretation is correct, it follows that indicators of social differentiation should be more evident at Pecan Point than at Upper Nodena.

We will, therefore, begin our analysis by assessing the assumption that the Pecan Point burial population—one of the largest such group of individuals recorded in the central Mississippi valley—exhibits patterning consistent with expectations for ranked societies. In doing so, we must note that we do not view the search for evidence of social ranking at Pecan Point as an important line of research in its own right. We are, however, interested in evaluating the traditional interpretation of Pecan Point as an apical site within an inferred hierarchical settlement system (e.g., D. Morse 1989, 1990; P. Morse 1981, 1990; Morse and Morse 1983).

Analysis of the Pecan Point mortuary data generally follows the format and methods used in our study of mortuary patterning at Upper Nodena (Fisher-Carroll 2001b; Fisher-Carroll and Mainfort 2000; Mainfort and Fisher-Carroll this volume). The modeled expectations for mortuary remains associated with prehistoric ranked societies presented therein are as follows:

1. There will be a division of the mortuary population into disproportionate segments, and the elite will be represented by a small minority.
2. Access to special burial locations will be limited to the elite segment.
3. Symbols of authority will be associated solely with the elite segment and will cut across age and sex distinctions therein.
4. There will be marked disparities between elite and non-elite burials with regard to the amount of wealth and, particularly, effort expended during mortuary ritual.

Although there have been important theoretical advances in the study of archaeological mortuary remains since the pioneering work of Saxe (1970), Binford (1971; see also Kamp 1998), and Brown (1971, 1981a), these expectations continue to be useful in the search for ranking among burials (cf. O'Shea 1984: 47) and are a reasonable baseline for examining the data from Pecan Point. As was the case for Upper Nodena, the quality of available mortuary data from Pecan Point limits the extent to which some of the expectations can be tested. This was also the case with Moundville and Spiro (e.g., Brown 1971, 1996; Peebles 1971; Peebles and Kus 1977), both key sites in the initial development of archaeological mortuary theory.

Note that our modeled expectations are essentially those used to assess mortuary variability at Moundville (Peebles 1971; Peebles and Kus 1977); interpretations of this site and the "chiefdom" concept of the 1960s and 1970s have had considerable influence on interpretations of late-period sites in northeast Arkansas (e.g., P. Morse 1981: 86). We will state again that for a variety of reasons, Moundville is not an appropriate analogue for the societies represented by the late-period archaeological record in the central Mississippi valley (Fisher-Carroll 2001b; Fisher-Carroll and Mainfort 2000). With the exception of shell beads, none of artifact classes associated with individuals that scholars infer to be the Moundville elite (i.e., the "superordinate dimension" of Peebles and Kus [1977]) are present at late-period sites in our study area. Mississippian copper axes, oblong copper gorgets, copper-covered shell beads, pearl beads, copper earspools, stone discs, bear-tooth pendants, and galena cubes (Peebles and Kus 1977: 438–439) do not occur (or at least have not been credibly reported). Of course, roughly comparable objects that served similar functions may have been present at Pecan Point, but the only likely candidates are two sociotechnic celts/axes (Gall et al. 2002; Mainfort et al. 2006), though the "stone ceremonial celts" found at Moundville are not associated with inferred high-status burials there (Peebles and Kus 1977: 438–439).

An important limitation that we cannot address in our analysis of the Upper Nodena mortuary data is that the specific locations of the Pecan Point burials were not recorded, rendering expectation number 2 above moot. We recognize that there might have been significant spatial differentiation within the site that was not recorded, but this will never be known. What is known is that Moore did not excavate in the large mound at Pecan Point. Note that at Moundville, individuals interpreted as apical burials were interred in mounds and that some socially valued goods (e.g., copper and stone ceremonial celts) were restricted to mound burials (Peebles 1971: 81–83; Peebles and Kus 1977: 438–439). There is no published, documentary, or anecdotal evidence in the central Mississippi valley of "high-status" mound burials or of the more impressive sociotechnic objects recorded at Moundville.

Moore did not record data on burial cards (Fisher-Carroll 2001a), but in contrast to earlier excavators, he did take notes on each individual (at least for the sites he excavated in northeast Arkansas), including the disposition and relative age of the skeleton, associated funerary objects, and the location of these objects relative to the human remains. Only rarely did Moore record depth below the surface. In some instances, additional information could be gleaned from the published descriptions of burials and artifacts (Moore 1911). Bioarchaeological data for Pecan Point are nonexistent; collecting human remains typically was not a priority of early excavators. Thus, we have only field identifications of individuals as adults or children, which we consider fairly reliable; the sex of the interred individuals is unknown. Although this is a significant limitation of this study, we faced similar, though less extreme, constraints in our analysis of mortuary behavior at Upper Nodena (Fisher-Carroll and Mainfort 2000; Fisher-Carroll 2001b).

Moore recorded relative ages for all burials for a sample of 274 adults and 75 subadults. As is commonly seen in prehistoric mortuary populations in the Eastern Woodlands, subadults are markedly underrepresented. Nearly 94 percent (n = 327) of the interred individuals at Pecan Point were placed in a supine extended position, a pattern seen at late-period sites throughout the region, including at Upper Nodena (Fisher-Carroll 2001a, 2001b). Other recorded burial positions were prone extended (n = 4) and partially flexed (n = 2); 16 burials were disturbed to some degree. Moore uncovered no examples of the individuals in a "sitting or squatting" position, as reported by Thomas (1894: 220). The individual in Burial 56 apparently died as a result of an arrow wound.

Burial Diversity Scores

Lacking spatial and bioarchaeological data, our analysis relies almost exclusively on funerary objects. Diversity scores have proved to be a useful tool for exploring archaeological mortuary differentiation (Fisher-Carroll 2001b; Fisher-Carroll and Mainfort 2000; Howell and Kintigh 1996). Scores for each burial are calculated by assigning a value of 1 to each specific artifact class associated with a burial, regardless of quantity; multiple objects of a single artifact class do not affect the scores, and there is no upper limit on the magnitude of scores. In calculating the diversity scores presented here, we also counted some unique or rare items. Unlike Howell and Kintigh (1996: 550–551), we make no claim that diversity scores are a proxy measure of the number of social roles held by individuals (see also Rosenwig 2000: 432–433). Rather, we use diversity scores as one device for revealing the co-occurrence of specific funerary objects with the dead, as discussed below.

The artifact classes used in computing artifact diversity scores for human burials at Pecan Point are the same as those used in the Upper Nodena study, save for a few items that were not found with any of the burials Moore excavated. Artifact classes include but are not limited to sociotechnic celt/axe; stone discoidal; clay disc/discoidal; shell bead necklace; shell bead bracelet; shell earplug; ceramic pipe; shell spoon; mussel shell; bone tool; bone dice; bird wing; stone point; other stone tool; plain bowl; plain bottle; painted bottle; other bottle; plain jar; decorated jar; compound vessel; kneeling-human-effigy vessel; other human-effigy vessel; fish-effigy vessel; bird-effigy vessel; frog-effigy vessel; and other zoomorphic vessel.

Ninety-four burials at Pecan Point have a diversity score of 1. With eight exceptions, all were accompanied by a single ceramic vessel. Two plain ceramic vessels of the same form (bottle, bowl, jar, or "vessel," as identified in Moore's notes) were found with Burials 65, 218, 255, 270, and 331. Three plain ceramic vessels of the same form were associated with Burials 27 and 293. Adjacent to the skull of Burial 202 were a pair of shell earplugs, and a bird-effigy bowl was placed with Burial 127.

One hundred thirty-six burials have a diversity score of 2. Most were accompanied by two ceramic vessels (of different shape and/or style). Three vessels (at least two of similar shape and/or style) were found with 14 burials, four vessels (in various combinations) with five individuals, and five vessels

Table 10.1. Burials at Pecan Point with a Diversity Score of 3 and at Least One Nonceramic Funerary Object

Burial No.	Funerary Objects
2	turkey wing, Nodena point, Campbell Incised compound bottle
25	limonite, plain bowl, plain bottle
74	shell earplugs, shell bead necklace, plain bottle
107	bone bead necklace, plain bowl, plain bottle
162	spatulate celt (cannel coal), chert "chisel," plain bottle
164	mussel shells, plain bowl, plain bottle
168	tortoise shell, 2 plain bottles, plain bowl
182	plain shell gorget, plain bowl, plain bottle
199	unidentified bird wing, plain bowl, plain bottle
222	red ochre, plain bowl, plain jar
248	unidentified bird wing, plain bowl, plain bottle
254	shell beads, plain bowl, plain bottle
311	perforated shell ornament, zoomorphic bowl, plain bowl
325	shell gorget, decorated bottle, plain bottle

with one burial. Interments with funerary objects other than ceramic vessels are Burial 4 (ceramic pipe and plain bowl), Burial 121 (pottery tool and plain bottle), Burial 138 (shell bead necklace and kneeling-human-effigy bottle), Burial 152 (red ochre and a frog-effigy jar), Burial 181 (mussel shell and two plain bottles), Burial 272 (one shell bead and a plain bottle), and Burial 333 (two stone discoidals and plain bowl). The only headpot Moore found at Pecan Point was with Burial 11, as was an Old Town Red bottle.

Thirty-five of the Pecan Point burials have a diversity score of 3. In 14 instances, at least one associated funerary object was not a ceramic vessel; these burials are listed in Table 10.1. The cannel coal spatulate celt with Burial 162 is one of only two large sociotechnic lithic artifacts associated with the burials Moore excavated. Among the burials in Table 10.1 are three of the seven interments at Pecan Point with whom large bird wings were placed.

Eleven burials have a diversity score of 4. With the exception of Burial 7, at least one funerary object placed with each individual was not a ceramic vessel. The funerary objects with all 11 burials are listed in Table 10.2. Note the sociotechnic axe found with Burial 300; a very large Nodena point also was placed with this individual. Four of the eight individuals at Pecan Point with red ochre have a diversity score of 4.

Five burials, each with at least one nonceramic funerary object, have a diversity score of 5. These are listed with their associated funerary objects in Table 10.3. Effigy bowls accompanied all five burials, but the interments are diverse in terms of other funerary objects.

Table 10.2. Burials at Pecan Point with a Diversity Score of 4

Burial No.	Funerary Objects
7	plain bottle, plain bowl, decorated jar, plain jar
13	shell bead necklace, stone discoidal, elk astragalus die, unidentified bird wing
28	2 "dumb-bell shaped"[a] shell beads, flat oblong shell bead "with crescentic incisions in four sides and two central perforations," multiple shell earplugs, plain jar
40	deer astragalus die, plain bottle, plain bowl, frog-effigy jar
85	red ochre, bone tool, compound bottle, plain bowl
101	shell bead, chert flakes, turtle-effigy bottle, plain bowl
185	flat stone, ogee bottle, plain bottle, plain bowl
300	sociotechnic axe (drilled), large (5 in) Nodena point, 2 plain bowls, plain jar
302	red ochre, stone chisel, hooded effigy bottle, plain bowl
309	red ochre, shell gorget, unidentified bone, plain bottle
340	red ochre, 2 shell beads, plain bowl, plain bottle

Note: [a]Quotation marks in tables for this chapter indicate direct quotes from the excavator's notes.

Table 10.3. Burials at Pecan Point with a Diversity Score of 5

Burial No.	Funerary Objects
82	shell bead necklace, multiple shell earplugs, 4 plain bowls, plain bottle, plain jar
160	2 flat circular stones, mussel shell spoon, large mussel shell, fish-effigy bowl, plain bowl
188	unidentified bird wing, ceramic disk, shell effigy bowl, plain bowl, Old Town Red bottle
305	stone "celt," mussel shell, fish-effigy bowl, frog-effigy bowl, zoomorphic bowl
326	ochre, bone "dagger," multiple antler tines, 2 shell effigy bowls, plain bottle

Three burials have a diversity score of 6 (see Table 10.4). The score for Burial 167 could be increased or decreased by one, depending on how the individual components of the necklace were counted. A nonplain ceramic vessel was found with each burial.

Only Burial 228 has a diversity score of 7. The associated funerary objects are a shell bead necklace, two sets of shell earplugs, a perforated stone ornament, a plain bowl, a plain bottle, and two plain jars (one miniature).

Burial 150 is the only one with a diversity score of 9. Its associated funerary objects are as follows: a shell bead necklace, a stone "bowl," a quartz crystal, a swan wing, a stone celt, three stone chisels, a large Nodena point, a kneeling-human-effigy bottle, and a plain(?) bottle. The very large (12.5 in) Nodena point is quite unusual, if not unique, among recorded late-period burials in northeast Arkansas.

The highest diversity score among the Pecan Point burials is 12, and only Burial 60 received that score. The associated funerary objects are a pair of shell

Table 10.4. Burials at Pecan Point with a Diversity Score of 6

Burial No.	Funerary Objects
104	4 astragalus dice (bison, 2 deer, elk), limonite discoidal, red ochre, stirrup bottle, plain bottle, plain bowl
167	shell earplugs, necklace consisting of a perforated conch shell, several perforated conch spires, and a shell gorget, 2 stone discoidals, ogee bottle, 2 plain jars
171	2 deer-astragalus dice, bone awl, unidentified stone, zoomorphic bowl, 3 plain bowls, 2 plain jars

earplugs, a necklace of shell beads, a small conch shell, three conch-spire ornaments, a "panther" canine, a stone "knife," limonite, and ten ceramic vessels (a raccoon effigy bowl, four unidentified zoomorphic bowls, a Nodena Red and White bottle, a compound vessel, a stirrup-neck bottle, a plain bowl, and a plain bottle).

Each individual in the three burials with the highest diversity scores wore a shell bead necklace, but there are no other commonalities, save for the presence of a ceramic vessel.

If Pecan Point represents the archaeological remains of an apical town, it would be reasonable to expect that burial diversity scores for the site would be higher than those at nonapical sites in the same region. Table 10.5 compares burial diversity scores from Pecan Point with those from Upper Nodena (Fisher-Carroll and Mainfort 2000: 111) and Middle Nodena (Mainfort and Fisher-Carroll, this volume), neither of which have been interpreted as api-

Table 10.5. Burial Diversity Scores for Pecan Point, Upper Nodena, and Middle Nodena

Diversity Score	Pecan Point (N = 349)	Upper Nodena (N = 893)	Middle Nodena (N = 255)
1	94 (26.9%)	280 (31.4%)	65 (25.5%)
2	136 (39.0%)	170 (19.0%)	124 (46.7%)
3	35 (10.0%)	32 (3.6%)	31 (12.2%)
4	11 (3.2%)	8 (0.9%)	6 (2.4%)
5	5 (1.4%)	3 (.3%)	5 (2.0%)
6	3 (1.7%)	4 (.4%)	2 (.8%)
7	1 (.3%)	2 (.2%)	0 (0%)
8	0 (0%)	1 (.1%)	1 (.4%)
9	1 (0.3%)	0 (0%)	0 (0%)
10	0 (0%)	0 (0%)	0 (0%)
11	0 (0%)	0 (0%)	0 (0%)
12	1 (.3%)	0 (0%)	0 (0%)

cal sites (Morse 1989, 1990). The scores for Pecan Point are higher than those for Upper Nodena, and the differences are statistically significant ($p < .001$; $\chi^2 = 42.627$, $df = 6$ [using only scores of 1–6 to avoid cells with $df = 0$]). Although this finding is in keeping with the stated expectation, the diversity scores for the smaller Middle Nodena site are not significantly different than those for Pecan Point ($p > .1$; $\chi^2 = 3.572$, $df = 6$). Further, the scores for Middle Nodena, like those for Pecan Point, are significantly higher than those for Upper Nodena ($p < .001$; $\chi^2 = 55.291$, $df = 6$). This is at odds with the stated expectation because site area of Middle Nodena is only about half that of Upper Nodena (cf. Morse 1989: 103) and no mounds have been reported at the site.

What are we to make of these seemingly contradictory findings? Based on our analysis of mortuary variation at Middle Nodena presented in chapter 8 of this volume, we view the higher scores for Pecan Point and Middle Nodena relative to Upper Nodena as primarily reflecting temporal differences rather than necessarily reflecting greater social differentiation (with the attendant implications of hierarchy). Specifically, the former sites have long been thought to postdate Upper Nodena and the higher scores for Pecan Point and Middle Nodena reflect an increase in the number of ceramic vessels per grave over time (Fisher-Carroll 2001a: 42).

Analysis of Burials by Artifact Class

Mortuary variability also can be examined using the occurrence of specific classes of artifacts and the objects associated with them. Because mortuary rites are rituals, objects placed with the dead can be viewed as symbols. The use of different combinations of symbols and differences between sites in the use of specific symbols by sex and/or age are likely to reflect differences in mortuary ritual and hence in group identity. Further, if certain artifact classes consistently co-occur, the various combinations may reflect various social roles that were symbolized during mortuary ritual (Howell and Kintigh 1996; Mainfort 1985).

At Pecan Point, Moore (1911: 449) noted the "curious custom" of placing "metacarpal bones of birds of considerable size" with the dead. Except for a very unusual burial at the Campbell site in extreme southeastern Missouri (Chapman and Anderson 1955), Pecan Point appears to represent the northern limit of this practice in the central Mississippi valley and is also the site with the greatest number of recorded examples. Although Moore found bird wings with only seven burials at Pecan Point (five adults, two children), this is a marked contrast with both Upper and Middle Nodena, where no bird wings are reported among recorded human burials (Fisher-Carroll-2001a, 2001b).

Table 10.6. Structure of Burials at Pecan Point Accompanied by Bird Wings

Burial No.	Age	Funerary Objects
2	adult	turkey wing, Nodena point, Campbell Incised compound bottle
13	child	unidentified bird wing, shell bead necklace, stone discoidal, elk astragalus (perhaps a die)
104	child	snow goose wing, shell bead necklace, raccoon baculum, 2 deer astragali, elk astragalus, bison astragalus, "limonite" discoidal, stirrup-neck bottle, plain bottle, plain bowl
150	adult	swan wing, shell bead necklace, stone "bowl," 3 chert "chisels," "celt" (probably flaked), large Nodena point, stone discoidal, quartz crystal, kneeling-human effigy bottle, plain bottle
188	adult	unidentified bird wing, ceramic disc, shell effigy bowl, Old Town Red bottle, plain bowl (disturbed)
199	adult	unidentified bird wing, plain bowl, plain bottle
248	adult	unidentified bird wing, plain bowl, plain bottle

Three wings were identified as turkey, snow goose, and swan (Moore 1911: 449, 451), and the remainder were not identified (though all reportedly were fairly large). The lack of raptors is noteworthy.

The structure of the Pecan Point burials with bird wings is summarized in Table 10.6. Location within the grave is variable, and there is no obvious pattern. Two wings were found near the head, and wings were found one time at the left thigh, one time at the left shoulder, and one time at the "near forearm." Location was not recorded for the bird wings associated with Burials 104 and 248.

All burials accompanied by bird wings have a diversity score of at least 3. Three of these individuals (two children, one adult) also wore a shell bead necklace and were accompanied by a stone discoidal; an elk astragalus had been placed with both children buried with bird wings.

We tentatively interpret bird wings as indicators of horizontal social differentiation, perhaps involving clan membership. The occurrence of bird wings with children suggests that they do not mark special social roles, such as shamans.

Stone discoidals were associated with five individuals, including four subadults, of the 349 recorded human burials at Pecan Point. The structure of each burial is summarized in Table 10.7. Discoidals occurred with one adult, a subadult, and three children. With the exception of Burial 333, all individuals with discoidals wore shell earplugs and a shell bead/object necklace. A bird wing was placed with three individuals. Location within the grave included near the right forearm (Burials 150 and 167), the left femur (Burial 13), the left skull (Burial 104), and the left pelvis (Burial 333).

Table 10.7. Structure of Burials at Pecan Point with Stone Discoidals

Burial No.	Age	Funerary Objects
13 (1 discoidal)	child	shell earplugs, shell bead necklace, unidentified bird wing, elk astragalus (die?)
104 (1 discoidal)	child	shell earplugs, shell bead necklace, snow goose wing, raccoon baculum, 2 deer astragali, elk astragalus, bison astragalus, stirrup-neck bottle, plain bottle, plain bowl
150 (1 discoidal)	adult	shell earplugs, shell bead necklace, swan wing, stone "bowl," 3 chert "chisels," "celt" (probably flaked), large Nodena point, quartz crystal, kneeling-human effigy bottle, plain bottle
167 (3 discoidals)	child	shell earplugs, necklace consisting of a perforated conch shell and 3 perforated conch spires and a triangular shell gorget, bottle with applied ogee motif, 2 plain jars
333 (2 discoidals)	subadult	plain bowl

At Upper Nodena, stone discoidals accompanied 10 interments, five adults and five children (Fisher-Carroll and Mainfort 2000: 115). Unlike at Pecan Point, shell earplugs were not found with any of the individuals at Upper Nodena with a stone discoidal.

Eight individuals—six children and two adults—wore a necklace of shell beads. The other funerary objects found with these burials are listed in Table 10.8. Not counted among these are Burial 28, a child with two "dumb-bell shaped" shell beads and a flat oblong shell bead "with crescentic incisions in

Table 10.8. Structure of Burials at Pecan Point with Shell Bead Necklaces

Burial No.	Age	Funerary Objects
13	child	shell earplugs, unidentified bird wing, stone discoidal, elk astragalus (die?)
60	child	shell earplugs; necklace of shell beads, a small conch shell, 3 conch spire ornaments, and a "panther" canine; stone "knife," limonite; 10 pots (including a raccoon-effigy bowl, four unidentified zoomorphic bowls, Nodena Red and White bottle, compound vessel, stirrup-neck bottle, plain bowl, plain bottle)
74	adult	shell earplugs, plain bottle
82	child	shell earplugs, 4 plain bowls, plain bottle, plain jar
104	child	shell earplugs, snow goose wing, raccoon baculum, 2 deer astragali, elk astragalus, bison astragalus, "limonite" discoidal, stirrup-neck bottle, plain bottle, plain bowl
138	child	kneeling human effigy bottle
150	adult	shell earplugs, swan wing, stone "bowl," 3 chert "chisels," "celt" (probably flaked), large Nodena point, stone discoidal, quartz crystal, kneeling-human effigy bottle, plain bottle
228	child	shell earplugs, perforated stone ("talc") ornament, plain bowl, plain bottle, 2 plain jars (1 miniature)

Table 10.9. Structure of Burials at Pecan Point with Shell Gorgets

Burial No.	Age	Funerary Objects
167	child	2 plain jars, bottle with ogee design, 2 shell earplugs, perforated conch shell, 3 perforated conch spires, 2 stone discoidals
182	child	plain bottle, plain bowl
309	adult	plain bottle, ochre, unidentified bone
325	adult	decorated bottle, plain bowl

four sides and two central perforations," and Burial 167, a child with a necklace consisting of a perforated conch shell, several perforated conch spires, and a triangular shell gorget. Multiple shell beads were located at the right humerus of Burial 119, where they were probably worn as a bracelet. The two shell beads found at the neck of Burial 340 probably represent a necklace; the location of the two with Burial 254 was not recorded. A single shell bead was found with Burials 101 and 272.

Moore found shell gorgets with four burials (two children, two adults) at Pecan Point (Table 10.9). Moore described the gorget with Burial 167 as triangular in shape; we suspect that it was a shell mask. This gorget was a component of a necklace that also included a perforated conch shell and three perforated conch spires. The gorget accompanying Burial 182 was "plain." At least two additional funerary objects occurred with all of the burials with a shell gorget, but potential sociotechnic objects accompanied only Burial 167 (shell earplugs, stone discoidals).

Moore found shell earplugs occurring as a pair with seven burials at Pecan Point. Most of these "somewhat resemble a mushroom in shape" (Moore 1911: 451), having a flat, narrow shaft and a roughly circular end (see Drooker 1997: 301; Morse and Morse 1983: 277). With Burial 228 was one set of earplugs of this style and a second set of the blunt-end style (Moore 1911: 455). Five of the seven individuals with shell earplugs were children, a remarkably high number given the paucity of excavated children.

The structure of the Pecan Point burials with shell earplugs is presented in Table 10.10. With the exception of Burial 202, all of these individuals also wore a shell bead or shell ornament necklace; the necklace worn by Burial 167 was particularly elaborate. Again excepting Burial 202, one or more ceramic vessels were placed with each individual with shell earspools.

Moore found two sociotechnic celts at Pecan Point, both with adults. A spatulate celt (described as "hoe-shaped," a term Moore consistently used in his writings about spatulate celts) made from a low grade of cannel coal was located at the right shoulder of Burial 162 (Moore 1911: 454–455), and a

Table 10.10. Structure of Burials at Pecan Point with Shell Earplugs

Burial No.	Age	Funerary Objects
28	child	2 dumbbell-shaped shell beads, flat oblong shell bead "with crescentic incisions in four sides and two central perforations," plain jar
60	child	necklace of shell beads, a small conch shell, 3 conch spire ornaments, and a "panther" canine; stone "knife"; limonite; 10 pots(including a raccoon-effigy bowl, four unidentified zoomorphic bowls, Nodena Red and White bottle, compound vessel, stirrup-neck bottle, plain bowl, plain bottle)
74	adult	shell bead necklace, plain bottle
82	child	shell bead necklace, 4 plain bowls, plain bottle, plain jar
167	child	necklace consisting of a perforated conch shell and 3 perforated conch spires, and a triangular shell gorget; 2 stone discoidals; bottle with an applied ogee motif; 2 plain jars
202	adult	(no other artifacts)
228	child	shell bead necklace, perforated stone ornament, plain bowl, plain bottle, 2 plain jars (1 miniature)

large, drilled (but not completely pierced) rectanguloid celt of "ferruginous shale" may have been grasped in the right hand of the individual in Burial 300 (Moore 1911: 455–456). These two burials are otherwise undistinguished except, perhaps, for the large (5-in.-long) Nodena point with Burial 300.

Finally, we must mention the previously unreported discovery of two copper beads at Pecan Point by W. P. Hall (Hall to W. H. Pratt, April 18, 1881, W. P. Hall Correspondence File, #3522a, Putnam Museum of History and Natural Science, Davenport, Illinois). Copper objects of any form are very rare among sites assigned to the traditional Nodena phase (Fisher-Carroll 2001a).

It should be evident from the discussion above that the Pecan Point mortuary data provide no compelling evidence for the existence of marked social differentiation. To be sure, a small number of burials have particularly high diversity scores, but these do not share a consistent pattern of allocation of funerary objects. Symbols of authority such as those associated with elite burials at Moundville have not been reported at Pecan Point, and if other objects served comparable symbolic functions, they have not been identified or preserved. In fact, relatively few objects other than pottery vessels were interred with the dead. There is no evidence of specialized burial modes among the burials excavated by Moore at Pecan Point, and the few individuals that received nonmodal burial treatment are otherwise undistinguished. Finally, although Moore did not produce a site map, he mentioned that he did not excavate in the large mound at Pecan Point. Thus, all of the excavated burials probably are, in a general sense, from comparable spatial contexts.

Additional Comparisons with Upper Nodena

Pecan Point is one of over 60 archaeological sites assigned to the Nodena phase (D. Morse 1989, 1990), a taxonomic construct that basically includes all late-period archaeological remains located relatively close to the Mississippi River in northeast Arkansas and southeast Missouri. The contemporary Parkin phase construct includes sites to the west and southwest along the St. Francis River and its tributaries (P. Morse 1981, 1990). Sites have been assigned to these and dozens of similar culture-historical constructs in the lower Mississippi valley based largely on variations in the frequency of types of ceramic potsherds in surface collections (Phillips 1970).

Without undertaking a lengthy review of the literature on the relationships between material culture, ritual, and ethnicity (e.g., Barth 1969; Jones 1997), we will simply make the claim that similarities in ritual behavior, specifically disposal of the dead, are likely to be more straightforward indicators of group identity than broken pieces of pottery from uncertain contexts. As an initial case study in this regard, we offer some observations on intersite mortuary variation between Pecan Point and Upper Nodena (Fisher-Carroll 2001b; Fisher-Carroll and Mainfort 2000). Both sites have been assigned to the Nodena phase construct (Phillips 1970: 934). Upper Nodena is located only 15 km north of Pecan Point (Figure 10.1), and the sites are roughly contemporary (D. Morse 1989: 103, 1990: 80; Morse and Morse 1983: 286–287). It would therefore be reasonable to expect archaeologically visible aspects of mortuary ritual to be similar at the two sites. We have already noted one major difference between Pecan Point and Upper Nodena: higher burial diversity scores at the former.

As is the case at virtually all of the 38 late-period sites in the central Mississippi valley with a moderate to large number of reported human burials (a total of approximately 5,000 human burials), the overwhelming majority of interments at both Pecan Point (96.1 percent) and Upper Nodena (91.5 percent) were placed in an extended supine position (Fisher-Carroll 2001a). A more interesting behavioral comparison between the sites is the number of ceramic vessels placed with the dead. As shown in Table 10.11, nearly half of the burials at Upper Nodena lacked an associated ceramic vessel, in contrast to less than 20 percent at Pecan Point. Over half (55 percent) of the reported burials at Pecan Point had two or more ceramic vessels—over 2.5 times as many as at Upper Nodena. Not surprisingly, this contrast is mirrored by the

Table 10.11. Percentage of Burials with 0, 1, 2, 3, and 4+ Ceramic Vessels at Pecan Point, Upper Nodena, and Middle Nodena

No. Vessels	Pecan Point	Upper Nodena	Middle Nodena
0	17%	49%	10%
1	28%	31%	29%
2	41%	17%	52%
3	10%	2%	6%
4+	4%	1%	7%

average number of ceramic vessels per burial at the two sites—1.6 at Pecan Point and .7 at Upper Nodena. We believe that the greater number of ceramic vessels at Pecan Point reflects a regional trend in which the average number of vessels interred with the dead increased over time at late-period sites in the central Mississippi valley (Fisher-Carroll 2001a: 42). Thus, we propose that Pecan Point postdates Upper Nodena. This inference is bolstered by data from Middle Nodena (see Table 10.11), which has long been considered to postdate Upper Nodena (D. Morse 1973: 2, 1989: 2, 1990: 77; cf. Williams 1980: 105).

Several more contrasts between Pecan Point and Upper Nodena merit particular consideration. These involve certain artifact classes that occur infrequently at both sites, which immediately raises concern about sampling issues. We share these concerns, but at the same time we wish to emphasize that although the number of burials discussed below are small, they must be considered in the context of overall sample sizes, namely 349 human burials at Pecan Point and nearly 900 at Upper Nodena. Moreover, as Davidson (2004: 329–376) has shown, distinctions observed in a relatively small number of individuals can be enormously important in understanding mortuary variability, especially with regard to symbolizing group identity.

Shell earplugs are more numerous (in absolute numbers and proportionately) at Pecan Point (n = 7 individuals) than at Upper Nodena, and five of the seven individuals with shell earplugs were children. In contrast, at Upper Nodena, earplugs were recorded with only five individuals, all adults, of which four were women (Fisher-Carroll and Mainfort 2000: 114). Further, at Upper Nodena, two of the five individuals with shell earplugs wore a shell bead necklace and/or bracelet, but at Pecan Point, six of the seven individuals with shell earplugs wore a shell bead necklace. Here we have clear distinctions between the two sites involving the overall frequency of shell earplugs, the relative ages of individuals with earplugs, and the co-occurrence of specific artifacts in burials with earplugs.

Of the interments Moore excavated at Pecan Point, six children and two adults wore a shell bead necklace. Shell earplugs were associated with seven of these individuals. At least five individuals in the Upper Nodena mortuary population wore a shell bead necklace—two adult females, two adults of unknown sex, and an infant. Among these, only an adult female also was accompanied by shell earplugs (cf. Fisher-Carroll and Mainfort 2000: 114). In fact, of the 14 burials with shell beads, only two individuals also wore shell earplugs. The overall frequency of shell bead necklaces, the relative ages of individuals with necklaces, and the co-occurrence of specific artifacts in burials with necklaces differ significantly between the sites.

Stone discoidals present another contrast between the two sites. At Pecan Point, discoidals were interred with four subadults and one adult; at Upper Nodena, discoidals occurred with five adults and five subadults. Moreover, in four instances (80 percent) at Pecan Point, discoidals co-occur with shell earplugs; at Upper Nodena, shell earplugs do not co-occur with stone discoidals.

Differences in the relative frequencies of shell earspools and shell bead necklaces might simply be a function of changing popularity over time, but differences involving differential allocation based on age as well as co-occurrence with other artifacts, both of which involve the manipulation of artifacts within a ritual context, are more likely to reflect differences in mortuary ritual at the two sites. Differences in ritual are more likely a function of group identity, such as ethnicity (e.g., Barth 1987; Schiller 2001; Smedal 1989).

Finally, we find two differences in material culture between Pecan Point and Upper Nodena to be striking, despite the relatively small numbers of objects involved. First, greenstone (Hillabee metabasite) is present at Upper Nodena (Gall et al. 2002) but is not represented in collections from Pecan Point. Second, large bird wings (fans?) were placed with the dead at Pecan Point but not at Upper (or Middle) Nodena. The lack of greenstone at Pecan Point might be attributable to temporal differences between the sites, specifically a relatively short window during which greenstone was transported to northeast Arkansas (Gall et al. 2002: 242). Placement of bird wings with the dead could also have a temporal aspect; it could be due not to availability but to changes in mortuary ritual over time. While not dismissing this possibility, we feel that it is more telling that Moore (1911) found bird wings with human burials at several sites south of Pecan Point (see also Perino 1966), thus suggesting a north-south geographical division in the placement of bird wings with the dead that may be a function of group identity.

Concluding Remarks

Based in part on the Soto chronicles and interpretations of social ranking and hierarchy at Moundville (Peebles 1971; Peebles and Kus 1977), the late-period societies of northeast Arkansas have been traditionally interpreted as chiefdoms (e.g., D. Morse 1989, 1990; P. Morse 1990). The subject of this chapter, the Pecan Point site, has been identified as the "capital town" of the province of Pacaha (which some researchers equate with the Nodena phase) mentioned in the Soto documents (e.g., Morse and Morse 1983: 311; Morse and Morse 1996: 131–132). Using the modeled expectations employed in our analysis of mortuary patterning at Upper Nodena (Fisher-Carroll 2001b; Fisher-Carroll and Mainfort 2000), one of our goals here was to assess these interpretations using the large body of mortuary data recorded by C. B. Moore (1911) at Pecan Point. Among sites assigned to the Nodena phase construct, only Upper Nodena has a larger sample of recorded burials. If the interpretation of Pecan Point as the "capital" of the Nodena phase is correct, indicators of social differentiation should be more evident at Pecan Point than at Upper Nodena.

As was the case at Upper Nodena (Fisher-Carroll 2001b; Fisher-Carroll and Mainfort 2000), the data fall considerably short of meeting the modeled expectations for the existence of social ranking in the society represented by the burial population. In fact, there is less compelling evidence of social hierarchy in the Pecan Point mortuary sample than that seen at Upper Nodena. At both sites, the degree of social differentiation almost certainly was of a much lower order than inferred for Moundville, which calls into question (but does not disprove) scenarios involving hierarchical settlement systems (D. Morse 1989: 103–105) and the collection of tribute (P. Morse 1981: 88). As an obvious caveat, we will add that it is possible that unrecorded apical burials may have been present at Pecan Point. This is a potential problem with mortuary data from all sites. That said, nothing in the sketchy notes of W. P. Hall and the Smithsonian field assistants or in the artifacts they collected from the site suggests the presence of such burials.

In his excellent dissertation on the Campbell site, which is located in the extreme southeast of Missouri, Holland (1991: 2) stated that "many of the larger well-known Nodena-phase (e.g., Nodena, Pecan Point) sites were excavated before the advent of modern archaeology, and the materials recovered, while interesting, lack context." This study, as well as our analysis of mortuary patterning at Upper Nodena, demonstrates that the available mortuary data (for all their limitations) and the associated funerary objects are much more than merely "interesting" and can add much to our understanding of the late-period societies in the central Mississippi valley.

Notes

1. In his field notes (C. B. Moore Field Notes 34, 1910–1911, p. 1), Moore states that the "causeway" was located on the west side of the mound.

2. That is, Capt. Hall's excavations; Moore specifically mentions Hall in his field notes (C. B. Moore Field Notes 34, 1910–1911, p. 2).

11

Mound Construction and Community Changes within the Mississippian Town at Town Creek

EDMOND A. BOUDREAUX III

The Mississippian Period was a time of significant political and social change within the native communities of the southeastern United States (Griffin 1985: 63; Smith 1986b: 56–63; Steponaitis 1986: 388–391). Political changes within Mississippian societies included increases in power and authority for community leaders and the establishment of multiple-community political entities known as chiefdoms (Hally 1996; Scarry 1996; Steponaitis 1986: 383). Relatively large settlements were established that were occupied for generations in some cases (Holley 1999). These large communities were formally arranged towns that contained clearly demarcated public and domestic spaces (Hally 1994: 233; Holley 1999: 28; Lewis et al. 1998). Significant architectural changes occurred within these towns during their occupation, and the most obvious change in many cases was the construction of one or more platform mounds on which public buildings were placed. It has been proposed that the placement of public buildings and residences on mound summits was a physical manifestation of concomitant social and political changes (Emerson 1997: 250; Lewis and Stout 1998: 231), namely the centralization of political authority that occurred during the process of establishing chiefdoms (Anderson 1994: 119–120, 1999: 220; DePratter 1983: 207–208; Rudolph 1984: 40). In particular, within the regional variant of Mississippian culture known as South Appalachian Mississippian (Ferguson 1971), platform mounds at a number of sites were preceded by a distinctive type of earth-embanked public building called an earthlodge (Crouch 1974; Fairbanks 1946; Larson 1994: 108–110; Rudolph 1984). Based on their architectural attributes and their analogy with the council houses of historic Indians (see Hudson 1976: 218–226), earthlodges in the Southeast have been interpreted as places where a council of community leaders came together to make decisions based on consensus (Anderson 1994: 120, 1999: 220; DePratter 1983: 207–208; Wesson 1998: 109). In contrast to the more inclusive function proposed for premound earthlodges, it has been argued that access to the buildings on top of Mississippian platform mounds was limited to the community's social and political elite (Anderson 1994: 119; Blitz 1993: 92; Brown 1997: 479; Holley 1999: 30; Lewis et al. 1998: 17; Steponaitis 1986: 390; but see Blitz 1993: 184).

While archaeological and ethnohistoric evidence from across the Southeast suggests that Mississippian mound summits supported buildings that served a variety of functions (Blitz 1999: 583; Knight 2004: 318–319; Lindauer and Blitz 1997), they primarily served as the locus of political power in many communities (Hally 1996, 1999). If mounds were the seats and symbols of political power within Mississippian societies and if ground-level earthlodges were more accessible than structures on the summits of mounds, then access to leaders and leadership may have decreased over time. Thus, the sequence of change for public architecture during the Mississippian Period may reflect a centralization of political power (Anderson 1994: 119–120, 1999: 220; DePratter 1983: 207–208; Rudolph 1984: 40). This especially would have been the case in communities where a leader was able to place a residence on top of an earthen mound, an act that has been interpreted as an expression of political power that made a clear statement that the person living on top of the mound was now associated with a powerful, traditional, community-oriented symbol and with the locus of political authority (Brown 1997: 475; Knight 1989a: 287, 1998: 60; Milanich et al. 1997: 118; Steponaitis 1986: 386).

While the idea that changes in public architecture within a Mississippian community reflect changes in relationships among individuals and groups certainly seems plausible, our ability to test this proposition against the archaeological record has been hindered by the limited nature of excavations in many cases. Although changes in public architecture have been documented at numerous Mississippian sites, investigations of contemporaneous nonmound contexts generally have been of a relatively limited scale that has not allowed the documentation of large portions of Mississippian communities. This essay focuses on the Town Creek site in North Carolina, where extensive excavations produced a large amount of data from public and domestic contexts that predate and postdate mound construction. I use mortuary and architectural data from the entire site to assess the proposition that changes in public architecture, namely the replacement of a ground-level earthlodge with buildings placed on a platform mound summit, reflect social and political changes within the community. I also use these data to evaluate the proposition that significant social and political changes accompanied the construction of a platform mound in this community and I compare the demographic and artifactual data of several burial groups to explore contemporaneous variation and changes through time. The architectural and mortuary data show that

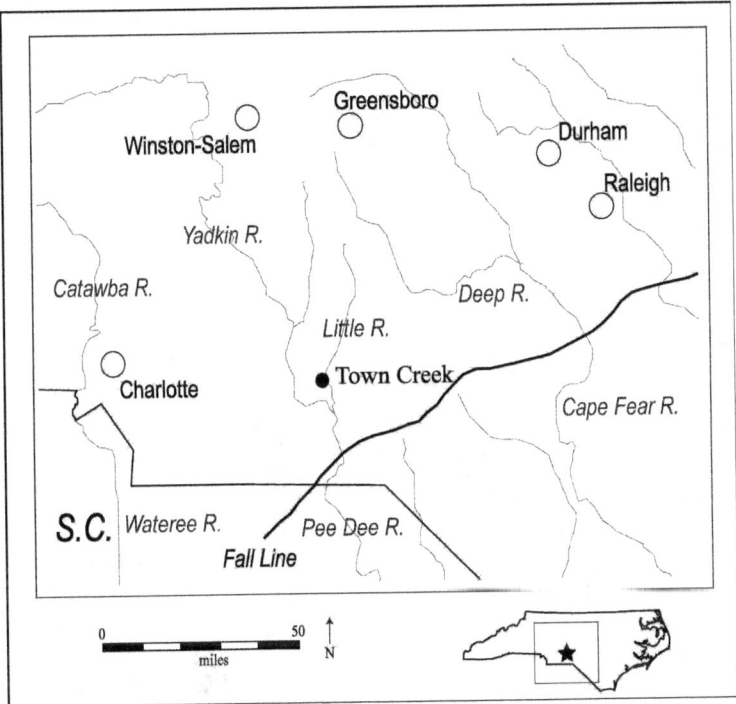

Figure 11.1. Map Showing the Location of the Town Creek Site.

significant changes did accompany mound construction at Town Creek. Some individuals may have played a more prominent social and political role within the community after mound construction, which would be consistent with an increase in authority for some community leaders. These changes, however, were not associated with an increase in political power or a more hierarchical social and political organization (see Fried 1967: 13). Instead, it seems that a heterarchical political organization in which power was shared and negotiated among multiple social groups (Crumley: 1987, 1995) existed throughout the history of the Town Creek community.

Town Creek Background

Town Creek is a single-mound site located on the Little River in the Piedmont of North Carolina (Figure 11.1). Fieldwork conducted there beginning in 1937 and ending in 1983 resulted in the excavation of almost the entire 3.5-m-tall platform mound, the documentation of thousands of archaeological features, the identification of tens of structures, and the excavation of over 200 burials (Figure 11.2) (Boudreaux 2005, 2007a; Coe 1995). While the site was used at

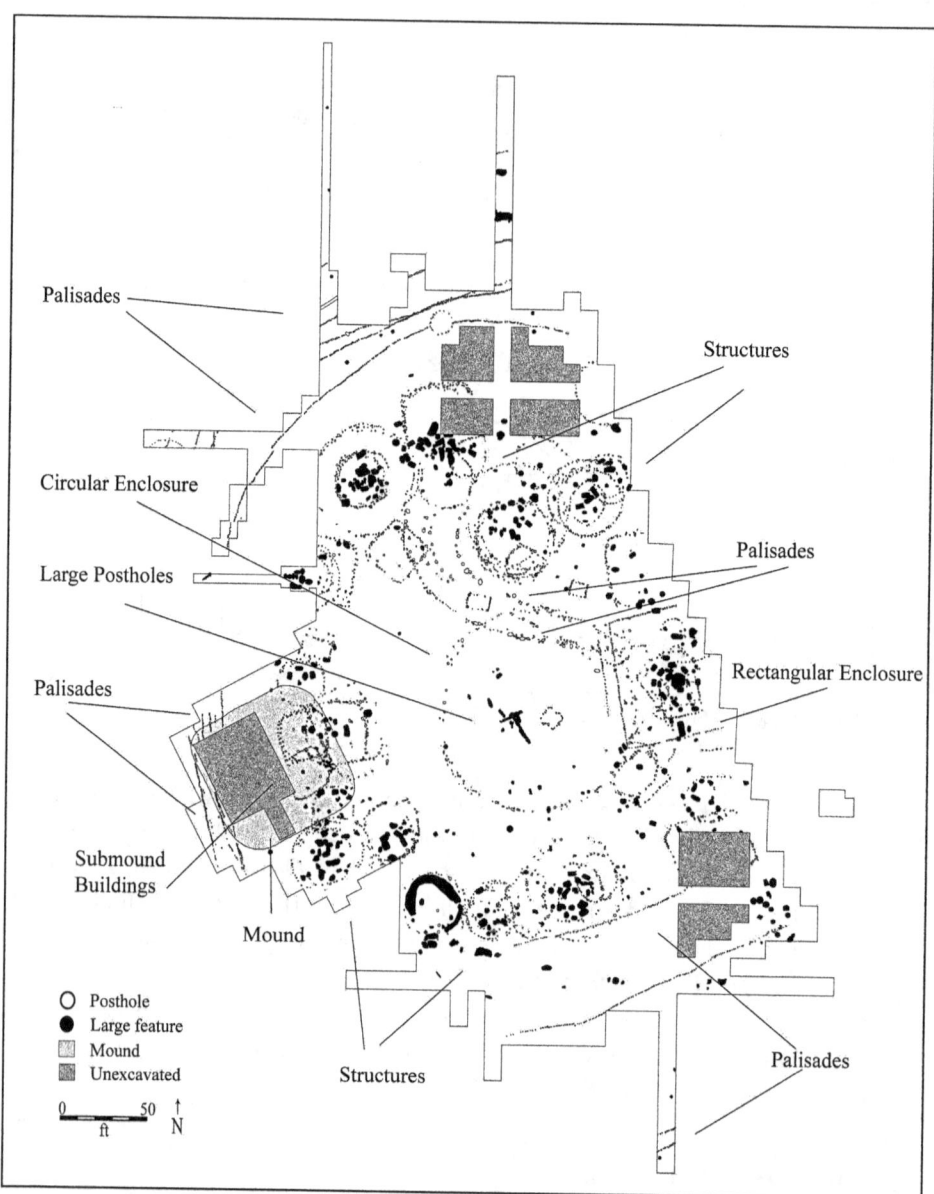

Figure 11.2. Identified Architectural Elements at Town Creek.

least intermittently from the Early Archaic through the Protohistoric periods, the overwhelming majority of contexts researchers encountered in excavations date to the Mississippian Period. Town Creek is considered a part of the regional variant of Mississippian culture known as South Appalachian Mississippian, which is characterized by paddle-stamped ceramics that are not shell-tempered (Caldwell 1958: 34; Ferguson 1971: 7–8; Griffin 1967: 190). Town Creek and other Mississippian sites in the Piedmont of the Carolinas and the Coastal Plain of South Carolina constitute a more localized cultural unit known as Pee Dee culture (Anderson 1982: 313; Coe 1952: 308–309; Judge 2003a). A ceramic chronology has been established for Pee Dee sites in the vicinity of Town Creek (Boudreaux 2007b; Oliver 1992), and a cultural chronology of the Town Creek site shows that it was a Mississippian town between A.D. 1050 and 1400 during the Town Creek (A.D. 1050–1300) and Leak (A.D. 1300–1550) phases (Boudreaux 2007a: 8–9).[1]

Leadership, Architecture, and Mortuary Analysis

Town Creek's rich mortuary record (Boudreaux 2005: 414–419; Davis et al. 1996; Driscoll 2001), which includes 218 Mississippian burials, is a critical data set for exploring the relationship between changes in public architecture and changes in the nature of leadership. The mortuary analysis presented here is based on the assumption that the spaces in which individuals were buried, the position in which they were placed, and the items that were interred with them reflect the statuses the individuals held in life and the social roles they played within their community (see Binford 1971: 13–15; Saxe 1970). Based on cross-cultural studies and the documentary record from the Southeast in particular, it is clear that an individual's social status strongly influenced their treatment at death (Binford 1971; Brown 1971: 104–105). A great deal of variability exists at Town Creek in the ways individuals were treated. This variability was expressed through the position of the body within the grave (e.g., flexed or extended), the location of the burial (e.g., in public or domestic contexts), and the kinds and quantities of associated artifacts.

It is assumed that community leaders will be identifiable in Town Creek's archaeological record based on distinctions in where they were buried, how they were buried, and the objects that were interred with them. Leadership is a status that is marked in many small-scale societies worldwide with the differential treatment of individuals at death (Feinman and Neitzel 1984: 57; Flannery 1999; Marcus and Flannery 1996; Whalen and Minnis 2000: 172). Artifact distributions can be useful in this regard. If objects signified particular statuses held in life, then burials of community leaders—as individuals who held the greatest number of roles in small-scale and middle-range societies—should contain a greater diversity of associated objects (Howell 1995: 129, 1996: 63; Howell and Kintigh 1996: 551; Kintigh 2000: 104). Therefore, one of the ways that Town Creek burials are compared is the number of artifact types included as grave goods (see Bennett 1984: 36; Driscoll 2002: 23–25). Also, artifacts that are distinctive within the context of a particular community have been recognized as symbols of particular leadership statuses in some Mississippian cases (Blitz 1993: 104; Brown 1971: 101; Peebles and Kus 1977: 439; Scarry 1992: 179). Another way to recognize leaders is by setting them apart physically from others, for example burying them in special places within the community such as in public spaces (Brown 1981a: 29; DePratter 1983: 189; Goldstein 1981: 57; Sullivan 1995: 117). Also, leaders may have been set apart by the arrangement of their body within the grave (e.g. orientation, seated vs. prone, extended vs. flexed, etc.) (Marcus and Flannery 1996: 84–85) as well as by the form of the grave itself (Sullivan 1995: 118–119).

The interpretations presented here are partially based on contrasting the individuals and artifacts associated with public buildings with those found in domestic structures. Mississippian towns generally can be thought of as being divided into domestic and public spheres (Hally 1994: 233; Holley 1999: 28; Lewis et al. 1998; Polhemus 1990: 134). The domestic sphere would have included the structures and facilities used and controlled by individual households to perform the production and consumption activities necessary to maintain the household (Wilk and Netting 1984). As the composite product of the entire community's daily activities, the domestic sphere constitutes the bulk of most archaeological collections. Since each household would have performed its activities largely independently, the domestic structures across a community should be characterized by repetitive facilities and assemblages (Winter 1976: 25). In the Southeast, Mississippian houses have been identified based on their similarity in size and style as well as on the presence of artifacts and ecofacts that are consistent with domestic activities (Hally and Kelly 1998: 53; Lewis and Kneberg 1946: 49).

Public buildings in historic southeastern native towns were architecturally, socially, and politically the most prominent buildings in the community. They were the loci of daily meetings concerning intracommunity and intercommunity decision-making (Braund 1999: 144; Lefler 1967: 42–43; Waselkov and Braund 1995: 62 and 102; Worth 1998: 93). They also often were the locations of important social events such as the entertaining and housing of significant guests and community-wide ceremonies (Lefler 1967: 43–47; Waselkov and Braund 1995: 85; Worth 1998: 93). It is clear in the ethnohistoric and ethnographic record that social proscriptions existed regarding who could access public buildings. In some cases, access was always limited to a certain social group (Kenton 1927: 427; McWilliams 1988: 92; Sattler 1995: 220; Waselkov and Braund 1995: 102 and 149; Worth 1998: 88). In others, access may have been more limited in some situations and more inclusive in others (Speck 1979: 120). Based on the documentation of the few funerals in public buildings in the historic record, it is clear that the person being interred in the public building in death was also a person who had access to the building during life (Swanton 1911: 138–157). Assuming that the public buildings at Town Creek were similar to those documented in the ethnohistoric record with regard to function and the social proscriptions that determined access, then the activities that took place within them probably involved primarily community-level decision making and the hosting of intracommunity social events. If it is also assumed that the people buried in public buildings were individuals who frequented those buildings in life, then it is likely that the people buried within public buildings at Town Creek were influential in the community's political life.

Early Town Creek Phase: The Community Before Mound Construction

The community at Town Creek was organized as a formal town beginning around A.D. 1050 (Boudreaux 2007a: 49–55). While the form and function of structures would change significantly throughout its history, the layout of the town was established at the outset, and it remained relatively unchanged throughout its existence. The site plan consisted of a large oval plaza surrounded by buildings. Public buildings and monuments were placed along a central east-west axis, and corporate group buildings were located to the north and south of this axis.

During the early Town Creek phase, the center of the plaza was occupied by a large monument that consisted of a circular enclosure (34 m in diameter) made of wooden posts with several massive posts near its center (Figure 11.3). Initially, with the exception of the western end, the plaza was surrounded by at least ten circular houses. These buildings have been classified as Small Circular Structures. This type of building was approximately 9 m in diameter, had walls made of single-set posts, and contained a relatively high density of interior burials (Figure 11.4) (Boudreaux 2005: 209, 2007a: 70–73). Three sets of paired rectilinear public buildings were constructed on the west side of the plaza, in the area where the mound would be built later (Figure 11.5). Each set of submound public buildings appears to have consisted of paired small and large rectilinear structures. The pair of public buildings used at the end of the early Town Creek phase immediately preceding mound construction (Struc-

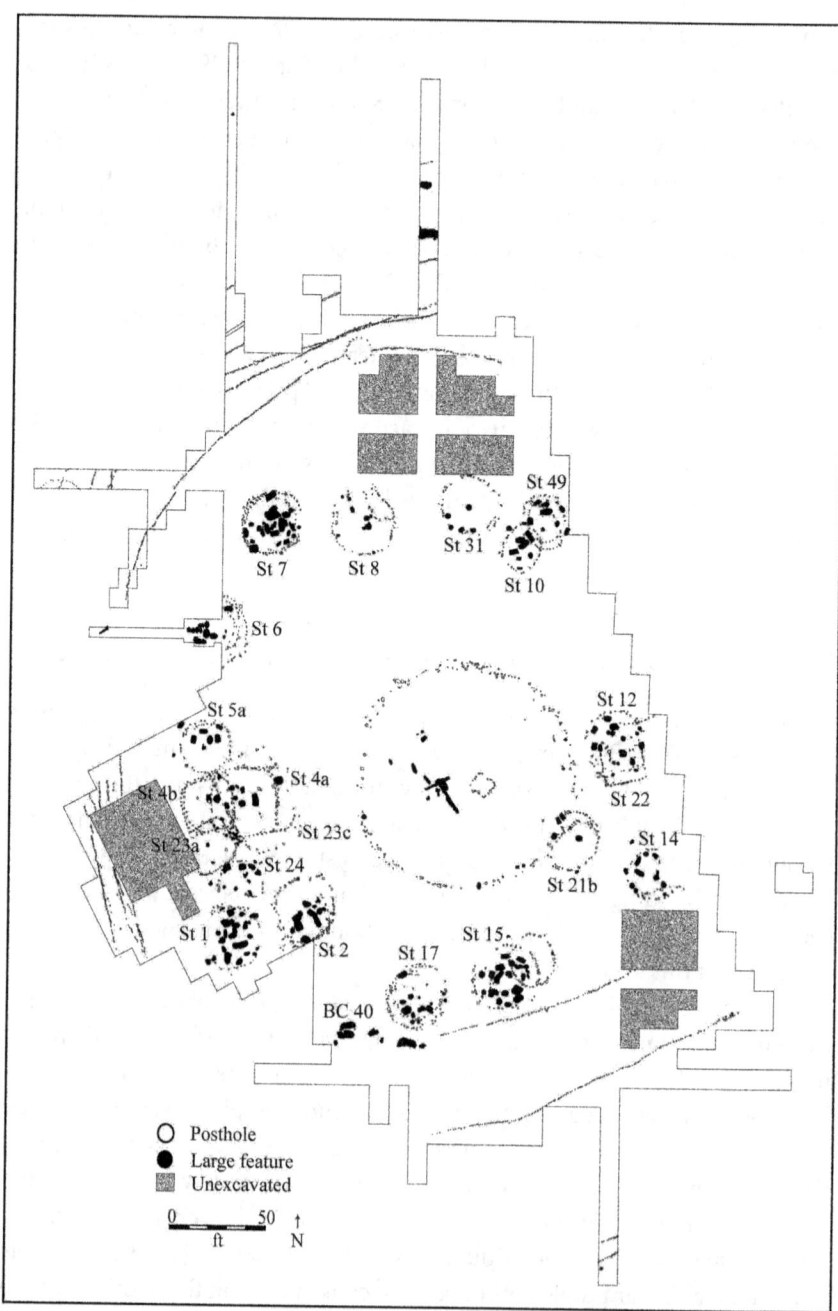

Figure 11.3. Early Town Creek Phase Architectural Elements.

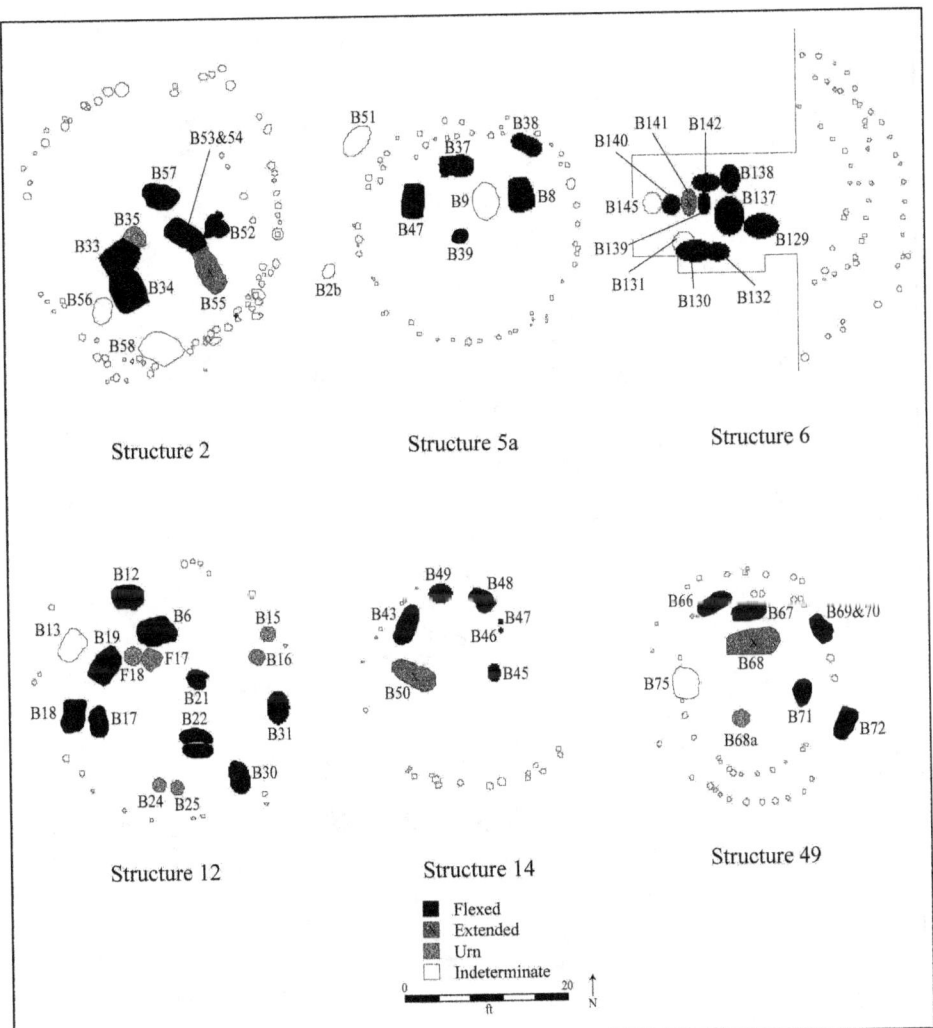

Figure 11.4. Burials in Small Circular Structures at Town Creek.

tures 23a and 23c) consisted of a large lightly constructed structure adjacent to the plaza with an adjoining smaller substantially built earth-embanked structure located on the west side of the mound farthest from the plaza. Another earth-embanked rectilinear structure was built on the eastern end of the plaza, probably also at the end of the early Town Creek phase. This building was placed along the axis shared by the other public buildings and the central circular monument and it faced these other public constructions.

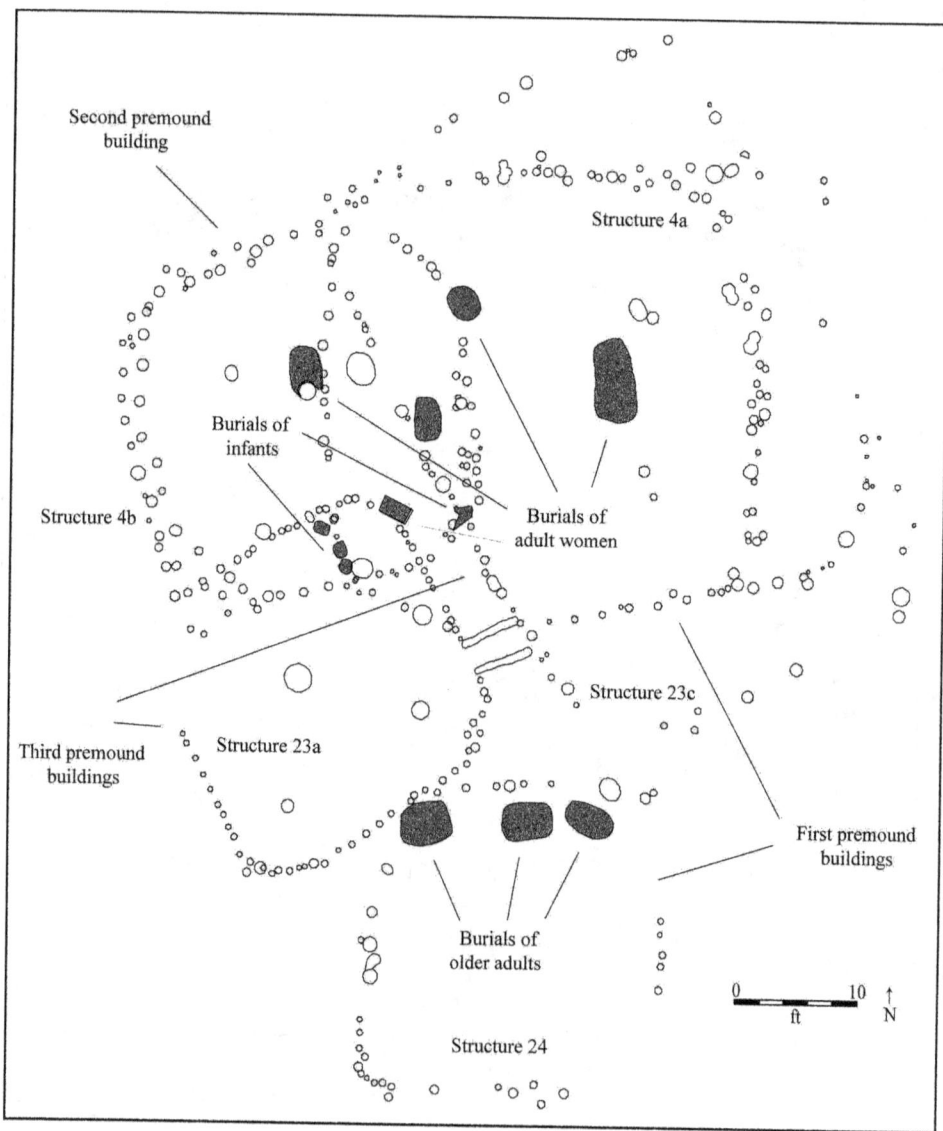

Figure 11.5. Premound Public Buildings and Associated Burials at Town Creek.

The earliest Mississippian public buildings at Town Creek were a large rectangular structure (Structure 4a) and a small square structure (Structure 24) that were oriented the same way and located next to each other on the western edge of the plaza (Figure 11.6). Structure 4a was associated with the burials of at least three and possibly four adult women and one adolescent (Table 11.1). Structure 4b, the building that succeeded Structure 4a, contained the burial of

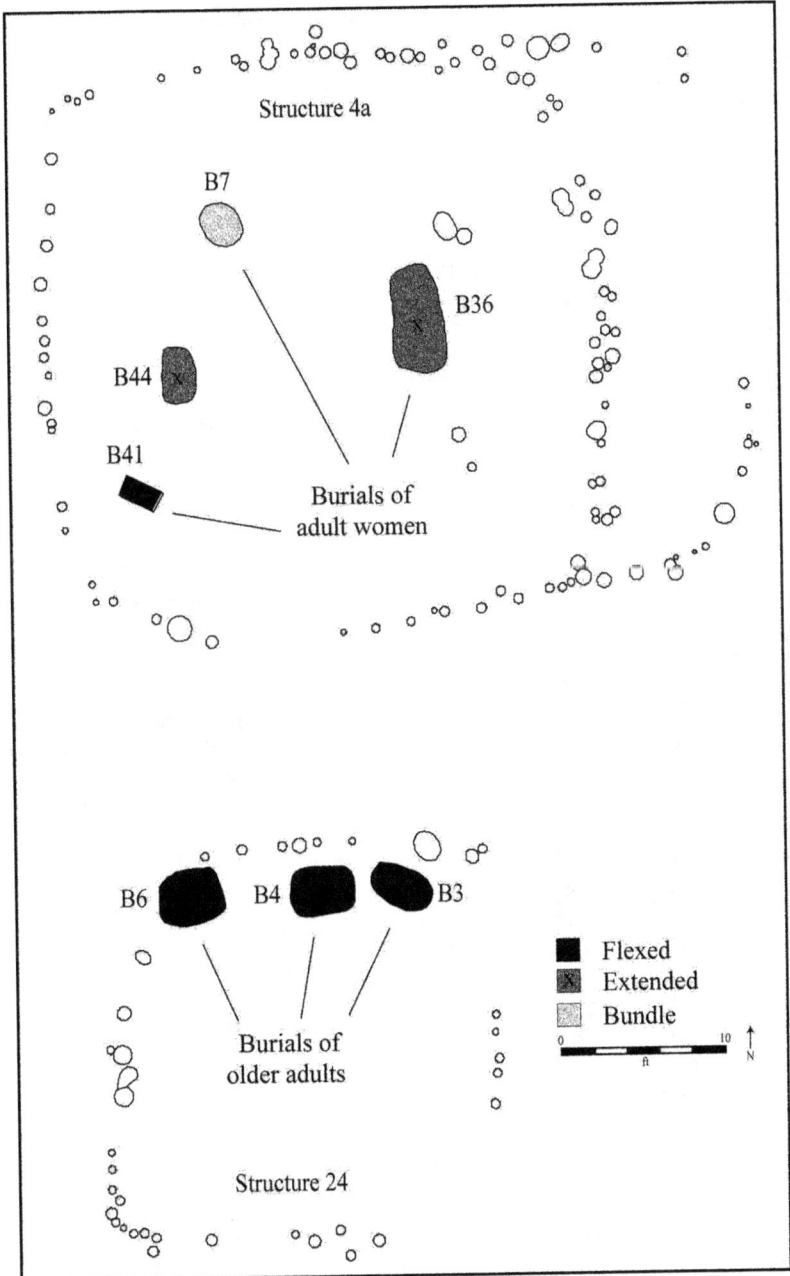

Figure 11.6. Burials Associated with Structures 4a and 24 at Town Creek.

Table 11.1. Mortuary Data from Mississippian Contexts at Town Creek

Context	Age Class[a]	Sex[b]	Burial Type[c]	NAT	Artifacts
Early Town Creek Phase					
Premound Public (Mg2)					
Burial 7	MA	F	B		
Burial 36	MA	F?	E		
Burial 41	MA	F	F	1	marine shell fragment
Burial 44	CH	Y	E	2	92 small columella beads, 2 stone beads
Burial 50	IND	IND	IND	1	1 ceramic vessel
Burial 45	YA	F	F		
Burial 46	CH	Y	F	1	6 shell pendants
Burial 10	CH	Y	ND		
Burial 42	CH	Y	F		
Burial 43	CH	Y	F	1	1 small columella bead, 13 medium columella beads
Burial 11	CH	Y	F		
Burial 3	OA	F?	F		
Burial 4	OA	M	F		
Burial 6	OA	M	F	2	76 small columella beads, 6 bone scratchers
Small Circular					
Burial 33	YA	M	F	1	1 stone projectile point
Burial 34	OA	M	F	1	1 small columella bead
Burial 35	IND	Y	U	2	marine shell beads, ceramic urn and cover
Burial 52	ADL	Y	F		
Burial 53	YA	F	F		
Burial 53a	CH	Y	ND		
Burial 54	MA	M	F		
Burial 55	MA	F?	E		
Burial 56	ADL	Y	IND		
Burial 57	YA	F?	F		
Burial 58	YA	IND	IND		
Burial 2b	YA	M?	IND		
Burial 8	MA	F?	F		
Burial 9	IND	IND	ND		
Burial 37	YA	IND	F		
Burial 38	YA	F	F		
Burial 39	CH	Y	F		
Burial 47	MA	IND	F	1	7 copper fragments
Burial 51	IND	IND	IND		
Burial 129a	ADL	Y	F		
Burial 129b	YA	M	ND		
Burial 130	MA	F	F		
Burial 130a	CH	Y	F		
Burial 130b	CH	Y	ND		

Context	Age Class[a]	Sex[b]	Burial Type[c]	NAT	Artifacts
Burial 131	YA	F?	F		
Burial 131a	CH	Y	ND		
Burial 132	YA	F	F	1	1 stone projectile point
Burial 137	OA	F	F		
Burial 138	ADL	Y	F	2	32 small columella beads, 1 pottery pipe
Burial 139	IND	IND	F		
Burial 140	YA	IND	F		
Burial 141	YA	F?	E		
Burial 142	OA	F	F		
Burial 142a	CH	Y	ND		
Burial 143	MA	M	F		
Burial 144	CH	Y	F		
Burial 145	YA	F?	IND		
Burial 6	MA	IND	F	1	2 rocks
Burial 12	MA	F?	F	1	1 quartzite pebble
Burial 13	CH	Y	IND		
Burial 15	CH	Y	U		
Burial 16	CH	Y	U	2	1 ceramic urn, 1 pebble
Burial 17	MA	M	F		
Burial 18	YA	F?	F		
Burial 19	MA	M	F	1	12 small columella beads
Burial 21	ADL	Y	F		
Burial 22	YA	IND	F		
Burial 24	CH	Y	U	2	1 small unmodified columella bead, 6 large unmodified columella beads, 1 ceramic urn
Burial 25	CH	Y	U	2	9 small columella beads, 1 ceramic urn
Burial 30	YA	F?	F	2	shell beads, copper fragments
Burial 31	ADL	Y	F		
Feature 17	NA	Y	U		
Feature 18	NA	Y	U		
Burial 43	MA	F	F	3	23 medium columella beads, 1 Pine Island shell gorget, 1 shell disc
Burial 45	YA	F?	F	1	pottery beads
Burial 46	OA	M	F		
Burial 47	YA	IND	F		
Burial 48	OA	M	F		
Burial 49	OA	F	F		
Burial 50	OA	M	E	3	20 large polished columella beads, 1 copper axe, 1 stone
Burial 77	ADL	Y	F	1	3 rocks
Burial 78	ADL	Y	F		
Burial 79	YA	IND	F		
Burial 66	YA	M	F		
Burial 67	MA	M?	F		
Burial 68	MA	F?	E	2	1 stone projectile point, 1 rock

continued

Table 11.1.—*Continued*

Context	Age Class[a]	Sex[b]	Burial Type[c]	NAT	Artifacts
Burial 68a	CH	Y	U	4	9 small columella beads, 1 Pine Island shell gorget, 1 ceramic urn, 1 quartz piece
Burial 69	OA	F	F		
Burial 70	OA	F?	F	2	1 rock, 1 celt blank
Burial 71	OA	F?	F		
Burial 72	OA	M	F		
Burial 75	ADL	Y	F	2	1 hammerstone, 1 rock
Unassigned					
Burial 126	ADL	Y	F		
Burial 127	CH	Y	IND		
Burial 133	YA	IND	F		
Burial 146	OA	M	E		
Burial 146a	CH	IND	ND		
Burial 147	OA	F	F	1	1 ceramic vessel
Burial 148a	CH	Y	IND		
Burial 148b	MA	IND	ND		
Burial 149	YA	M	F		
Burial 150	IND	IND	IND		
Burial 151	ADL	Y	IND	1	1 rock

Late Town Creek–Leak Phases

Mound Summit (Mg2)

Context	Age Class[a]	Sex[b]	Burial Type[c]	NAT	Artifacts
Burial 59	YA	M	F	6	13 sm. columella beads, 10 very large unmodified beads, 2 stone projectile points, 3 mica ornaments, 2 rattles, 1 lump of ochre
Burial 61	YA	IND	F	1	2 quartz pieces
Burial 60	ADT	U	F	2	mica fragments, 1 rattle
Burial 48	YA	F	B	1	1 shell hairpin or earpin
Burial 49	YA	IND	B		

Enclosure 1 (Mg3)

Context	Age Class[a]	Sex[b]	Burial Type[c]	NAT	Artifacts
Burial 9	YA	IND	F	2	1 large columella bead, 1 large cobble
Burial 20	ADT	M	F	6	1 small columella bead, 1 raccoon skull, 1 pottery pipe, 4 stone projectile points, mica fragments, 1 rattle
Burial 23	YA	IND	F	2	16 medium unmodified columella beads, mica fragments
Burial 29	YA	IND	IND		
Burial 32	IND	U	IND		
Burial 1	CH	Y	ND		
Burial 1a	YA	F	F	2	shell fragments, 1 ceramic urn
Burial 2a	ADT	IND	IND		
Burial 3	CH	Y	IND		

Context	Age Class[a]	Sex[b]	Burial Type[c]	NAT	Artifacts
Burial 4	YA	IND	IND		
Burial 5	YA	F	F	3	4 conch shoulder gorgets, 3 stone projectile points, 1 rattle
Burial 7	CH	Y	F	1	shell beads
Burial 8	OA	M	F		
Burial 10	MA	F	F		
Burial 33	YA	F?	F	1	2 stone ear discs
Burial 36	CH	Y	IND	4	2 ceramic discs, 1 stone disc (ear spool?), 2 copper-covered wooden earspools, 1 rattle
Burial 37	MA	F	E	3	98 small columella beads, 4 bracket-style shell earpins, 1 copper-covered wooden earspool
Burial 38	YA	IND	F		
Burial 39	MA	F?	F		
Burial 40	ADL	Y	F		
Burial 41	IND	IND	F	1	deer ulna

Enclosed Circular

Context	Age Class[a]	Sex[b]	Burial Type[c]	NAT	Artifacts
Burial 1a	MA	IND	F		
Burial 1b	MA	F	F		
Burial 2a	CH	Y	U	2	22 small columella beads, 1 ceramic urn and cover
Burial 5	YA	F	F		
Burial 12	ADL	Y	F		
Burial 12a	ADL	Y	ND		
Burial 12b	CH	Y	ND		
Burial 13	YA	F	F		
Burial 14a	YA	F	IND		
Burial 14b	YA	M	F		
Burial 14c	CH	Y	ND		
Burial 15	MA	F	F		
Burial 16	OA	M	F		
Burial 17	YA	M	F		
Burial 18	IND	IND	F		
Burial 19	IND	IND	F		
Burial 20	ADT	M	E		
Burial 21	OA	M	F		
Burial 22	YA	IND	F		
Burial 23	OA	IND	F	1	2 stone projectile points
Burial 24	MA	M	F		
Burial 25	OA	M	F		
Burial 26	OA	M	F		
Burial 27	OA	M	F	1	1 antler projectile point
Burial 28	MA	F?	D		
Burial 29	MA	M	F		
Burial 29a	MA	IND	ND		
Burial 30	YA	F	B	1	copper fragments

continued

Table 11.1.—*Continued*

Context	Age Class[a]	Sex[b]	Burial Type[c]	NAT	Artifacts
Burial 31	ADL	Y	F		
Burial 32	YA	IND	E		
Burial 86	OA	F	IND	1	1 awl
Burial 87	OA	M	F	1	1 rock
Burial 87a	ADT	IND	ND		
Burial 88	CH	Y	F	1	154 small columella beads
Burial 89	OA	M	F	1	2 rocks
Burial 90	YA	M	E		
Burial 91	CH	Y	F		
Burial 92	OA	M	F	1	copper fragments
Burial 93	CH	Y	E		
Burial 94	CH	Y	F	1	69 small columella beads, 4 medium columella beads
Burial 95	MA	F	F		
Burial 96	OA	F	F		
Burial 97	CH	Y	U	2	31 small columella beads, 1 ceramic urn and cover
Burial 98	CH	Y	U	2	1 ceramic urn, 1 rock
Burial 99	OA	F	F		
Burial 100	ADL	Y	F	1	44 small columella beads, 7 medium columella beads
Burial 101	OA	F	F	2	27 small columella beads, 1 marginella bead
Burial 102	CH	Y	ND		
Burial 102a	CH	Y	U	1	1 ceramic urn and cover
Burial 103	CH	Y	U	1	urn
Burial 104	CH	Y	IND		
Burial 105	YA	M	F		
Burial 106	MA	M	F		
Burial 107	YA	M	F		
Burial 108	ADL	Y	F	1	2 ceramic vessels
Burial 109	CH	Y	IND	3	10 small columella beads, 63 marginella beads, pottery beads
Burial 109a	CH	Y	IND		
Burial 110	OA	M	F		
Burial 111	CH	Y	F	2	829 small columella beads, 16 medium columella beads, 2 conch shoulder gorgets
Burial 112	ADL	Y	F	2	1 small columella bead, 1 bone bead
Burial 112a	CH	Y	ND		
Burial 113	CH	Y	U	2	3 small columella beads, 1 ceramic urn and cover
Burial 114	OA	M	F		
Burial 115	OA	M	F		
Burial 116	YA	M?	IND		
Burial 117	MA	F	E		
Burial 118a	CH	Y	IND	1	2 conch shoulder gorgets
Burial 118b	CH	Y	IND		
Burial 118c	CH	Y	IND		

Context	Age Class[a]	Sex[b]	Burial Type[c]	NAT	Artifacts
Burial 118d	CH	Y	IND		
Burial 119	OA	F	F	1	40 small columella beads
Burial 120	CH	Y	F	3	8 medium columella beads, 10 large columella beads, 2 marginella beads, 1 celt
Burial 121	CH	Y	U	2	132 small polished columella beads, 1 ceramic urn and cover
Burial 122	CH	Y	IND	1	84 small columella beads
Burial 123	OA	F	F	2	2 marginella beads, 1 rock
Burial 124	CH	Y	U	2	1 bone bead, 1 ceramic urn and cover
Burial 124a	CH	Y	IND	5	2 sm. columella beads, 1 med. polished columella bead, 2 disc columella beads, 1655 marginella beads, 92 pottery beads
Burial 125	OA	M	F	2	1 small columella bead, 1 stone projectile point
Burial 125a	CH	Y	ND		
Burial 125b	IND	IND	ND		

Large Rectangular

Context	Age Class[a]	Sex[b]	Burial Type[c]	NAT	Artifacts
Burial 61	YA	F	F		
Burial 62a	ADL	Y	D	2	1 deer jaw, 1 pottery disc
Burial 62b	ADL	Y	D		
Burial 62c	YA	IND	D		
Burial 62d	ADT	IND	D		
Burial 63	YA	F?	ND		
Burial 80	CH	Y	F		
Burial 81	ADL	Y	F		
Burial 82	ADL	Y	F		
Burial 11	OA	F?	F	1	1 quartzite pebble
Burial 26	YA	F	F		
Burial 27	YA	IND	F		
Burial 28	MA	M	F		
Burial 83	OA	F	F		

Unassigned

Context	Age Class[a]	Sex[b]	Burial Type[c]	NAT	Artifacts
Burial 65	YA	IND	B	1	7 small columella beads
Burial 65a	CH	Y	ND		
Burial 65b	ADL	Y	ND		
Burial 73	ADL	Y	IND		
Burial 74	ADT	IND	IND		
Burial 40	ADL	Y	IND		
Feature 35	IND	IND	IND		
Burial 76	ADL	Y	F		
Burial 84	MA	IND	F	2	29 small columella beads, 1 bone awl
Burial 85	CH	Y	F		

Notes: [a]CH-child, ADL-adolescent, YA-young adult, MA-mature adult, OA-older adult, ADT-adult, IND-indeterminant
[b]F-female, M-male, Y-youth, IND-indeterminant
[c]B-bundle, E-extended, D-disarticulated, F-flexed, U-urn, IND-indeterminant, ND-no data

a young adult female and a child.² The exclusive association of adult women with these public buildings and the absence of adult men is uncommon in Mississippian contexts (Sullivan 2001: 110). It is not what one would expect from reading the ethnohistoric record in which men predominantly (and in many communities exclusively) met in councils to make political decisions (Braund 1999: 145; Lefler 1967: 49; Sattler 1995: 220; Speck 1979: 120; Waselkov and Braund 1995: 62, 105, and 149; Worth 1998: 88 and 94). Indeed, it is a very different pattern from what has been observed archaeologically at other southeastern sites (Rodning 1999: 12, 2001: 94–97).

Gender, along with kinship, was a fundamental social distinction that affected virtually every aspect of individual's lives in southeastern native groups (Eastman and Rodning 2001; Hudson 1976: 260; Perdue 1998: 8). A gendered division of labor within these groups was based upon strong social proscriptions regarding the behaviors considered appropriate for each gender group (Claassen 2001: 20–25; Rodning and Eastman 2001: 3; Thomas 2001: 34). In general, men's roles included intercommunity activities, such as warfare and trading, and women's roles included intracommunity activities, such as food production and household responsibilities (Rodning 2001: 80–82; Thomas 2001: 29–34). Ethnohistoric accounts indicate that men generally occupied community leadership roles, although accounts of female chiefs are not uncommon (Sullivan 2001: 102; Waselkov and Braund 1995: 153; Worth 1998: 88). While men are most frequently discussed as leaders in written accounts, male political power was not absolute, nor were women absent from the political process (Sullivan 2001: 102). In many southeastern communities, it is likely that men and women drew from different complementary sources of political power and that each group served as a check to the power of the other (Perdue 1998: 13; Rodning 2001: 81–82; Sullivan 2001: 103).

If males generally were the preferred leaders in Mississippi and historic period communities (see Worth 1998: 88), why are only women interred in one of the early Town Creek phase public buildings? Ethnohistoric accounts clearly indicate that women played prominent social and political roles in many native communities as the leaders of households, kin groups, and clans (Sullivan 2001: 110). Also, women could be political leaders outright (Clayton et al. 1993: 278; Worth 1998: 86). Even if they did not occupy a formal political role, there is ample evidence that women could influence the male-dominated realms of warfare and politics as clan and lineage leaders (Perdue 1998: 52; Sattler 1995: 222). Additionally, it was through female ancestors that kin-group membership was determined among most southeastern Indians. Being a member of a kin group was essential to participation in community life because kin groups—in the forms of clans and local lineages—were directly associated with rights and obligations within the community (Hudson 1976: 189; Knight 1990: 6 and 10; Perdue 1998: 24, 46, and 47). The fact that access to community life was determined by kinship through women is clearly demonstrated by the practice of adoption; it was women who decided if prisoners would be killed to atone for the deaths of clan members or adopted to replace a member and given full rights within the clan (Perdue 1998: 53–54; Sattler 1995: 222). Clearly, participation in society was made possible by one's membership in a lineage through a relationship, either natal or adoptive, with a woman (Perdue 1998: 54). Thus, women must have had a great deal of influence in native communities because they provided access to the kin groups that constituted much of the social and political structure of these communities. The presence of women exclusively in an early Town Creek phase public building suggests that women could be community leaders and that they played a prominent role in the political decision-making process at that time. The fact that women's political power within native southeastern societies likely derived from leadership roles within kin groups suggests that community political leadership and kin-group leadership were inextricably related during the early Town Creek phase.

Structure 4a was paired with Structure 24, which contained the burials of three older adults. Two of these individuals are males and the third is a female. The association of older adults with a public building is consistent with observations about southeastern societies in the ethnohistoric record. Older individuals, especially those who had distinguished themselves through their achievements, were esteemed in native communities (Gearing 1958: 1149; Lefler 1967: 43; Sattler 1995: 225; Waselkov and Braund 1995: 118). A council of older adults (primarily men) who advised the chief was a recurrent feature of political organization among historic groups (Hudson 1976: 225; Muller 1997: 83). The presence during the early Town Creek phase of a public building with older adults of both sexes indicates that older individuals, both men and women, were esteemed at a community-wide level and that these individuals probably participated in the political process at this time.

The last set of premound public buildings (Structures 23a and 22) faced each other across the plaza. They were not associated with adult burials, although several infant burials were present. These are the only public buildings not associated with adult burials. It is unclear why these structures were distinctive in this way from the public buildings that preceded and followed them.

The burials within Small Circular Structures probably represent household groups, assuming that households would have consisted of subadults and adults and both males and females (see Brown 1981a: 30; Howell and Kintigh 1996: 541). Although the proportions vary a great deal among structures, males and females are present in all Small Circular Structures, and subadults are present in all of them with the exception of Structure 14. This structure is superimposed by a protohistoric burial cluster, though, and it is possible that a subadult burial included with the former was actually associated with the latter (Boudreaux 2005: 166). Overall, in contrast to the more restricted demographic profiles of the submound public buildings, all five age classes and both sexes are represented in the burials found in Small Circular Structures. Several Small Circular Structures included urn burials, interments of children in large ceramic jars that were placed in structure floors. This practice has been documented at several Pee Dee sites (Coe 1952: 309; Ferguson 1971: 206). Urn burials occurred in Small Circular Structures during the early Town Creek phase, but they were absent in public buildings. This suggests that placing children in urns was an important part of household or kin group mortuary rituals but that it was not a part of the rituals that took place in public buildings.

Burial in the flexed position (n = 61), which constituted 79 percent of identifiable burial positions, was the most common practice at Town Creek during the early Town Creek phase. Seven individuals are distinctive because they were interred in an extended burial position. Four extended burials were found in Small Circular Structures, one in a burial cluster not associated with a building, and two in a premound public building (Structure 4a). Nearly all of the individuals buried in the extended position during the early Town Creek phase were adults (n = 6), with the exception of one child who was buried in Structure 4a. There are two indications that the extended burial position marks an important status, although exactly what that status was is unknown. First, with the exception of the public building Structure 4a, only one individual per structure or burial cluster was treated in this way. Second, extended burials were generally placed in a central location within an architectural element. Whatever the status may have been, it does not seem to have been determined by sex because two of the early Town Creek phase extended burials are males and four are females. The six adult burials represent all three stages of adulthood, so the status being expressed may not have been associated with a particular age group either. These burials were distinguished by their position and location but not by durable objects because in the early Town Creek phase community only two of the six extended adult burials had artifacts. Interestingly, one of these (Burial 50) had some of the most unusual artifacts at the site, including polished columella beads and a copper axe.

The presence of no more than one extended adult burial in each architectural element suggests that only one adult could occupy the particular role manifested by this burial position throughout the use-life of the structure.

If Small Circular Structures were used for 20 to 30 years and rebuilt in place, as may have been the case with structures at other Mississippian sites (see Hally 2002: 91), then perhaps one person in a generation occupied the role signified by an extended burial position. The distribution of extended burials across the site suggests that the status marked by this burial position existed in many of the social groups that constituted the Mississippian community at Town Creek, perhaps in each household or matrilineage. Among historic native groups in the Southeast, regional tribal units were subdivided into a small number of clans (Gearing 1958: 1150; Knight 1990; Swanton 1993: 79). Clan membership was matrilineal; each person became a member of their mother's clan at birth (Hudson 1976: 185). Clans were manifested at the local level as matrilineages that often consisted of a single household or group of closely related households organized around a matriarch (Hudson 1976: 189; Knight 1990: 6). Historic native communities were composed of multiple matrilineages that represented several different clans (Hudson 1976: 190; Knight 1990: 6). While clans were only weakly corporate groups, members of matrilineages met often, and it was matrilineages that controlled access to particular economic resources such as agricultural land (Hudson 1976: 193; Knight 1990: 5–6). It is possible that the single extended burials found within each burial group in the early Town Creek phase community are those of important or senior lineage members. If the extended burials represent individuals who were distinctive within their kin groups, the general absence of artifacts associated with them is consistent with cross-cultural patterns in which kin-based statuses are generally expressed through organic artifacts that are not preserved archaeologically or through a distinctive body posture or orientation (O'Shea 1981: 49–50).

The distribution of early Town Creek phase adult burials by the number of artifact types (NAT) included as grave goods (see Howell 1995: 129, 1996: 63; Kintigh 2000: 104) is continuous. Assuming that there was a correlation between the number of artifact types interred with a person and the number of different roles they played within the community, then no individuals clearly stand out as potential community leaders based on NAT. It is interesting that the individuals buried in the early Town Creek phase public structures are not distinguished by either the quality or quantity of their associated artifacts. Generally, the placement of some early Town Creek phase individuals within public buildings rather than their grave accompaniments is most distinctive. This resembles historic Cherokee communities in which burials of community leaders are distinguished only by their placement in the vicinity of the townhouse (Sullivan 1995: 117). In contrast, an older adult male in the early Town Creek phase village (Structure 14) was buried with a copper axe, the only such artifact at Town Creek. This type of artifact is distinctive in Mississippian contexts because it is generally associated with mound burials in conjunction with other unusual artifacts that are often made from exotic materials (Brain and Phillips 1996: 362). Copper axes have been interpreted as symbols of political authority at other Mississippian sites (Brain and Phillips 1996: 362; Fox 2004; Peebles 1971: 82; Scarry 1992: 178–179). If this was also the case at Town Creek, then it appears that one of the community's political leaders was not buried in a public building but was instead interred in what appears to be a house.

Late Town Creek–Leak Phases: The Post–Mound Construction Community

Significant architectural changes occurred across the entire Town Creek site during the late Town Creek and early Leak (A.D. 1250–1350) phases (Boudreaux 2007a: 55–60). A platform mound was built on the western side of the plaza over the community's earlier public buildings at the beginning of the late Town Creek phase around A.D. 1250 (Figure 11.7). At some point after mound construction, the circular monument in the middle of the plaza was removed, although the large central post may have remained. Also after mound construction, a rectangular enclosure containing at least one rectilinear building and several burial clusters was built across the plaza next to the river.

The mound consisted of at least four construction stages, and mound use continued at least into the late Leak phase (Boudreaux 2007a: 31–33). The western part of two mound-stage summits (farthest from the plaza) contained two smaller earth-embanked structures joined by an entrance trench (Figure 11.8). Unfortunately, the remains of any structures on the eastern part of the mound adjacent to the plaza were destroyed by looters prior to 1937 (Coe 1995: 8). Although it is impossible to identify a complete set of mound-summit buildings for any stage, a conjecture can be made based on three factors: evidence of such architecture from the early Leak phase that was preserved, the configuration of submound public buildings, and patterns observed at other South Appalachian Mississippian sites (Hally 1994: 157; Polhemus et al. 1987: 1213–1214, 1990: 131; Smith 1994: 38 and Figure 11.14). It is possible that a large lightly constructed building similar to premound building Structure 23c occupied the eastern part of the mound summit adjacent to the plaza and that two smaller earth-embanked structures were located on the western part of the summit farthest from the plaza (Boudreaux 2007a: 33–38).

The placement of an enclosure that encompassed a number of burials on the eastern side of the plaza is a significant change that occurred during the

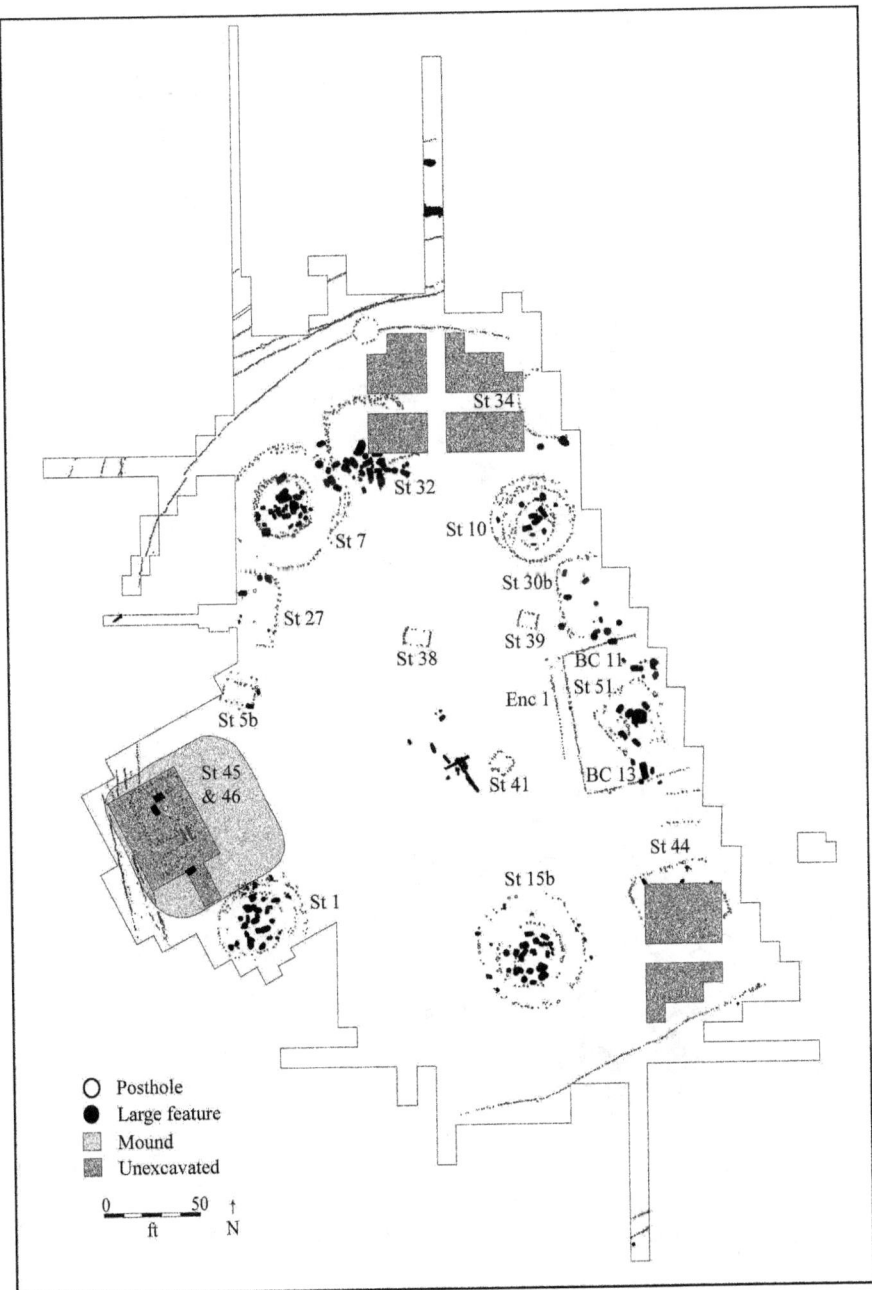

Figure 11.7. Late Town Creek–Early Leak Phase Architectural Elements.

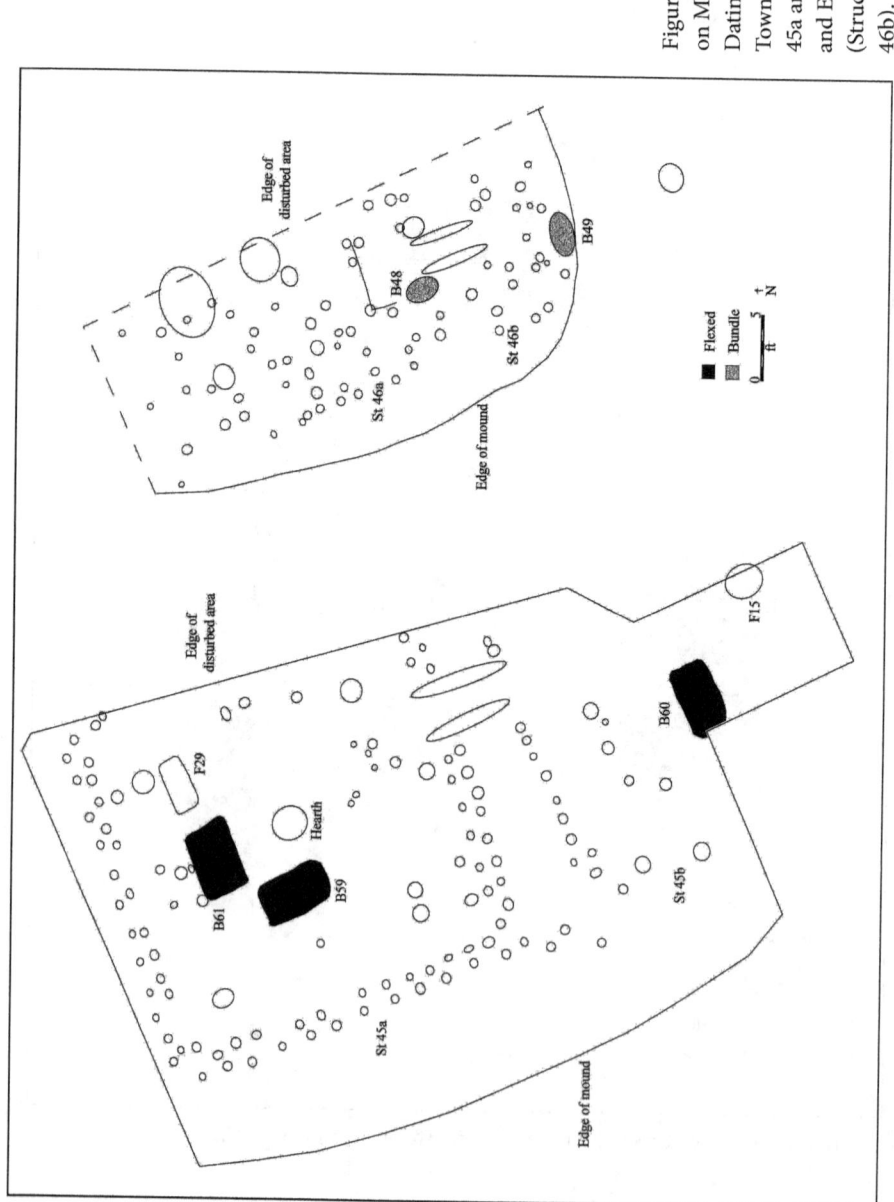

Figure 11.8. Structures on Mound Summits Dating to the Late Town Creek (Structures 45a and 45b) Phase and Early Leak Phase (Structures 46a and 46b).

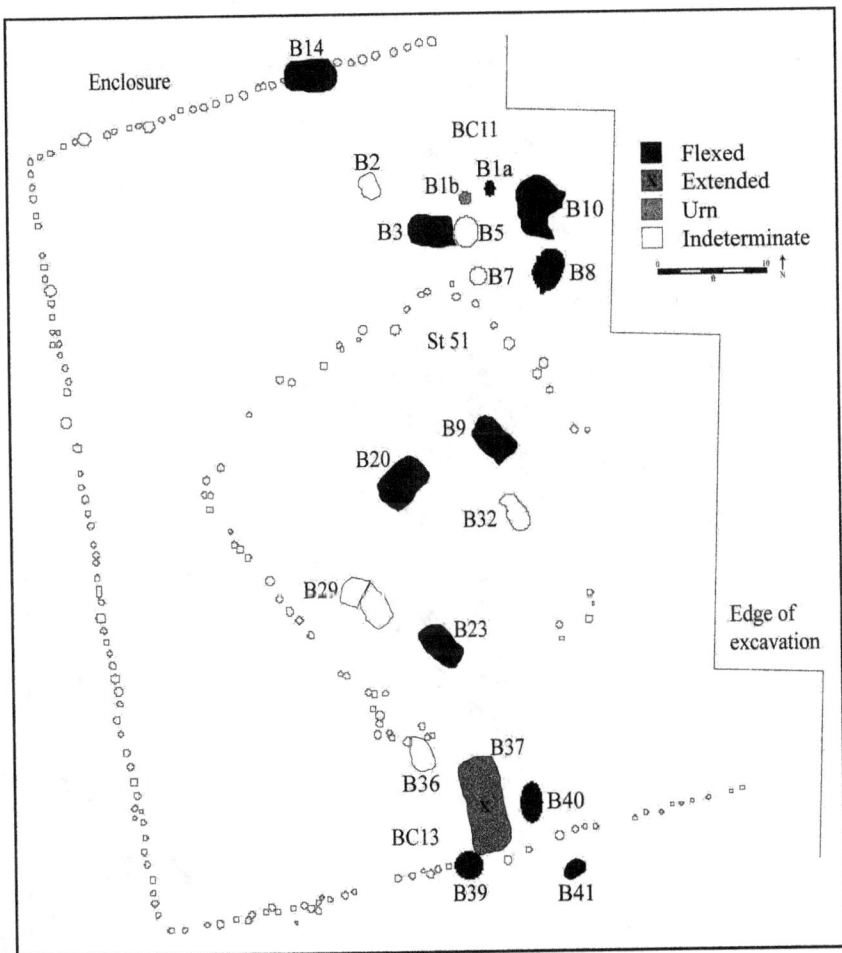

Figure 11.9. Burials Associated with Enclosure 1 and Structure 51 at Town Creek.

late Town Creek–Leak phase (Figure 11.9). Enclosure 1 contains burials within one structure and two burial clusters. Individuals of both sexes and all five age classes are present. The patterns are interesting, though, when the contexts within the enclosure are considered independently. Structure 51 contains only young adults. The two burial clusters outside Structure 51 contain all age groups and both sexes, although they include one of the highest proportions of females at Town Creek.

Significant changes occurred in the site's domestic sphere after the mound was built when two new types of structures appeared (Boudreaux 2005: 249–255). One new type is the Enclosed Circular Structure, which includes buildings that are approximately 18 m in diameter and house a relatively high

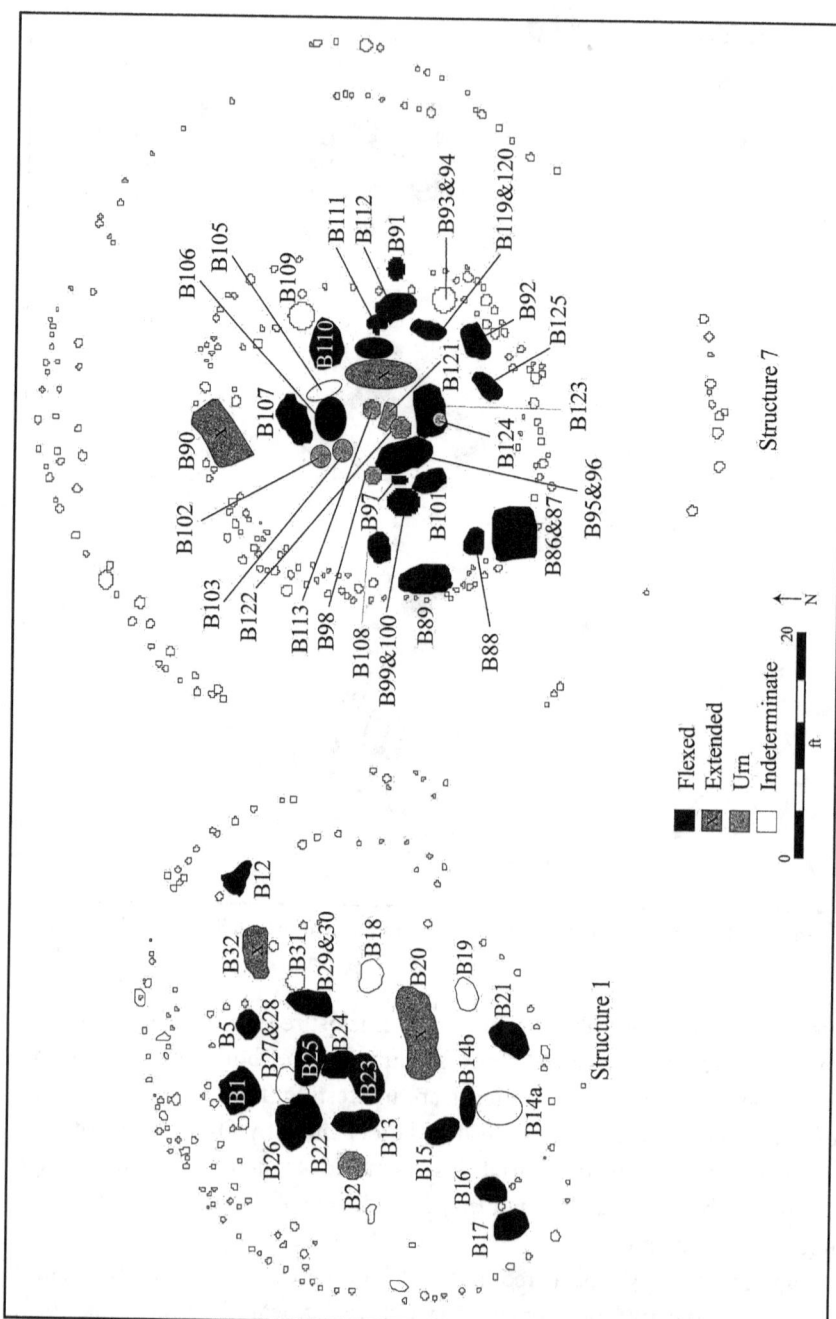

Figure 11.10. Burials in Enclosed Circular Structures at Town Creek.

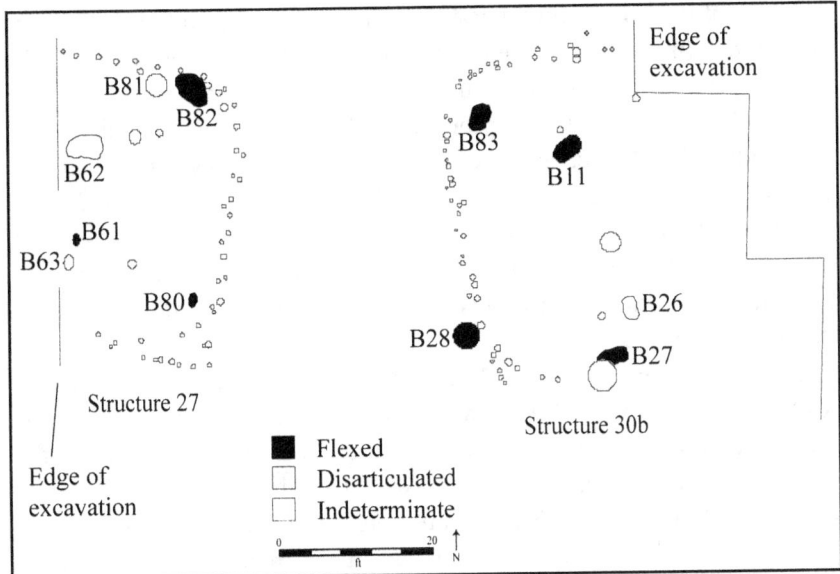

Figure 11.11. Burials in Large Rectangular Structure at Town Creek.

density of interior burials (Boudreaux 2007a: 18–23). The two excavated Enclosed Circular Structures each contained 30 and 50 individuals. Enclosed Circular Structures appear to be former house sites that were encircled with an enclosure of wooden posts and used as cemeteries (Figure 11.10). At least four former house sites were maintained as cemeteries, probably by the corporate groups that lived there before the mound was built. Each circular enclosed cemetery appears to have been paired with a Large Rectangular Structure, the other new type of structure (Figure 11.11). The floor areas of Large Rectangular Structures exceeded 305 m^2, and these structures had relatively low burial densities (Boudreaux 2007a: 23).

Enclosed Circular Structures and Large Rectangular Structures appear to alternate around the plaza. Based on their contemporaneity and complementary distribution, these structure types may have been paired together. The facts that there were multiple examples of Enclosed Circular and Large Rectangular Structures at Town Creek and that they were located in the domestic portion of the site suggests that these structures were used by kin-based groups, most likely clan-based matrilineages. It is possible that each structure pair represents public buildings—a cemetery and an adjacent area for large group gatherings—associated with one of the several corporate groups that constituted the Town Creek community. The demographic profile of Enclosed Circular Structures suggests that burial within these buildings was open to all members of the social group because all five age classes and both sexes are represented. In contrast to the more representative nature of Enclosed Circular Structures, the burials within Large Rectangular Structures are almost exclusively females. While the proportion of males in Small Circular Structures and Enclosed Circular Structures is nearly identical, fewer women were buried in Enclosed Circular Structures (56 percent) than in Small Circular Structures (83 percent) because they were placed in Large Rectangular Structures instead. For whatever reason, it was important after mound construction for some women to be buried outside of the former house sites and in Large Rectangular Structures.

Infants were buried in urns in Enclosed Circular Structures but not in Large Rectangular Structures. Urn burials are absent in clearly public spaces—the mound summit and within the enclosure next to the river. If placing children in urns was something that did not take place in buildings that were more public in nature, then the absence of urn burials in Large Rectangular Structures could mean that these buildings served a more public function within individual kin groups.

The flexed burial position ($n = 67$) remained the most common following mound construction (74 percent). Some adults ($n = 4$) interred within Enclosed Circular Structures were distinctive because they were placed in an extended position. Unlike in Small Circular Structures, though, two individuals within each Enclosed Circular Structure were distinguished in this way. If Enclosed Circular Structures began as houses that were later maintained as cemeteries and if the status signified by the extended burial position was filled by one person per generation in each group, then the presence of two extended burials in each of the Enclosed Circular Structures would be consistent with the notion that the use-life of these structures was longer than the use-life of Small Circular Structures, which would be expected if the former were cemeteries located in the same place as the latter.

Discussion

The overall political organization of the early Town Creek phase community appears to have been relatively diffuse, spread among many individuals and multiple social groups. These groups are represented by the adult women buried in two public buildings, the older adult men and women buried in another public building, and the older adult man buried with a copper axe in a house. The association of adult women with one public building and older adults with another implies that both groups participated in the political process. If the political power of adult women in some native communities was based on their role as clan or lineage leaders (Perdue 1998: 41; Rodning 2001: 96; Sattler 1995: 222; Sullivan 2001: 107), then the inclusion of adult women in a public building at Town Creek may reflect their status as representatives of their kin groups. If the older adults represent a group of esteemed individuals that served as a council, a common political feature in southeastern societies (Braund 1999: 144; Lefler 1967: 204; Muller 1997: 81; Hudson 1976: 225; Moore 1988: 32; Waselkov and Braund 1995: 118), then it seems that individuals could also participate in the political process based on lifetime achievements. The fact that all three adult age classes are represented in premound public buildings indicates that the political process involved individuals from all stages of adulthood. Early Town Creek phase public contexts contain an equal representation of mature adults and older adults, while young adults are the least well represented. This suggests that adults in the latter two stages of their lives were preferred for positions of leadership during the early Town Creek phase, which is consistent with the importance of achievement as a factor in filling community leadership roles at this time.

It is clear from the ethnohistoric record that political relationships within and among kin groups were a major component of a community's political structure (Hudson 1976: 184–185; Knight 1990; Muller 1997: 190–192; Sullivan 2001: 105). The extended burial position of one of the adult women in an early Town Creek phase public building may also speak to a relationship between kinship and politics. The overall distribution of extended burials and their location near the center of Small Circular Structures indicates that individuals buried in this way were distinctive within their kin groups. If the extended burial position signifies some important kinship-based status, then the presence of an extended burial in an early Town Creek phase public building may indicate the importance of kinship within the realm of community leadership at this time. It may have been that the representation of kin groups was an important element of the political process. Also, it is likely that the leaders of households and lineages, perhaps individuals distinguished by the extended burial position and placement near the center of household burial clusters, also participated in community politics during the early Town Creek phase. The fact that an individual who likely was a community leader (based on artifacts—the older adult male with the copper axe) was buried in an extended position in a house rather than a public building is consistent with the importance of kinship in the political process in that at least some community leaders' political roles were equal to their roles within their own households. The fact that the individual with the copper axe was an older adult speaks to the relationship between lifetime achievement and leadership during the early Town Creek phase.

An examination of the people buried in public places during the late Town Creek–Leak phases suggests a somewhat different political situation than that of the premound community. The mound-summit burials for which age could be determined (n = 4) were all young adults. This pattern contrasts with premound public buildings where young adults represented the lowest percentage of any age category. If the mound was the locus of political decision-making within the community, then the exclusive presence of young adults in summit buildings could indicate that a change in the nature of leadership followed the construction of the mound.

Public buildings at Town Creek are overwhelmingly associated with young adults after mound construction. While only 4 percent of young adults in the premound community were buried in public buildings, 37 percent of young adults were buried in public contexts after mound construction. Related to this is the fact that the proportion of the community's older adults buried in public contexts decreased after mound construction, from 19 percent to 5 percent. One possible explanation for the association of young adults with the mound and the rectangular enclosure is that leaders after mound construction may have been associated with risky behaviors that might lead to death at an early age. This could mean that participation in warfare was a prominent activity for leaders; for males, young adulthood was the time when they were most likely to distinguish themselves in this way (Sullivan 2001: 124). The presence of young adult females is more perplexing, though, because the avenues available for women to enhance their status through achievement likely were open during later stages of life (Eastman 2001: 73; Sullivan 2001: 120).

One of the major differences thought to have existed between the political organization of Mississippian and other societies in the Southeast is a transition from informal leadership positions, which were based primarily on the charisma and ability of a singular individual who built and maintained a following, to a formally defined office of leadership, which existed independently of any one person (Scarry 1996: 4; Service 1971: 146; Steponaitis 1986: 983). The absence in the mound of individuals from age categories other than young adult could mean that the status of community leader may not have been held for life following mound construction. Perhaps political leaders gave way to younger rivals at some point and only individuals who died while occupying the status of leader were eligible for mound burial (see Driscoll 2002: 25–26). This is consistent with the idea that an office of "community leader" existed at Town Creek after the mound was built.

Although the leadership positions that existed after mound construction may have been more formal, these positions were not clearly associated with increased political power. An important manifestation of political power in

Mississippian communities would have been the placement of a residence on the summit of a platform mound, the community's symbol of political authority (Anderson 1994: 119–120, 1999: 220; DePratter 1983: 207–208; Milanich et al. 1997: 118; Rudolph 1984: 40; Steponaitis 1986: 386). If the mound was used as a residence, it could be expected that the demographic profiles of the burials on the summit of the mound would be relatively inclusive (Boudreaux 2007a: 88–89). Instead, only one age class is represented on the mound summit and subadults are completely absent. The more restrictive demographic profile associated with the mound summit, unlike the much more representative populations within the enclosed cemeteries around the plaza, is not consistent with the notion that the summit served as a residence for a family (see Brown 1981a: 30; Howell and Kintigh 1996: 538). Another indication that the summit buildings were not domestic is the fact that their spatial configuration was likely very similar to those of the public buildings that immediately preceded mound construction, all of which were clearly distinct from contemporaneous domestic structures (Boudreaux 2005: 236–245). Additionally, although this issue is not discussed here, the vessel data from the mound summit are not consistent with the idea that a residence was located there (Boudreaux 2007a: 99–104). Collectively, the components of the submound public buildings and public buildings on the mound summit at Town Creek do not resemble houses but instead are reminiscent of historically documented sets of public buildings in the Southeast that consisted of a large pavilion used for public meetings that involved feasting and an enclosed building to which access was limited (Waselkov and Braund 1995: 104–105, Figures 21 and 22).

While the individuals buried in premound public buildings were mostly indistinguishable in terms of the kinds and quantities of artifacts with which they were associated, several notable changes within burials in public spaces following mound construction suggest changes in the nature of leadership. It was after the mound was built that some individuals became more distinctive based not only on where but also with what they were buried. All adults during the early Town Creek phase had a NAT value of three or less. Most adults during the late Town Creek–Leak phases also had a NAT value of three or less, but two males who were buried with six artifact types each were distinct from all of the others (Figure 11.12). Assuming that artifact types placed in a burial represent a role played by the individual during life, then the two individuals with the highest NAT values may have been political leaders within the late Town Creek–Leak phase community (see Howell 1995: 129, 1996: 63; Kintigh 2000: 104). This idea is supported by the fact that these two individuals were buried in public spaces, perhaps two of the most exceptional locations in the community after mound construction. One of these individuals was buried on

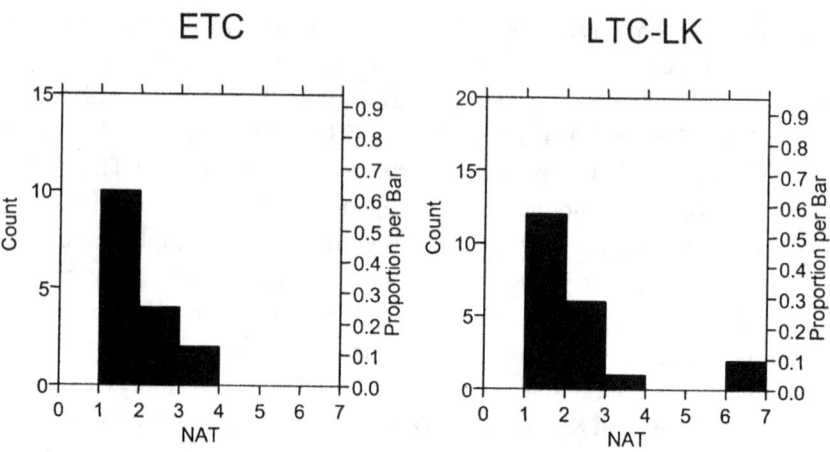

Figure 11.12. Histograms of NAT for Early Town Creek and Late Town Creek–Leak Phase Burials with Grave Goods.

the mound summit (Burial 59) and the other was placed in Structure 51 at the center of the rectangular enclosure across the plaza (Burial 20).

It is possible that the two adult men buried with unique artifacts occupied the same leadership role within the late Town Creek–Leak phase community as the man buried with the copper axe in the early Town Creek phase community. However, the location of the two later burials and the variety of their associated artifacts shows a marked change from the early Town Creek phase pattern in which no individuals were distinguished by their NAT values and in which one of the individuals who most likely represented a community leader based on the evidence of artifacts was buried in a house rather than a public building. The placement of these men with distinctive artifact assemblages in public places, which implies an association with the whole community, rather than in their houses, which implies a primary association with their own families, is consistent with the idea that after mound construction the leadership role they occupied was an office connected with the political institutions of the town rather than something based solely on the abilities of a singular individual who still had strong ties to his own kin group.

Another change regarding artifacts has to do with the percentage of burials that contained grave goods. The percentage of burials with grave goods in the mound (80 percent) is much higher than in both premound public buildings (43 percent) and contemporaneous village burials (33 percent) (Figure 11.13). Also, a comparison of NAT by structure type, standardized by the number of burials, shows that the mound and the rectangular enclosure contain much higher densities of artifact types (Figure 11.14). If grave goods generally can be seen as markers of roles occupied by individuals in life, then the higher per-

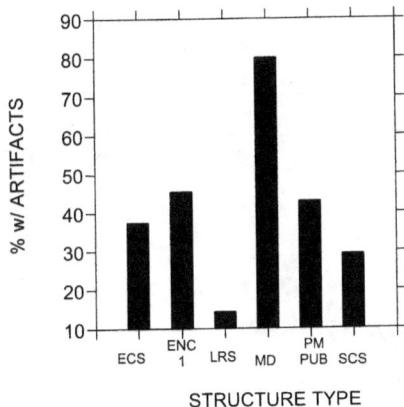

Figure 11.13. Bar Chart Showing Percentages of Burials with Artifacts by Structure Type or Burial Area at Town Creek.

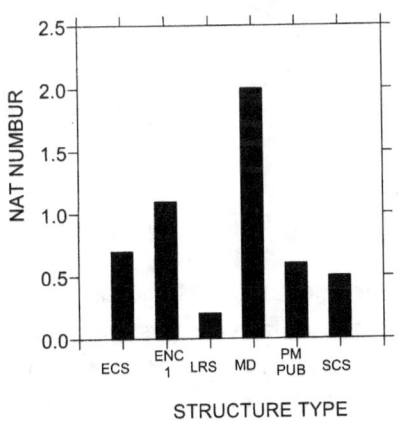

Figure 11.14. NAT Density (NAT/Number of Burials) by Structure Type or Burial Area at Town Creek.

centage of burials in public spaces with grave goods and the higher density of artifact types in contexts after mound construction could mean that individuals buried in public spaces played a more prominent role in the community after mound construction than did their contemporaries who were buried in domestic contexts and their early Town Creek phase predecessors.

The concentration of unusual artifacts within the two primary public spaces is another change that occurred after the mound was built. During the early Town Creek phase, burials in public buildings were not characterized by an association with unusual artifacts. In contrast, distinctive artifacts during the late Town Creek–Leak phases were found only in burials on the mound sum-

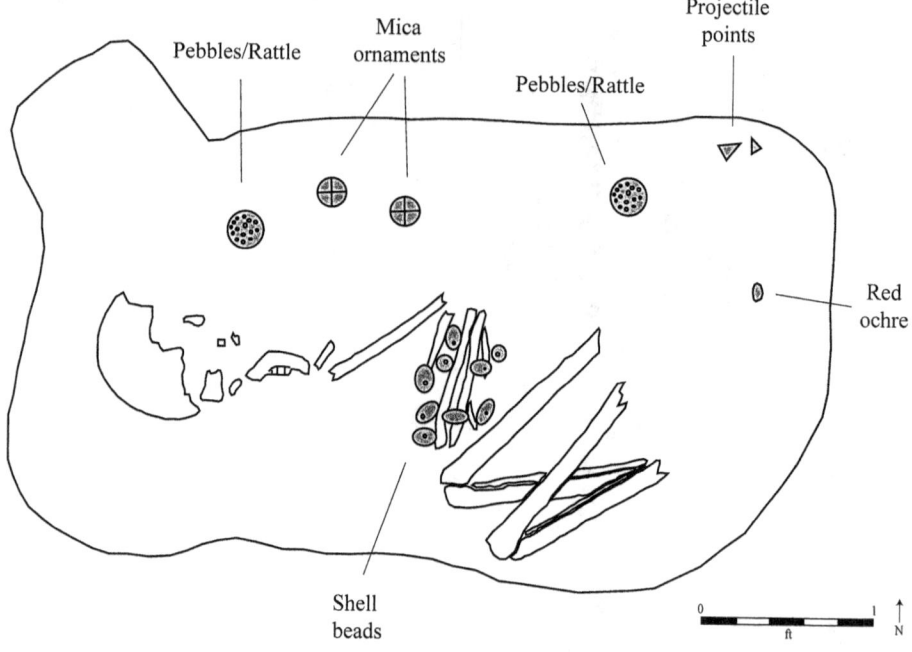

Figure 11.15. Burial 59/Mg2.

mit or within the rectangular enclosure across the plaza (Boudreaux 2007a: 91–93; Driscoll 2002: 22–23). These distinctive artifacts are mostly made from nonlocal materials and include rattles, mica objects, and ear ornaments made from polished stone, copper-covered wooden discs, or marine shell. Most of the individuals associated with these distinctive artifacts (83 percent) were young adults (n = 5). This is not surprising, though, since the unusual artifacts are found only in public buildings, which have a high proportion of young adults. The status signified by these artifacts does not seem to have been linked to sex since they are found with both women and men. The fact that an infant was buried with four types of unusual artifacts, which is a relatively rich grave within the Town Creek burial population, suggests that there may have been an ascriptive element to the status signified by them (see Larson 1971: 66).

The types of artifacts found with some of the public-space burials during the late Town Creek–Leak phases can give us insights into the roles that the individuals buried with them may have played within their communities. The two most distinctive burials (Burials 59/Mg2 and 20/Mg3) both contained rattles and mica (Figures 11.15 and 11.16). Rattles were often used among historic Indians in dances that were a part of social and ritual events (Swanton

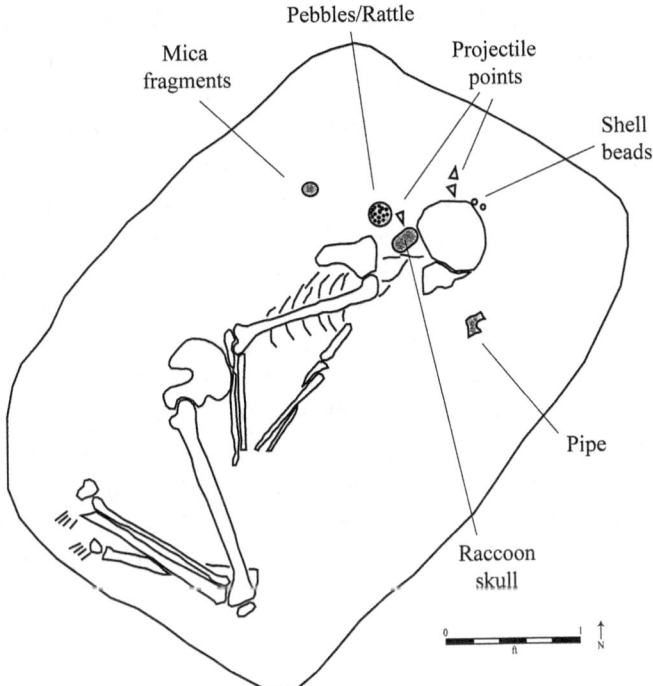

Figure 11.16. Burial 20/Mg3.

1979: 626–627). Based on iconographic depictions, artifact associations, and the ethnohistoric record, it is clear that high-status individuals in at least some Mississippian communities played critical roles in community rituals (Blitz 1993: 92; Dye 2000: 11; Emerson 1997: 258; Kenton 1927: 427; Knight 1989b: 209; Larson 1957: 9, 1989: 140; McWilliams 1988: 92; Pauketat 1994: 183–184). The association of rattles exclusively with public spaces during the late Town Creek–Leak phases at Town Creek and their presence in the burials of community leaders is consistent with this idea. The distribution of mica during the late Town Creek–Leak phases, which may have been part of regalia worn during rituals (Blitz 1993: 86; Larson 1989: 140), is also consistent with the idea that the mound summit and the rectangular enclosure at Town Creek contained burials of individuals who played important roles in rituals. Additionally, the distinctive burial on the mound also contained a lump of red ochre, a mineral thought to have been important as a pigment in various ritual contexts (Blitz 1993: 86). In addition to mica fragments and a rattle, the distinctive burial at the center of the rectangular enclosure also contained a ceramic pipe and a raccoon skull. Among historic groups, pipes were an integral part of meetings that took place in public buildings (Waselkov and Braund 1995: 50, 72, 102, and 104). Raccoons were frequently depicted in Mississippian iconography (Phillips and Brown 1978: 136 and 154–155), indicating that they were an important part of the belief system. Interestingly, southeastern Indians made pouches from their hides (Swanton 1979: 250). The presence of a skull is consistent with the fact that the animal's head sometimes figured prominently into the design of a pouch (Swanton 1979: 480). The raccoon skull was found near a cluster of pebbles that indicated the presence of a rattle, an item that could have been enclosed in a pouch. Among southeastern Indians, pouches were used by ritual practitioners to hold a variety of sacred objects (Dye 2000: 11; Hudson 1976: 370; Moore 1988: 42–43; Swanton 1979: 477–479). Although the exact significance of the raccoon skull will never be known, the fact that it was from an animal that was depicted in religious art and that it may have been part of a pouch that contained a rattle is consistent with the idea that the man buried at the center of the rectangular enclosure played a prominent role in the ritual life of the community at Town Creek after the construction of the mound.

Conclusion

An important assumption underlying many interpretations of Mississippian societies is that the presence of a mound signifies major differences in population dynamics as well as social and political organization (Anderson 1994: 80; Hally 1999; Holley 1999: 33–35; Lewis and Stout 1998: 231–232; Lindauer and Blitz 1997; Milner and Schroeder 1999: 96; Muller 1997: 275–276; Steponaitis 1978, 1986: 389–392). The archaeological record from Town Creek has provided an opportunity to evaluate this assumption with community-wide architectural and mortuary data from public and domestic contexts that preceded and followed mound construction. The premound mortuary data suggest that decision making was shared among multiple contexts and by multiple social groups. There is no indication from the archaeological data that any one of these groups—the women in public buildings, the older adults in public buildings, the older adult male with the copper axe, or the adult men and women at the center of household burial clusters—played a more prominent role in the community's political decision-making process than did any other group. The seemingly diffuse nature of political power within the early Mississippian community at Town Creek is consistent with the concept of heterarchy, a form of societal organization in which power is shared or counterpoised among multiple groups (Crumley 1987, 1995). Heterarchy, which was introduced as an alternative or complement to the concept of hierarchy, describes situations in which social and political relationships are complex but not necessarily hierarchical (Crumley 1995: 3). Political decision making within the early Town Creek phase community may have consisted of negotiations among kin group leaders, a council of older adults, and an individual recognized as a community leader or chief. Political power also could have been situational, with one group holding more sway under certain conditions, such as at ritual events or during times of war (Knight 1990: 6; Sullivan 2001: 104).

The architectural and mortuary patterns from Town Creek indicate that significant changes were associated with mound construction. The mound appears at or about the same time that corporate group cemeteries and public buildings replaced houses around the plaza. Mortuary data indicate that there were changes in the nature of leadership as well. The differences in the composition of the burial populations between premound public buildings (which emphasized older and mature adults) and postmound public buildings (which emphasized young adults), coupled with the presence of new artifact types suggests that the people buried in public spaces after mound construction occupied new social and political roles. The distinctiveness of public-space burials after mound construction in terms of the kinds and quantities of associated artifacts suggests that these people may have played more prominent roles within the ritual life of the community, which is consistent with an increase in political authority (see Brown 1981a: 29).

Although community leaders after mound construction may have had more authority, there does not appear to have been a concomitant increase in power. Mississippian platform mounds were communal monuments that symbolized group identity, among other things (Knight 1989a: 287). Although leaders in some Mississippian societies were able to co-opt the power and symbolism of earthen mounds by placing residences on their summits (Brown 1997: 475; Knight 1998: 60; Steponaitis 1986: 386), the data from Town Creek do not support the idea that a residence was located on the mound summit there (Boudreaux 2007a: 114). The mortuary evidence shows age-class biases that are not consistent with the burials on the mound representing a household group (Brown 1981a: 30; Howell and Kintigh 1996: 541). The demographically restricted burial population associated with the mound is unlike the much more representative populations associated with the circular structures and enclosed cemeteries around the plaza, which probably represent households or kin-based groups. Another indication that the summit buildings were not domestic is that their configuration was likely very similar to those of the public buildings that immediately preceded mound construction, all of which were clearly distinct in several ways from contemporaneous domestic structures. Also, the ceramic evidence, which is not presented here (see Boudreaux

2005, 2007a: 99–104), shows that the mound summit assemblage was not like other domestic assemblages at the site. The composition of the assemblage is consistent with cooking for and serving large groups, which suggests that the mound may have been the locus of large group gatherings that were integrative in purpose (Boudreaux 2005: 393–394, 2007a: 103). The absence of houses around the plaza after mound construction indicates that settlement within the Town Creek community was more dispersed at this time. The individuals buried in public spaces with unusual artifacts probably played prominent roles in the ritual life of the community, and these rituals may have integrated a larger or more dispersed population following mound construction.

The absence of a residence on the mound summit and the location of multiple social groups in prominent locations within the community suggest that Town Creek's political structure was still heterarchical after the mound was built, even though the burial treatments of some individuals were more distinctive. The political situation of the community before mound construction appears to have been heterarchical, complexly but not hierarchically organized (see Crumley 1995: 3). Different social and political elements were present after mound construction, but these may have been heterarchically arranged as well. As was the case before the mound was built, multiple social groups occupied preeminent positions within the community after mound construction. The people buried in the mound, the rectangular enclosure, the kin-group cemeteries, and the kin-group public buildings may all represent distinctive social groups that participated in the political process following mound construction.

At many Mississippian sites, mound construction was used by emerging leaders as an arena for political competition within the context of existing kinship/corporate group relationships (Knight 1998: 59–60). At the Moundville site in Alabama, for example, emergent political leaders competed within the existing kinship structure by incorporating their residences into corporate group buildings on the summits of mounds (Knight 1998: 60). While corporate group public buildings were built around the plaza at Town Creek as well, a key difference is that public buildings did not serve as residences, indicating that at Town Creek there was not an exclusive link between an individual or a particular family and a public building. Knight (1998: 60) argues that the spatial arrangement of mounds at Moundville, primarily the construction of a massive mound that was the residence of a leader on the site's central axis, reflects the ability of leaders to transcend the traditional kinship structure and assume the role of a paramount chief. While corporate groups and their public buildings also were the fundamental components of the community at Town Creek, it seems that the absence of intense economic, political, and social competition meant that public buildings were not exclusively associated with particular leaders. Instead, a heterarchical political organization and the use of the platform mound as an integrative facility that remained a symbol of group identity seems to have persisted throughout the existence of the Town Creek community.

Notes

1. All dates are based on uncorrected radiocarbon dates. See Boudreaux 2007a: Table 1.1 for calibrated dates. See Boudreaux 2005 and 2007b for an extended discussion of both the calibrated and uncalibrated dates.

2. Age and sex information comes primarily from Patricia Lambert's analysis of the human skeletal remains for the site's Native American Graves Protection and Repatriation Act inventory (Davis et al. 1996). Age and sex determinations for individuals not included in Lambert's analysis came from Elizabeth Driscoll's (2001) dissertation. Lambert and Driscoll's age determinations were used to assign each individual to an age class. The classes are children (5 years of age and younger), adolescents (6 to 14 years), young adults (15 to 24 years), mature adults (25 to 34 years), and older adults (35 years and older).

12

Mortuary Practices and Cultural Identity at the Turn of the Sixteenth Century in Eastern Tennessee

LYNNE P. SULLIVAN AND MICHAELYN S. HARLE

Culturally ascribed identity groups "are based on the expression of a real or assumed shared culture and common descent" (Jones 1997: 84). Cultural identity can be correlated with suites of cultural practices or traditions, especially those related to ritual and symbolic practices (Beck 1995), and those that differentiate various social dimensions, such as gender and status differentiation or the organization of space (see Eriksen 1991). The importance of cultural identity as a social boundary and the impact it can have on human relationships encourages efforts to examine such differences among peoples in the prehistoric past.

Data concerning mortuary practices are well suited for making observations related to cultural identity. Mortuary practices are among the most symbolically charged cultural practices that can be archaeologically observed (Beck 1995; Emberling 1997; Emerson and Hargrave 2000). Mortuary practices also can provide insights into ritual and into differentiation across social dimensions such as gender and status. But just as differences in pottery styles may not correlate directly with social boundaries (Wobst 1977; but see Bowser 2000), differences in mortuary practices alone may not reflect difference in cultural identity. A case must be built that uses mortuary practices to recognize multiple dimensions of cultural practice and tradition. This case should be bolstered with analyses from other data classes that can indicate cultural differences so profound that they likely relate to past peoples' constructions of differing cultural identities.

We examine multiple dimensions of mortuary practices observed at two contemporaneous late Mississippian sites in order to revisit a long-standing discussion in the archaeology of Eastern Tennessee about the relationship and cultural identities of the Mouse Creek and Dallas phases. In the 1940s, Lewis and Kneberg (1946) correlated these archaeological complexes with differing cultural groups, the Yuchi and Creek, respectively. Mortuary practices were among the traits they used to make this distinction. We now know that Lewis and Kneberg's uncritical use of the direct historic approach and the absence of a more finely tuned understanding of regional chronologies and cultural attributes seriously undermine this correlation (Boyd and Boyd 1991: 84; Sullivan 2007a, 2007b). Our exploratory and more nuanced analysis allows us to suggest that Lewis and Kneberg's basic observation—that these archaeological complexes likely correlate with different cultural groups—was correct, but for all the wrong reasons.

Cultural Identity and Archaeological Perception

Cultural identity often is equated or conflated with ethnicity, but the two actually are distinct concepts and, as Eriksen notes, "there is no one-to-one relationship between culture and ethnicity" (Eriksen 1992: 43). While *cultural identity* can reference an "ensemble of cultural features that collectively constitutes the larger reality with which a person or group is identified through a certain name" (Gleason 1996: 480), *ethnicity* connotes kinship. The two are not necessarily congruent. Eriksen (1992: 43) further points out that

> cultural differences cut across ethnic boundaries, and ... ethnic identity is based on *socially sanctioned notions* of cultural differences, not "real" ones. While ethnic identity should be taken to refer to a notion of shared ancestry (a kind of fictive kinship), culture refers to shared representations, norms and practices. One can have deep ethnic differences without correspondingly important cultural differences ... and one can have cultural variation without ethnic boundaries.

One only has to contemplate "northern" versus "southern" in modern-day American culture to grasp the difficulties in distinguishing cultural differences in ethnicity, nationality, race, regionalism, and historical processes as factors in differences in dialect, cuisine, and political persuasions, among other variations in cultural practices (Sollors 1996). Yet one cannot overlook the significance of these differences—perceived or real—in constructing cultural identity. Accordingly, we adhere to the term "cultural identity" because it subsumes multiple scales along which differences in identity can be perceived or constructed but that may or may not include real or fictive kinship.

On a smaller scale, distinct social enclaves often exist within a broader cultural tradition that may or may not relate to ethnicity (Gulliver 1969: 22–3; Hill et al. 2004). Such enclaves may have their own dialects and their own versions of cultural practices that distinguish them from other such groups within the larger tradition. Such differences are well known among native groups in the Southeast. Groups that we may more readily correlate with conventional notions of ethnicity, such as the Cherokee, to this day maintain enclaves with distinct dialects and cultural practices, as did the historically known Overhill, Middle, Out, and Valley towns (King 1979). As a result, one can be both "Cherokee" and a member of a distinct community or enclave within the larger cultural tradition. Membership in these culturally distinct units is deeply integral to an individual's social persona and his or her interactions with others, both within and outside the larger group.

Regardless of these distinctions between ethnicity and cultural identity, much anthropological thinking about ethnic groups and ethnicity is applicable to distinctions in cultural identity, broadly writ (e.g., Banks 1996). Cohen (1978: 378) notes that like cultural identity, the perception and expression of ethnic identity also is scalar and "can vary in different situations depending on the context and scale of interaction, resulting in a series of nesting dichotomizations." Both ethnic and cultural identity can become altered or blended through interaction with others. Persons or groups can shift their identities for many reasons, including social, political, or economic relationships (Barth 1969). This multidimensional and rather fluid nature of identity makes it especially difficult to recognize in the archaeological record because identity can be a moving target that can shift depending on temporal, spatial, and circumstantial contexts.

Nevertheless, the cultural differences that inform constructions of cultural identity have to be systematic and enduring to varying degrees because these differences inform the ways people of differing identity interact, and interactions confirm the differences. As Jones reminds us, cultural identity is "reproduced and transformed in the ongoing processes of social life" (Jones 1997: 84), and as a process, cultural identity reproduces and transforms "basic classificatory distinctions between groups of people who perceive themselves to be in some respect culturally distinct" (Jones 1997: 84). Tradition thus is bound up with cultural identity because tradition materializes ways of "being and doing" that connote cultural differences (Pauketat 2001b: 2-3; S. J. Shennan 1993).

The archaeological problem in identifying differences in cultural identity, then, is to identify classificatory or cultural distinctions that prehistoric peoples perceived segregated themselves from other peoples, to the extent that these differences created perceptions of distinct identities. As noted above, it is likely that such distinctions involved basic cultural constructs and traditions such as gender and status differentiation, the organization of space, or ritual and symbolic practices (Eriksen 1992: 6-7, 50). To the archaeologist, such distinctions are most obvious across large expanses of space and time.

When there is direct cultural interaction and some shared technologies, ideologies, or symbolism, such as among Mississippian groups, it can be more difficult to recognize significant and important differences that may relate to cultural identity. We suggest that the degree to which archaeologically defined and observed suites of cultural practices suggest programs of differing cultural traditions and differing trajectories of cultural development may well correlate with the degree to which people consider(ed) themselves as having shared or separate identities in a scalar way.

Identifying cultural identity in archaeology is thus by nature a comparative process, and any such analysis must examine multiple data classes (Jones 1997: 126), both to identify possible distinctions in cultural practices and to assess the degree to which such distinctions may have segregated or unified the groups being compared. Spatially bounded nonurban settlements[1] that provide evidence of a wide variety of cultural practices beyond the individual household level may be one archaeological entity that offers a clear point of comparison. Such residential communities also imply a certain degree of social boundedness, although it is the connections between these communities that are of interest in regard to cultural identity.

Comparing archaeological sites to determine their similarities or differences is certainly not new to archaeology. We suggest that the focus of comparisons that seek to identify culturally distinct groups must move beyond simple comparisons of material culture types to comparisons of the cultural practices for which constellations of material culture are the signature. With this goal in mind, archaeologists can bridge the study of material culture with the realm of systematic cultural comparisons. There have been some forays into such archaeological ethnology with large-scale comparisons of the development of Mississippian political systems (e.g., King 2001; Wilson et al. 2006), but these differ from the smaller-scale detailed comparisons that must be made to discover differences in cultural identity, especially when sites are in relatively close spatial proximity.

The Ledford Island and Fains Island Sites

For this exploratory study, we compare several cultural practices (especially those that can be discerned from mortuary practices) of two contemporary groups—the mid- to late-fifteenth-century inhabitants of the Fains Island and Ledford Island sites. Both sites are on islands in tributaries of the Tennessee River. Ledford Island is in the lower Hiwassee River, while Fains Island is approximately 100 miles north in the lower French Broad River (see Figure 1.1). Both sites were excavated in the 1930s by Works Progress Administration

238 Lynne P. Sullivan and Michaelyn S. Harle

Table 12.1. Dates for the Ledford Island and Fains Island Sites

Site	Conventional Radiocarbon Age	Calibrated Intercept[a]	1 sigma (probability)	2 sigma (probability)
Ledford Island (40BY13)[b]	450±50	A.D. 1445	A.D. 1414–A.D. 1481 (100%)	A.D. 1334–A.D. 1336 (0%)
				A.D. 1398–A.D. 1524 (88%)
				A.D. 1559–A.D. 1564 (0%)
				A.D. 1570–A.D. 1631 (12%)
Fains Island (40JE1)[c]	370±30	A.D. 1490	A.D. 1454–A.D. 1518 (72%)	A.D. 1447–A.D. 1527 (58%)
			A.D. 1594–A.D. 1619 (28%)	A.D. 1553–A.D. 1633 (42%)

Notes: [a]Stuiver et al. 1998
[b]The date is from wood charcoal from a typical structure (Sullivan 1986).
[c]The AMS date is from a bone awl in a feature in the upper half of the platform mound (Harle 2003).

(WPA) crews under the direction of University of Tennessee archaeologists before Tennessee Valley Authority reservoirs were impounded. Ledford Island is now in the Chickamauga Reservoir while Fains Island is in Douglas Reservoir. The Fains Island site was a town with a platform mound (Harle 2003). Ledford Island did not have a mound but also was a central town (Sullivan 1987, 1989).

In the 1940s, Lewis and Kneberg (1946) recognized differences between the sites and assigned the Ledford Island site to the Mouse Creek phase and Fains Island to the Dallas phase (Harle 2003). However, Lewis and Kneberg's understanding of the temporal and spatial contexts of these sites and of the Dallas and Mouse Creek phases was flawed. Both phases originally were defined based on excavations and analyses of sites in the Chickamauga Basin (Lewis and Kneberg 1946; Lewis et al. 1995) and were thought to be contemporary there. We now know based on further analyses and radiocarbon dating that the Dallas phase actually predates the Mouse Creek phase in the Chickamauga Basin (Sullivan 2007a, 2007b). The Dallas phase in Chickamauga dates to the fourteenth and early fifteenth centuries, while the Mouse Creek phase dates to the mid-fifteenth and early sixteenth centuries. Elsewhere in the Upper Tennessee Valley, including along the French Broad River, the Dallas phase has not been segmented and encompasses the fourteenth through sixteenth centuries. The Mouse Creek phase can thus be considered the latter part of

"Dallas" in the Chickamauga Basin. Furthermore, biocultural studies have shown that Mouse Creek phase and Dallas phase populations from Chickamauga Reservoir sites are not biologically distinct (Boyd and Boyd 1991), and radiocarbon dates show that the Mouse Creek phase Ledford Island site and the Dallas phase Fains Island site are contemporary (Table 12.1).

Site Comparisons

Our comparisons cover several aspects of the community plan and spatial dimensions of the mortuary practices as well as the deposition of burials and the use of funerary objects as they relate to status and gender distinctions. (Of course, many more aspects could be explored.) We first describe the observed patterns and then discuss the implications for cultural practices, including differentiation of status and gender roles, the overall character of the mortuary programs, and the implications for distinctive rituals. All of these data sets and comparisons relate to cultural traditions and symbolism and are fundamentally different from the trait lists of material culture differences Lewis and Kneberg made (1946: 169–179). The trait lists emphasized artifact attributes and typologies but not the contexts of the objects, such as mortuary associations based on sex and age. Lewis and Kneberg's lists do include a few traits more directly indicative of cultural practices, such as burial placement and deposition, but they did not contextualize these practices and consider them to be aspects of cultural traditions related to status, gender roles, and ritual, as our comparison strives to do. Finally, we include some preliminary observations on ceramic assemblages that may correlate with differential trajectories of cultural development.

Community Plan and Spatial Dimensions of Mortuary Practices

We know more about the overall community plan of the Ledford Island site than we do for Fains Island. The palisaded Ledford Island site included a large central plaza surrounded by domestic structures and a large public building located on the plaza's north side (Figure 12.1). There are no sites with platform mounds associated with the Mouse Creek phase. Ledford Island was the central town for several contemporary villages located on the lower Hiwassee and adjacent sections of the Tennessee River.

Fains Island also likely was a central town for several smaller sites. It had a platform mound surrounded by a village. The WPA crews excavated the entire mound but dug only a small trench through the village deposits. We can presume (but we do not know) that it had a central plaza surrounded by

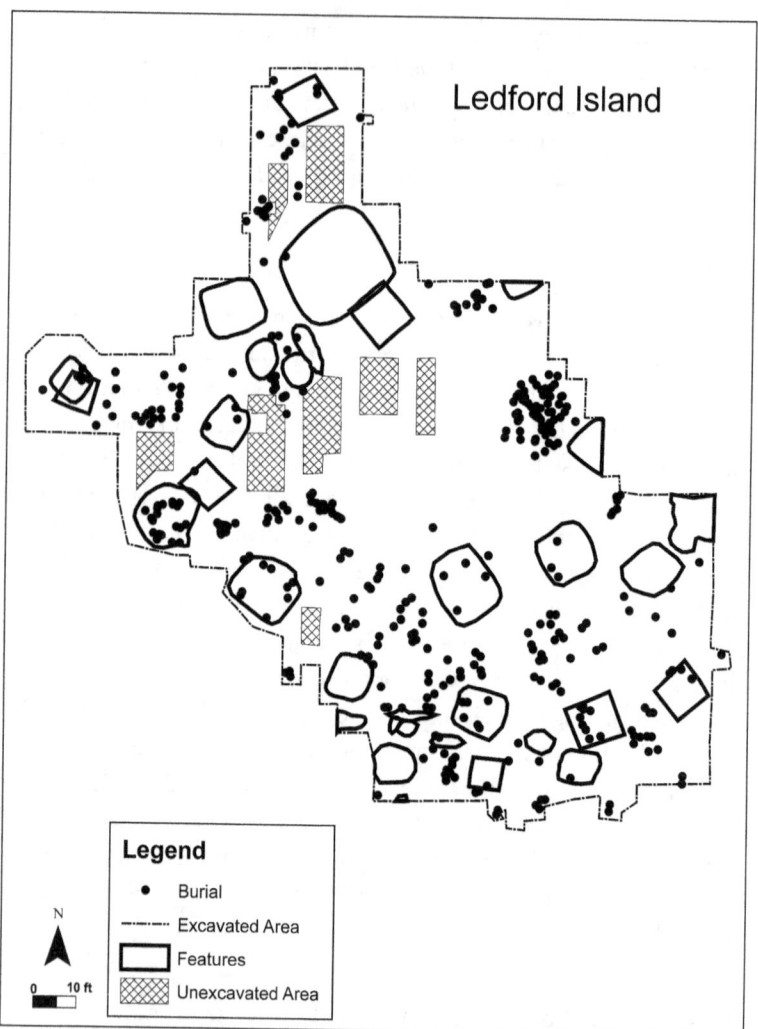

Figure 12.1. Ledford Island Site Plan.

domestic structures, as at other Dallas sites. The Fains Island mound consisted of three construction stages, each topped with a single large building (Figure 12.2). This structure was rebuilt or refurbished in five episodes.

The spatial placement of burials is very different at the two sites. At Ledford Island, most burials were placed in and around domestic household structures, but a large group of individuals was interred in a spatially segregated cemetery on the northeastern edge of the plaza. One burial, an infant, was interred in a corner of the large building on the plaza. The burials associated with households were placed either in the floors of the primary (winter) dwellings or in small cemeteries around secondary (summer) structures that likely

At the Turn of the Sixteenth Century in Eastern Tennessee   241

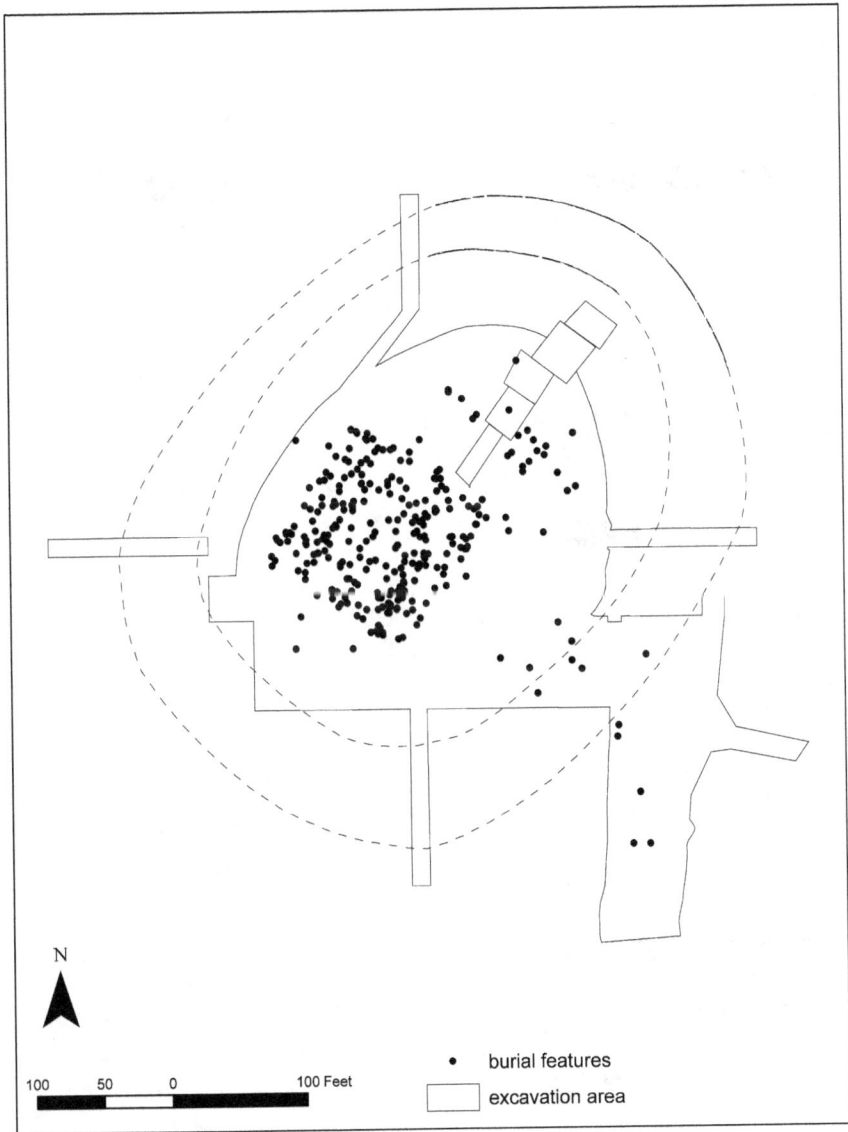

Figure 12.2. Fains Island Site Plan.

served as activity areas in warm weather (Sullivan 1987). Although we do not know the patterning of any burials in the village area at Fains, the mound included the largest burial population in any excavated Dallas phase mound (a point to which we will return). All but seven individuals in the mound were interred in the floors of one of the single large buildings built on the mound summits (Harle 2003).

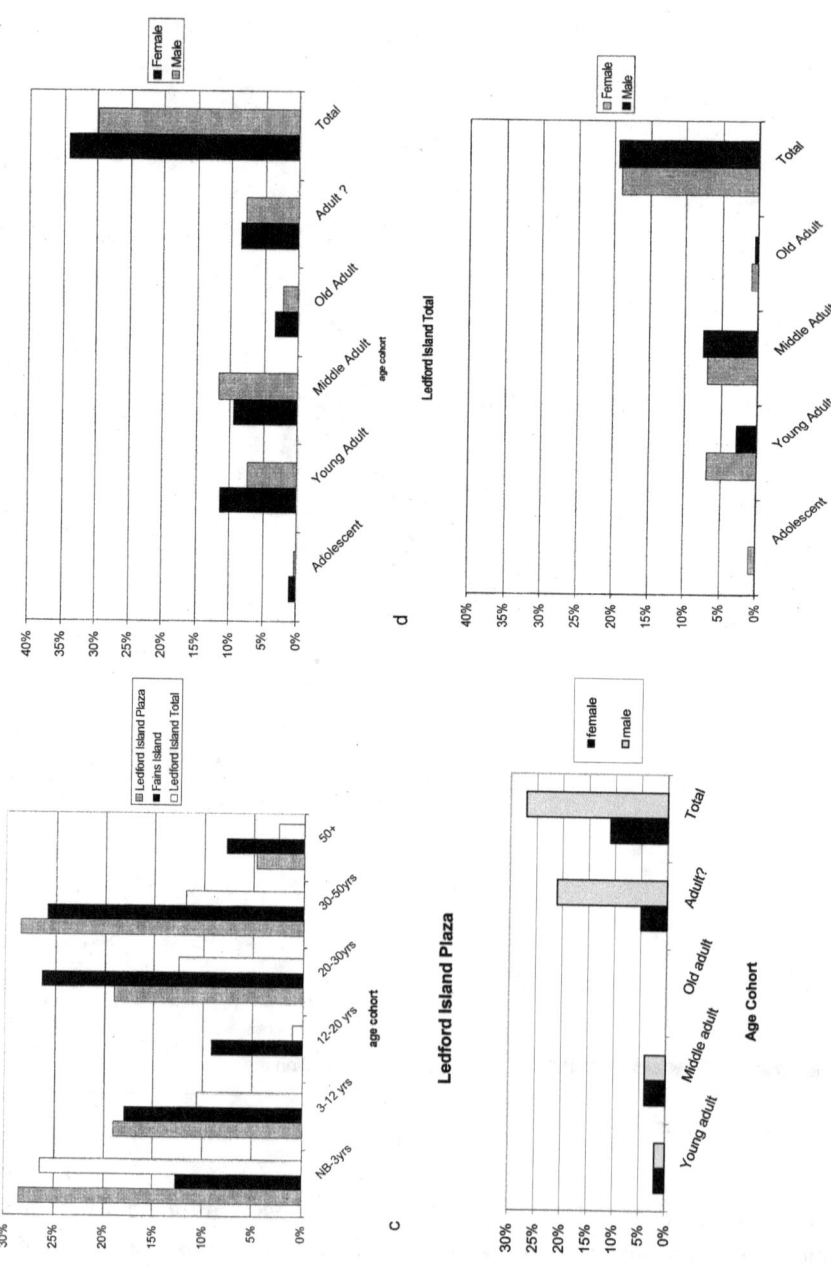

Figure 12.3. Comparison of the Demographic Profiles of the Ledford Island and Fains Island Burials. Age groups at both sites (a); age and sex of Fains Island total individuals (b); age and sex of Ledford Island plaza group (c); age and sex of Ledford Island total individuals (d).

Patterns in age and sex demographics as they relate to the spatial patterning of burials at the two sites also are quite different. Let us first presume that interment in the plaza cemetery at Ledford Island is comparable to burial in the mound at Fains because both are public places of burial (Figure 12.3a). The Ledford Island cemetery included 86 individuals, of which 60 percent (20) of the sexable individuals are adult males (Figure 12.3b). Very few subadults (10) and adult females (9) were interred in this cemetery (Sullivan 1986). In contrast, the 338 individuals in the Fains Island mound include a more equitable representation of both sexes and all age groups, and in fact, adult women are more numerous than adult men, although not in statistically significant numbers (Figure 12.3c). Of the sexable individuals, 75 were males and 84 were females (Harle 2003).

If we consider the entire burial sample at Ledford Island and look at the spatial patterning of the household burials, we see that the individuals buried in the floors of the winter houses were infants and young children. Older children and adults were interred around the summer structures (Sullivan 1986, 1987). The burial population from the entire excavated area at Ledford Island is demographically similar to the burial population in the Fains Island mound (Figure 12.3a, d). Given the relatively short use span of the Fains Island mound and given the size of mound burial populations at other Dallas phase sites that appear to have been occupied for much longer periods of time, such as Toqua in the Little Tennessee Valley (Polhemus et al. 1987), we have to wonder if the mound at Fains was used as the place of interment for most residents (Harle 2003). As a point of reference, the mounds at the Toqua site included less than 100 individuals each. It is unlikely that people were being brought from outlying villages to be buried in the Fains Island mound because the mound burials are primary interments and there are graves at contemporary villages in the surrounding area (Polhemus n.d.; Rowe and Whiteford n.d.).

Burial Deposition and the Use of Funerary Objects

Another aspect of mortuary practice that is quite different at the two sites is burial deposition (Figure 12.4). This difference was, in fact, one of the traits Lewis and Kneberg (1946; Lewis et al. 1995) used to differentiate the Mouse Creek and Dallas phases. The vast majority of individuals at the Ledford Island site—both in the plaza cemetery and in the households—were buried in an extended position (Sullivan 1986), while those at Fains were buried in flexed positions (Harle 2003).

The occurrences and uses of funerary objects are also somewhat different in the two "public" cemeteries, that is, the Ledford Island plaza cemetery and

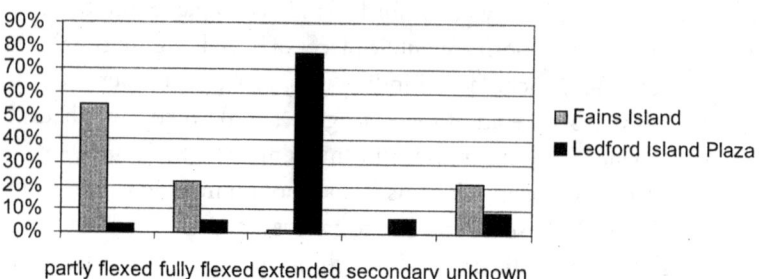

Figure 12.4. Burial Deposition at Ledford Island Plaza Cemetery and Fains Island Mound.

the Fains Island mound (Figure 12.5). The majority of sexed and aged individuals in the Ledford Island plaza cemetery are adult males, and 40 percent of these individuals have associated objects. The few subadults buried in the Ledford Island plaza cemetery have no associated funerary objects, and only one of the nine females in this cemetery has associated objects (Sullivan 1986). In the Fains Island mound, like the Ledford Island plaza cemetery, adult males are the most likely group to have preserved funerary objects. But the incidence was much higher at Fains Island than at Ledford Island: at Fains Island, 70 percent of the adult males were interred with some type of object.

When the entire burial samples from the two sites are compared, the differences hold for the males but not for the females and subadaults. There are significantly fewer adult males with associated objects (30 percent) at Ledford Island than in the Fains Island mound. However, the percentages of adult females and subadults with associated objects are similar; as at Ledford Island, at Fains Island, about 30 percent of both adult females and subadults were buried with associated objects (Harle 2003).

Some of these differences have to do with funerary objects that relate to personal ornamentation. Again, many more individuals were interred with ornaments (beads, hairpins, earpins, pendants, and gorgets) at Fains Island than in the Ledford Island plaza (Figure 12.6). This difference is exaggerated because at other Dallas phase–related sites, ornaments most typically are associated with women and children, and both of these groups are seriously underrepresented in the Ledford Island plaza cemetery. Nonetheless, more adult males with ornaments than females with ornaments are in the Fains Island mound. The Fains Island adult males also are more likely to have ornaments than their contemporaries at all three large Mouse Creek phase sites—Ledford Island, Rymer, and Mouse Creek—that have been excavated on the lower Hi-

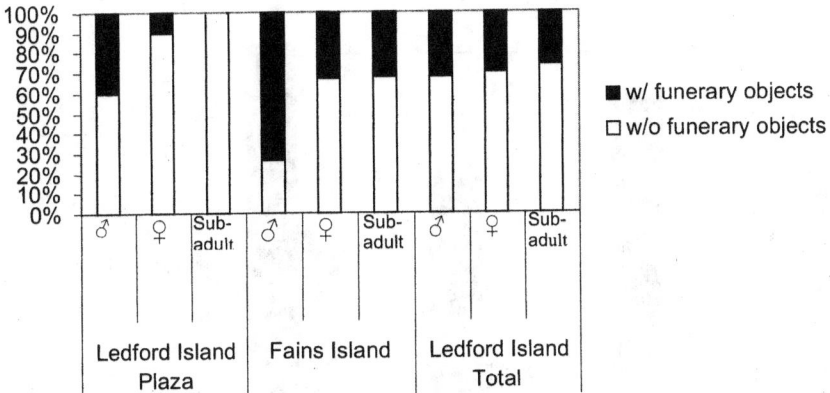

Figure 12.5. Occurrence of Funerary Objects by Age and Sex at Ledford Island and Fains Island.

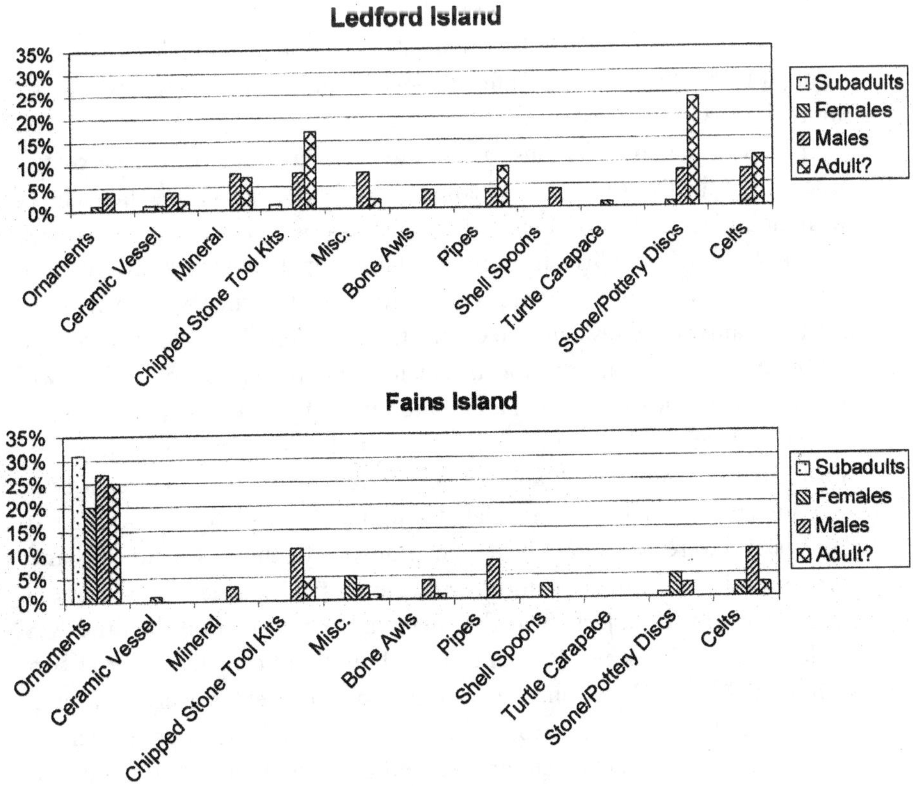

Figure 12.6. Occurrence of Objects by Age and Sex in the Fains Island Mound and the Ledford Island Plaza Cemeteries.

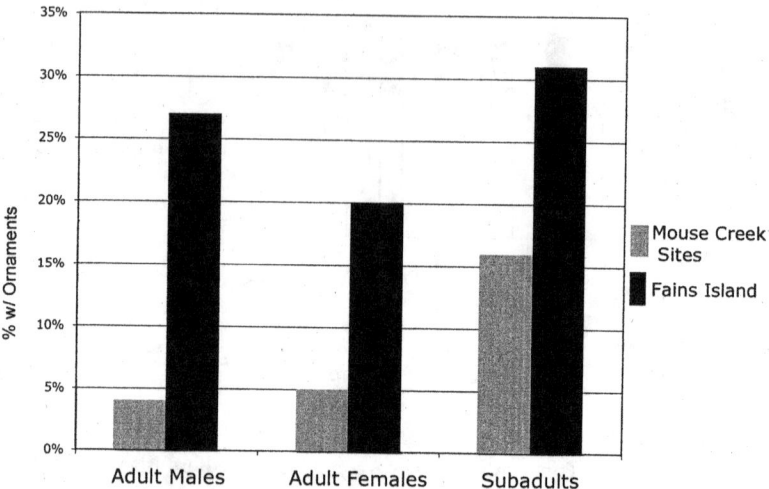

Figure 12.7. Occurrence of Ornaments by Age and Sex in the Fains Island Mound and Three Mouse Creek Phase Sites.

wassee River (Figure 12.7). In fact, there also are more adult males with ornaments at Fains Island than adult females or subadults with ornaments at these three Mouse Creek phase sites.

These comparisons demonstrate significant differences in the mortuary programs at the Fains Island and Ledford Island sites. Fains Island had a platform mound topped with a building in which people of both sexes and all age groups were interred. Given the number of individuals and the relatively short duration of mound use, the mound may have been the primary place of interment for Fains Island residents. In contrast, the residents of Ledford Island did not build a mound. They did construct a large building adjacent to the town plaza, but with the exception of an infant burial, this structure did not serve as a place for graves. Instead, a select group of individuals, mainly adult males, was buried in a cemetery that was also adjacent to the plaza. Other people were interred in cemeteries associated with households. Most individuals at Fains Island were interred in flexed positions, while those at Ledford Island were buried in extended positions. Adult males at Fains Island were more often interred with objects related to personal ornamentation than those at Ledford Island (in either the plaza or the household cemeteries) or at two additional Mouse Creek phase sites that have been extensively excavated (Lewis et al. 1995; Sullivan 1986). Adult males at Fains Island also were more often buried with ornaments than were either adult females or subadults at the three, extensively excavated, Mouse Creek phase sites on the Hiwassee River.

Implications for Cultural Practices

These differences in mortuary practices suggest interesting differences between the prehistoric residents of Fains Island and Ledford Island. Gender role distinctions among the two groups appear to be reflected in differing ways in the mortuary programs. At Fains, there are more females in the mound than males, but women are less likely to have associated preserved artifacts (Harle 2003). At Ledford Island, women are less likely to be buried in the plaza cemetery, but they are as likely to be buried with nonperishable objects as men (Sullivan 1986). Nuances of age and types of funerary objects are yet to be explored among the gender groups. In any case, while there clearly are gendered distinctions in the mortuary programs, neither program suggests dominance of one gender over the other.

Another gender-related distinction is how objects of personal adornment were placed with adult males at Fains Island. While we cannot say that these objects were actually worn by the men, it is nonetheless tempting to suggest that the Fains Island men used such ornamentation as a way to express their personal and possibly their cultural identities. Within the cultural tradition at Fains Island, men may have used certain ornamentation to display certain social statuses. The fact that the Mouse Creek phase men did not share this tradition indicates a difference in cultural practice that possibly was related to cultural identity (see Joyce 2005). Even if the ornaments were not part of actual costumes worn by men in life, the tradition of interring such objects with the dead clearly differed between the Fains Island and Mouse Creek phase sites.

Other differences in mortuary practices suggest that differing rituals were conducted at the two sites. These differences include body placement in the grave (flexed vs. extended), and the use of a mound-top building for the burial of many (if not the vast majority of) Fains Island residents, as opposed to use of a plaza cemetery at Ledford Island for certain individuals and household burial for others. The composition of the audiences for burial ceremonies at the two sites also may have differed. While the mound-top building at Fains Island is in a public space, actual burial may have been a more private affair, removed from village life by virtue of being indoors and on a mound. However, the actual act of burial could well have been removed from other more public ceremonies for the dead. It is hard to imagine a burial ceremony in the plaza at Ledford Island being anything other than a public affair. Interment in a house floor or household cemetery was likely more private, but as with burial in the building on the Fains Island mound, public ceremonies for the dead could have been held separately from actual burial of the body.

Interaction Spheres, Cultural Identity, and Scales of Difference

Before we delve further into the magnitude of these differences between the mortuary programs at these two sites as they may relate to cultural identity, we need to contextualize the sites in the possible effects of regional interaction spheres on trajectories of cultural development. The geographical locations of the Fains Island and Ledford Island sites are close to sites of archaeological complexes that are not related to the Dallas phase. Many Pisgah phase sites are known upstream from Fains Island on the French Broad River, while the Chickamauga Basin is near the Lamar phase sites of northern Georgia. There are a few Pisgah sherds in the Fains Island ceramic assemblage, while Lamar series complicated stamped sherds are known at Chickamauga Basin sites (especially sherds of the earlier Etowah and Wilbanks phases; Sullivan 2007b). There are no Pisgah sherds known at Chickamauga Basin sites and likewise there are no sherds more common to northern Georgia at Fains Island (Howell 2005). The presence of these types of sherds suggests that Fains Island residents likely interacted with groups to the east while Ledford Island's prehistoric inhabitants had interaction spheres that extended to the south.

These differing spheres of interaction undoubtedly were a factor in the differences in the cultural practices of the Fains Island and Ledford Island inhabitants. Interaction spheres are catalysts for change, through incorporation of, alteration of, or resistance to new ideas. Exposure to differing interaction spheres thus is a process that can create differing trajectories of cultural development and is related to the shifting and fluid nature of cultural identities (Haselgrove 1990).

Factoring together the differing interaction spheres and the differences in cultural practices we observed in our exploratory comparison of mortuary practices, we think it is very likely that the residents of Fains Island and Ledford Island did indeed consider themselves to be culturally distinct. We are unclear as to the degree or scale of difference. Did the prehistoric residents of these two islands consider themselves as completely distinct peoples or as separate and distinct groups within a larger cultural tradition that encompassed other distinct contemporary enclaves in the upper Tennessee Valley?

Given the historically known differences among Cherokee groups in the region, we cannot discount the possibility that groups associated with Fains Island and Ledford Island may have perceived themselves as part of a similar larger cultural identity. Are the distinctions we are seeing simply of degree and not of kind? As a counter to Lewis and Kneberg's (1946) correlation of Dallas with historically known Creek groups and Mouse Creek with the Yuchi, Joffre Coe (1961) argued that the difference between *all* Dallas phase sites and Pisgah and Qualla sites in western North Carolina was a matter of degree and not kind as they related to development of the Cherokee.

Whether or not the late prehistoric inhabitants of these two islands considered themselves as completely separate or somehow related peoples, the archaeological perception that "Dallas Culture" sites are similar and that "Dallas Culture people" shared cultural practices is an impediment to understanding cultural diversity in the upper Tennessee Valley. The archaeological notion of a "Dallas Culture" was based mainly on gross similarities in material culture—especially in pottery and architectural styles—and a limited understanding of chronology. Our comparisons will be more satisfying if we use the material culture to look at suites of cultural practices rather than comparisons of artifact typologies because the former can provide insights into how culture was constructed. Furthermore, how these practices did or did not differ across space and time provides clues to how closely past peoples interacted. Comparisons of trajectories or histories of cultural development also can help us understand how differing traditions came to be and how prehistoric peoples used traditions to shape unique and distinct identities.

Notes

1. See recent literature regarding social enclaves at Cahokia (e.g., Emerson and Hargrave 2000; Pauketat 1998, 2000).

13

The Mortuary Assemblage from the Holliston Mills Site, a Mississippian Town in Upper East Tennessee

JAY D. FRANKLIN, ELIZABETH K. PRICE, AND LUCINDA M. LANGSTON

After extensive archaeological investigations at Phipps Bend on the Holston River in upper East Tennessee, Lafferty (1981: 520) concluded that "the Mississippian occupation appears to be quite *unintense*." The Mississippian Period in the area was characterized by small, scattered settlements with no evidence for corn agriculture. Lafferty's volume stands out as a thorough and remarkable body of scholarship. However, it is clear that Lafferty was unaware of the archaeology of the Mississippian towns that once dotted the Holston River terraces immediately upstream of Phipps Bend. Lafferty (1981: xxii) also stated, "I would be surprised if all of the conclusions reached in this monograph remain unmodified, and I am certain that much greater detail is possible through more analysis and excavation." Toward that end, we introduce the archaeology of the nearby Holliston Mills site (40HW11), a Mississippian town in upper East Tennessee, with particular focus on mortuary patterning. We end by suggesting that the Mississippian occupation in the region was both intense and extensive if not prototypical of Mississippian occupations elsewhere in the greater Southeast.

The Holliston Mills site is located on the north bank of the Holston River south of Kingsport in Hawkins County, Tennessee (Figure 13.1). The site was excavated by members of the Tennessee Archaeological Society between 1968 and 1972. It was excavated in 10-foot blocks using six-inch levels, revealing a large late prehistoric (and perhaps protohistoric) town represented by least two palisades, more than 660 burials, a large public structure, and several smaller domestic structures. Richard Polhemus (personal communication, 2005) remembers multiple palisades and abundant structures. No mounds have been recorded at this locale (Figure 13.2).

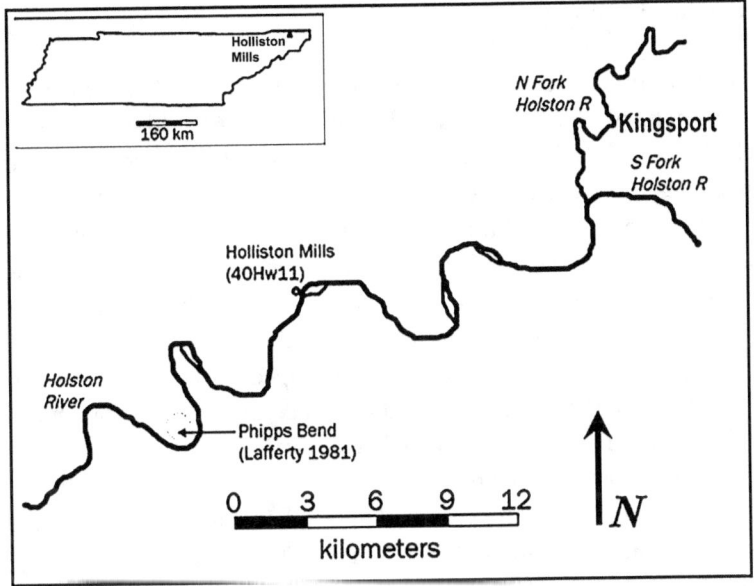

Figure 13.1. Location of the Holliston Mills Site.

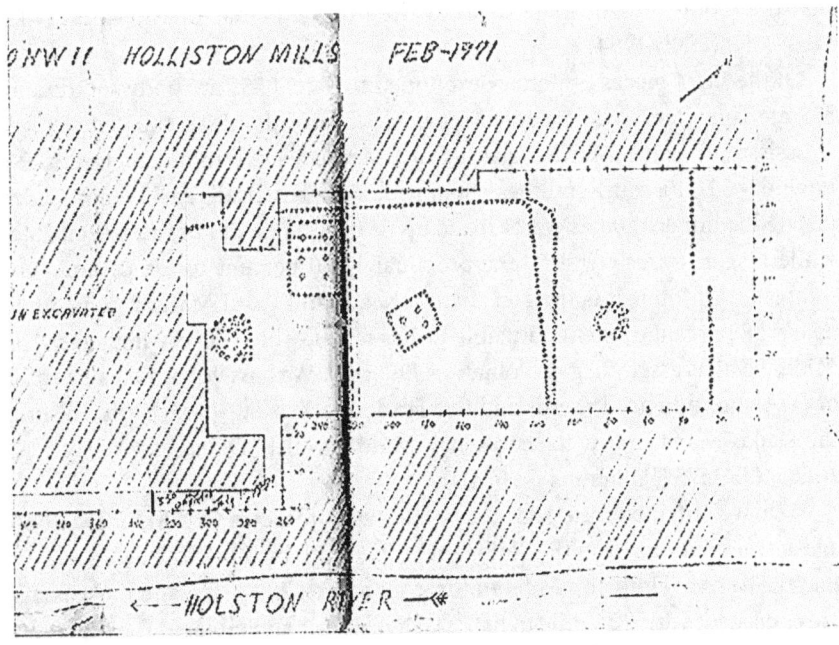

Figure 13.2. Plan View Map of the Holliston Mills Site.

Ceramics and Chronology

The excavators initially reported the recovery of what they believed to be Cobb Island pottery (see Polhemus and Polhemus 1966) in the plow zone and much Dallas material from the level excavations, but they also noted that the site had been looted prior to their excavations. Ceramic analysis is ongoing, but we can clearly say that the Holliston Mills site certainly had multiple components. There is little, if any, Cobb Island pottery, but there are some Pisgah ceramics. The rectilinear stamped pottery from Holliston Mills is not shell tempered (i.e., Cobb Island) but rather is sand and grit tempered. Thus, it is better characterized as Pisgah Rectilinear Stamped, Design A narrow and broad (Dickens 1976: 172–177). Dallas and Pisgah ceramics occur contemporaneously in both feature contexts and archaeological levels; there is no stratigraphic delineation between the two.

The Pisgah "phase" spans the period of about A.D. 1000 to 1550, and the Dallas phase typically from about A.D. 1300 to 1600. The ceramics from Holliston Mills fall later in these spans (i.e., A.D. 1400–1540). We have also recorded several Lamar curvilinear stamped sherds as well as several cazuela bowl fragments with typical middle Lamar incising along the rim and large reed punctations just below. The presence of these Lamar ceramics suggests that the Holliston Mills site dates to the Middle Lamar phase, about A.D. 1450–1550 (Hally 1994).

Of the 1,894 pieces of pottery examined to date, 1,555 are body sherds and 339 are rim sherds. Six accepted types have been identified thus far: Dallas (Mississippi) Plain, McKee Island Cord Marked, DeArmond Incised (Salo 1969: 62–63), Pisgah Rectilinear Stamped, Lamar Incised, and Lamar Complicated Stamped. Dallas wares make up nearly 70 percent of the assemblage, while Pisgah wares constitute approximately 30 percent of the ceramic assemblage. Of interest is the fact that McKee Island Cord Marked constitutes nearly 58 percent of the identifiable Dallas wares, which is very high even for Middle Dallas assemblages (Polhemus 1990: 41). We have identified a handful of DeArmond Incised sherds and two fabric-marked salt-pan sherds. In sum, the Dallas wares appear to represent a Middle to Late Dallas assemblage, ca. A.D. 1400–1525 (Polhemus 1990: 41).

We have obtained nine accelerator mass spectrometry (AMS) radiocarbon age determinations from the Holliston Mills site (Table 13.1). The dates suggest that the town at Holliston Mills endured for at least 200 years, and most assays are consistent with a Middle to Late Dallas ceramic assemblage. The first assay obtained comes from charred corn recovered from a probable smudge pit. At 1 sigma, it calibrates to A.D. 1423 (with a 2 sigma weighted mean of A.D. 1416).

Table 13.1. Radiocarbon (AMS) Determinations from the Holliston Mills Site

Laboratory ID	Material	Provenance	Measure (rcBP)	Calibrated 1 sigma (AD)	2 sigma (AD)	2 sigma weighted (AD)
AA67861[a]	Burned river cane (*Arundinaria* sp.)	Feature 64 ("burned house")	361 ± 32	1495, 1600	1485, 1590	1538
AA67862	Charred corn cob	smudge pit	505 ± 33	1423	1335, 1420	1416
AA71781	Mammal bone	Feature 159	552 ± 35	1335, 1405	1335, 1410	1375
AA71782	Mammal bone	Feature 23	380 ± 36	1480, 1605	1485, 1590	1527
AA71784	Mammal bone	Feature 161	549 ± 35	1333, 1408	1335, 1410	1378
AA71785	Mammal bone	40L130 pit	580 ± 35	1335, 1398	1355	1355
AA71786	Mammal bone	70L130, Level 3	478 ± 35	1430	1433	1433
AA71787	Mammal bone	60L400, Level 3	481 ± 35	1430	1430	1430
AA71788	Mammal bone	Feature 13	579 ± 35	1335, 1398	1360	1360

Note: [a]AA: National Science Foundation/University of Arizona AMS Facility

The smudge pits and the charred corn are clear evidence that corn agriculture was practiced in the region (contra Lafferty 1981: 520). The latest date was obtained from river cane from Feature 64, a burned house. The 2 sigma weighted mean is A.D. 1538, about the time that the De Soto entrada came through the region. A sheet copper or brass cone, or conical "tinkler," and a lead ball were recovered from Holliston Mills, but in plow zone contexts. The brass cone may date to the sixteenth century (Richard Polhemus, personal communications 2005, 2006). There is no archaeological evidence to suggest that either of the sixteenth-century Spanish entradas (De Soto or Pardo) ventured this far west in upper East Tennessee. Still, it is a possibility (Hudson 1990: 28).

To our knowledge, the substantial mix of Dallas and Pisgah ceramics is not well documented elsewhere except for a few sites. Seventy percent of the Mississippian assemblage at the McCullough Bend site was comprised of shell-tempered wares while 22 percent was grit-tempered complicated stamped (Polhemus and Polhemus 1966: 13, 15). Very little grit-tempered Cobb Island/Pisgah Complicated Stamped pottery was present at the Loy site, farther down the Holston, and most is tempered with shell rather than grit (Polhemus 1998, personal communication 2006). The Late Mississippian ceramic assemblage from the Fains Island site on the upper French Broad River includes about 15 percent Pisgah wares (Howell 2005).

The mix of Dallas and Pisgah wares at Holliston Mills may have implications for the cultural identity of the inhabitants of the site as well as their socio-political strategy. We believe that the two ware groups were contemporaneous. Instrumental neutron activation analysis of carefully selected ceramic samples was conducted by the Archaeometry Laboratory at the University of Missouri Research Reactor (MURR). The compositional analyses clearly distinguished between the shell-tempered (Dallas) and grit-tempered (Pisgah) wares. Dallas wares contain higher concentrations of chromium, arsenic, cesium, antimony, aluminum, and iron and low concentrations of tantalum, hafnium, sodium, and zirconium. The Pisgah pottery has exactly the opposite pattern of relative concentrations (Ferguson, Rosania, and Glascock 2007: 5). Ferguson et al. have noted that "this appears to be a meaningful difference in the materials used to manufacture the pottery, but it is difficult to determine if this is due to different sources of clay, temper, or both" (Ferguson et al. 2007: 6). An in-depth discussion of the compositional analyses of the Holliston Mills pottery is beyond the scope of this chapter, but we think these differences are culturally meaningful. Given the ubiquity of river mussel shell along the Holston in this area, it is difficult to believe that the presence of grit-tempered ceramics represents a necessity rather than cultural interactions (e. g., trade). We return to the notion of cultural identity in our summary and conclusions.

The Holliston Mills Mortuary Assemblage

More than 660 burials were excavated at Holliston Mills from 1968 to 1972. We have information and generated data from 565 of the burials. All were flexed to varying degrees. We note here that the age and sex determinations were made by a local physician in conjunction with the avocational archaeologists in charge of the excavations from 1968 to 1972. The potential unreliability of such determinations is a factor noted by other scholars in their Mississippian mortuary research (e. g., Fisher-Carroll and Mainfort 2000: 110). We believe our data are comparable, but in any case, the age and sex structure of the Holliston Mills population is not particularly germane to our central arguments. The distribution by sex in the Holliston Mills burial assemblage does not appear to be anomalous (Table 13.2). The number of identifiable male and female burials is equal, 137 each, although we are skeptical of the sex designations for individuals under 13 years of age. Ten burials also were tentatively designated as males and eight tentatively designated as females. Nearly half (48 percent), or 273 burials, could not be or were not sexed. The age structure appears to represent a community of people of all ages perhaps over several generations. There is no obvious skewing of the burial population by age structure except for the typical lack of subadults in an archaeological sample.

In the 1970s, Hatch (1975, 1976a, 1987) developed a "social status typology" for the Dallas phase of East Tennessee based on differences in funerary objects and, more important, the spatial segregation of high-status burials, particularly in mounds (Table 13.3). Hatch (1975: 133–134) delineated high-status burial objects for Dallas phase peoples, including ceramic bottles, (massive) columella beads, conch-shell vessels, copper headdresses and/or earspools, ceremonial celts, and bone pins. However, these items are confined to mound contexts (Hatch 1975: 134). Items that indicate age and/or sex status are bifa-

Table 13.2. Overall Burial Population Structure at Holliston Mills by Age and Sex

Age/Sex	Male	Male(?)	Female	Female(?)	Indeterminate	Totals
<1 yr	0	0	1	0	94	95
1–3 yrs	0	0	1	0	14	15
3–6 yrs	3	1	1	1	22	28
6–13 yrs	6	0	5	0	46	57
13–18 yrs	5	1	5	0	11	22
18–21 yrs	9	0	11	1	1	22
21–35 yrs	88	8	103	5	25	229
35–55 yrs	12	0	5	1	2	20
Indeterminate	14	0	5	0	58	77
Totals	137	10	137	8	273	565

Table 13.3. Mortuary Indicators of Dallas Social Status

High Status[a]	Age/Sex Status[a]	General Population[a]
confined to mound context	bifacially flaked flint blades: adult males	"commoners" regardless of location
ceramic bottles		males: pipes, celts, artifacts associated w/stone tool-making kit
columella beads		
conch-shell vessels	rattlesnake shell gorgets: subadults	
copper headdresses/earspools		females & subadults: utilitarian pottery & non-exotic (?) shell artifacts
ceremonial celts		
bone pins		

Note: [a]After Hatch 1975:133–134

cially flaked flint blades (adult males) and rattlesnake-shell gorgets (subadults and perhaps adult females). Hatch (1975) noted that utilitarian items were interred with most individuals, regardless of location. Males tended to be buried with pipes, celts, and artifacts associated with flintknapping. Females typically were buried with utilitarian pottery vessels and non-exotic shell items (Hatch 1975: 133–134).

As we have noted, there was no mound at Holliston Mills. Further, as the burial distributions from the site indicate, there is no spatial segregation of burials based on the distribution of funerary objects of any type or on demographic factors such as age and sex (Tables 13.4 and 13.5). The people at Holliston Mills were buried within their village and in and around their houses, much like the Pisgah community at the Warren Wilson site in western North Carolina (Dickens 1976). The lack of spatial segregation of burials with funerary objects vis-à-vis those with none is noteworthy because of the emphasis Hatch (1975: 134) placed on spatial segregation as a delineation of social and political status in Dallas society (Figure 13.3).

Other researchers also have discussed the importance of spatial segregation of burials in examining several kinds of social differentiation (Brown 1981a; Charles and Buikstra 1983; Fisher-Carroll and Mainfort 2000: 108; Sullivan 2001, 2006; Sullivan and Rodning 2001). The mortuary assemblage from the Holliston Mills site does not, however, compare favorably with analyses that posit spatial segregation based on rank because funerary objects, including those that are considered "high status," are common at Holliston Mills and there is no spatial segregation of individuals interred with such items.

Of the 565 burials on which we have useful information, 225 (40 percent) had associated funerary objects (Table 13.4). Funerary objects at Holliston

Table 13.4. General Distribution of Burial Items at Holliston Mills by Age and Sex

Age/Sex	Male	Male(?)	Female	Female(?)	Indeterminate	Totals
<1 yr	0	0	1	0	48	49
1–3 yrs	0	0	1	0	4	5
3–6 yrs	3	1	0	0	9	13
6–13 yrs	5	0	3	0	21	29
13–18 yrs	1	0	1	0	2	4
18–21 yrs	2	0	3	1	0	6
21–35 yrs	36	4	35	3	2	80
35–55 yrs	3	0	3	1	0	7
Indeterminate	6	0	3	0	23	32
Totals	56	5	50	5	109	225

Table 13.5. General Age/Sex Distributions of Individuals at Holliston Mills Without Burial Items

Age/Sex	Male	Male(?)	Female	Female(?)	Indeterminate	Totals
< 1 year	0	0	0	0	46	46
1–3 years	0	0	0	0	10	10
3–6 years	0	0	1	1	13	15
6–13 years	1	0	2	0	25	28
13–18 years	4	1	4	0	9	18
18–21 years	7	0	8	0	1	16
21–35 years	52	4	68	2	23	149
35–55 years	9	0	2	0	2	13
Indeterminate	8	0	2	0	35	45
Totals	81	5	87	3	164	340

Mills include shell beads, bone artifacts, celts, shell gorgets, pipes, ceramic vessels, mica disks, discoidals, pipes, turtle carapaces, turtle-shell bowls, flaked stone points, and some copper. Copper artifacts were recovered from only three burials. All of the pottery vessels are shell-tempered Dallas vessels. In fact, all mortuary vessels that we have been able to identify are shell-tempered Dallas types, even though the site's ceramic assemblage is composed of a significant mix of Dallas and Pisgah wares.

The most common type of burial item was shell beads. Of the burials with funerary objects, approximately 67 percent contained some kind of shell beads. These include columella, *Marginella*, and whelk varieties. One hundred fifty-seven burials (ca. 28 percent) contained shell beads (Table 13.6). There is no clear patterning of bead types across age or sex groups. Males appear to have been buried more often with columella beads than females (Table 13.7).

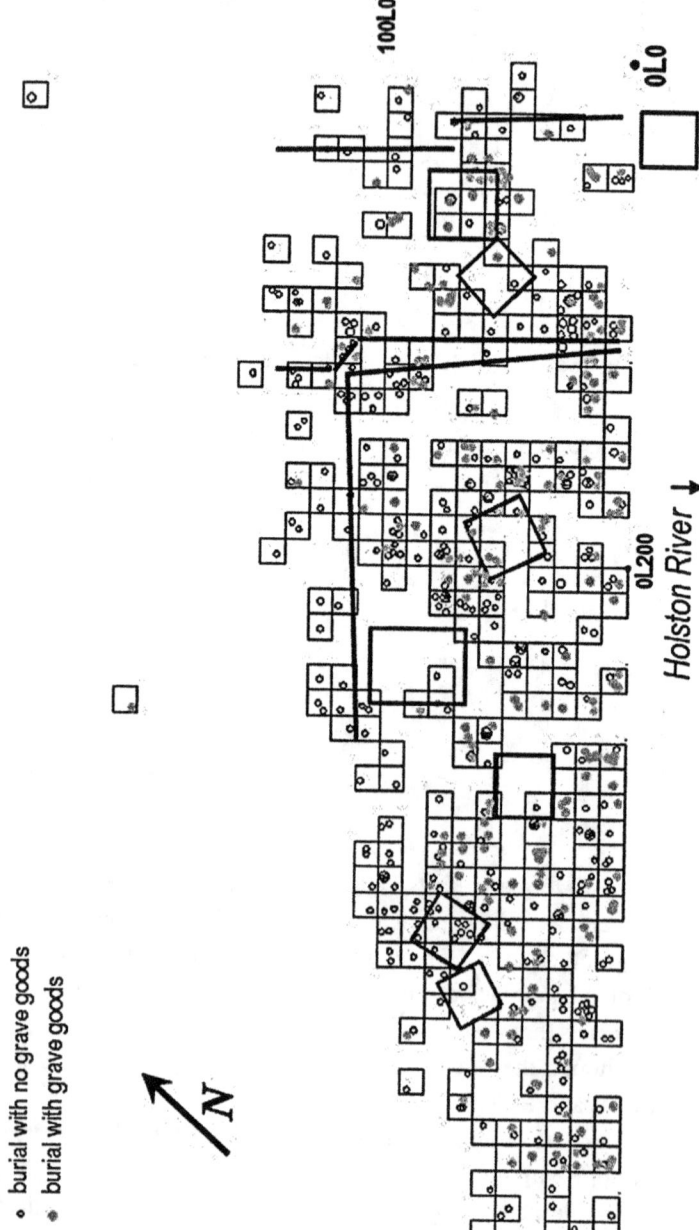

Figure 13.3. Distribution of Burials with Grave Goods vis-à-vis Burials Without Grave Goods at Holliston Mills. Grave goods indicated by gray dots; burials without grave goods indicated by open circles.

Table 13.6. General Distribution of Burials at Holliston Mills with Shell Beads

Age/Sex	Male	Male(?)	Female	Female(?)	Indeterminate	Totals
<1 yr	0	0	0	0	36	36
1–3 yrs	0	0	1	0	4	5
3–6 yrs	3	1	0	0	6	10
6–13 yrs	5	0	2	0	20	27
13–18 yrs	1	0	2	0	1	4
18–21 yrs	1	0	1	0	0	2
21–35 yrs	26	2	19	1	2	50
35–55 yrs	1	0	2	1	0	4
Indeterminate	4	0	1	0	14	19
Totals	41	3	28	2	83	157

However, we would point out two things: 1) the largest number of burials with columella beads is of indeterminate sex; and 2) we only have information from field burial forms, and in many cases the type of beads found with a particular burial was not listed.

The distribution of burials with shell beads is roughly the same as the distribution of funerary objects in general (Figure 13.3). These results contrast with findings at Upper Nodena in the central Mississippi valley, where marine-shell beads were statistically more likely to be found in "mound" burials than in nonmound contexts (Fisher-Carroll and Mainfort 2000: 109). Fisher-Carroll and Mainfort (2000: 116) arrive at the same conclusions for mortuary behavior at Upper Nodena that we draw for Holliston Mills. That is, no particular efforts were made to separate high-status individual burials from others in the community, but some individuals were interred with larger arrays of items than others. For example, in Burial 44a, a male about 10–12 years of age was

Table 13.7. Age and Sex Distributions of Burials at Holliston Mills with Columella Beads

Age/Sex	Male	Male(?)	Female	Female(?)	Indeterminate	Totals
<1 yr	0	0	0	0	12	12
1–3 yrs	0	0	1	0	2	3
3–6 yrs	1	1	0	0	3	5
6–13 yrs	0	0	0	0	3	3
13–18 yrs	0	0	1	0	0	1
18–21 yrs	0	0	0	0	0	0
21–35 yrs	13	6	0	0	0	19
35–55 yrs	0	0	1	0	0	1
Indeterminate	0	0	0	0	3	3
Totals	14	7	3	0	23	47

buried with five pottery vessels (one bottle, two jars, and two bowls), one celt, 1,622 beads, two rattlesnake gorgets, and two bone pins.

Shell gorgets are remarkably common in the Holliston Mills mortuary assemblage and indicate either considerable time depth or curation of these objects by the site's inhabitants or both. Seventy-nine shell gorgets were recovered (Table 13.8). These range in dating from the late twelfth to the early sixteenth centuries. Subadults and infants were most often interred with shell gorgets. The occurrence with males and females was nearly equal (n = 14, n = 16), but more subadult males than females had gorgets.

At least 19 Lick Creek–style rattlesnake gorgets were found at Holliston Mills. Muller (2000: 17) describes this style as "a fairly naturalistic form that dates to the mid-fifteenth century to the north of Knoxville, Tennessee." Sullivan (2007b) has obtained AMS dates from the Dallas site in southeastern Tennessee that place these gorgets in the fourteenth century. Muller (1997: 376; 2007: 31–32) also notes that small and "transitional" Lick Creek–style gorgets continue to be made into the sixteenth century, consistent with radiocarbon determinations from Holliston Mills (Table 13.1).

Hatch (1975) correlated rattlesnake gorgets with age status among Dallas peoples because his analysis showed that these gorgets were interred with subadults and infants. This pattern does not occur at Holliston Mills. At least nine rattlesnake gorgets were associated with adults (Table 13.8). Perhaps age status at Holliston Mills was symbolized differently than at other Dallas phase sites.

Turkey-cock, facemask, and quadrilobed gorgets also were found at Holliston Mills. Hatch (1975: 133) places turkey-cock gorgets in mound burial contexts. One turkey-cock gorget was found with a female aged 18–21 at Holliston Mills. Based on an AMS date from the Hixon site in southeastern Tennessee, Sullivan (2007b) places these gorgets in the thirteenth century. Facemask gorgets were the second most common type at Holliston Mills. The majority was found with adult male burials, but they were also buried with adult females and subadults. These gorgets typically are dated to the sixteenth century (Hally 2007; Smith and Smith 1989). One quadrilobed gorget was found at Holliston Mills. It is somewhat similar to those from the Warren Wilson site in western North Carolina (Dickens 1976: 166, 168), but the specimen from Holliston Mills is more stylized with a cross-in-circle motif in the center. A quadrilobed gorget with similar designs was recovered from premound deposits at the Hixon site. Sullivan (2007b) places these deposits in the late twelfth century. Hally (2007) dates the quadrilobed Bennett- and Moorehead-style gorgets to the thirteenth and fourteenth centuries but places the Warren Wilson forms in the fifteenth and early sixteenth centuries.

Table 13.8. Holliston Mills Burials with Shell Gorgets

Age and Sex	Gorget Type						
	Rattlesnake	Facemask	Birdman	Disc	Turkey-Cock	Unidentified	Totals
<1 yr							
Male	0	0	0	0	0	0	0
Female	0	0	0	0	0	0	0
Indeterminate	3	0	0	9	0	8	20
1–3 yrs							
Male	0	0	0	0	0	0	0
Female	0	0	0	0	0	0	0
Indeterminate	0	0	0	0	0	0	0
3–6 yrs							
Male	0	0	0	0	0	0	0
Female	0	0	0	0	0	0	0
Indeterminate	2	1	0	0	0	0	3
6–13 yrs							
Male	2	0	0	0	0	3	5
Female	0	0	0	0	0	2	2
Indeterminate	1	1	0	0	0	9	11
13–18 yrs							
Male	1	0	0	0	0	0	1
Female	0	0	0	0	0	1	1
Indeterminate	0	0	0	0	0	3	3
18–21 yrs							
Male	0	0	0	0	0	0	0
Female	0	1	0	0	1	0	2
Indeterminate	0	0	0	0	0	0	0
21–35 yrs							
Male	1	4	1	0	0	3	9
Female	5	2	0	0	0	2	9
Indeterminate	0	0	0	0	0	2	2
35–55 yrs							
Male	0	0	0	0	0	0	0
Female	0	0	0	0	0	0	0
Indeterminate	0	0	0	0	0	0	0
Indeterminate							
Male	1	0	0	0	0	0	1
Female	0	0	0	0	0	0	0
Indeterminate	3	1	0	1	0	5	10
Totals	19	10	1	10	1	38	79

A gorget that is not listed in Table 13.8 was associated with Burial 359 at Holliston Mills. It has a hand with a cross-in-circle motif on the back side of the hand. While both the hand and the cross-in-circle motif are common in Mississippian iconography, the association of the two motifs on a shell gorget appears to be unique (Jan Simek, personal communication 2006).

Sociopolitical Organization at Holliston Mills and in Upper East Tennessee

Mississippian societies are typically characterized as chiefdom societies in which rank is hereditary. Peebles and Kus (1977) discussed several archaeological correlates of ranked (e. g. Mississippian) societies including differential status as reflected in mortuary practices and burial objects, monumental or large-scale architecture, settlement hierarchy, and part-time craft specialization.

We attempt to address these characteristics (except for craft specialization) using the Holliston Mills data and limited information from other sites in the region. We already have suggested that the lack of evidence for social rank differentiation in the mortuary data does not compare favorably with a chiefly sociopolitical structure or lineage. While there are a number of burials with several types of shell gorgets, these objects typically are not correlated with differentiation of social rank (Muller 2000). Three burials possessed copper earspools, items more often associated with emblems of high rank, but these individuals were not otherwise differentiated. Several individuals also were interred with celts, but these objects appear more utilitarian than ceremonial. There are no flint blades or spatulate axes at Holliston Mills.

We can address public works and settlement hierarchy to varying degrees. Hally (1993, 1996) and others (Meyers 2002: 182; Beck and Moore 2002: 193; King 2006: 193) argue that mound construction may be viewed as an archaeological correlate of chiefdom-level societies in the Southeast. Hally (1993) also developed a settlement model based on his research in northern Georgia in which the geographic spacing of mounded settlements gives some indication of political structure. Contemporaneous mounds located within 31 km of each other were likely part of the same chiefdom. Mound centers separated by more than 31 km suggest distinct chiefdoms.

As at Holliston Mills, other identified Mississippian settlements in upper East Tennessee lacked mounds (Figure 13.4). There are no mound sites or centers within a 31 km radius of Holliston Mills in any direction (Figure 13.5). This radius includes the so-called Chiaha/Olamico (Zimmerman's Island) site

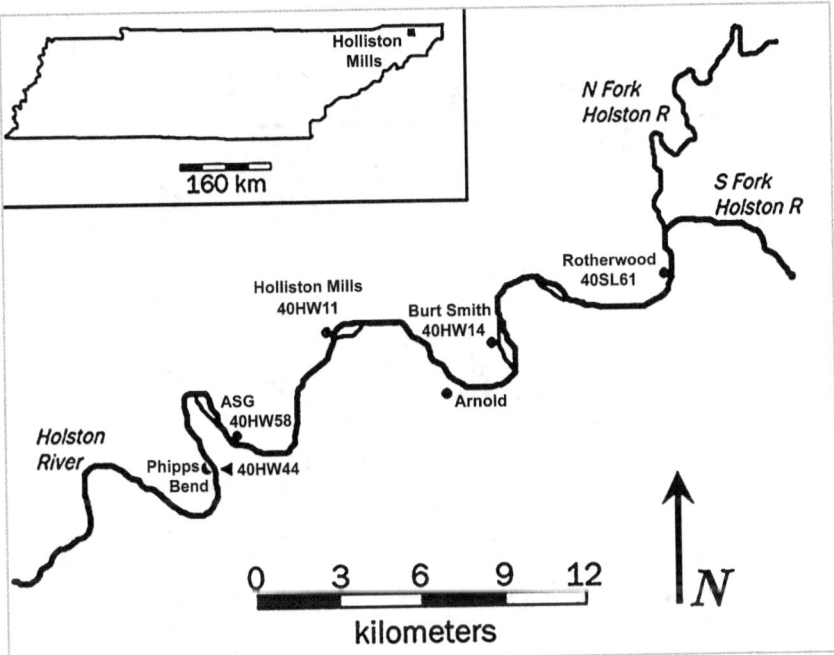

Figure 13.4. Other Mississippian Period Sites in the Immediate Vicinity of Holliston Mills.

to the south, mound centers in the Norris basin to the west, Pisgah sites in western North Carolina, and southwestern Virginia (Site 44SC8).

Based on Hally's (1993) model, two conclusions may be drawn. First, Holliston Mills itself was not a chiefdom, at least in the prototypical sense. Second, given the fact that contemporaneous mound centers are more than 32 km distant, Holliston Mills was seemingly not subject to any chiefdom in the southern Appalachians. Therefore, the site does not conform to the stereotypical chiefdom model that has been used to broadly characterize the Mississippian Period.

However, a number of likely contemporary sites are in relatively close proximity to Holliston Mills. The ceramic assemblages from these sites exhibit mixes of pottery styles similar to that at Holliston Mills. At the ASG site, just downstream, there are Dallas ceramics (McKee Island Cord Marked and Laurel Incised) as well as Lamar (or perhaps Qualla) ceramics with large reed punctations. These resemble the Lamar Incised pottery from Holliston Mills, but the ASG ceramics are sand tempered. A single AMS determination from a smudge pit at the ASG site has yielded a measure of 359 Å 34 BP with a 2 sigma weighted mean of A.D. 1542, indicating that the ASG site was roughly

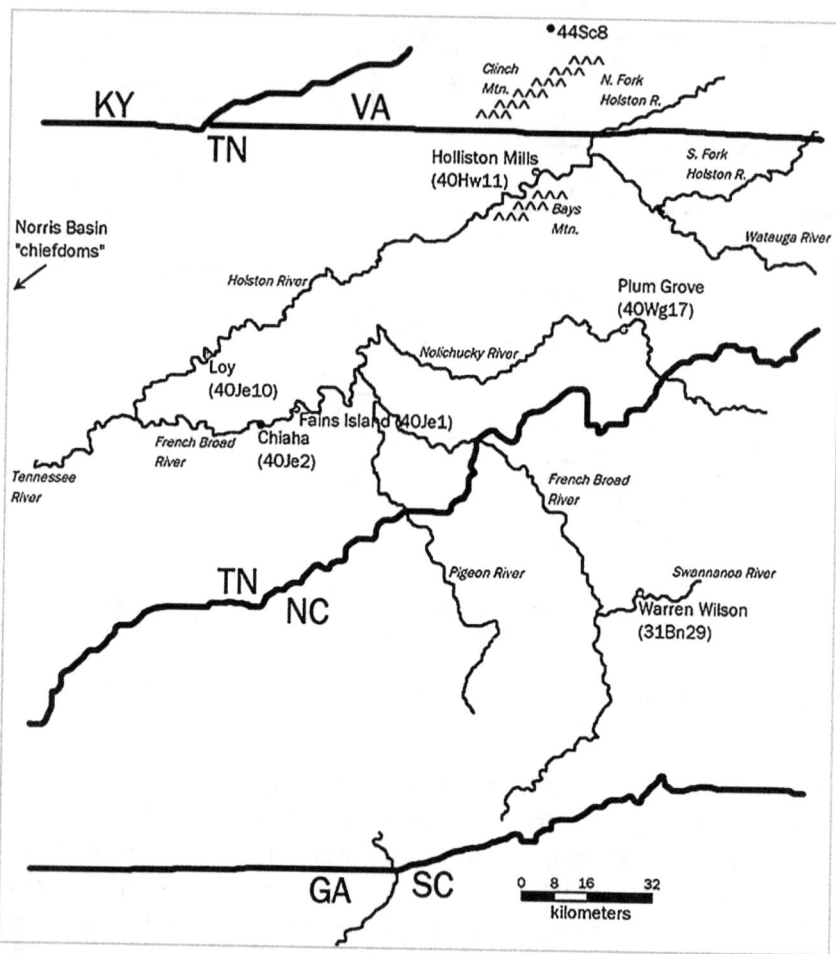

Figure 13.5. Prominent Mississippian Period Sites in the Region Surrounding Holliston Mills.

contemporary with Holliston Mills. Approximately 6 km downstream from Holliston Mills and one riverbend downstream from ASG is site 40HW44 on Phipps Bend. A radiocarbon assay on material from a midden containing Pisgah ceramics (Lafferty 1981: 487–489) calibrates to A.D. 1335 at the 2 sigma level, suggesting that the Pisgah component at this site is contemporary with Holliston Mills. Given the proximity of the two sites, it is not surprising that Lafferty (1981: 520) did not find an "intensive" Mississippian site on Phipps Bend.

Just upstream from Holliston Mills is the Bert Smith site. This poorly known site has produced both Pisgah and shell-tempered incised pottery. Farther upstream is the Rotherwood site. Limited excavations at this site yielded some limestone-tempered Pisgah sherds. The body sherds are rectilinear stamped and the rim sherds are the classic collared and thickened rims with series of diagonal punctations (Dickens 1976: 178). Shell-tempered ceramics also were recovered. Across the river from Holliston Mills is the Arnold site, where excavations revealed houses and produced Dallas pottery (e.g., McKee Island Cord Marked, Laurel Incised). Clearly there were several Mississippian settlements in the immediate vicinity of Holliston Mills, but the relationships between these are unknown at present. A settlement hierarchy is not obvious. The hybrid ceramic assemblages that include both Dallas and Pisgah wares are a key link between these sites.

Data from the Nelson site on the nearby Nolichucky River, the McCullough Bend site on the Clinch River, and Cobb Island on the Holston and Cobb Island sites suggest that Pisgah pottery makers were in upper East Tennessee before Dallas pottery makers, although there is evidence that the two types are contemporary at Cobb Island (Dickens 1976; Polhemus and Polhemus 1966). An AMS assay on a grit-tempered, rectilinear stamped Pisgah sherd that was heavily sooted from the Nelson site (40WG7) yielded a calibrated means of A.D. 1245 and 1233 (1 sigma and 2 sigma, respectively). This date is earlier than Holliston Mills, but Dallas (Mississippi) Plain sherds and sand-tempered plain sherds also have been collected from the site (McIlhany 1978: 68). At Cobb Island, Dickens (1976: 94) reports that "a single burial, accompanied by two Dallas Cord Marked vessels, was found near the . . . structure. The burial fill contained nine Pisgah Complicated Stamped sherds." This use of Dallas vessels in mortuary contexts is very similar to the practice at Holliston Mills, where all of the burial vessels appear to be Dallas wares but there are also significant amounts of Pisgah wares.

Comparisons

We initially attempted to compare the mortuary assemblage from Holliston Mills to those from two other Dallas phase sites in upper East Tennessee: Fains Island along the upper French Broad River and the Loy site on the Holston, both in Jefferson County. However, the excavations that produced the large burial assemblage at Fains Island (see Sullivan and Harle, this volume) were restricted to mound contexts and the limited excavations at Loy produced a small data set, so the assemblages are not comparable (Price and Langston 2007).

The Plum Grove and Warren Wilson sites in North Carolina appear to be more comparable to Holliston Mills. A late Pisgah phase (ca. A.D. 1300–1600) component was identified at the Plum Grove site, located on the Nolichucky

Table 13.9. Burial Items Recovered from the Plum Grove Site

Pisgaha	"Qualla"[a]
ground stone discs &celts	columella shell beads
cut mica discs	*Marginella*-shell beads
columella shell beads	mask style shell gorgets
small tubular shell beads	Citico rattlesnake gorgets
Lick Creek rattlesnake gorgets	undecorated disc-shell gorgets
turtle carapace rattles	small disc-shell beads
Pisgah pottery (sherds)	historic trade items (2)

Note: [a]After Dickens 1980:19; Boyd 1986a.

River some 45 km southeast of Holliston Mills, Associated Pisgah wares were grit-tempered rectilinear stamped and plain varieties (Boyd 1986a: 84). The Pisgah phase spans several hundred years at the site. Calibrated radiocarbon dates for the Pisgah phase at Plum Grove are A.D. 975 (2 sigma), A.D. 1377 (2 sigma weighted mean), and A.D. 1580 (2 sigma weighted mean) (Boyd 1986b: 67). The densest part of the site covers approximately three acres (Dickens 1980: 13). Plum Grove includes a protohistorical component represented by both shell-tempered (Dallas) wares and sand-tempered wares that have been called the Nolichucky Series (Boyd 1986a: 53; Earnest n.d.). Some soapstone-tempered Burke Series ceramics also were recovered (Boyd and Riggs 1986: 60–61; Beck and Moore 2002).

Thirty-six burials were initially excavated at Plum Grove (Dickens 1980: 20) and five were excavated later (Boyd 1986a: 83). Only some very general mortuary comparisons with Holliston Mills are possible. Table 13.9 lists the general descriptions for both Pisgah and "Qualla" burials at Plum Grove (Dickens 1980: 19). The most common funerary objects at both sites were columella and *Marginella* beads. Rattlesnake and mask gorgets also were common at both locations. In short, the burial items are consistent with those found at Holliston Mills, and it appears that the sites were contemporary and similar in configuration.

The Warren Wilson site is a Pisgah phase site more than 100 km south of Holliston Mills (Figure 13.5). The village covered approximately two to three acres and included several houses and multiple palisades (Dickens 1976: 25). There was no mound. Only 35 human burials were excavated, far fewer than at Holliston Mills. Nonetheless, site structure at both locations is similar. The relative abundance of burial items appears to be greater and more evenly distributed at Holliston Mills. Eleven (ca. 31 percent) of 35 burials at Warren Wilson had associated funerary objects. Of these, nine contained ornamental items (Dickens 1976: 127). Males were more often buried with grave goods than were females. According to Dickens, "shell gorgets were found only with infants or young children" (Dickens 1976: 127–128), which contrasts with Holliston Mills, where infants, adults of both sexes, and occasionally adolescents were interred with shell gorgets (Table 13.8). Households at Warren Wilson appear to have been differentially associated with funerary objects, leading Dickens (1976: 128) to conclude that the variation might represent differential kin-group and household status or temporal variation in burial customs. While we find Dickens's conclusions intriguing, the excavation and burial data from Holliston Mills do not permit such a fine-grained assessment. The town at Holliston Mills also persisted for at least 200 years, making it difficult to sort out temporal variation.

Summary and Conclusions

We agree with Fisher-Carroll and Mainfort (2000: 116) that there are inherent problems in using mortuary data as a one-to-one correlate for social status. Mortuary data are a useful beginning point for systematically addressing regional-scale sociopolitical dynamics in the Holston valley during the Mississippian Period. Based on the mortuary data and (to a limited extent) on Hally's (1993) model, we do not believe that the chiefdom model is a good fit for Mississippian sociopolitical organization in the Holston valley. If we were to use the corporate/network strategy dichotomy (Blanton et al. 1996), which King used (2006: 185) to look at Mississippian sociopolitical strategies in eastern Tennessee and northern Georgia, we would argue for a corporately structured, or community-based, population at Holliston Mills. King (2006) summarized these differences, which we list in Table 13.10. We cannot yet appropriately address items 1 through 3, but we believe we have used the mortuary data from Holliston Mills to address item 4 regarding status and wealth indicators. While a few individuals have more burial items than most of the others, nothing else suggests a hierarchical sociopolitical structure. There is no spatial segregation of individuals buried with status items and a large number of the population (40 percent) is buried with funerary objects. Status symbols and/or wealth appear to have been fairly evenly distributed at Holliston Mills.

In sum, the residents of the Holliston Mills site had their own Mississippian lifestyle and cultural practices that may flag them as a distinct cultural group (see Hudson 1990: 90). The mix of Dallas and Pisgah ceramics suggests cultural hybridity (Alt 2006) between upper Tennessee Valley and western Blue Ridge groups. Some elements of the Dallas ceramics appear to be regionally distinct, such as modeled appliqué "faces" over cord marking on jars (Figure 13.6). Polhemus (personal communication 2005) notes that only a "couple of

Table 13.10. Mississippian Political Economy Structures

Network[a]	Corporate[a]
1. Decision making: individual	1. Decision making: shared
2. Sources of power: participating in external networks of social ties	2. Sources of power: social solidarity and interdependence
3. Mobilized surplus: used to acquire prestige goods and fund displays aggrandizing the leader	3. Mobilized surplus: used to fund solidarity-building communal rites of intensification
4. Status/wealth indicators: clearly marked	4. Status/wealth indicators: personal wealth and status secondary to importance of the community

Note: [a]After King 2006: 185 sensu Blanton et al. 1996.

Figure 13.6. Modeled Appliqué Face Cord-Marked Sherd from Holliston Mills.

vessels" with this decorative form were found in all of the Tellico Project work along the Little Tennessee River south of Knoxville.

On the other hand, much work remains to be done to explain the mix of Pisgah and Dallas wares. While archaeologists often tend to equate particular pottery styles with particular ethnic groups and/or archaeological cultures (Hally 1994: 144; Beck and Moore 2002: 193, 196), this often is not a demonstrable correlation. Trade and other cultural processes must also be considered. As far as we are aware, no chemical characterizations (e. g., trace element analyses) of ceramics from the Appalachian Summit region exist (see Steponaitis, Blackman, and Neff 1996 for general southeastern patterns in Mississippian ceramics). Dallas ceramic assemblages also vary greatly. For example, Dallas sherds from Holliston Mills that we submitted for trace element analyses did not match any Mississippian sherds in the MURR database, including sherds from the McMahan site near Sevierville, Tennessee, and Bussell Island at the mouth of the Little Tennessee River (Ferguson et al. 2007: 5; Steponaitis, Blackman, and Neff 1996).

In sum, we do not believe that the archaeological evidence at Holliston Mills supports an interpretation of a chiefdom society with a chiefly lineage. Differential social status at Holliston Mills likely fell out along kin groups within a corporately structured community. To paraphrase a colleague, the inhabitants of Holliston Mills may have been a group of "wealthy businesspeople." This notion would be consistent with Hudson's (1990; Hudson et al. 1985: 731) notion of the late prehistoric native peoples of upper East Tennessee as traders. Such an interpretation would explain the diversity of ceramics.

14

Caves as Mortuary Contexts in the Southeast

JAN F. SIMEK AND ALAN CRESSLER

From early in the history of European settlement in the Southeast, it was observed that the region's caves and karsts were used by the ancients as places for interring the dead. At the dawn of the nineteenth century, discoveries in the deep caves of Tennessee and Kentucky caught the imagination of the American intelligentsia, leading to intensive efforts to uncover the remarkable treasures that Appalachia's caves clearly held hidden within their fastnesses. In 1811, for example, there was an impressive find of the bones of a giant ground sloth (*Megalonyx jeffersonii*) in Big Bone Cave, Tennessee, which site was named for the discovery. This skeleton, now curated at the Academy of Natural Sciences in Philadelphia, represents the only known specimen of a giant ground sloth with a complete pelvis (Mercer 1897). As we shall see, human remains were also discovered in Big Bone Cave at about the same time. Other sites in Kentucky and in Tennessee yielded extraordinary evidence of past use as mortuaries, and as time went on, it became clear that the complexity of prehistoric cave use was considerable (Watson 1969, 1974), including use as burial locales. Despite this growing evidence for complexity, however, archaeologists only rarely concerned themselves with cave burials in considering regional mortuary practices.

Yet the prehistoric use of caves as burial places in the Appalachian Plateau region was remarkable and significant. Beginning in the Archaic Period, increasing in the Woodland Period, and culminating in the Mississippian Period, cave burials represent a varied set of contexts that link mortuary practices with complex ritual behaviors including elaborate preparation of the remains, extensive illumination of the cave burial locations, and in some cases, the production of specific parietal art motifs. Cave burials were clearly solemn and significant for the people who produced them and they were distinctive in relation to contemporary exterior interments. Understanding caves as mortuary contexts in the Southeast is thus central to understanding aspects of ancient culture that archaeologists traditionally see in mortuary behavior: social stratification, class, and religion, among other things.

Before we turn to prehistoric cave burials in Appalachia, we offer a few conditions for our presentation. First, the Eastern Band of Cherokee Indians, through the tribal historic preservation officer, has issued guidelines for recording and discussing prehistoric human remains in areas of their interest, including the region we consider in this chapter. Based on those guidelines, we will not reveal the locations of any cave that contains human burials, nor will we show photographs of human remains. Second, even though this is a book on Mississippian mortuary behavior, we hope to show that the prehistoric practice of cave burial has a long, continuous chronological trajectory in Appalachia that transcends and links standard period designations. Thus, we believe the phenomena are best considered over time, and while we will highlight Mississippian cave use when appropriate, we will try to understand it as it relates to practices that originated in and were continuous with earlier time periods.

Background: Historical Views of Archaeological Caves in Appalachia, 1800–1950

It is clear from early nineteenth-century accounts that the prehistoric record in Appalachian caves was at one time quite extraordinary. Conditions in the exceedingly dry nitrate-rich caverns of the Cumberland Plateau preserved cordage, weavings, basketry, feathers, and human bodies to a degree unknown elsewhere in the Southeast, except perhaps some waterlogged sites in the gulf region (cf. Vietzen & Vietzen 1956). One of the first and most notable discoveries of this type occurred in 1810 in Big Bone Cave, Tennessee. In September of that year, nitrate miners exploiting the cave for gunpowder ingredients (Big Bone contains the best-preserved industrial niter works in the east; Smith 2004) uncovered two human bodies that were mummified in the desiccating sediments (George 1990, 1994). This find ignited the interest of the country (see Figure 14.1). In 1812, Pleasant Miller wrote about the bodies in the *Medical Repository*, and because of the detail of his description and the remarkable nature of the discoveries being described, Miller's letter deserves extended quotation:

> On the 2nd day of September last [1810], some persons were digging in a copperas cave (in the county of Warren, state of Tennessee,) situated on what is usually called the Caney Fork of Cumberland River, 10 miles below the falls. That at about six feet below the surface of the bottom of the cave, something like clothing was discovered, which, upon proper examination, was found to be the shrouding of some dead bodies. Upon further investigation, the bodies were found to be two in

number, a male and female, which, as he [Miller refers to an unnamed correspondent here] expressed it, they judged to have been buried in ancient times. They [Miller's correspondents are unnamed] supposed the male to have been at the time of his decease about 25 years of age. He was enveloped in the following manner: first, with a fine linen shirt. His legs were drawn up, then five deer skins were closely bound round his body. A twilled blanket, wrapped around them, and a cane mat sixty feet long, wrapped round the whole. His frame was entire except for the bowels; his hair, of a fair complexion; his teeth, remarkably sound; his stature, above the common. The body of the female was found interred about three feet from that of the other. Its position of lying was similar to that of the male. The carcase was enveloped first with two undressed deer skins, under which, upon the face, was found a small cane mat. Then four dressed deer skins were wrapped round it, over which was folded a cane mat large enough to cover the whole. There were then five sheets, supposed to be made of nettle lint, wrought up curiously around each side with feathers of various kinds and colours. Two fans of feathers were found next, upon the breast. The body, with the whole of the before described wrapping, was found on what was believed to be a hair trunk or box, with a cane cover, which was wound up in two well-dressed deerskins of the largest kind; the whole girthed with two straps: the female is supposed to have been from 12 to 15 years of age: her hair short and black; the body entire; the eyes as full and prominent as if alive." (Miller 1812)

It is truly unfortunate that the artifacts and remains that Miller described are lost today. Shortly after the discovery of these burials, they and others found at about the same time (see below) were removed and began long, convoluted, and destructive journeys that saw them systematically mislabeled, misused, and misrepresented. Some were lost outright to disasters such as museum fires; others disappeared into the sands of time simply because they changed hands and identities once too often (George 1994). At least part of this sad history was due to the great public interest the remains excited and the greed that interest incited in certain individuals. Little if anything remains of these discoveries today. Preservation in Big Bone Cave was such that these remarkable discoveries *could* well have been present, as is clear from materials recovered in the cave during more recent archaeological projects, such as the woven fiber bag depicted in Figure 14.2 (Crothers 1987). And while this level of preservation, and that in the descriptions, might suggest that these artifacts and the Big Bone Cave burials are relatively recent in age, a ^{14}C date made directly on the woven bag places it firmly within the Middle Woodland Period.

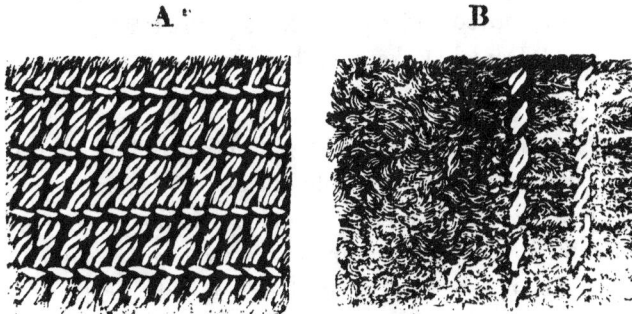

Figure 14.1. Drawing by Constantine Rafinesque of a Prehistoric Mummy from Short Cave, Kentucky, and Woven Fiber Artifacts Found with It. From Rafinesque 1824.

Figure 14.2. Late Woodland Period Woven Fiber Bag from Big Bone Cave, Tennessee. At the Frank H. McClung Museum, The University of Tennessee.

The Big Bone Cave finds were not the only ones during this time period. Also in 1811, the body of a child was found in Short Cave, Kentucky, "again enveloped in a deer skin ... but on exposure to the open atmosphere, it in a few hours crumbled to its natural dust" (J. Clifford, Lexington, Kentucky, to B. Barton, Philadelphia, September 4, 1811, quoted in George 1990). And it is likely that two or more mummies were found in Short Cave in 1811, one of which, "Fawn Hoof," was moved and represented to tourists as being from Mammoth Cave. In 1812, Daniel Drake described two more bodies from a Tennessee cave:

> In digging for saltpeter in 1811, on Dutch River, Smith Co. Tennessee, a large stone was discovered across the mouth of a cave. On entering the cave, which appeared natural in a limestone rock, resembling a vault or ancient sepulcher, the bodies of two human persons were discovered. They were male and female, and each in a curious wrought basket made of splits of cane. The bodies were in a setting posture. Around each body was wrapped a kind of large shroud [?] or plaid [?] seemingly wrought with the fingers and made of the best matting resembling wild nettles or Indian hemp. Both bodies and shroud were entire. The bodies were

consolidated (notes by Daniel Drake from The Daniel Drake Papers of the Draper Manuscripts #2 O 30, curated by the State Historical Society of Wisconsin, quoted in George 1990. According to George [1990: 52], this could be the reference seen by Pleasant Miller [Miller 1812:147] in a Nashville newspaper in 1810.

It is clear from these descriptions that an extraordinary archaeological record existed in the caves of the Southeast at the time the area was settled by Europeans. It is unfortunate that no modern archaeologists have seen anything like the examples of intentional burials described in the preceding passages. It is true that mummified corpses have been discovered in the modern era (Lost John was found in Mammoth cave in 1935), but these were the results of accidental deaths and depositions (Meloy 1984; Watson 1974). At best, only faint traces of the rich early record remain today. We have no idea of the chronological position of these remains.

As more caves in the Southeast were explored, it became clear that a variety of types of cave burials existed in the region. In 1885, for example, J. R. Stubblefield reported in a letter to the *Nashville Union* newspaper on his discovery in Grundy County, Tennessee of "at least 20 skulls all touching each other, besides which was a bed of bones beneath and around them of all parts of the human skeleton" (Stubblefield 1885). Mica sheets, mineral ore, a bead, projectile points, a stone pipe, polished stones, and a piece of copper were all found in association within this mass grave; these artifacts would suggest a Woodland Period association. We have visited this site, affirmed the past presence of human burials (although the site has been heavily looted since its discovery), and documented a series of painted red ochre dots on the cave wall above the area where the grave was located. In 1895, two Pickett County, Tennessee, hunters followed their dogs after an animal and "began digging near a large rock closing the entrance to a cave" (Parris 1946: 59). Further investigation found "Indian burials which lay upon the floor of this sealed natural vault.... There were pipes, gorgets, pottery bowls and other objects of Indian manufacture" (ibid.). A Dr. Shelton initiated heavy excavations in 1895, and W. G. Parris excavated the remaining deposits in 1919. Both discovered thousand of shell beads, several ceramic vessels, and bone artifacts in association with human bones. These associations indicate at least a Woodland Period age. This cave was small (only 2 m in diameter) and apparently represented a sealed prehistoric burial chamber containing numerous human remains. Parris discovered several other such small burial chambers containing several human internments along with similar grave goods, all in the Pickett County area (Lewis 1947).

Under the auspices of the United States National Museum, Gerard Fowke carried out a rather quixotic and unsystematic archaeological survey of caves in several midwestern and southeastern states in 1922 (Fowke 1922). Relying as much on unverified local informants as on personal observation, Fowke recorded five caves in Kentucky that were reported to contain human burials, at least two with multiple internments, out of the total of 39 caves he cataloged (13 percent). (One of these five, Fowke's Bell's Cave, was later referred to as Glovers Cave by Vietzen and Vietzen [1956]; see below). Curiously, Fowke cataloged Short Cave but did not refer to the important burials discovered there in the nineteenth century. Of the 16 caves he lists for Tennessee, only one, Caldwell's Cave is reported on secondhand information to contain human remains (6 percent of Fowke's total for Tennessee). We do not know today where Caldwell's Cave was, although it certainly has a different and more recent name. For Fowke, Alabama had the richest cave burial record; out of 26 caves he recorded, six contained human remains (23 percent of the sample), although only one explicitly lists more than a single body and only one is listed as containing grave goods in the form of pottery. At least two of the Alabama sites were sealed with walls or rocks at the openings. Thus, Fowke identified a widespread cave burial tradition in the Southeast, one that might contain multiple or single burials and that could involve the walling or sealing of burial caves. These characteristics would be expanded and elaborated by later research.

In 1946, E. F. Hassler reported on three burial caves in northern Tennessee, including one that was purportedly sealed by a large stone at the entrance that, when opened, revealed "many skeletons lying on cane scaffolds" (Hassler 1946; see Figure 14.3a). In another cave close by, Hassler found two burials, including one interred against the cave wall and another covered only by a layer of *eboulis sec* (Hassler 1946). In association with the second of these he found shell beads, a shell earplug, and two shell gorgets (Figure 14.3b). In a third cave some distance away, "the most spectacular cave in this immediate region," Hassler uncovered nearly 30 individual skeletons in anatomical position: "All had been deposited near the right-hand and left-hand walls at right angles to them and with heads next to the walls. . . . Burial accompaniments were mostly in the form of shell beads and ornaments, although a few stone objects were present" (Hassler 1946: 16). The grave associations in these three caves suggest Woodland or Early Mississippi period use. As Hassler shows, organization and patterning in the disposition of some cave burial assemblages was evident.

Hassler was not the only one to record these complex burial caves. Amateur artifact collector Raymond Vietzen excavated Glover's Cave in Todd County,

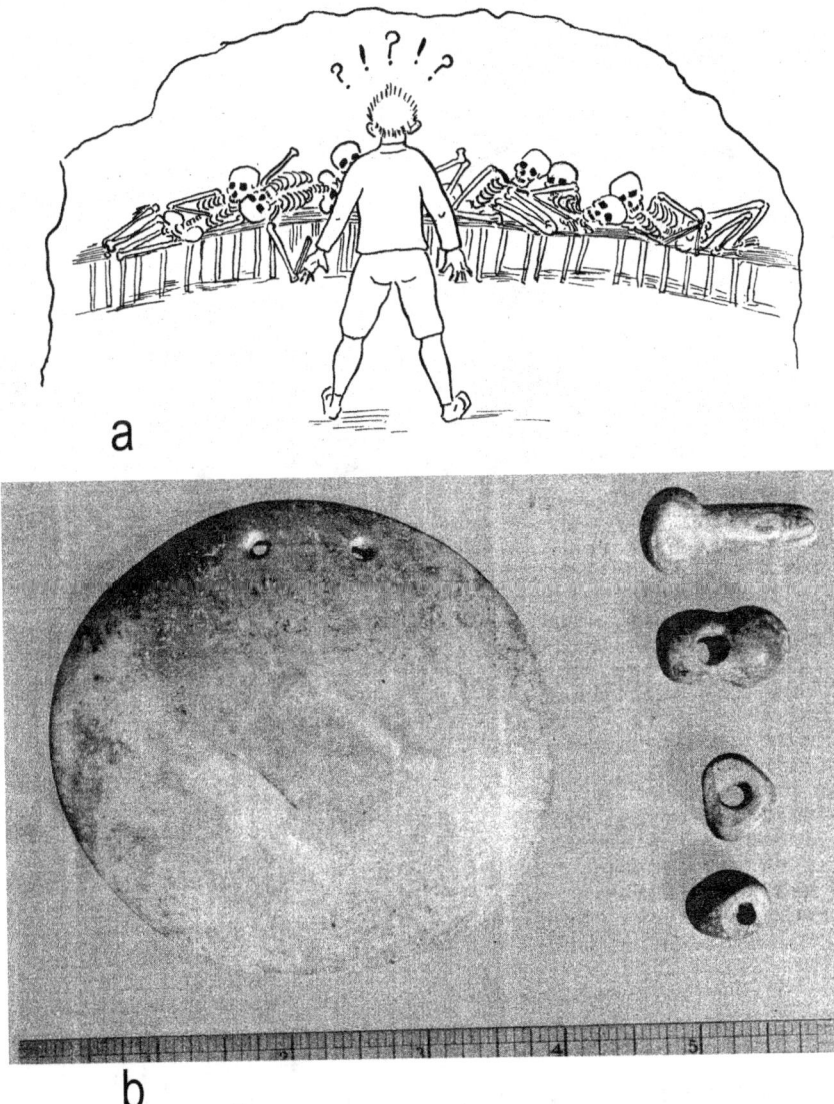

Figure 14.3. Illustrations by E. F. Hassler from His Description of a Tennessee Burial Cave. Skeletons lying on scaffolds (a); artifacts from the same cave (b). From Hassler 1946.

Kentucky, from 1941 to 1951 (Vietzen and Vietzen 1956). This remarkably preserved mortuary cave site contained numerous cremations, bundle burials, and burials in anatomical position (Figure 14.4), numbering more than 200 individuals, according to Vietzen (1956: 59). Five dog burials, some of which were possibly associated with grave goods and one with stone slabs, were also present. Grave associations were sparse, but it is clear from Vietzen's descrip-

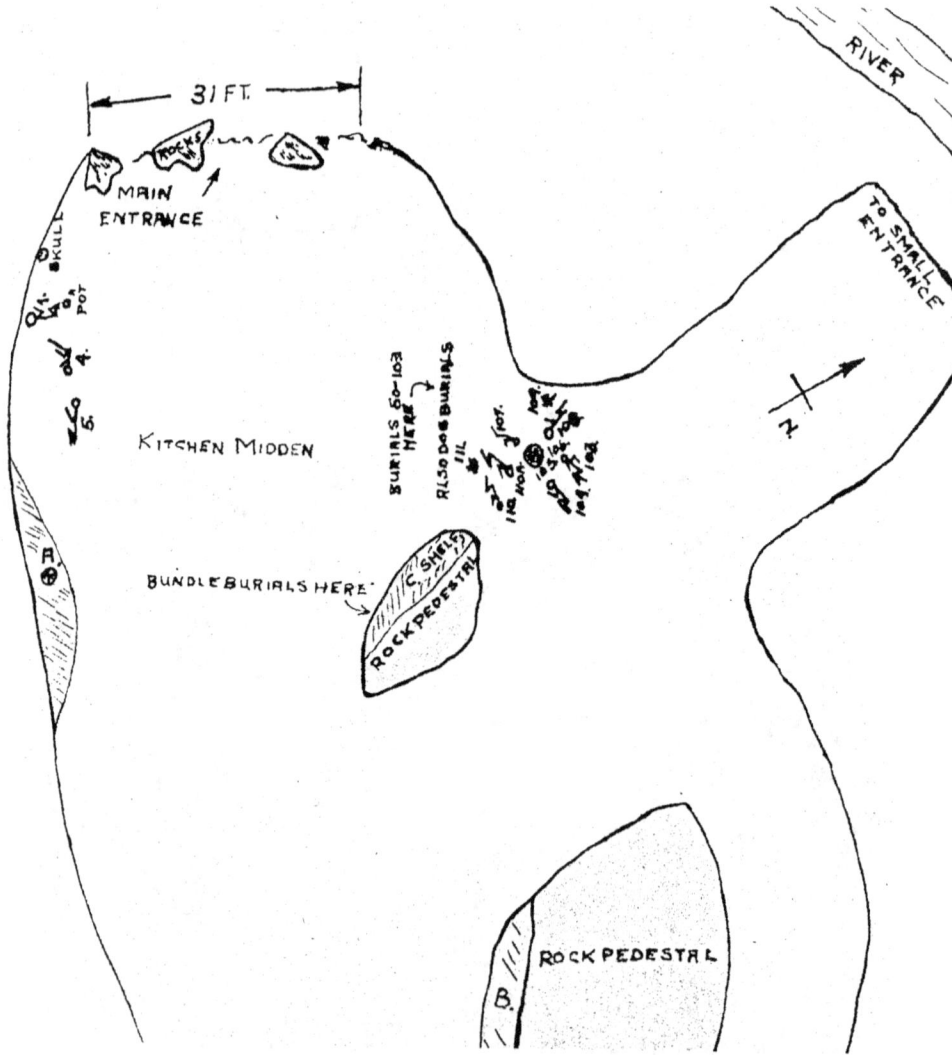

Figure 14.4. Map of Glover's Cave Burials. After Vietzen and Vietzen (1956).

tions that these included both Archaic (the most common) and Woodland Period artifacts along with a great variety of preserved cordage and textiles.

T. B. Hay described an elaborate multiple internment in a cave in Montgomery County, Tennessee, not far from Glovers Cave. This site included 12 bodies (Figure 14.5) associated with bedrock mortars, artifact caches, and a series of post molds at the cave mouth that may represent an artificial cloture (Hay 1958). Hay attributed this assemblage to the Archaic Period on stylistic grounds with agreement from T. M. N. Lewis and M. Kneberg (Hay 1958: 15).

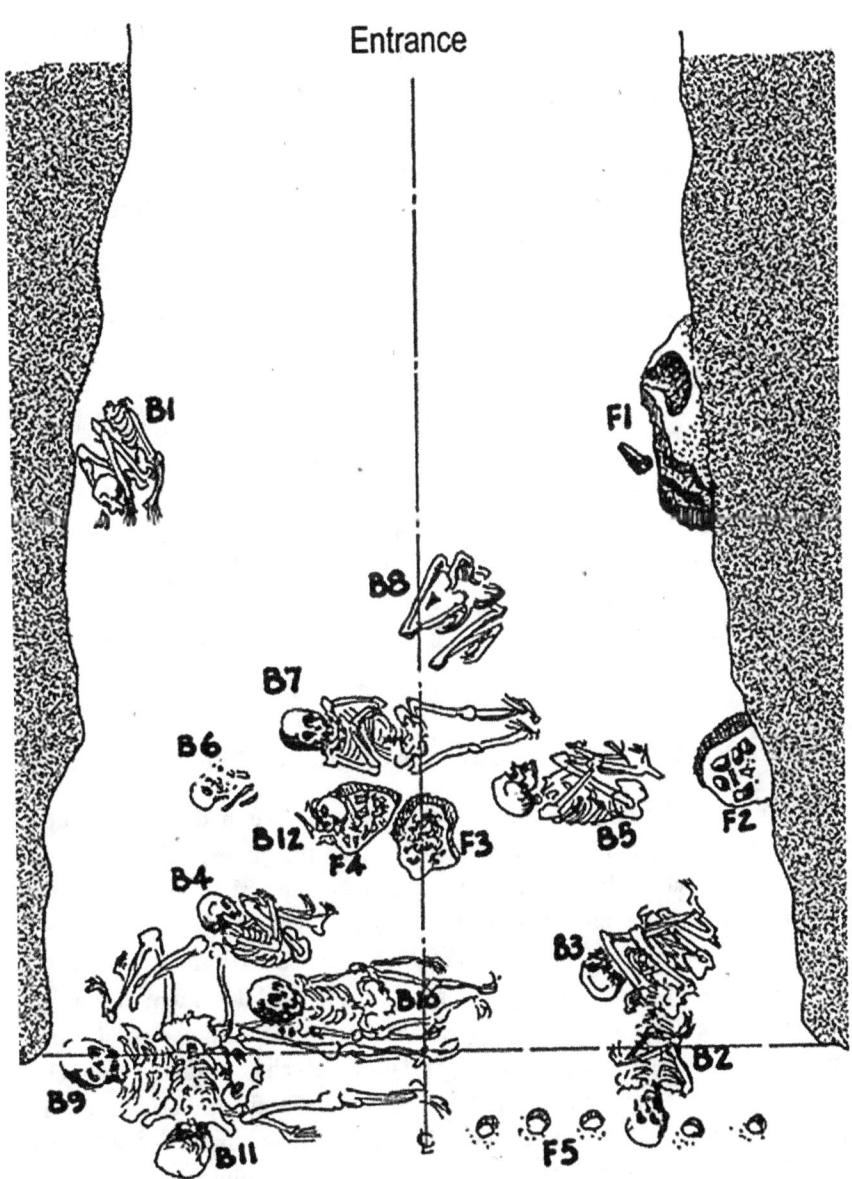

Figure 14.5. Map of Prehistoric Burials in Coleman Cave, Tennessee. After Hay 1958.

Finally, Virgil Owens excavated four bundle burials from the wet inner chamber of "Saltpeter Cave" in Bedford County, Tennessee (Owens 1958), found in association with *Anculosa* shell beads, atlatl weights, and shell pendants. These all suggest an Archaic Period mortuary. We have revisited this cave, now completely looted, and identified a single human tooth left in the deep chamber that yielded the original samples.

Thus, early archaeological work in the nineteenth and twentieth centuries revealed a long-term and complex use of caves for mortuary purposes in the Appalachian Plateau region. Cave burial began in the Archaic and continued into the Mississippian periods. In some cases, numerous graves were disposed in an organized fashion around the interior of caves. Grave goods were common and (in some cases) very elaborate and sometimes involved preparation of the body. Cremations, bundle burials, and articulated bodies were all included. Single burials also occurred and could also entail grave artifacts. In some cases, architectural elements were deployed to support the bodies on constructed scaffolding or to close the caves, including large boulders that had no evident modification, dry rock walls, and perhaps closures made from posts and coverings. In short, complicated mass burials in caves have been known from the Southeast for many years since early in the history of archaeology in the area. What has not been clear is the extent and scale of this practice.

Current Research on Southeastern Cave Burials, 1950 to the Present

In more recent years, professional archaeologists have made notable studies of cave burials in the Southeast using modern techniques of recovery and analysis. Excavations beginning in 1953 yielded a rich archaeological sequence in Russell Cave, Alabama, that included some burials; these studies focused on the Archaic Period (Griffin 1974). This sequence most directly addresses the use of the cave's vestibule area for the occasional internment of the dead instead of the deepest recesses of the dark zone; the vestibule was also used for habitation. Much the same can be said for the Archaic sequence from Dust Cave, Alabama (Sherwood et al. 2004). For the Woodland Period, Walthall and DeJarnette's 1974 publication on the Copena cave burials of the Tennessee River Valley in Alabama cataloged 28 caves containing elaborate burials that included wooden grave furniture, mica, galena, and other exotic grave goods (Walthall and DeJarnette 1974). More recently, Boyd and colleagues in Virginia have identified more than 50 prehistoric mortuary caves, primarily in the southwestern portion of the state (Boyd and Boyd 1997; Boyd et al. 2001). For the most part, these Virginia cave burials date to the Late Woodland

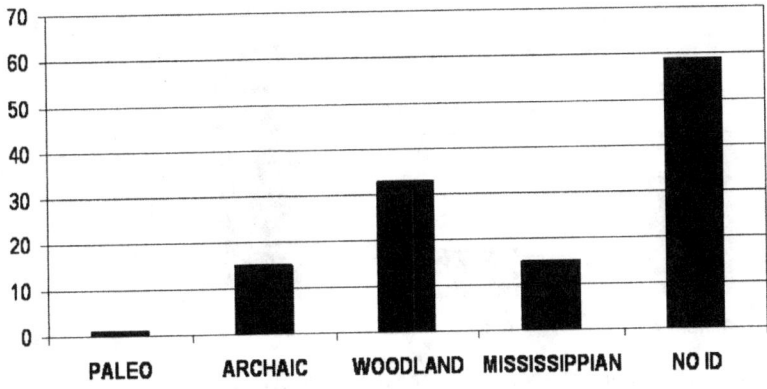

Figure 14.6. Count of Burial Caves Known Today by Time Period. (N = 103)

Period (ca. A.D. 900–1600), and all sexes and ages were buried in a variety of burial forms. The same is true for Lake Hole Cave, a heavily vandalized burial site in extreme northeastern Tennessee (near those described in Virginia by the Boyds) that underwent intensive professional salvage excavations in 1991 (Whyte and Kimball 1997). Lake Hole contained more than 99 individual burials, including possible cremations and bundles as well as articulated interments. All ages from infants to adults and both sexes are represented at Lake Hole, and the cave may have been sealed originally with limestone slabs.

Our own survey work in the caves of the Southeast indicates that cave burials are more frequent than might be suspected, and they constitute a significant portion of the archaeological record of prehistoric mortuary practices in the region. This assertion is based on more than two decades of cave inventory by archaeologists from the University of Tennessee, beginning with Charles Faulkner and P. Willey in the 1980s and continuing today with the University of Tennessee Cave Archaeology Research Team (CART). As of 2005, CART has visited nearly 1,500 caves in North Georgia, North Alabama and Tennessee, surveying cave vestibules and dark-zone passages as deeply as is physically possible. We have identified 103 caves as sites of dark-zone burials.

We do no excavation in these caves because the archaeological record is rarely in jeopardy, so we must rely on finding chronologically diagnostic artifacts to give us temporal parameters (Figure 14.6). In some cases we do have ^{14}C age determinations from the charcoal of river-cane torches, but most of our absolute dates were made in association with cave art because of our funding context. Thus, 59 of our 103 burial caves have no chronological information. Of the other 44, only Dunbar Cave in Tennessee (Simek et al. 2006) has

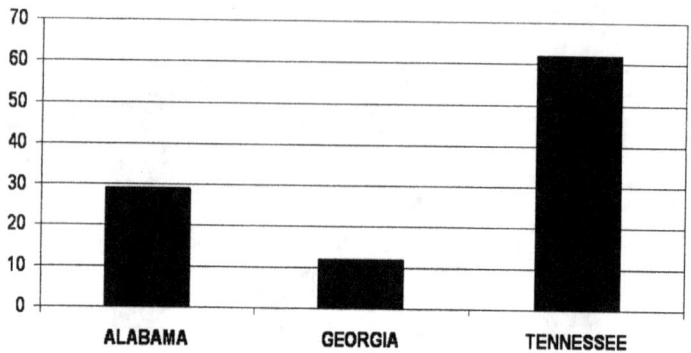

Figure 14.7. Count of Burial Caves Known Today by State. (N = 103)

PaleoIndian artifacts; these were found in the cave vestibule, not inside the cave, where burials were found. At Dunbar, a Beaver Lake point came from the base of a four-meter-deep sequence underlying rich Archaic, Woodland, and Mississippian levels. Fifteen caves have Archaic associations, but the Woodland Period has the most frequent chronological indicators (33). Surprisingly, given conventional wisdom (Crothers, et al. 2002), cave burials are associated with the Mississippi Period as often as they are for the Archaic, which has 15 such associations.

Figure 14.7 shows the distribution of the 103 burial caves by state. Alabama has 29 sites in our sample, but we note that these include only sites we have visited. A number of the Copena caves documented in Walthall and DeJarnette are not included here. Alabama surely has many more cave burial sites than we have in our sample. Georgia has yielded only a dozen sites. The Appalachian karst region has only a limited presence in both Alabama and Georgia, so it is likely that there are fewer caves there than to the north, in Tennessee and Kentucky. For obvious reasons, we have visited many more caves in Tennessee than in the adjacent states to the south; 1,000 caves in our sample come from Tennessee. This represents a little over 10 percent of the nearly 9,000 caves recorded by Tennessee Cave Survey, Inc., an avocational organization that seeks and documents caves in the state. More than 250 (about 25 percent of the sample total) contain some evidence of prehistoric human use. If this proportion is representative, then there may be some 2,200 dark-zone cave archaeological sites in Tennessee, a number that would comprise some 15 percent of the recorded prehistoric archaeological record in the state. Obviously, this is a significant but underrepresented aspect of the region's archaeological record. Of the archaeological sites already surveyed, 62 caves in our Tennessee sample (6 percent) were used for burial of the dead. If this sample proportion is representative, there may be as many as 550 burial caves in Tennessee alone. These are impressive numbers, and they could be replicated to greater or lesser extent in Kentucky, West Virginia, Virginia, Georgia, Alabama, Missouri, and Arkansas—anywhere where karst geomorphology is present.

The context of southeastern cave burial sites is quite variable. Of the 103 caves in our sample, the great majority (65) include multiple bodies. Thirty-eight sites contain only a single individual, but some of these (such as Indian Cave in Grainger County, Tennessee) are probably accidental deaths in caves like some of the early mummy finds in Kentucky. Seven multiple burial caves were clearly ledge burials, not as elaborate but similar to those Hassler described in the 1940s. Eleven caves have evidence that can be interpreted as grave goods associated with burials, but no such associations can be made in any of the other cases. Four caves include calcined human bones in some quantity, suggesting that caves may have received cremated remains along with uncremated bodies. One of the Alabama caves in our sample has evidence of a wooden grave box, suggesting another Copena burial cave as described by Walthall and DeJarnette in 1974.

We believe that another contextual variable is important. In nearly one in five of the caves in our sample, human remains were deposited into a vertical pit, usually to a depth that precluded access by the living. Often multiple individuals (sometimes a considerable number) are present in such pits, and these do not seem to be specific as to age or gender. It is clear that articulated bodies were introduced into pits in some but not all of these cases. Rarely are artifacts associated with these pit burials, and 15 of these sites have no chronological information. But the four that have artifacts include two with Archaic and two with Mississippian associations. It is not clear what differentiates the people who were buried in pits from those laid out more formally in caves or, for that matter, those buried outside caves. It is clear that this practice, like cave burial more generally, spans much of the prehistoric sequence in the Southeast.

In half our sample, cave burials are not the only activities in the cave. Many burial caves show evidence of exploration in other parts of the dark zone, perhaps related to burial placement in the cave (or it may reflect other times or activities). In a few burial caves, people mined for minerals and resources such as clay, although it is unclear that these activities were related, since they are always located in different parts of the cave. Finally, the most common activity associated with cave burials (occurring over 20 percent of the burial cave sample), is the production of dark-zone cave art.

Human Burials and Cave Art

The relationship between parietal art and human internment is surely complex; sometimes the activities coincide in space and sometimes they do not. Our analysis of this relationship is just beginning, but we have made at least one correlation, concerning the association between a particular cave art motif and the presence of human burials in caves. In all likelihood, this relationship developed during the Late Woodland Period in Tennessee and continued into the Mississippian. We have published a detailed paper on this issue that considered six sites, four in Tennessee, one in Georgia, and one in West Virginia (Simek, Cressler, and Pope 2004). In this chapter, we will briefly review the sites we have previously presented (except for the West Virginia site, which is outside the southeastern sphere) and will discuss three additional sites that may exhibit this relationship. The motif that is associated with burials is an elongated closed oval with a series of vertical lines crossing perpendicular to the oval's long axis. We refer to the figure as a "toothy mouth." We have labeled this image as a mouth because in several cases it forms the mouth of a human face. Thus, we interpret the oval as the mouth and the vertical segments as teeth inside the mouth. In nearly every case where we have found the toothy mouth, the cave housing the glyph contains multiple human burials or there is evidence that it once did so. Currently we know of eight southeastern cave sites that contain this image.

5th Unnamed Cave is a small cave with two entrances, one a vertical pit drop and the second a tight horizontal passage that joins the main chamber below the pit. As we showed in 2004, there are two engraved petroglyphs on the wall of the cave and the cave floor contained a number of intact human remains, including at least one whole cranium. (In 1997, looters destroyed the interior of the cave.) The more complex of the two glyphs is an anthropomorph with a box-shaped torso, narrow arms that extend out from the shoulders and then bend down, and short legs. The second image is a detached toothy mouth with no associated head or body (Figure 14.8a). The mouth is slightly above the human effigy, and the human remains are in the talus below, probably dropped into the pit entrance, given their location within the cave.

6th Unnamed Cave is very close to 5th Unnamed Cave, and like that example is quite small (60 m in total length). Also like its neighbor, 6th Unnamed Cave has two entrances, a pit and a horizontal talus entrance. Thus, burials could have been introduced both by dropping bodies down the pit and by carrying them into the cave. Human remains were found in the main chamber (especially below the pit) and for some distance down two connecting horizontal side passages. It is therefore likely that bodies were introduced

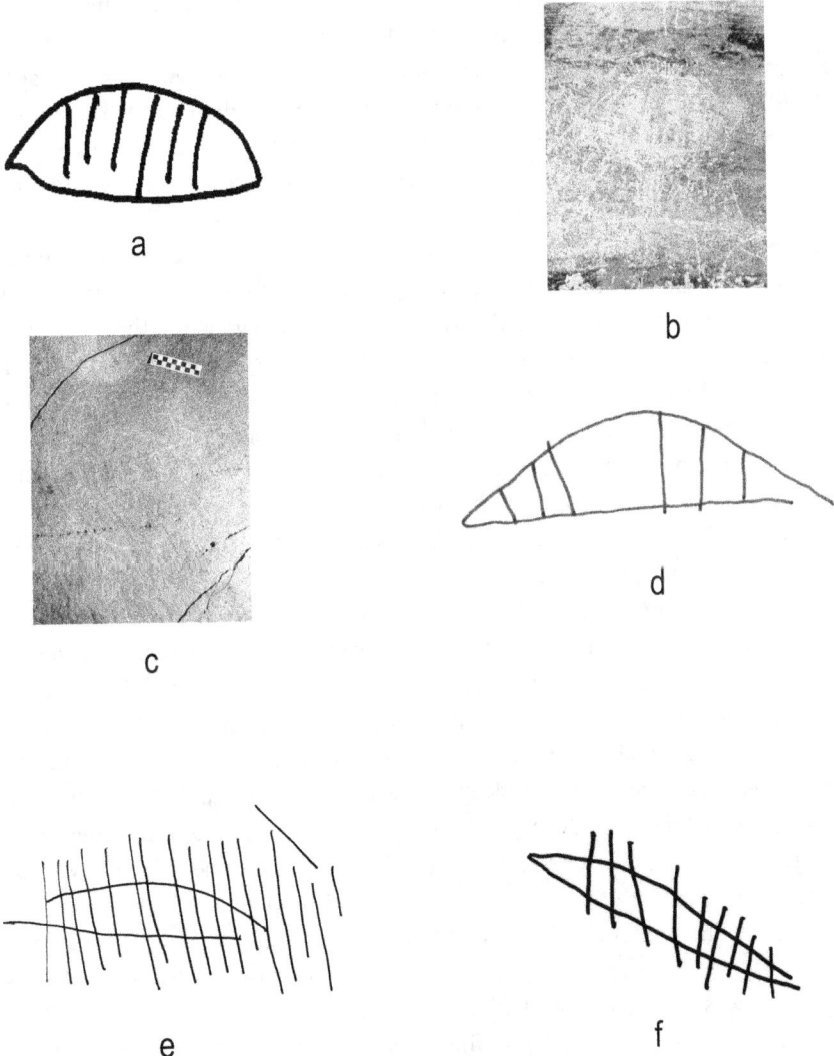

Figure 14.8. Examples of the Toothy Mouth Motif from Caves Discussed in the Text. Disembodied mouth from 5th Unnamed Cave, Tennessee (a); mouth in a face effigy from 6th Unnamed Cave, Tennessee (b); mouth in a face effigy from 11th Unnamed Cave, Tennessee (c); disembodied mouth from 34th Unnamed Cave, Tennessee (d); disembodied mouth from 38th Unnamed Cave, Tennessee (e); disembodied mouth from 12th Unnamed Cave, Tennessee (f). All were produced as engraved petroglyphs.

through both horizontal and vertical entrances. No diagnostic artifacts were recovered from the site. This cave was clearly the site of multiple human internments, and the biological anthropologist who first studied its assemblage, P. Willey, counted a human minimum number of individuals (MNI) of at least 15 people (Willey, Crothers, and Faulkner 1988). All ages and sexes are represented, including nine adults, one adolescent, three children, and two infants. Some of the bones are so burned as to indicate cremation, while other bones are entirely unburned. Two ^{14}C age determinations were made on human remains from the site, one on a burned specimen and the other on unburned bone. The burned bone yielded a Middle Woodland age while the unburned bone dates to the Mississippi Period. At least five petroglyphs, including four human heads, were carved on a single wall of the main chamber in 6th Unnamed Cave. At least one of the faces has a toothy mouth (Figure 14.8b). Two of the faces have no mouths, and a single disembodied mouth is also present. For reasons we have discussed (Simek, Cressler, and Pope 2004), it is most likely that the art in 6th Unnamed Cave is contemporary with the Mississippian (uncremated) burials at the site.

The archaeological record from 11th Unnamed Cave in Tennessee presents an impressive and diverse array of human activities (Simek et al. 2001). These are almost certainly profound and ceremonial in nature. They include elaborate illumination (a series of burning torches was mounted on the cave floor and ceiling), clay mining, art, burial of the dead, and perhaps hunting. We have discussed this site in detail elsewhere (Simek et al. 2001), so we will confine ourselves to the toothy mouth images and human burial evidence. A series of radiocarbon age determinations indicates that classic period Mississippian peoples were responsible for this record. Two glyphs in particular are relevant to this chapter. One is a remarkable petroglyph depicting a round face with weeping eyes and a pronounced toothy mouth (Figure 14.8c). A second face was drawn as a black pictograph a little farther into the cave. At two points in the cave where deep sediment deposits were cut by erosion, we observed a human phalanx and a fibula from two different adults. We saw other human bones in the back dirt from looters' pits outside the cave vestibule.

15th Unnamed Cave in Georgia is the southernmost of all the caves showing the toothy mouth motif in association with human graves. As we saw in other cases, this cave has several entrances, including both vertical pit and horizontal openings. Two unburned human teeth, both adult premolars, possibly from the same individual, were found in an area of the main cave passage heavily eroded by the action of an interior stream flowing toward the cave mouth. Not far from the location of the bones, and in the same stream passage, 15th Unnamed Cave also contains more than dozen petroglyphs arranged in two panels within sight of the cave opening. These include geometric shapes, a number of rayed circles ("suns"), at least one human face effigy without a toothy mouth, and several toothy mouth motifs.

Prehistoric glyphs in 34th Unnamed Cave include at least ten finely engraved petroglyphs that are difficult to discern without sources of raking light. Most are simple sets of straight or curved lines, cross-hatching, or "comb" figures. Two toothy mouths are also present (Figure 14.8d shows one of them). These glyphs are positioned in the middle of a long array of ledge burials in the cave. An MNI of seventeen people is calculated from human remains found commingled in a side passage, where nineteenth-century saltpeter miners displaced them and where we observed bones in situ on ledges. Adults and children of both sexes are present. As in 6th Unnamed Cave, some of the bones are burned, and the surfaces suggest cremation. Other bones are unburned. The fact that several grit-tempered ceramic sherds were found with the commingled remains suggest that the cave activity took place in the Woodland Period.

38th Unnamed Cave is the most recent discovery among the burial caves that exhibits the toothy mouth motif. This site was found in late 2003 and was not included in our 2004 publication on the motif; it is reported here for the first time. The cave has unfortunately been the site of heavy looting; this, coupled with a complex geology in which archaeological materials that were deposited at the opening in the karst system eroded down into a lower wet level by mass wasting and human (pothunter) bioturbation has all but eliminated deposits that can reliably inform us about the archaeological sequence at the site. We have been able to see some of the artifacts removed from the site, thanks to the owners of 38th Unnamed Cave, who borrowed materials from persons who dug there. These include two greenstone trapezoidal pendants, three shell pendants of diverse shapes, a steatite celt with fine line segments engraved around one face in groups of three or four, and a small ground limestone disk with a cross engraved on both faces, sometimes referred to as a "gaming piece." Also in the collection was a very long (22cm) polished-bone hairpin and several Archaic period lithic projectile points. In addition, a Jack's Reef corner-notched point and a Hamilton point indicate Late Woodland/Early Mississippi occupation. While we observed no human remains either in the cave or in the collection at first hand, the owners assured us that the pothunters claimed to have uncovered several burials during the course of their work, and we think this is almost certain, given the artifacts just described. In any case, these artifacts indicate a multicomponent occupation sequence at 38th Unnamed Cave featuring Archaic and Early Mississippi periods. Burials were probably present from at least the later prehistoric period.

This last fact is particularly important, given the presence in 38th Unnamed Cave of 21 petroglyphs disposed in five panels along the right side of the upper (entrance) passage. These glyphs, located in the twilight zone of the cave, are very faint and can only be seen when oblique light is focused on them. Many of the glyphs are abstract complex signs, cross-hatching, and/or geometric shapes. Several are representational, including an anthropomorph with a box-shaped body (Figure 14.9a), a large rendering of a bird's body, a figure that resembles a fringed textile (Figure 14.9b), and a typical toothy mouth (Figure 14.8e). The latter image is most germane here, since we are convinced by the site's contents and reported history that it contained human burials at one time.

In subject matter and production format, the 38th Unnamed Cave petroglyphs are quite similar to at least two other cave art sites we have recorded but that were not included in our 2004 paper on the toothy mouth motif; both of these sites are within a dozen kilometers of 38th Unnamed Cave and both of these also contain toothy mouth images. The first of these is 7th Unnamed Cave (Simek and Cressler 2008), located in a valley just below 38th Unnamed Cave. 7th Unnamed Cave contains a rich assemblage of finely incised petroglyphs, including avimorphs (more than 30 turkeys are depicted on the cave walls), a dancing bird-human image in the deepest part of the cave, and at least one image of a cross in a circle. Several toothy mouths are concentrated in one wall panel. Despite the fact that the cave has been heavily looted, we have observed human bones at various places around the cave floor, and it is certain that more than one individual is represented. We have not seen collections from this site and have not collected materials from it except for five fragments of burned animal bone from different areas of the cave floor. These were sampled and submitted for ^{14}C age determination by AMS (Simek and Cressler 2001; Simek and Cressler 2005). The average of these determinations indicates a calibrated date range of A.D. 680–A.D. 940, within this region's Late Woodland/Early Mississippi periods. In sum, 7th Unnamed Cave is another example of mass human burials in association with the toothy mouth motif.

Perhaps the most elaborate cave art site in Tennessee is 12th Unnamed Cave, also very close to the preceding sites. This small karst passage contains the largest assemblage of images that we have seen in an individual cave, rivaled only in its richness by Picture Cave in Missouri (Diaz-Granados et al. 2001; Diaz-Granados and Duncan 2004). Filled with petroglyphs that are very similar to those in 38th and 7th Unnamed caves, this site includes nearly 400 finely worked drawings that include avimorphs (many turkeys as well as raptors and other birds), box-shaped and conventionally shaped anthropomorphs, several

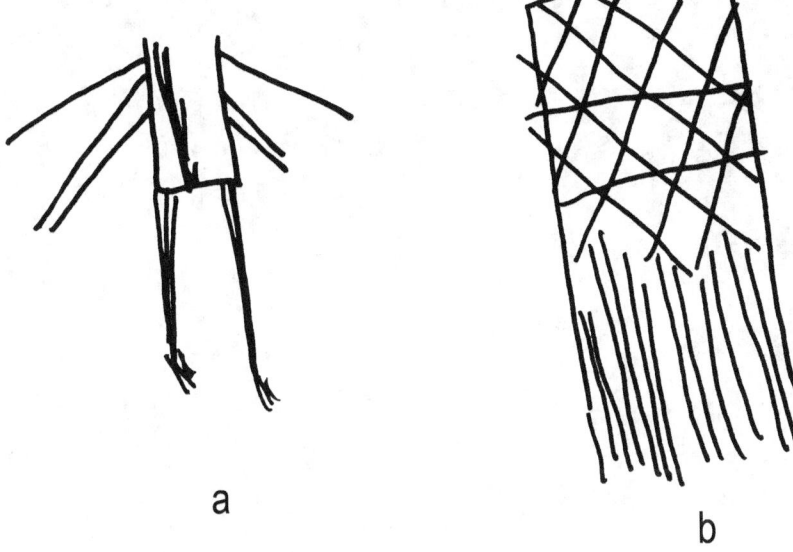

Figure 14.9. Petroglyphs from 38th Unnamed Cave, Tennessee. Box-shaped anthropomorph (a); woven bag motif (b).

images of fringed textiles identical to the one we saw in 38th Unnamed Cave (Figure 14.10), and a number of serpents, including one with antlers. A single toothy mouth image (Figure 14.8f) is present in the array. We have seen no human remains in this cave and we have not heard of looters finding human bones there. However, because it has been known as an archaeological site for a long time and is easy to access without detection, numerous parties have heavily looted the sediment deposits in the cave over the years, and few intact deposits remain today. The collections at the University of Tennessee contain one specimen sent to the Department of Anthropology in the 1980s labeled using the site's common local name (which we will not give here). This name is not uncommon in Tennessee, and only the residence of the sender would link this particular human cranial fragment to 12th Unnamed Cave. Still, it is possible (but not certain) that there were human burials in the cave at one time. Eleven ^{14}C age determinations from this site place it at the Late Woodland/Early Mississippi boundary for Middle Tennessee (Simek and Cressler 2001; Simek and Cressler 2005). 12th Unnamed Cave may be another cave that associates human burials with the toothy mouth cave art motif.

Although this evidence is difficult to quantify, it is our impression after examining more than 50 prehistoric cave art sites in the Southeast that these

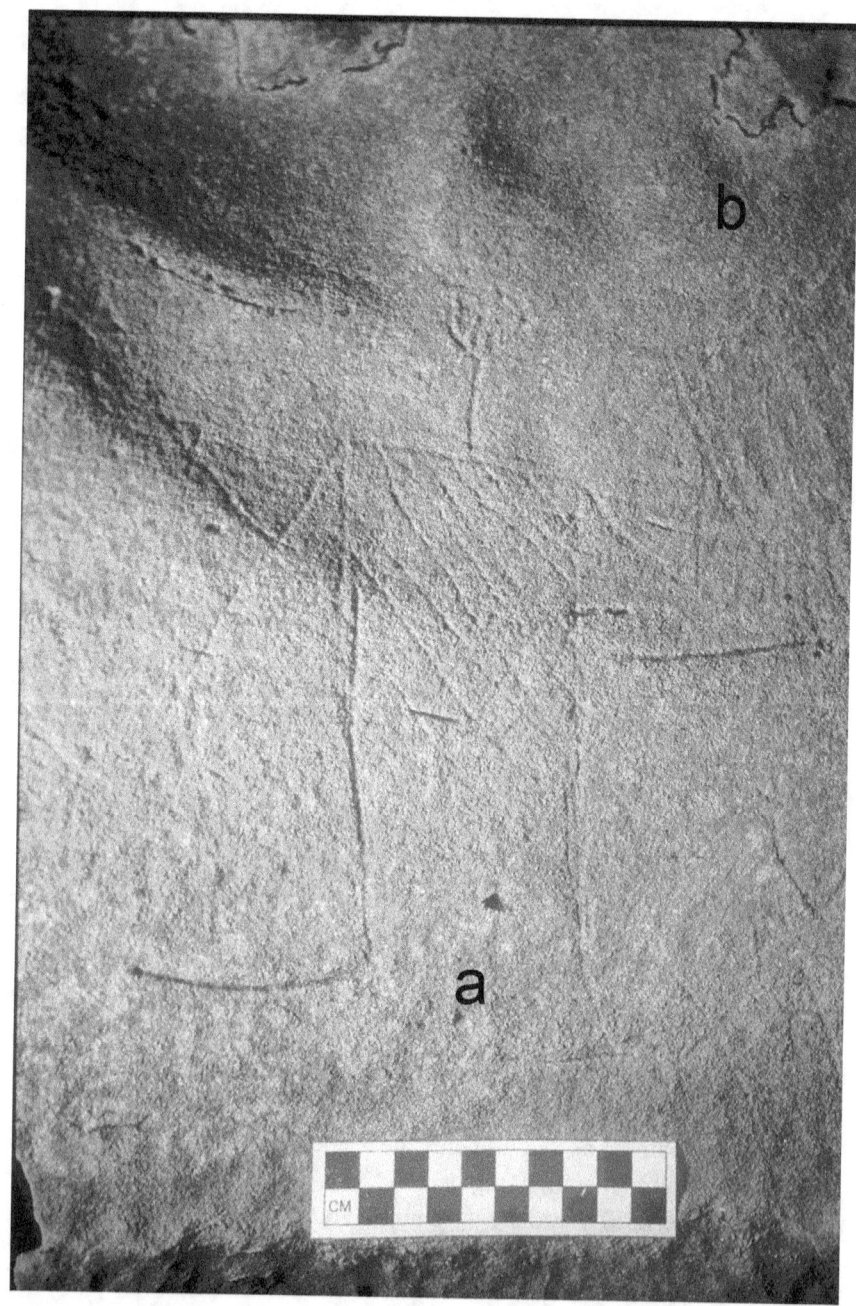

Figure 14.10. Petroglyphs from 12th Unnamed Cave, Tennessee. Box-shaped anthropomorph (a); woven bag motif (b).

last three are the most similar to each other in style, execution, and subject matter (as well as location) and may well have been produced by the same local cultural group or individual artists; this is an admittedly impressionistic assertion, a "gut feeling" based on a great deal of experience with these sites.

Comparative analysis of numerous prehistoric cave sites in the Southeast, then, shows a patterned relationship between the presence of a particular motif (an oval with multiple vertical lines filling the interior) and multiple human interments in the cave. This motif can occur as an isolated figure on the cave wall or can be incorporated into a human face effigy as the mouth (thus the name we have given it). There is some variability in chronology suggesting that this relationship may have its origins in the Middle Woodland Period and extend into the Mississippi. There is variability in burial method; pit-drop, cremation, and ledge burial techniques were used. Yet the basic association so far is fairly clear.

Conclusion

The prehistoric use of caves in the Southeast for human burial is a more common aspect of the archaeological record than has been recognized. Systematic survey demonstrates that the dark zones of many hundreds of caves were used for burial, beginning at least in the Archaic and continuing through the Mississippian Period. Burial practices were complex and varied, including possible sealing of the cave opening with natural boulders or constructed architectural features; open placement of the dead on cave floors, sometimes wrapped in cane matting or placed in baskets; construction of platforms to hold the dead; interment in sedimentary deposits; covering by rock cairns; and placement in inaccessible vertical fissures. Grave goods were sometimes (but not always) associated with burials. Other activities might be carried out in the cave, including the production of cave art, and at least some of the art was related to—and maybe "marked"—the presence of burials. Cave burial had a long and continuous tradition in the Southeast, suggesting indigenous origins and development. One interesting problem is how these sites relate to other contemporary burial options, such as mound burials and cemeteries. Integration of this evidence into the wider archaeological record, while a complicated undertaking, will be required if the true nature of complex prehistoric ritual landscapes in the Southeast is to be comprehended. At present, there is no indication that particular people were selected over others for underground mortuary treatment, at least according to age or gender, but it is surely significant that this practice occurred as one method of burial among many options at each point in time. And this is perhaps the most intriguing and enigmatic question about prehistoric cave burial in the Southeast: Exactly who was it that warranted eternal rest at the gateways to the underworld? The ultimate answer to this question will, we believe, tell us much about the cosmology of prehistoric people in the region and their own view of their place in the universe.

References Cited

Adams, R. L., and S. M. King (editors)
2010 *Residential Burial: A Multi-Regional Exploration.* Archeological Papers of the American Anthropological Association No. 20. Washington, D.C. In press.

Ahler, S. A., and P. J. DePuydt
1987 *A Report on the 1931 Powell Mound Excavations, Madison, County, Illinois.* Reports of Investigations, No. 43. Springfield: Illinois State Museum.

Alcock, S. E.
1993 *Graecia Capta: The Landscapes of Roman Greece.* Cambridge: Cambridge University Press.

Alt, S. M.
2001 Cahokian Change and the Authority of Tradition. In *The Archaeology of Traditions,* edited by T. R. Pauketat, pp. 141–56. Gainesville. University Press of Florida.
2002 Identities, Traditions, and Diversity in Cahokia's Uplands. *Midcontinental Journal of Archaeology* 27: 217–236.
2006 The Power of Diversity: The Roles of Migration and Hybridity in Culture Change. In *Leadership and Polity in Mississippian Society,* edited by B. M. Butler and P. D. Welch, pp. 289–308. Center for Archaeological Investigations Occasional Paper No. 33. Carbondale, Illinois: Southern Illinois University.

Alt, S. M., and T. R. Pauketat
2007 Sex and the Southern Cult. In *The Southeastern Ceremonial Complex,* edited by A. King. Tuscaloosa: University of Alabama Press.

Ambrose, S. H., J. Buikstra, and H. W. Krueger
2003 Status and Gender Differences in Diet at Mound 72, Cahokia, Revealed by Isotopic Analysis of Bone. *Journal of Anthropological Archaeology* 22: 217–226.

Anderson, D. G.
1982 *The Mattassee Lake Sites: Archeological Investigations along the Lower Santee River in the Coastal Plain of South Carolina.* Commonwealth Associates Inc. Submitted to United States Department of the Interior, Contract Number C54030(80). National Park Service, Interagency Archeological Services, Atlanta, Georgia.
1994 *The Savannah River Chiefdoms: Political Change in the Late Prehistoric Southeast.* Tuscaloosa: University of Alabama Press.
1997 The Role of Cahokia in the Evolution of Southeastern Mississippian Society. In *Cahokia: Domination and Ideology in the Mississippian World,* edited by T. R. Pauketat and T. E. Emerson, pp. 248–268. Lincoln: University of Nebraska Press.

1999 Examining Chiefdoms in the Southeast: An Application of Multiscalar Analysis. In *Great Towns and Regional Polities in the Prehistoric American Southwest and Southeast*, edited by J. E. Neitzel, pp. 215–241. Albuquerque: University of New Mexico Press.

Anderson, K.
1994 The Aztalan Site: A Human Skeletal Inventory and Excavation History. Unpublished M.A. Thesis, Department of Anthropology, University of Chicago.

Bailey, G. A.
1995 *The Osage and the Invisible World: From the Works of Francis La Flesche*. Norman: University of Oklahoma Press.

Banks, Marcus
1996 *Ethnicity: Anthropological Constructions*. New York: Routledge.

Barker, A. W.
2004 Some Preliminary Observations on the Quick and the Dead at Mound C, Etowah. Paper presented at the 61st Annual Meeting of the Southeaster Archaeological Conference, St. Louis, Missouri.

Barker, A. W., C. E. Skinner, M. S. Shackley, M. D. Glascock, and J. D. Rogers
2002 Mesoamerican Origin for an Obsidian Scraper from the Precolumbian Southeastern United States. *American Antiquity* 67: 103–8.

Barrett, S. A.
1933 *Ancient Aztalan*. Bulletin of the Public Museum of the City of Milwaukee, 13. Milwaukee, Wisconsin.

Barrett, J. C.
1999 The Mythical Landscapes of the British Iron Age. In *Archaeologies of Landscape: Contemporary Perspectives*, edited by W. Ashmore and A. B. Knapp, pp. 253–265. Oxford: Blackwell.

Barth, F.
1969 Introduction. In *Ethnic Groups and Boundaries. The Social Organization of Culture Difference*, edited by F. Barth, pp. 5–38. Prospect Heights, California: Waveland Press.
1987 *Cosmologies in the Making*. Cambridge: Cambridge University Press.

Barth, F. (editor)
1969 *Ethnic Groups and Boundaries*. Boston, Mass.: Little, Brown.

Beck, L. A.
1995 Regional Cults and Ethnic Boundaries in "Southern Hopewell." In *Regional Approaches to Mortuary Analysis*, edited by L.A. Beck, pp. 167–184. New York: Plenum Press.

Beck, R. A., Jr. (editor)
2007 *The Durable House: House Society Models in Archaeology*. Center for Archaeological Investigations, Occasional Paper No. 35. Carbondale, Illinois: Southern Illinois University.

Beck, R. A., D. J. Bollander, J. A. Brown, and T. K. Earle
2007 Eventful Archaeology: The Place of Space in Structural Transformation. *Current Anthropology* 48: 833–860.

Beck, R. A., Jr., and D. G. Moore
2002 The Burke Phase: A Mississippian Frontier in the North Carolina Foothills. *Southeastern Archaeology* 21: 192–205.

Bennett, L. J.
1984 A Mortuary Analysis of Early Mississippian Status Structure Along the Tombigbee River. Unpublished M.A. thesis, Department of Anthropology, State University of New York at Binghamton. Binghamton, New York.

Binford, L. R.
1964 *Archaeological Investigations on Wassam Ridge*. Archaeological Salvage Report 17. Carbondale, Illinois: Southern Illinois University.
1971 Mortuary Practices: Their Study and Their Potential. In *Approaches to the Social Dimensions of Mortuary Practices*, edited by J. A. Brown, pp. 6–29. Memoir 25. Salt Lake City: Society for American Archaeology.
1972 *An Archaeological Perspective*. New York: Seminar Press.

Birmingham, R. A., and L. G. Goldstein
2005 *Aztalan: Mysteries of an Ancient Indian Town*. Madison, Wisconsin: University of Wisconsin Press and Wisconsin Historical Society.

Blanton, R. E., G. M. Feinman, S. A. Kowalewski, and P. N. Peregrine
1996 A Dual-Processual Theory for the Evolution of Mesoamerican Civilization. *Current Anthropology* 37: 1–14.

Blitz, J. H.
1993 *Ancient Chiefdoms of the Tombigbee*. Tuscaloosa: University of Alabama Press.
1999 Mississippian Chiefdoms and the Fission-Fusion Process. *American Antiquity* 64: 577–592.

Bloch, M., and J. Parry
1982 Introduction: Death and the Regeneration of Life. In *Death and the Regeneration of Life*, edited by M. Bloch and J. Parry, pp. 1–44. Cambridge: Cambridge University Press.

Boudreaux, E. A.
2005 The Archaeology of Town Creek: Chronology, Community Patterns, and Leadership at a Mississippian Town. Unpublished Ph.D. dissertation, Department of Anthropology, University of North Carolina, Chapel Hill.
2007a *The Archaeology of Town Creek*. Tuscaloosa: University of Alabama Press.
2007b A Mississippian Ceramic Chronology for the Town Creek Region. *North Carolina Archaeology* 56:1–57.

Bowser, B. J.
2000 From Pottery to Politics: An Ethnoarchaeological Study of Political Factionalism, Ethnicity, and Domestic Pottery Style in the Ecuadorian Amazon. *Journal of Archaeological Method and Theory* 7:219–248.

Boyd, C. C., Jr.
1986a *The 1986 Salvage Excavations at the Plum Grove Site (40Wg17), Washington County, Tennessee*. Report Submitted to the U. S. Forest Service, Cherokee National Forest, Cleveland, Tennessee and the Center for Appalachian Stud-

ies, East Tennessee State University, Johnson City. Department of Sociology/Anthropology, Radford University, Virginia.
1986b   An Evolutionary Approach to the Prehistory of Upper East Tennessee and Adjacent Areas. Unpublished Ph.D. Dissertation, Department of Anthropology, The University of Tennessee, Knoxville.

Boyd, C. C., Jr., and D. C. Boyd
1991   A Multidimensional Investigation of Biocultural Relationships Among Three Late Prehistoric Societies in Tennessee. *American Antiquity* 56: 75–88.
1997   Osteological Comparison of Prehistoric Native Americans from Southwest Virginia and East Tennessee Mortuary Caves. *Journal of Cave and Karst Studies* 39:160–165.

Boyd, C. C., Jr., and B. H. Riggs
1986   Ceramic Artifact Analysis. In *Archaeological Investigations in the Watauga Reservoir, Carter and Johnson Counties, Tennessee*, edited by C. C. Boyd, Jr., pp. 15–69. Tennessee Valley Authority, Publications in Anthropology, No. 46. Department of Anthropology Report of Investigations No. 44, University of Tennessee, Knoxville: Tennessee Valley Authority.

Boyd, C. C., D. C. Boyd, M. B. Barber, and D. A. Hubbard
2001   Southwest Virginia's Burial Caves: Skeletal Biology, Mortuary Behavior, and Legal Issues. *Midcontinental Journal of Archaeology* 26: 219–231.

Bradley, R.
1993   *Altering the Earth: The Origins of Monuments in Britain and Continental Europe.* Monograph Series 8. Edinburgh: Society of Antiquities of Scotland.
1998   *The Significance of Monuments: On the Shaping of Human Experience in Neolithic and Bronze Age Europe.* London: Routledge.

Brain, J. P., and P. Phillips
1996   *Shell Gorgets: Styles of the Late Prehistoric and Protohistoric Southeast.* Cambridge, Mass.: Peabody Museum Press.

Braun, D. P.
1979   Illinois Hopewell Burial Practices and Social Organization: A Reexamination of the Klunk-Gibson Mound Group. In *Hopewell Archaeology: The Chillicothe Conference*, edited by D. S. Brose and N. Greber, pp. 66–79. Kent, Ohio: Kent State University Press.

Braund, K. E. Holland (editor)
1999   *A Concise Natural History of East and West Florida*, by Bernard Romans. Tuscaloosa: University of Alabama Press.

Bridges, P. S.
1996   Warfare and Mortality at Koger's Island, Alabama. *International Journal of Osteoarchaeology* 6: 66–75.

Bridges, P. S., K. P. Jacobi, and M. L. Powell
2000   Warfare-Related Trauma in the Late Prehistory of Alabama. In *Bioarchaeological Studies of Life in the Age of Agriculture: A View from the Southeast*, edited by P. M. Lambert, pp. 35–62. Tuscaloosa: University of Alabama Press.

Brose, D. S., J. A. Brown, and D. W. Penney
1985 *Ancient Art of the American Woodland Indians.* New York: Henry N. Abrams.

Broster, J. B.
1972 The Ganier Site: A Late Mississippian Village on the Cumberland River. In *The Middle Cumberland Culture*, edited by R. B. Ferguson, pp. 51–78. Publications in Anthropology 3. Nashville, Tennessee: Vanderbilt University.

Brown, I.
1981 A Study of Stone Box Graves in Eastern North America. *Tennessee Anthropologist* 6: 1–26.

Brown, J. A.
1971 The Dimensions of Status in the Burials at Spiro. In *Approaches to the Social Dimensions of Mortuary Practices*, edited by J. A. Brown, pp. 92–112. Memoir 25. Salt Lake City: Society for American Archaeology.
1975 Spiro Art and its Mortuary Contexts. In *Death and the Afterlife in Pre-Columbian America*, edited by E. P. Benson, pp. 1–32. Washington, D.C.: Dumbarton Oaks Research Library and Collections.
1976 The Southern Cult Reconsidered. *Midcontinental Journal of Archaeology* 1:115–135.
1981a The Search for Rank in Prehistoric Burials. In *The Archaeology of Death*, edited by R. Chapman, I. Kinnes, and K. Randsborg, pp. 25–37. Cambridge: Cambridge University Press.
1981b The Potential of Systematic Collections for Archaeological Research. In *The Research Potential of Anthropological Museum Collections*, edited by A.-M. E. Cantwell, J. B. Griffin & N. A. Rothschild, pp. 65–76. Annals of the New York Academy of Science 376.
1990 Archaeology Confronts History at the Natchez Temple. *Southeastern Archaeology* 9: pp. 1–10.
1995 On Mortuary Analysis–with Special Reference to the Saxe-Binford Research Program. In *Regional Approaches to Mortuary Analysis*, edited by L. A. Beck, pp. 3–26. New York: Plenum.
1996 *The Spiro Ceremonial Center: The Archaeology of Arkansas Valley Caddoan Culture in Eastern Oklahoma.* Memoirs of the Museum of Anthropology No. 29. Ann Arbor: University of Michigan.
1997 The Archaeology of Ancient Religion in the Eastern Woodlands. *Annual Review of Anthropology* 26: 465–485.
2001 Human Figures and the Southeastern Ancestor Shrine. In *Fleeting Identities: Perishable Material Culture in Archaeological Research*, edited by P. B. Drooker, pp. 76–93. Center for Archaeological Investigations Occasional Paper No. 28. Carbondale, Illinois: Southern Illinois University Press.
2003 The Cahokia Mound 72Sub1 Burials as Collective Representation. In "A Deep-Time Perspective: Studies in Symbols, Meaning, and the Archaeological Record," edited by J. D. Richards and M. L. Fowler. *Wisconsin Archeologist* 84: 81–97.

2004a The Cahokia Expansion: Creating Court and Cult. In *The Hero, Hawk, and the Open Hand: American Indian Art of the Ancient Midwest and South*, edited by R. F. Townsend and R. Sharp, pp. 108–123. Chicago: Art Institute of Chicago.

2004b Exchange and Interaction to A.D. 1500. *Handbook for North American Indians, Volume 14–Southeast*, edited by R. D. Fogelson, pp. 677–685. Washington, D.C.: Smithsonian Institution Press.

2006a Where's the Power in Mound Building?–An Eastern Woodland Perspective. In *Leadership and Polity in Mississippian Society*, edited by B. M. Butler and P. D. Welch, pp. 197–213. Center for Archaeological Investigations Occasional Paper No. 33. Carbondale, Illinois: Southern Illinois University Press.

2006b On the Identity of the Birdman within Mississippian Art. In *Ancient Objects and Sacred Realms*, edited by F. K. Reilly, III and J. F. Garber, pp. 56–106. Austin: University of Texas Press.

2007a The Social House in Southeastern Archaeology. In *The Durable House: House Society Models in Archaeology*, edited by R. A. Beck, Jr. Center for Archaeological Investigations, Occasional Paper No. 35. Carbondale, Illinois: Southern Illinois University Press.

2007b On the Identity of the Birdman within Mississippian Period Art and Iconography. In *Ancient Objects and Sacred Realms: Interpretations of Mississippian Iconography*, edited by F. K. Reilly III, and J. F. Garber, pp. 56–106. Austin: University of Texas Press.

2007c Chronological Implications of the Bellows-shaped Apron. In *Southeastern Ceremonial Complex: Chronology, Content, Context*, edited by A. King, pp. 38–56. Tuscaloosa: University of Alabama Press.

Brown, J. A. (editor)
1971 *Approaches to the Social Dimensions of Mortuary Practices*. Memoir 25. Salt Lake City: Society for American Archaeology.

Brown, James A., and David H. Dye
2007 Severed Heads and Sacred Scalplocks: Mississippian Iconographic Trophies. In *The Taking and Displaying of Human Trophies by Amerindians*, edited by R. J. Chacon and D. H. Dye, pp. 274–294. Norwell, Mass.: Kluwer Academic/Plenum Publishers.

Brown, J. A., and J. D. Rogers
1999 AMS Dates on Artifacts of the Southeastern Ceremonial Complex at Spiro. *Southeastern Archaeology* 18: 134–141.

Brown, J. A., and J. E. Kelly
2000 Cahokia and the Southeastern Ceremonial Complex. In *Mounds, Modoc, and Mesoamerica: Papers in Honor of Melvin L. Fowler*, pp. 469–510. Scientific Papers, Volume 28. Springfield: Illinois State Museum.

Brown, J. A., R. A. Kerber, and H. D. Winters
1990 Trade and the Evolution of Exchange Relations at the Beginning of the Mississippian Period. In *The Mississippian Emergence*, edited by B. D. Smith, pp. 251–280. Washington, D.C.: Smithsonian Institution Press.

Brown, J. E.
1953   *The Sacred Pipe: Black Elk's Account of the Seven Rites of the Oglala Sioux.* Norman: University of Oklahoma Press.

Burnett, E. K.
1945   The Spiro Mound Collection in the Museum. *Contributions from the Museum of the American Indian* 14:9–47. New York: Heye Foundation.

Butler, J.
1993   *Bodies That Matter: On the Discursive Limits of "Sex."* London: Routledge.

Byers, A. M.
2006   *Cahokia: A World Renewal Cult Heterarchy.* Gainesville: University Press of Florida.

Caldwell, J. R.
1958   *Trend and Tradition in the Prehistory of the Eastern United States.* Memoir Number 88. Springfield, Illinois: American Anthropological Association.

Cannon, Aubrey
1989   The Historic Dimension in Mortuary Expressions of Status and Sentiment. *Current Anthropology* 30(4):437–458.

Carr, C.
1995   Mortuary Practices: Their Social, Philosophical-Religious, Circumstantial, and Physical Determinants. *Journal of Archaeological Method and Theory* 2:105–200.

Carsten, J., and S. Hugh-Jones
1995   Introduction. In *About the House: Lévi-Strauss and Beyond,* edited by J. Carsten and S. Hugh-Jones, pp. 1–46. Cambridge: Cambridge University Press.

Champion, S.
1982   Exchange and Ranking: The Case of Coral. In *Ranking Resource, and Exchange: Aspects of the Archaeology of Early European Society,* edited by C. Renfrew and S. Shennan, pp. 67–72. Cambridge: Cambridge University Press.

Chapman, C. H., and L. O. Anderson
1955   The Campbell Site: A Late Mississippi Town Site and Cemetery in Southeast Missouri. *Missouri Archaeologist* 17.

Chapman, J.
2000   *Fragmentation in Archaeology: People, Places and Broken Objects in the Prehistory of South-Eastern Europe.* London: Routledge.

Chapman, R. W.
2005   Mortuary Analysis: A Matter of Time? In *Interacting with the Dead,* edited by G. M. Rakita, J. E. Buikstra, L. A. Beck, S. R. Williams, pp. 25–40. Gainesville: University Press of Florida.

Chappell, S. A. Kitt
2002   *Cahokia: Mirror of the Cosmos.* Chicago: University of Chicago Press.

Charles, D. K.
1995   Diachronic Regional Social Dynamics: Mortuary Sites in the Illinois River Valley/American Bottom. In *Regional Approaches to Mortuary Analysis,* edited by L. A. Beck, pp. 77–100. New York: Plenum Press.

Charles, D. K., and J. E. Buikstra
1983   Archaic Mortuary Sites in the Central Mississippi Drainage: Distribution, Structure, and Behavioral Implications. In *Archaic Hunters and Gatherers in the American Midwest*, edited by J. L. Phillips and J. A. Brown, pp. 117–145. New York: Academic Press.

Cherry, J. F.
2009   *The Headpots of Northeast Arkansas and Southern Pemiscot County, Missouri.* Fayetteville: University of Arkansas Press.

Clark, J. E., and M. Blake
1994   The Power of Prestige: Competitive Generosity and the Emergence of Rank Societies in Lowland Mesoamerica. In *Factional Competition and Political Development in the New World*, edited by E. M. Brumfiel and J. W. Fox, pp. 17–30. Cambridge: Cambridge University Press.

Claassen, C.
2001   Challenges for Regendering Southeastern Prehistory. In *Archaeological Studies of Gender in the Southeastern United States*, edited by J. M. Eastman and C. B. Rodning, pp. 10–26. Gainesville: University Press of Florida.

Clay, R. Berle
1976   Tactics, Strategy, and Operations: The Mississippian System Responds to its Environment. *Midcontinental Journal of Archaeology* 1: 137–162.

Clayton, L. A., V. J. Knight, Jr., and E. C. Moore (editors)
1993   *The De Soto Chronicles: The Expedition of Hernando de Soto to North America in 1539–1543.* Tuscaloosa: University of Alabama Press.

Clements, F. E.
1945   Historical Sketch of the Spiro Mound. *Contributions to the Museum of American Indian, Heye Foundation* 14: 48–68.

Cobb, C. R.
2003   Mississippian Chiefdoms: How Complex? *Annual Review of Anthropology* 32:63–84.

Cobb, C. R., and B. M. Butler
2002   The Vacant Quarter Revisited: Late Mississippian Abandonment of the Lower Ohio Valley. *American Antiquity* 67(4): 625–642.

Coe, J. L.
1952   The Cultural Sequence of the Carolina Piedmont. In *Archeology of Eastern United States*, edited by J. B. Griffin, pp. 301–311. Chicago: University of Chicago Press.

1961   Cherokee Archaeology. In *Symposium on Cherokee and Iroquois Culture*, edited by J. Gulick, pp. 53–60. Bureau of American Ethnology, Bulletin 180. Washington, D.C.: Government Printing Office.

1995   *Town Creek Indian Mound: A Native American Legacy.* Chapel Hill: University of North Carolina Press.

Cohen, R.
1978   Ethnicity: Problem and Focus in Anthropology. *Annual Review of Anthropology* 7:385. Palo Alto, California: Stanford University Press.

Cole, F.-C., R. Bell, J. Bennett, J. Caldwell, N. Emerson, R. MacNeish, K. Orr, and R. Willis
1951   *Kincaid: A Prehistoric Illinois Metropolis*. Chicago: University of Chicago Press.

Colwell-Chanthaphonh, C., and T. J. Ferguson
2006   Rethinking Abandonment in Archaeological Contexts. *The SAA Archaeological Record* 6(1): 37–41.

Conrad, L.
1993   Two Elaborate Middle Mississippian Graves from the Kingston Lake Site, Peoria County, Illinois. *Illinois Archaeology* 5(1–2):297–330.

Cook, R. A.
2004   Upper Mississippian Village Structure and Formation: Spatial Analysis of SunWatch, A Fort Ancient Site in Southwest Ohio. Unpublished Ph.D. dissertation, Department of Anthropology, Michigan State University, East Lansing.
2007   Single Component Sites with Long Sequences of Radiocarbon Dates: The Sun Watch Site and Middle Fort Ancient Village Growth. *American Antiquity* 72: 439–460.
2008   *SunWatch: Fort Ancient Development in the Mississippian World*. Tuscaloosa: University of Alabama Press.

Cook, R. A., and L. F. Fargher
2007   Fort Ancient-Mississippian Interaction and Shell-Tempered Pottery at the SunWatch Site. *Journal of Field Archaeology* 32: 1–12.
2008   The Incorporation of Mississippian Traditions into Fort Ancient Societies: A Preliminary View of the Shift to Shell-Tempered Pottery Use in the Middle Ohio Valley. *Southeastern Archaeology* 27(2): 222–237.

Cosgrove, D.
1993   Landscapes and Myths, Gods and Humans. In *Landscape: Politics and Perspectives*, edited by B. Bender, pp. 281–306. Providence, Rhode Island: Berg.

Cowan, C. W.
1987   *First Farmers of the Middle Ohio Valley: Fort Ancient Societies, A.D. 1000–1670*. Cincinnati: The Cincinnati Museum of Natural History.

Cowan, C. W., S. Dunavan, J. P. Nass, Jr., and S. Scott
1990   The Schomaker Site, a Middle Period Fort Ancient Town on the Great Miami River, Hamilton County, Ohio. *West Virginia Archaeologist* 42: 11–35.

Crouch, Daniel J.
1974   South Appalachian Earth Lodges. Unpublished M. A. Thesis. Department of Anthropology, University of North Carolina, Chapel Hill.

Crothers, G. M.
1987   *An Archaeological Survey of Big Bone Cave, Tennessee and Diachronic Patterns of Cave Utilization in the Eastern Woodlands*. Knoxville: University of Tennessee.

Crothers, G., C. H. Faulkner, J. F. Simek, P. J. Watson, and P. Willey
2002   Woodland Period Cave Use in the Eastern Woodlands. In *The Woodland*

Southeast, edited by D. G. Anderson and R. C. Mainfort, Jr. Tuscaloosa: University of Alabama Press.

Crumley, C. L.
1979   Three Locational Models: An Epistemological Assessment of Anthropology and Archaeology. *Advances in Archaeological Method and Theory* 2: 141–173.
1987   A Dialectical Critique of Hierarchy. In *Power Relations and State Formation*, edited by T. C. Patterson and C. Ward, pp. 155–169. Washington: American Anthropological Association.
1995   Heterarchy and the Analysis of Complex Societies. In *Heterarchy and the Analysis of Complex Societies*, edited by R. M. Ehrenreich, C. L. Crumley and J. E. Levy, pp. 1–5. Archeological Papers 6. Washington: American Anthropological Association.

Dalan, R. A., G. R. Holley, W. I. Woods, H. W. Watters, Jr., and J. A. Koepke
2003   *Envisioning Cahokia: A Landscape Perspective*. DeKalb, Illinois: Northern Illinois University Press.

Davidson, J. M.
2004   Mediating Race and Class Through the Death Experience: Power relations and Resistance Strategies of an African-American Community, Dallas, Texas (1869–1907). Unpublished Ph.D. dissertation, Department of Anthropology, University of Texas, Austin.

Davis, R. P. S., Jr., P. M. Lambert, V. P. Steponaitis, C. S. Larsen, and H. T. Ward
1996   *NAGPRA Inventory of Human Remains and Funerary Objects from Town Creek Indian Mound*. Chapel Hill: Research Laboratories of Anthropology, University of North Carolina.

DeBoer, W. R.
1993   Like a Rolling Stone: The Chunkey Game and Political Organization in Eastern North America. *Southeastern Archaeology* 12: 83–92.

Decker, D. A.
1969   Early Archaeology on Catalina Island: Potential and Problems. *Archaeological Survey Annual Report* 11:69–84. Los Angeles: University of California.

DePratter, C. B.
1983   Late Prehistoric and Early Historic Chiefdoms in the Southeastern United States. Unpublished Ph.D. dissertation, Department of Anthropology, University of Georgia, Athens.

Diaz-Granados, C., M. W. Rowe, M. Hyman, Duncan J. R., and J. R. Southon
2001   Radiocarbon Dates for Charcoal from Three Missouri Pictographs and Their Associated Iconography. *American Antiquity* 66: 481.

Diaz-Granados, C., and J. R. Duncan
2004   Reflections of Power, Wealth, and Sex in Missouri Rock Art Motifs. In *The Rock-Art of Eastern North America: Capturing Images and Insight*, edited by C. Diaz-Granados and J. R. Duncan, pp. 145–158. Tuscaloosa: University of Alabama Press.

Dickens, R. S., Jr.
1976   *Cherokee Prehistory: The Pisgah Phase in the Appalachian Summit Region.* Knoxville: University of Tennessee Press.
1980   Preliminary Report on Archaeological Investigations at the Plum Grove Site (40Wg17), Washington County, Tennessee. Laboratory of Archaeology, Department of Anthropology, Georgia State University, Atlanta. Manuscript on file, Archaeology Laboratory, East Tennessee State University, Johnson City.

Dillehay, T. D.
1995   Mounds for the Social Death: Araucanian Funerary Rites and Political Succession. In *Tombs for the Living: Andean Mortuary Practices*, edited by T. D. Dillehay. Washington, D.C.: Dumbarton Oaks.

Dobres, M.-A.
2000   *Technology and Social Agency.* Blackwell, Oxford.

Dobres, M.-A., and J. E. Robb
2000   Agency in Archaeology: Paradigm or Platitude? In *Agency in Archaeology*, edited by M.-A. Dobres and J. E. Robb, pp. 3-18. London: Routledge.

Donnan, C. B.
1995   Moche Funerary Practice. In *Tombs for the Living: Andean Mortuary Practices*, edited by T. D. Dillehay, pp. 111-159. Washington, D.C.: Dumbarton Oaks.

Dornan, J. L.
2002   Agency and Archaeology: Past, Present, and Future Directions. *Journal of Archaeological Method and Theory* 9: 303-329.

Dorsey, G. A.
1969   *Traditions of the Skidi Pawnee.* Memoir 8, American Folklore Society. New York: Houghton and Mifflin.
1997   *The Pawnee Mythology.* Lincoln: University of Nebraska Press.

Douglas, M.
1967   Primitive Rationing: A Study in Controlled Exchange. In *Themes in Economic Anthropology*, edited by R. Firth, pp. 119-147. London: Tavistock.

Douglas, W. A.
1969   *Death in Murelaga.* Monograph 49. Seattle: American Ethnological Society.

Dragoo, D. W.
1963   *Mounds for the Dead.* Annals of the Carnegie Museum Vol. 37. Pittsburgh: Carnegie Museum.

Driscoll, E. M.
2001   Bioarchaeology, Mortuary Patterning, and Social Organization at Town Creek. Unpublished Ph.D. dissertation, Department of Anthropology, University of North Carolina, Chapel Hill.
2002   Mortuary Patterning and Social Organization at Town Creek Mound and Village. In *The Archaeology of Native North Carolina: Papers in Honor of H. Trawick Ward*, edited by J. M. Eastman, C. B. Rodning, and E. A. Boudreaux, III, pp. 18-27. Special Publication 7. Biloxi, Mississippi: Southeastern Archaeological Conference.

Drooker, P. B.
1997   *The View from Madisonville: Protohistoric Western Fort Ancient Interaction Patterns.* Memoirs 31. Ann Arbor: Museum of Anthropology, University of Michigan.

Duff, A.
1996   Ceramic Micro-Seriation: Types or Attributes? *American Antiquity* 61: 89–101.

Duffield, L. F.
1973   The Oklahoma Craig Mound: Another Look at an Old Problem. *Bulletin of the Oklahoma Anthropological Society* 22: 1–10.

Dunnell, Robert C.
1971   *Systematics in Prehistory.* New York: The Free Press.

Durham, J.
1989   Excavations at Nodena in 1932. In *Nodena,* edited by D. F. Morse, pp. 23–29. Research Series No. 30. Fayetteville: Arkansas Archeological Survey.

Dye, D. H.
2000   The Accouterments of High Office: Elite Ritual Paraphernalia from Pickwick Basin. Paper presented at the 57th Annual Meeting of the Southeastern Archaeological Conference, Macon, GA.
2004   Art, Ritual, and Chiefly Warfare in the Mississippian World. In *Hero, Hawk, and Open Hand,* edited by R. F. Townsend and R. V. Sharp, pp. 191–206. New Haven: Yale University Press.

Earnest, H.
n. d.   Preliminary Analysis of Cherokee Ceramics from Ten Sites on the Nolichucky River. Department of Anthropology, University of Tennessee, Knoxville. Manuscript on file, Archaeology Laboratory, East Tennessee State University, Johnson City.

Eastman, J. M.
2001   Life Course and Gender among Late Prehistoric Siouan Communities. In *Archaeological Studies of Gender in the Southeastern United States,* edited by J. M. Eastman and C. B. Rodning, pp. 57–76. Gainesville: University Press of Florida.

Eastman, J. M., and C. B. Rodning (editors)
2001   *Archaeological Studies of Gender in the Southeastern United States.* Gainesville: University Press of Florida.

Ehernreich, R. M., C. L. Crumley, and J. E. Levy (editors)
1995   *Heterarchy and the Analysis of Complex Societies.* Archeological Papers of the American Anthropological Association No. 6. Washington: American Anthropological Association.

Eisenberg, L. E.
1989   On Gaming Pieces and Culture Contact. *Current Anthropology* 30: 345.

Emberling, G.
1997   Ethnicity in Complex Societies: Archaeological Perspectives. *Journal of Archaeological Research* 5:295–344.

Emerson, T. E.
1997 *Cahokia and the Archaeology of Power.* Tuscaloosa: University of Alabama Press.

Emerson, T. E., and E. Hargrave
2000 Strangers in Paradise: Recognizing Ethnic Mortuary Diversity on the Fringes of Cahokia. *Southeastern Archaeology* 19:1–23.

Emerson, T. E., and R. E. Hughes
1999 Figurines, Flint Clay Sourcing, the Ozark Highlands, and Cahokian Acquisition. *American Antiquity* 65: 79–101.

Emerson, T. E., E. Hargrave, and K. Hedman
2003 Death and Ritual in Early Rural Cahokia. In *Theory, Method, and Technique in Modern Archaeology,* edited by R. J. Jeske, and D. K. Charles. Westport, Conn.: Bergin and Garvey.

Emerson, T. E., R. E. Hughes, M. R. Hynes, and S. U. Wisseman
2003 The Sourcing and Interpretation of Cahokia-Style Figurines in the Trans-Mississippi South and Southeast. *American Antiquity* 68: 287–313.

Emerson, T. E., and T. R. Pauketat
2002 Embodying Power and Resistance at Prehistoric Cahokia. In *Power in Archaeology,* edited by M. O'Donovan, pp. 105–125. Center for Archaeological Investigations Occasional Paper No. 30. Carbondale: Southern Illinois University.

Eriksen, T. H.
1991 The Cultural Contexts of Ethnic Differences. *Man,* n.s. 26:127–144.
1992 *Us and Them in Modern Societies: Ethnicity and Nationalism in Trinidad, Mauritius and Beyond.* London: Scandinavian University Press.
2001 Ethnic Identity, National Identity and Intergroup Conflict: The Significance of Personal Experiences. In *Social Identity, Intergroup Conflict, and Conflict Reduction,* edited by R. D. Ashmore, L. J. Jussim, and D. Wilder, pp. 42–70. Oxford: Oxford University Press.

Essenpreis, P. S.
1978 Fort Ancient Settlement: Differential Response at a Mississippian-Late Woodland Interface. In *Mississippian Settlement Patterns,* edited by B. D. Smith, pp. 143–167. New York: Academic Press.

Fairbanks, C. H.
1946 The Macon Earth Lodge. *American Antiquity* 12(2): 94–108.
2003 *Archaeology of the Funeral Mound: Ocmulgee National Monument, Georgia.* Tuscaloosa: University of Alabama Press (original 1956).

Feinman, G., and J. Neitzel
1984 Too Many Types: An Overview of Sedentary Prestate Societies in the Americas. In *Advances in Archaeological Method and Theory,* Vol. 7, edited by M. B. Schiffer, pp. 39–102. Orlando, Florida: Academic Press.

Ferguson, J. R., C. N. Rosania, and M. D. Glascock
2007 Instrumental Neutron Activation Analysis of Pottery, Holliston Mills Site, Upper Eastern Tennessee. Manuscript on file, Archaeometry Laboratory

(MURR), Columbia, Missouri and the Archaeology Laboratory, East Tennessee State University, Johnson City.

Ferguson, L. G.
1971 South Appalachian Mississippian. Unpublished Ph.D. dissertation, Department of Anthropology, University of North Carolina, Chapel Hill.

Ferguson, Robert B.
1972 The Arnold Village Site Excavations of 1965–1966. In *The Middle Cumberland Culture*, edited by R. B. Ferguson, pp. 1–50. Publications in Anthropology 3. Nashville, Tennessee: Vanderbilt University.

Finger, C. J., Jr.
1989 The University of Arkansas Museum Excavations at Middle Nodena. In *Nodena*, edited by D. F. Morse, pp. 31–32. Research Series No. 30. Fayetteville: Arkansas Archaeological Survey.

Fisher-Carroll, R.
2001a Environmental Dynamics of Drought and its Impact on Sixteenth Century Indigenous Populations in the Central Mississippi Valley. Unpublished Ph.D. dissertation, Environmental Dynamics Program, University of Arkansas, Fayetteville.
2001b *Mortuary Behavior at Upper Nodena*. Research Series 59. Fayetteville: Arkansas Archeological Survey.

Fisher-Carroll, R., and R. C. Mainfort, Jr.
2000 Late Prehistoric Mortuary Behavior at Upper Nodena. *Southeastern Archaeology* 19:105–119.

Flannery, K. V.
1999 Chiefdoms in the Early Near East: Why It's So Hard to Identify Them. In *The Iranian World: Essays on Iranian Art and Archaeology, Presented to Ezat O. Negahban*, edited by A. Alizadeh, Y. Majidzadeh, and S. M. Shahmirzadi, pp. 44–58. Tehran: Iran University Press.

Fletcher, A. C., and F. La Flesche
1992 *The Omaha Tribe*. Vols. 1–2. Lincoln: University of Nebraska Press.

Ford, J. A.
1963 *Hopewell Culture Burial Mounds Near Helena, Arkansas*. Anthropological Papers of the American Museum of Natural History 50(1). New York: American Museum of Natural History.

Foucault, M.
1979 *Discipline and Punish: The Birth of the Prison*. New York: Vintage Books.

Fowke, G.
1922 *Archeological Investigations, I. Cave Explorations in the Ozark Region of Central Missouri. II. Cave Explorations in Other States. III. Explorations Along the Missouri River Bluffs in Kansas and Nebraska. IV. Aboriginal House Mounds. V. Archeological Work in Hawaii*. Bureau of American Ethnology Bulletin 76. Washington: Government Printing Office.

Fowler, C.
2004   *The Archaeology of Personhood: An Anthropological Approach.* New York: Routledge.

Fowler, M. L.
1997   *The Cahokia Atlas: A Historical Atlas of Cahokia Archaeology.* Studies in Archaeology, Number 2, Illinois Transportation Archaeological Research Program, University of Illinois, Urbana.

Fowler, M. L. (editor)
1996   The Ancient Skies and Sky Watchers of Cahokia: Woodhenges, Eclipses, and Cahokian Cosmology. *Wisconsin Archeologist* 77(3–4).

Fowler, M. L., J. C. Rose, B. Vander Leest, and S. R. Ahler
1999   The Mound 72 Area: Dedicated and Sacred Space in Early Cahokia. Reports of Investigations, No. 54. Springfield: Illinois State Museum.

Fox, J. A.
1902   *Mississippi County in the St. Francis Basin of Arkansas.* Osceola, Arkansas: J. A. Fox.

Fox, W. A.
2004   The North-South Copper Axis. *Southeastern Archaeology* 23(1): 85–97.

Fried, M. H.
1960   On the Evolution of Social Stratification and the State. In *Culture in History: Essays in Honor of Paul Radin*, edited by S. Diamond, pp.713–731. New York: Columbia University Press.
1967   *The Evolution of Political Society.* New York: Random House.

Gall, D. G., R. C. Mainfort, Jr., and R. Fisher-Carroll
2002   The Occurrence of Greenstone at Late Period Sites in Northeast Arkansas. *Southeastern Archaeology* 21(2):235–244.

Gearing, F.
1958   The Structural Poses of 18th Century Cherokee Villages. *American Anthropologist* 60: 1148–1157.

Geertz, C.
1966   Religion as a Cultural System. In *Anthropological Approaches to the Study of Religion*, edited by M. Banton, pp. 1–46. A. S. A. Monograph No. 3. London: Tavistock.
1980   *Negara: The Theatre State in Nineteenth-Century Bali.* Princeton, New Jersey: Princeton University Press.

Gell, Alfred
1998   *Art and Agency: An Anthropological Theory.* Oxford: Clarendon.

George, A.
1990   *Prehistoric Mummies from the Mammoth Cave Area.* Louisville, Kentucky: George Publishing.
1994   *Mummies, Catacombs, and Mammoth Cave.* Louisville, Kentucky: George Publishing.

Gillespie, S. D.
2000   Beyond Kinship: An Introduction. In *Beyond Kinship: Social and Material Reproduction in House Societies*, edited by R. A. Joyce and S. D. Gillespie, pp. 1–21. Philadelphia: University of Pennsylvania Press.
2001   Personhood, Agency, and Mortuary Ritual: A Case Study from the Ancient Maya. *Journal of Anthropological Archaeology* 20:73–112.

Gleason, P.
1996   Identifying Identity: A Semantic History. In *Theories of Ethnicity: A Classical Reader*, edited by W. Sollors, pp. 460–487. Ipswich, Suffolk: Ipswich Book Company. Reprinted from Journal of American History 69:910–31 (1983).

Goldstein, L. G.
1976   Spatial Structure and Social Organization: Regional Manifestations of Mississippian Society. Unpublished Ph.D. dissertation, Department of Anthropology, Northwestern University, Evanston, Illinois.
1979   An Archaeological Survey of Portions of the Crawfish and Rock River Valleys near Their Confluence in Jefferson County, Wisconsin. Reports of Investigations 32. Milwaukee: University of Wisconsin-Milwaukee Archaeological Research Laboratory.
1980   *Mississippian Mortuary Practices: a Case Study of Two Cemeteries in the Lower Illinois Valley*. Evanston, Illinois: Northwestern University Archeological Program.
1981   One-Dimensional Archaeology and Multi-Dimensional People: Spatial Organization and Mortuary Analysis. In *The Archaeology of Death*, edited by R. Chapman, I. Kinnes, and K. Randsborg, pp. 53–69. Cambridge: Cambridge University Press.
1989   Is Secondary Disposal a Mortuary Practice? Paper presented at the 1989 Theoretical Archaeology Group, Newcastle upon Tyne.
1991   The Implications of Aztalan's Location. In *New Perspectives on Cahokia: Views from the Periphery*, edited by J. B. Stoltman, pp. 209–228. Madison, Wisconsin: Prehistory Press.
1997   Exploring Aztalan and Its Role in Mississippian Societies. In *Research Frontiers in Anthropology: Archaeology*, vol. 2, edited by C. R. Ember, M. Ember, and P. N. Peregrine, pp. 159–186. New York: Prentice Hall.
2000   Mississippian Ritual as Viewed Through the Practice of Secondary Disposal of the Dead. In *Mounds, Modoc, and Mesoamerica: Papers in Honor of Melvin L. Fowler*, edited by S. Ahler, pp. 193–206. Scientific Papers, Volume 28. Springfield: Illinois State Museum.

Goldstein, L. G. (editor)
1999   *Aztalan Research: Preparing for Park Interpretation & Planning*. Report prepared for the Wisconsin Department of Natural Resources, Archaeology Office, Madison.

Goldstein, L. G., and J. E. Freeman
1997   Aztalan: A Middle Mississippian Village. *Wisconsin Archeologist* 78(1–2): 223–248.

Goldstein, L. G., and D. H. Gaff
2002   Recasting the Past: Examining Assumptions About Aztalan. In *Current Issues in the Archaeology of the Western Great Lakes: Problems and Progress*, edited by R. Jeske. Wisconsin Archeologist 83: 98–110.

Goldstein, L. G., and N. Sullivan
1986   People as Food, Bone as Ritual: Rethinking Old Data. Paper presented at the 51st Annual Meeting of the Society for American Archaeology, New Orleans.

Goodenough, W. H.
1965   Rethinking "Status" and "Role": Toward a General Model of the Cultural Organization of Social Relationships. In *The Relevance of Models for Social Anthropology*, edited by M. Blanton, pp. 1–20. A.S.A. monographs, 1. New York: F. A. Praeger.

Gougeon, R.
2006   Different but the Same: Social Integration of Households in Mississippian Chiefdoms. In *Leadership and Polity in Mississippian Society*, edited by B. Butler and P. Welch, pp. 178–194. Occasional Paper 33. Carbondale: Center for Archaeological Investigations, Southern Illinois University. Carbondale.

Greber, N.
1976   Within Ohio Hopewell: Analyses of Burial Patterns from Several Classic Sites. Unpublished Ph.D. dissertation, Department of Anthropology, Case Western Reserve University, Cleveland, OH.

Griffin, J. B.
1943   *The Fort Ancient Aspect: Its Cultural and Chronological Position in Mississippi Valley Archaeology*. Anthropological Papers 28. Ann Arbor: Museum of Anthropology, University of Michigan.
1952   Prehistoric Cultures of the Central Mississippi Valley. In *Archeology of Eastern United States*, edited by J. B. Griffin, pp. 226–238. Chicago: University of Chicago Press.
1967   Eastern North American Archaeology: A Summary. *Science* 156(3772): 175–191.
1985   Changing Concepts of the Prehistoric Mississippian Cultures of the Eastern United States. In *Alabama and the Borderlands: From Prehistory to Statehood*, edited by R. R. Badger and L. A. Clayton, pp. 40–63. Tuscaloosa: University of Alabama Press.
1992   Fort Ancient Has No Class: The Absence of an Elite Group in Mississippian Societies in the Central Ohio Valley. In *Lords of the Southeast: Social Inequality and the Native Elites of Southeastern North America*, edited by A. W. Barker and T. R. Pauketat, pp. 53–59. Archaeological Papers 3. Washington: American Anthropological Association.

Griffin, J. W.
1974   *Investigations in Russell Cave, Russell Cave National Monument, Alabama*. Washington: U. S. National Park Service.

Gulliver, P. H.
1969 Introduction. In *Tradition and Transition in East Africa*, edited by P. H. Gulliver, pp. 5–38. Berkeley: University of California Press.

Hall, R. L.
1997 *An Archaeology of the Soul: North American Indian Belief and Ritual*. Urbana: University of Illinois Press.
2000 Sacrificed Foursomes and Green Corn Ceremonialism. In *Mounds, Modoc, and Mesoamerica: Papers in Honor of Melvin L. Fowler*, edited by S. R. Ahler, pp. 245–253. Scientific Papers, Volume 28. Springfield: Illinois State Museum.

Hallam, E., and J. Hockey
2001 *Death, Memory and Material Culture*. Oxford: Berg.

Hally, D. J.
1975 Introduction to the Symposium: The King Site and Its Investigation. *Southeastern Archaeological Conference Bulletin* 18: 48–54.
1988 Archaeology and Settlement Plan of the King Site. In *The King Site: Continuity and Contact in Sixteenth-Century Georgia*, edited by R. Blakely, pp. 3–16. Athens: University of Georgia Press.
1993 The Territorial Size of Mississippian Chiefdoms. In *Archaeology of Eastern North American: Papers in Honor of Stephen Williams*, edited by J. B. Stoltman, pp. 143–168. Archaeological Report No. 25. Jackson: Mississippi Department of Archives and History.
1994 An Overview of Lamar Culture. In *Ocumulgee Archaeology, 1936–1986*, edited by D. J. Hally, pp. 144–174. Athens: University of Georgia Press.
1996 Platform Mound Construction and the Instability of Mississippian Chiefdoms. In *Political Structure and Change in the Prehistoric Southeastern United States*, edited by J. F. Scarry, pp. 92–127. Gainesville: University Press of Florida.
1999 The Settlement Pattern of Mississippian Chiefdoms in Northern Georgia. In *Settlement Pattern Studies in the Americas: Fifty Years Since Virú*, edited by B. R. Billman and G. M. Feinman, pp. 96–115. Washington, D.C.: Smithsonian Institution Press.
2002 "As caves below the ground": Making Sense of Aboriginal House Form in the Protohistoric and Historic Southeast. In *Between Contact and Colonies: Archaeological Perspectives on the Protohistoric Southeast*, edited by C. B. Wesson and M. A. Rees, pp. 90–109. Tuscaloosa: University of Alabama Press.
2004 Mortuary Patterns at a Sixteenth-Century Town in Northwestern Georgia. *Southeastern Archaeology* 23: 166–177.
2007 Mississippian Shell Gorgets in Regional perspective. In *Southeastern Ceremonial Complex: Chronology, Content, Context*, edited by A. King, pp. 185–231. Tuscaloosa: University of Alabama Press.
2008 *King: The Social Archaeology of a Late Mississippian Town in Northwestern Georgia*. Tuscaloosa: University of Alabama Press.

Hally, D. J., and H. Kelly
1998   The Nature of Mississippian Towns in Georgia: The King Site Example. In *Mississippian Towns and Sacred Spaces: Searching for an Architectural Grammar*, edited by R. B. Lewis and C. B. Stout, pp. 49–63. Tuscaloosa: University of Alabama Press.

Hally, D. J., and J. B. Langford
1988   *Mississippi Period Archaeology of the Georgia Valley and Ridge Province*. University of Georgia, Laboratory of Archaeology Series, Report 25. Athens: Department of Anthropology, University of Georgia.

Hamilton, H. W.
1952   The Spiro Mound. *Missouri Archaeologist* 14: 17–106.

Hammerstedt, S. W.
2005a   Mississippian Construction, Labor, and Social Organization in Western Kentucky. Unpublished Ph.D. dissertation, Department of Anthropology, Pennsylvania State University. University Park.
2005b   Mississippian Status in Western Kentucky: Evidence from the Annis Mound. *Southeastern Archaeology* 24:11–27.

Hampson, J. K.
1989   The Nodena Site. In *Nodena*, edited by D. F. Morse, pp. 9–21. Research Series No. 30. Fayetteville: Arkansas Archeological Survey.
n.d.a   Notes on Nodena, etc. Unpublished manuscript (typescript). Copy on file, Arkansas Archeological Survey, Fayetteville.
n.d.b   Untitled catalog of the Hampson collection (3 volumes). Xerographic copy on file, Arkansas Archeological Survey, Fayetteville, North Carolina.

Harle, M. S.
2003   A Bioarchaeological Analysis of Fains Island. Unpublished M.A. thesis, Department of Anthropology, University of Tennessee, Knoxville.

Harn, A. D.
1980   *The Prehistory of Dickson Mounds: The Dickson Excavation*. 2nd ed. Reports of Investigations, No. 35. Springfield: Illinois State Museum.

Harn, A. D.
1991   The Eveland Site: Inroad to Spoon River Mississippian Society. In *New Perspectives on Cahokia: Views from the Periphery*, edited by J. B. Stoltman, pp. 129–153. Madison, Wisconsin: Prehistory Press.

Harris, Marvin
1968   *The Rise of Anthropological Theory: A History of Theories of Culture*. New York: Thomas Y. Crowell.
1979   *Cultural Materialism: The Struggle for a Science of Culture*. New York: Random House.

Hart, J. P., and H. J. Brumbach
2003   The Death of Owasco. *American Antiquity* 68: 737–752.

Haselgrove, C.
1990   The Romanization of Belgic Gaul: Some Archaeological Perspectives. In *The*

Early Roman Empire in the West, edited by T. Blagg and M. Millett, pp. 45–71. Oxford: Oxbow.

Hassler, E. F.
1946 The Burials of Bone Cave, Speck Cavern, and Bunkam Cave. *Tennessee Archaeologist* 3: 15–17.

Hatch, J. W.
1974 Social Dimensions of Dallas Mortuary Pattern. Unpublished M.A. thesis, Department of Anthropology, Pennsylvania State University. University Park.
1975 Social Dimensions of Dallas Burials. *Southeastern Archaeological Conference Bulletin* 18: 132–138.
1976a Status in Death: Principles of Ranking in Dallas Culture Mortuary Remains. Unpublished Ph.D. dissertation, Department of Anthropology, Pennsylvania State University. University Park.
1976b The Citico Site: A Synthesis. *Tennessee Anthropologist* 1:74–103.
1987 Mortuary Indicators of Organizational Variability Among Late Prehistoric Chiefdoms in the Southeastern U.S. Interior. In *Chiefdoms in the Americas*, edited by R. D. Drennan and C. A. Uribe, pp. 9–16. Lanham: University Press of America.

Hay, T. B.
1958 The Coleman's Cave Investigation. *Tennessee Archeologist* 14: 9–15.

Hayden, D.
1995 *The Power of Place: Urban Landscapes as Public History*. Cambridge, Mass.: MIT Press.

Heckenberger, M. J.
2004 *The Ecology of Power: Culture, Place, and Personhood in the Southern Amazon, A.D. 1000–2000*. New York: Routledge.

Heilman, J. M., and R. Hoefer
1981 Possible Astronomical Alignments in a Fort Ancient Settlement at the Incinerator Site in Dayton, Ohio. In *Archaeoastronomy in the Americas*, edited by R. Williamson, pp. 157–171. Menlo Park, California: Ballena.

Heilman, J. M., M. C. Lileas, and C. A. Turnbow (editors)
1988 *A History of 17 Years of Excavation and Reconstruction: A Chronicle of 12th Century Human Values and the Built Environment*. Dayton, Ohio: Dayton Museum of Natural History.

Helms, M. W.
1988 *Ulysses' Sail: An Ethnographic Odyssey of Power, Knowledge, and Geographical Distance*. Princeton: Princeton University Press.
1993 *Craft and the Kingly Ideal: Art, Trade, and Power*. Austin: University of Texas Press.

Henderson, A. G.
1992 Capitol View: An Early Madisonville Horizon Settlement in Franklin County, Kentucky. In *Current Archaeological Research in Kentucky*, vol. 2, edited by D. Pollack and A. G. Henderson, pp. 223–240. Frankfort: Kentucky Heritage Council.

1998   Middle Fort Ancient Villages and Organizational Complexity in Kentucky. Unpublished Ph.D. dissertation, Department of Anthropology, University of Kentucky, Lexington.

Hendon, J.
2000   Having and Holding: Storage, Memory, Knowledge, and Social Relations. *American Anthropologist* 102: 42–53.

Hill, J. B., J. Clark, W. Doelle, and P. Lyons
2004   Prehistoric Demography in the Southwest: Migration, Coalescence, and Hohokam Population Decline. *American Antiquity* 69:689–716.

Hillier, B.
1996   *Space Is the Machine*. Cambridge: Cambridge University Press.

Hodder, I., and C. Cessford
2004   Daily Practice and Social Memory at Çatalhöyük. *American Antiquity* 69:17–40.

Holcomb, G.
1952   An Analysis of Human Remains from Aztalan. Unpublished M.A. thesis, Department of Anthropology, University of Wisconsin-Madison.

Holley, G. R.
1999   Late Prehistoric Towns in the Southeast. In *Great Towns and Regional Polities in the Prehistoric American Southwest and Southeast*, edited by J. E. Neitzel, pp. 22–38. Albuquerque: University of New Mexico Press.

Holland, T. D.
1991   An Archaeological and Biological Analysis of the Campbell Site. Unpublished Ph.D. dissertation, Department of Anthropology, University of Missouri. Columbia.

Holmes, W. H.
1886   Ancient Pottery of the Mississippi Valley. *Proceedings of the Davenport Academy of Natural Sciences* 4:123–196.

House, J. H.
1991   Monitoring Mississippian Dynamics: Time, Settlement and Ceramic Variation in the Kent Phase, Eastern Arkansas. Unpublished Ph.D. dissertation, Department of Anthropology, Southern Illinois University. Carbondale.

Howard, J. H.
1968   *The Southern Ceremonial Complex and Its Interpretation*. Memoir 6. Columbia: Missouri Archaeological Society.

Howell, C.
2005   Ceramic Analysis of Fains Island (40JE1), A Late Dallas Phase Mississippian Site in Upper East Tennessee. Paper Presented at the 62nd Southeastern Archaeological Conference, Columbia, South Carolina.

Howell, T. L.
1995   Tracking Zuni Gender and Leadership Roles across the Contact Period. *Journal of Anthropological Research* 51: 125–147.
1996   Identifying Leaders at Hawikku. *Kiva* 62(1): 61–82.

Howell, T. L., and K. W. Kintigh
1996 Archaeological Identification of Kin Groups Using Mortuary and Biological Data: An Example from the American Southwest. *American Antiquity* 61:537–554.

Howland, Henry R.
1877 Recent Archaeological Discoveries in the American Bottom. *Buffalo Society of Natural Sciences Bulletin* 3(5): 204–211.

Hudson, C.
1976 *The Southeastern Indians*. Knoxville: University of Tennessee Press.

Hudson, C.
1990 *The Juan Pardo Expeditions: Exploration of the Carolinas and Tennessee, 1566–1568*. Tuscaloosa: University of Alabama Press.

Hudson, C., M. T. Smith, D. Hally, R. Polhemus, and C. DePratter
1985 Coosa: A Chiefdom in the Sixteenth-Century Southeastern United States. *American Antiquity* 50: 723–737.

Hutchinson, D. L., and L. V. Aragon
2002 Collective Burials and Community Memories: Interpreting the Placement of the Dead in the Southeastern and Mid-Atlantic United states with Reference to Ethnographic Cases from Indonesia. In *The Space and Place of Death*, edited by H. Silverman and D. B. Small, pp. 27–54. Archaeological Papers of the American Anthropological Association 11. Arlington, Virginia.

Hyer, N. F.
1837 Ruins of the Ancient City of Aztalan. *The Milwaukee Advertiser*, February 25, 1837, p. 2.

Inomata, T., and L. S. Coben (editors)
2006 *Archaeology of Performance: Theaters of Power, Community, and Politics*. Walnut Canyon, California: AltaMira.

Jackson, J. B.
1984 *Discovering the Vernacular Landscape*. New Haven, Conn.: Yale University Press.

Jacobi, K. P., and D. H. Dye
2000 Headless in Alabama. Presented at the 57th Annual Meeting of the Southeastern Archaeological Conference. Macon, GA.

Jeter, M. D. (editor)
1990 *Edward Palmer's Arkansaw Mounds*. Fayetteville: University of Arkansas Press.

Johnson, G.
1982 Organizational Structure and Scalar Stress. In *Theory and Explanation in Archaeology*, edited by C. Renfrew, M. J. Rowlands, and B. A. Segraves, pp. 389–423. New York: Academic Press.

Jones, Siân
1997 *The Archaeology of Ethnicity: Constructing Identities in the Past and the Present*. London: Routledge.

Joyce, R. A.
2000 Girling the Girl and Boying the Boy: The Production of Adulthood in Ancient Mesoamerica. *World Archaeology* 31: 473–483.
2005 Archaeology of the Body. *Annual Review of Anthropology* 34:139–158.

Joyce, R. A., and S. D. Gillespie (editors)
2000 *Beyond Kinship: Social and Material Reproduction in House Societies*. Philadelphia: University of Pennsylvania Press.

Judge, C.
2003a An Overview of the Mississippian Ceramic Sequence for the Wateree River Valley, South Carolina. Paper presented at the Sixtieth Annual Meeting of the Southeastern Archaeological Conference, Charlotte, North Carolina.
2003b Concrete Memories: Fragments of the Past in the Classic Maya Present (500–1000 A.D.). In *The Archaeologies of Memory*, edited by R. M. Van Dyke and S. E. Alcock, pp. 104–126. Malden, Mass.: Blackwell.

Kammerer, C. A., and N. Tannenbaum
2003 Introduction. In *Founders' Cults in Southeast Asia: Ancestors, Polity, and Identity*, edited by N. Tannenbaum and C. A. Kammerer, pp. 1–14. New Haven, Conn.: Yale University Southeast Asia Studies.

Kamp, K. A.
1998 Social Hierarchy and Burial Treatments: A Comparative Assessment. *Cross-Cultural Research* 32:79–115.

Kay, M., and G. Sabo, III
2006 Mortuary Ritual and Winter Solstice Imagery of the Harlan-Style Charnel House. *Southeastern Archaeology* 25: 29–47.

Kehoe, A. B.
2002 Theaters of Power. In *The Dynamics of Power*, edited by M. O'Donovan, pp. 259–272. Center for Archaeological Investigations Occasional Paper No. 30. Carbondale, Illinois: Southern Illinois University.

Kelly, A. R., and L. H. Larson
1957 Explorations at the Etowah Indian Mounds Near Cartersville, Georgia: Seasons 1954, 1955, 1956. *Archaeology* 10:39–48.

Kelly, J. E.
1994 The Archaeology of the East St. Louis Mound Center: Past and Present. *Illinois Archaeology* 6: 1–57.
2006 The Ritualization of Cahokia: The Structure and Organization of Early Cahokia Crafts. In *Leadership and Polity in Mississippian Society*, pp. 236–263. Occasional Paper 33. Carbondale: Center for Archaeological Investigations, Southern Illinois University.

Kenton, E. (editor)
1927 *The Indians of North America: From "The Jesuit Relations and Allied Documents: Travels and Explorations of the Jesuit Missionaries in New France, 1610–1791,"* edited by Reuben Gold Thwaites, Vol. 2. New York: Harcourt, Brace.

Kerber, R. A.
1986 Political Evolution in the Lower Illinois Valley: A.D. 400–1000. Unpublished Ph.D. dissertation, Department of Anthropology, Northwestern University, Evanston, Illinois.

Kidd, K. E.
1953 The Excavation and Historical Identification of a Huron Ossuary. *American Antiquity* 18: 359–379.

King, A.
2001 Long-Term Histories of Mississippian Centers: The Developmental Sequence of Etowah and Its Comparison to Moundville and Cahokia. *Southeastern Archaeology* 20: 1–17.

2003 *Etowah: The Political History of a Chiefdom Capital.* Tuscaloosa: University of Alabama Press.

2004 Deciphering Etowah's Mound C: The Construction History and Mortuary Record of a Mississippian Burial Mound. *Southeastern Archaeology* 23(2): 153–165.

2006 The Historic Period Transformation of Mississippian Societies. In *Light on the Path: The Anthropology and History of the Southeastern Indians*, edited by T. J. Pluckhahn and R. Ethridge, pp. 179–195. Tuscaloosa: University of Alabama Press.

2007 The Southeastern Ceremonial Complex: From Cult to Complex. In *Southeastern Ceremonial Complex: Chronology, Iconography, and Style*, edited by A. King, pp. 1–14. Tuscaloosa: University of Alabama Press.

King, D. H.
1979 The Origin of the Eastern Cherokees as a Social Political Entity. In *The Cherokee Indian Nation: A Troubled History*, edited by D. H. King, pp. 164–180. Knoxville: University of Tennessee Press.

King, M. E., and J. S. Gardner
1981 The Analysis of Textiles from Spiro Mound, Oklahoma. In *The Research Potential of Anthropological Museum Collections*, edited by A.-M. E. Cantwell, J. B. Griffin and N. A. Rothschild, pp. 123–139. Annals of the New York Academy of Sciences 376.

King, T. F.
1976 Political Differentiation among Hunter-Gathers: An Archaeological Test. Unpublished Ph.D. dissertation, Department of Anthropology, University of California, Riverside.

Kintigh, Keith W.
2000 Leadership Strategies in Protohistoric Zuni Towns. In *Alternative Leadership Strategies in the Prehispanic Southwest*, edited by B. J. Mills, pp. 95–116. Tucson: University of Arizona Press.

Kintigh, K. W., and A. Ammerman
1982 Heuristic Approaches to Spatial Analysis in Archaeology. *American Antiquity* 47: 41–63.

Kirchhoff, P.
1959 The Principles of Clanship in Human Society. In *Readings in Anthropology*, vol. 2, edited by M. Fried, pp. 260–270. New York: Thomas Y. Crowell.

Knapp, A. B., and W. Ashmore
1999 Archaeological Landscapes: Constructed, Conceptualized, Ideational. In *Archaeologies of Landscape: Contemporary Perspectives*, edited by A. B. Knapp and W. Ashmore, pp. 1–30. Malden, Mass.: Blackwell.

Knight, V. J., Jr.
1989a Symbolism of Mississippian Mounds. In *Powhatan's Mantle: Indians in the Colonial Southeast*, edited by P. H. Wood, G. A. Waselkov, and M. T. Hatley, pp. 279–291. Lincoln: University of Nebraska Press.
1989b Some Speculations on Mississippian Monsters. In *The Southeastern Ceremonial Complex: Artifacts and Analysis*, edited by P. Galloway, pp. 206–210. Lincoln: University of Nebraska Press.
1990 Social Organization and the Evolution of Hierarchy in Southeastern Chiefdoms. *Journal of Anthropological Research* 46: 1–23.
1997 Some Developmental Parallels between Cahokia and Moundville. In *Cahokia: Domination and Ideology in the Mississippian World*, edited by T. R. Pauketat and T. E. Emerson, pp. 229–247. Lincoln: University of Nebraska Press.
1998 Moundville as a Diagrammatic Ceremonial Center. In *Archaeology of the Moundville Chiefdom*, edited by V. J. Knight, Jr., and V. P. Steponaitis, pp. 1–25. Washington: Smithsonian Institution Press.
2004 Characterizing Elite Midden Deposits at Moundville. *American Antiquity* 69: 304–321.
2006 Farewell to the Southeastern Ceremonial Complex. *Southeastern Archaeology* 25:1–5.
2007 The Social Significance of Mound Assemblages at Moundville. Paper presented at the 64th annual meeting of the Southeastern Archaeological Conference. Knoxville, Tennessee.

Knight, V. J., Jr., and V. P. Steponaitis
1998 A New History of Moundville. In *Archaeology of the Moundville Chiefdom*, edited by V. J. Knight, Jr., and V. P. Steponaitis, pp. 1–25. Washington: Smithsonian Institution Press.

Konigsberg, L. W.
1985 Demography and Mortuary Practice at Seip Mound 1. *Midcontinental Journal of Archaeology* 10(1): 123–148.

Kozuch, L.
2002 Olivella Beads from Spiro and the Plains. *American Antiquity* 67: 697–709.

Kroeber, A. L.
1927 Disposal of the Dead. *American Anthropologist* 29: 308–315.

Kuijt, I.
2000 Keeping the Peace: Ritual, Skull Caching, and Community Integration in the Levantine Neolithic. In *Life in Neolithic Farming Communities: Social Orga-*

nization, Identity, and Differentiation, edited by I. Kuijt, pp. 137–164. Kluwer Academic Publishers, Norwell, Mass.: Kluwer Academic.

Kuttruff, J. T.
1993 Mississippian Period Status Differentiation through Textile Analysis: A Caddoan Example. *American Antiquity* 58: 125–145.

Lafferty, R. H., III
1981 *The Phipps Bend Archaeological Project*. Research Series 4, Office of Archaeological Research, University of Alabama, and Tennessee Valley Authority Publications in Anthropology 26, Knoxville: Tennessee Valley Authority.

Lapham, Increase A.
1855 *The Antiquities of Wisconsin*. Smithsonian Contributions to Knowledge 7. Washington, D.C.: Government Printing Office.

Lankford, George E.
1987 *Native American Legends: Southeastern Legends–Tales from the Natchez, Caddo, Biloxi, Chickasaw, and Other Nations*. Atlanta: August House.
2007a Some Cosmological Motifs in the Southeastern Ceremonial Complex. In *Ancient Objects and Sacred Realms*, edited by F. K. Reilly, III, and J. F. Garber, pp. 8–38. Austin: University of Texas Press.
2007b The "Path of Souls": Some Death Imagery in the Southeastern Ceremonial Complex. In *Ancient Objects and Sacred Realms*, edited by F. K. Reilly, III and J. F. Garber, pp. 174–212. Austin: University of Texas Press.
2007c The Great Serpent in Eastern North America. In *Ancient Objects and Sacred Realms: Interpretations of Mississippian Iconography*, edited by F. Kent Reilly, III, and James F. Garber, pp. 107–135. University of Texas Press

Larson, Lewis H.
1957 An Unusual Wooden Rattle from the Etowah Site. *The Missouri Archaeologist* 19: 7–11.
1959 A Mississippian Headdress from Etowah, Georgia. *American Antiquity* 25:109–122.
1971 Archaeological Implications of Social Stratification at the Etowah Site, Georgia. In *Approaches to the Social Dimensions of Mortuary Practices*, edited by J. A. Brown, pp. 58–67. Memoir 25. Washington, D.C.: Society for American Archaeology.
1989 The Etowah Site. In *The Southeastern Ceremonial Complex: Artifacts and Analysis*, edited by Patricia Galloway, pp. 133–141. Lincoln: University of Nebraska Press.
1993 An Examination of the Significance of a Tortoise-Shell Pin from the Etowah Site. In *Archaeology of Eastern North America: Papers in Honor of Stephen Williams*, edited by J. Stoltman, pp. 169–185. Archaeological Report No. 25. Jackson: Mississippi Department of Archives and History.
1994 The Case for Earth Lodges in the Southeast. In *Ocmulgee Archaeology 1936–1986*, edited by D. J. Hally, pp. 105–115. Athens: University of Georgia Press.

2004 The Submound and Mound Architecture and Features of Mound C, Etowah, Bartow County, Georgia. *Southeastern Archaeology* 23(2):127–141.

Latour, B.
1999 *Pandora's Hope: Essays on the Reality of Science Studies*. Cambridge: Harvard University Press.

Lefler, H. T. (editor)
1967 *A New Voyage to Carolina*. Chapel Hill: University of North Carolina Press.

Lewis, G. H.
1979 *Day of Shining Red*. Cambridge University Press, Cambridge.

Lewis, R. B.
1988 Old World Dice in the Protohistoric Southern United States. *Current Anthropology* 29(5):759–768.
1989 On Astragalus Dice and Culture Contact: A Reply to Eisenberg. *Current Anthropology* 31(4):410–413.

Lewis, R. B., and C. Stout
1998 The Town as Metaphor. In *Mississippian Towns and Sacred Spaces: Searching for an Architectural Grammar*, edited by R. B. Lewis and C. Stout, pp. 227–241. University of Alabama Press.

Lewis, R. B., C. Stout, and C. B. Wesson
1998 The Design of Mississippian Towns. In *Mississippian Towns and Sacred Spaces: Searching for an Architectural Grammar*, edited by R. B. Lewis and C. Stout, pp. 1–21. Tuscaloosa: University of Alabama Press.

Lewis, T. M. N.
1947 Kiesling Cave. *Tennessee Archeologist* 3: 33–34.

Lewis, T. M. N., and M. Kneberg
1946 *Hiwassee Island*. Knoxville: University of Tennessee Press.

Lewis, T. M. N., M. K. Lewis, and L. P. Sullivan (editors)
1995 *The Prehistory of the Chickamauga Basin in Tennessee*. 2 vols. Knoxville: University of Tennessee Press.

Leone, M.
1984 Interpreting Ideology in Historical Archaeology: The William Paca Garden in Annapolis, Maryland. In *Ideology, Power and Prehistory*, edited by D. Miller and C. Tilley, pp. 25–36. Cambridge: Cambridge University Press.

Lightfoot, K. G., and A. Martinez
1995 Frontiers and Boundaries in Archaeological Perspective. *Annual Review of Anthropology* 24: 471–492.

Lindauer, O., and J. H. Blitz
1997 Higher Ground: The Archaeology of North American Platform Mounds. *Journal of Archaeological Research* 5: 169–207.

Lorant, S. (editor)
1946 *The New World: The First Pictures of America*. New York: Duell, Sloan and Pearce.

Lorenz, Karl G.
1997 A Re-examination of Natchez Sociopolitical Complexity: A View from the Grand Village and Beyond. *Southeastern Archaeology* 16: 97–112.
2000 The Natchez of Southwest Mississippi. In *Indians of the Greater Southeast: Historical Archaeology and Ethnohistory*, edited by B. G. McEwan, pp. 142–177. Gainesville: University Press of Florida.

McCleary, T. P.
1997 *The Stars We Know: Crow Indian Astronomy and Lifeways.* Prospect Hills, Illinois: Waveland.

McGee, W. J.
1897 The Siouan Indians: A Preliminary Sketch. In *Fifteenth Annual Report of the Bureau of American Ethnology*, pp. 153–204. Washington, D.C.: Government Printing Office.

McGuire, R. H.
1988 Dialogues with the Dead: Ideology and the Cemetery. In *The Recovery of Meaning in Historical Archaeology*, edited by M. P. Leone and P. B. Potter, Jr., pp. 435–480. Washington: Smithsonian Institution Press.
1992 *Death, Society, and Ideology in a Hohokam Community.* Boulder, Colorado: Westview.

McIlhany, C. W., III
1978 An Archaeological Survey of the Middle Nolichucky River Basin. Unpublished M. A. Thesis, Department of Anthropology, University of Tennessee, Knoxville.

McWilliams, R. G. (translator and editor)
1988 *Fleur de Lys and Calumet.* Tuscaloosa: University of Alabama Press.

Mainfort, R. C., Jr.
1979 *Indian Social Dynamics in the Period of European Contact.* Anthropological Series 1(4). East Lansing, Michigan: The Museum, Michigan State University.
1985 Wealth, Space, and Status in a Historic Indian Cemetery. *American Antiquity* 50: 555–579.
1996 Time and the Fletcher Site. In *Investigating the Archaeological Record of the Great Lakes State*, edited by M. B. Holman, J. G. Brashler, and K. E. Parker, pp. 415–454. Kalamazoo, Michigan: New Issues Press.
2001 The Late Prehistoric and Protohistoric Periods in the Central Mississippi Valley. In *Societies in Eclipse*, edited by D. S. Brose, C. W. Cowan, and R. C. Mainfort, Jr., pp. 173–189. Washington, D.C.: Smithsonian Institution Press.
2003 Late Period Ceramic Rim Variation in the Central Mississippi Valley. *Southeastern Archaeology* 22(1):33–46.
2005 Architecture at Upper Nodena: Structures Excavated by Dr. James. K Hampson. *Arkansas Archeologist* 44:21–30.

Mainfort, R. C., Jr. (editor)
2003 Archaeological Investigation at Upper Nodena: 1973 Field Season. Project completion report submitted to the Arkansas Natural and Cultural Resources Council, Little Rock.

Mainfort, R. C., Jr., J. M. Compton, and K. H. Cande
2007   1973 Excavations at the Upper Nodena Site. *Southeastern Archaeology* 26:108–123.

Mainfort, R. C., Jr., R. Fisher-Carroll, and D. G. Gall
2006   Sociotechnic Celts from the Upper Nodena Site, Northeast Arkansas. *Midcontinental Journal of Archaeology* 31:323–343.

Marcus, J., and K. V. Flannery
1996   *Zapotec Civilization*. London: Thames and Hudson.

Marshall, John B.
1992   The St. Louis Mounds Group: Historical Accounts and Pictorial Depictions. *Missouri Archaeologist* 53:43–79.

Maschner, H. D. G. (editor)
1996   *Darwinian Archaeologies*. New York: Plenum.

Maxwell, M. S.
1952   Clay Ear Spools from the Aztalan Site. *American Antiquity* 18: 61–63.

Meggitt, M. J.
1965   The Mae-Enga of the Western Highlands. In *Gods, Ghosts and Men in Melanesia*, edited by P. Lawrence and M. J. Meggitt, pp. 105–131. New York: Oxford University Press.

Meloy, H.
1984   *Mummies of Mammoth Cave*. Shelbyville, Indiana: Micron Publishing.

Mercer, H. C.
1897   The Finding of the Remains of Fossil Sloth at Big Bone Cave, Tennessee, in 1896. *Proceedings of the American Philosophical Society* 36: 36–70.

Merriam, L. G., and C. J. Merriam
2004   *The Spiro Mound: A Photo Essay*. Oklahoma City: Merriam Station Books.

Meskell, L.
2004   *Object Worlds in Ancient Egypt: Material Biographies Past and Present*. Oxford: Berg.

Metcalf, P., and R. Huntington
1991   *Celebrations of Death*. 2nd ed. Cambridge: Cambridge University Press.

Milanich, J. T., A. S. Cordell, V. J. Knight, Jr., T. A. Kohler, and B. J. Sigler-Lavelle
1997   *Archaeology of Northern Florida, A.D. 200–900: The McKeithen Weeden Island Culture*. Reprinted. Gainesville: University Press of Florida. Originally published 1984, Academic Press.

Milner, G. R.
1984   Social and Temporal Implications of Variation among American Bottom Mississippian Cemeteries. *American Antiquity* 49: 468–488.
1998   *The Cahokia Chiefdom: The Archaeology of a Mississippian Society*. Washington: Smithsonian Institution Press.

Miller, P. M.
1812   Preservation of Human Bodies in a Cave, in Tennessee: In a Letter from Pleasant M. Miller, Esq. of Knoxville, Dated May 1st, 1811. *Medical Repository* 3: 147–149.

Milner, G. R., and S. Schroeder
1999 Mississippian Sociopolitical Systems. In *Great Towns and Regional Polities in the Prehistoric American Southwest and Southeast*, edited by J. E. Neitzel, pp. 95–107. Albuquerque: University of New Mexico Press.

Mississippi River Commission
ca. 1915 Survey of the Mississippi River, Chart Number 17. Baltimore: A. Hoen and Co. Lithographers.

Moore, A. (editor)
1988 *Nairne's Muskhogean Journals: The 1708 Expedition to the Mississippi River*. Jackson: University Press of Mississippi.

Moore, C. B.
1905 Certain Aboriginal Remains of the Black Warrior River. *Journal of the Academy of Natural Sciences of Philadelphia* 13: 124–244.
1907 Moundville Revisited. *Journal of the Academy of Natural Sciences of Philadelphia* 13: 334–405.
1911 Some Aboriginal Sites on Mississippi River. *Journal of the Academy of Natural Sciences of Philadelphia* 14:367–478.
1916 Additional Investigations on Mississippi River. *Journal of the Academy of Natural Sciences of Philadelphia* 16:492–508.

Moorehead, W. K.
1932 *The Etowah Papers*. Andover Mass.: Phillips Academy.

Morris, I.
1987 *Burial and Ancient Society*. Cambridge: Cambridge University Press.
1991 The Archaeology of Ancestors: The Saxe/Goldstein Hypothesis Revisited. *Cambridge Archaeological Journal* 1: 147–169.

Morse, D. F.
1990 The Nodena Phase. In *Towns and Temples Along the Mississippi*, edited by D. H. Dye and C. A. Cox, pp. 69–97. Tuscaloosa: University of Alabama Press.

Morse D. F. (editor)
1973 *Nodena: An Account of 90 Years of Archeological Investigation in Southeast Mississippi County, Arkansas*. Research Series 4. Fayetteville: Arkansas Archeological Survey.
1989 *Nodena: An Account of 90 Years of Archeological Investigation in Southeast Mississippi County, Arkansas*. Revised. Research Series 30. Fayetteville: Arkansas Archeological Survey.

Morse, D. F., and P. A. Morse
1983 *Archaeology of the Central Mississippi Valley*. New York: Academic Press.
1996 Northeast Arkansas. In *Prehistory of the Central Mississippi Valley*, edited by C. H. McNutt, pp. 119–135. Tuscaloosa: University of Alabama Press.

Morse, P. A.
1981 *Parkin*. Research Series 13. Fayetteville: Arkansas Archeological Survey.

1990 The Parkin Site and the Parkin Phase. In *Towns and Temples Along the Mississippi*, edited by D. H. Dye and C. A. Cox, pp. 118–134. Tuscaloosa: University of Alabama Press.

Muller, J.
1997 *Mississippian Political Economy*. New York: Plenum.
2000 Contradictions in the Interpretation of the Southeastern Ceremonial Complex. Paper presented at the 65th Annual Society for American Archaeology meeting, Philadelphia, Pennsylvania.

Munson, C. A. (editor)
1994 Archaeological Investigations at the Southwind Site, a Mississippian Community in Posey County, Indiana. Report submitted to Indiana Department of Natural Resources, Division of Historic Preservation and Archaeology, Indianapolis.

Nass, J. P., Jr., and R. W. Yerkes
1995 Social Differentiation in Mississippian and Fort Ancient Communities. In *Mississippian Communities and Households*, edited by J. D. Rogers Mississippian and Bruce D. Smith, pp. 58–80. Tuscaloosa: University of Alabama Press.

Neitzel, R. S.
1965 Archeology of the Fatherland Site, the Grand Village of the Natchez. *Anthropological Papers* 51(1). New York: American Museum of Natural History.

Nora, Pierre
1989 Between Memory and History: Les Lieux de Mémoire [1984]. *Representations* 26: 7–25.

O'Shea, J.
1981 Social Configurations and the Archaeological Study of Mortuary Practices: A Case Study. In *The Archaeology of Death*, edited by R. Chapman, I. Kinnes, and K. Randsborg, pp. 39–52. Cambridge: Cambridge University Press
1984 *Mortuary Variability*. New York: Academic Press.
1995 Mortuary Custom in the Bronze Age of Southeastern Hungary: Diachronic and Synchronic Perspectives. In *Regional Approaches to Mortuary Analysis*, edited by L. A. Beck, pp. 125–145. New York: Plenum.

Oehler, C.
1973 *Turpin Indians: A Revised Report of the Findings of the Cincinnati Museum of Natural History's Archaeological Exploration of the Turpin Site, Hamilton County, Ohio 1946 to 1949*. Popular Publication Series 1. Cincinnati: Cincinnati Museum of Natural History.

Oliver, B. L.
1992 Settlements of the Pee Dee Culture. Unpublished Ph.D. dissertation, Department of Anthropology, University of North Carolina, Chapel Hill.

Orr, K. G.
1946 The Archaeological Situation at Spiro, Oklahoma: A Preliminary Report. *American Antiquity* 11: 228–255.

Owens, V. S.
1958   A Bedford County Cavern Investigation. *Tennessee Archeologist* 14: 16–22.

Parker Pearson, M.
1982   Mortuary Practices, Society and Ideology: An Ethnoarchaeological Study. In *Symbolic and Structural Archaeology*, edited by I. Hodder, pp. 99–113. Cambridge: Cambridge University Press.
1999   *The Archaeology of Death and Burial*. Stroud, Gloucestershire: Sutton Publishing Ltd.

Parris, W. G.
1946   A Cave Site in Pickett County. *Tennessee Archeologist* 2: 59–60.

Pauketat, T. R.
1994   *The Ascent of Chiefs: Cahokia and Mississippian Politics in Native North America*. Tuscaloosa: University of Alabama Press.
2000   The Tragedy of the Commoners. In *Agency in Archaeology*, edited by M.-A. Dobres and J. Robb, pp. 113–129. London: Routledge.
2001a   Practice and History in Archaeology: An Emerging Paradigm. *Anthropological Theory* 1: 73–98.
2001b   A New Tradition in Archaeology. In *The Archaeology of Historical Processes: Agency and Tradition Before and After Columbus*, edited by T. R. Pauketat, pp. 1–16. Gainesville: University Press of Florida.
2003   Resettled Farmers and the Making of a Mississippian Polity. *American Antiquity* 68: 39–66.
2004   *Ancient Cahokia and the Mississippians*. Cambridge: Cambridge University Press.
2005a   The Forgotten History of the Mississippians. In *North American Archaeology*, edited by T. R. Pauketat and D. D. Loren, pp. 187–212. Blackwell, Oxford: Blackwell.
2005b   Mounds, Buildings, Posts, Palisades, and Compounds. In *The Archaeology of the East St. Louis Mound Center. Part I: The Southside Excavations*, edited by T. R. Pauketat, pp. 113–192. Transportation Archaeological Research Reports No. 21, Illinois Transportation Archaeological Research Program, University of Illinois, Urbana, Illinois.
2007   *Chiefdoms and Other Archaeological Delusions*. Walnut Canyon, California: AltaMira.
2008   Founders' Cults and the Archaeologies of Wa-kan-da. In *Memory Work: The Archaeologies of Material Practice*, edited by B. J. Mills and W. H. Walker, pp. 61–80. Santa Fe: School of American Research Press.
2009   *Cahokia's Big Bang and the Story of Ancient North America*. New York: Viking-Penguin.

Pauketat, T. R. (editor)
2001   *The Archaeology of Historical Processes: Agency and Tradition Before and After Columbus*. Gainesville: University Press of Florida.

Pauketat, T. R., and S. M. Alt
2003 Mounds, Memory, and Contested Mississippian History. In *Archaeologies of Memory*, edited by R. M. Van Dyke and S. E. Alcock, pp. 151–179. Oxford: Blackwell.
2005 Agency in a Postmold? Physicality and the Archaeology of Culture-Making. *Journal of Archaeological Method and Theory* 12: 213–236.

Pauketat, T. R., and A. W. Barker
2000 Mounds 65 and 66 at Cahokia: Additional Details of the 1927 Excavations. In *Mounds, Modoc, and Mesoamerica: Papers in Honor of Melvin L. Fowler*, edited by S. Ahler, pp. 125–140. Illinois State Museum Scientific Papers, Volume 28. Springfield: Illinois State Museum.

Pauketat, T. R., and M. A. Rees
1996 *Early Cahokia Project 1994 Excavations at Mound 49, Cahokia (11-S-34-2)*. Illinois Historic Preservation Agency.

Payne, C.
2006 The Foundations of Leadership in Mississippian Chiefdoms: Perspectives from Lake Jackson and Upper Nodena. In *Leadership and Polity in Mississippian Society*, edited by B. Butler and P. Welch, pp. 91–111. Occasional Paper 33. Carbondale: Center for Archaeological Investigations, Southern Illinois University.

Peebles, C. S.
1971 Moundville and Surrounding Sites: Some Structural Considerations of Mortuary Practices, II. In *Approaches to the Social Dimensions of Mortuary Practices*, edited by J. A. Brown, pp. 68–91. Memoir No. 25. Washington: Society for American Archaeology.
1974 Moundville: The Organization of a Prehistoric Community and Culture. Unpublished Ph.D. dissertation, Department of Anthropology, University of California-Santa Barbara.
1978 Determinants of Settlement Size and Location in the Moundville Phase. In *Mississippian Settlement Patterns*, edited by B. D. Smith, pp. 369–416. New York: Academic Press.
1979 *Excavations at Moundville, 1905–1951*. Ann Arbor: University of Michigan Press.
1983 Moundville: Late Prehistoric Sociopolitical Organization in the Southeastern United States. In *The Development of Political Organization in Native North America*, edited by E. Tooker, pp. 183–201. Proceedings of the American Ethnological Society. Washington, D.C.

Peebles, C. S., and S. M. Kus
1977 Some Archaeological Correlates of Ranked Societies. *American Antiquity* 42: 421–448.

Perdue, T.
1998 *Cherokee Women: Gender and Culture Change, 1700–1835*. Lincoln: University of Nebraska Press.

Peregrine, P. N.
1992　*Mississippian Evolution: A World-System Perspective.* Madison, Wisconsin: Prehistory Press.

Perino, G.
1966　*The Banks Village Site, Crittenden County, Arkansas.* Memoir No. 4, Missouri Archaeological Society. Columbia, Missouri: Missouri Archaeological Society.

1971a　The Mississippian Component at the Schild Site No. 4, Greene County, Illinois. In *Mississippian Site Archaeology in Illinois I: Site Reports from the St. Louis and Chicago Areas*, pp. 1–148. Bulletin 8. Urbana: Illinois Archaeological Survey.

1971b　The Yokem Site, Pike County, Illinois. In *Mississippian Site Archaeology in Illinois I: Site Reports from the St. Louis and Chicago Areas*, pp. 149–191. Bulletin 8. Urbana: Illinois Archaeological Survey.

Phillips, P.
1970　*Archaeological Survey in the Lower Yazoo Basin, Mississippi, 1949–1955.* Papers of the Peabody Museum of American Archaeology and Ethnology, Vol. 60. Cambridge, Mass.: Harvard University.

Phillips, P., and J. A. Brown
1978　*Pre-Columbian Shell Engravings from the Craig Mound at Spiro, Oklahoma.* Part 1. Cambridge, Mass.: Peabody Museum Press, Harvard University.

Phillips, P., J. A. Ford, and J. B. Griffin
1951　*Archaeological Survey in the Lower Mississippi Alluvial Valley, 1940–1947.* Papers of the Peabody Museum, Vol. 25. Cambridge, Mass.: Harvard University.

Polhemus, R. R.
1990　Phase Characteristics: East Tennessee River. In *Lamar Archaeology: Mississippian Chiefdoms in the Deep South*, edited by M. Williams and G. Shapiro, pp. 39–41. Tuscaloosa: University of Alabama Press.

1998　Activity Organization in Mississippian Households: A Case Study from the Loy Site in East Tennessee. Unpublished doctoral dissertation, Department of Anthropology, University of Tennessee, Knoxville.

n.d.　Unpublished Field Notes for the Loy Site (40JE10) Excavations. Manuscript on file at the Frank H. McClung Museum, University of Tennessee, Knoxville.

Polhemus, R. R., and J. H. Polhemus
1966　The McCullough Bend Site. *Tennessee Archaeologist* 12(1): 13–24.

Polhemus, R. R., A. E. Bogan, and J. Chapman
1987　*The Toqua Site: 40MR6: A Late Mississippian Dallas Phase Town.* Report of Investigations Number 41, Department of Anthropology, University of Tennessee and Publications in Anthropology 44. Knoxville: Tennessee Valley Authority.

1990　Dallas Phase Architecture and Sociopolitical Structure. In *Lamar Archaeol-*

ogy: Mississippian Chiefdoms in the Deep South, edited by M. Williams and G. Shapiro, pp. 125–138. Tuscaloosa: University of Alabama Press.

Pollack, D.
2004   *Caborn-Welborn*. Tuscaloosa: University of Alabama Press.

Pollack, D., and A. G. Henderson
1992   Toward a Model of Fort Ancient Society. In *Fort Ancient Cultural Dynamics in the Middle Ohio Valley*, edited by A. G. Henderson, pp. 281–294. Madison, Wisconsin: Prehistory Press.
2000   Insights into Fort Ancient Culture Change: A View from South of the Ohio River. In *Cultures Before Contact: The Late Prehistory of Ohio and Surrounding Regions*, edited by R. A. Genheimer, pp. 194–215. Columbus: Ohio Archaeological Council.

Pollack, D., A. G. Henderson, and C. T. Begley
2002   Fort Ancient/Mississippian Interaction on the Northeastern Periphery. *Southeastern Archaeology* 21: 206–220

Porubcan, P. J.
2000   Human and Nonhuman Surplus Display at Mound 72, Cahokia. In *Mounds, Modoc, and Mesoamerica: Papers in Honor of Melvin L. Fowler*, edited by S. R. Ahler, pp. 207–225. Scientific Papers Vol. 28. Springfield: Illinois State Museum.

Powell, M. L.
1988   *Status and Health in Prehistory: A Case Study of the Moundville Chiefdom*. Washington, D.C.: Smithsonian University Press.
1989   The Nodena People. In *Nodena*, edited by D. F. Morse, pp. 65–96. Research Series 30. Fayetteville: Arkansas Archaeological Survey.
1990   Health and Disease at Nodena: A Late Mississippian Community in Northeast Arkansas. In *Towns and Temples Along the Mississippi*, edited by D. H. Dye and C. A. Cox, pp. 98–117. Tuscaloosa: University of Alabama Press.

Precourt, W. E.
1984   Mortuary Practices and Economic Transaction: A Holgeistic Study. *Research in Economic Anthropology* 6:161–170.

Price, E. K., and L. M. Langston
2007   A Skeletal Analysis and Comparative Study of Three Mississippian Period Sites in Upper East Tennessee. Unpublished manuscript on file, Archaeology Laboratory, East Tennessee State University, Johnson City.

Radin, P.
1948   *Winnebago Hero Cycles: A Study in Aboriginal Literature*. Baltimore: Waverly.

Rafinesque, C. S.
1824   *Ancient History, or Annals of Kentucky: With a Survey of the Ancient Monuments of North America*. Whitefish, Montana: Kessinger Publishing.

Rakita, G. F. M.
2001   Social Complexity, Religious Organization, and Mortuary Ritual in the Casas Grandes of Chihuahua, Mexico. Unpublished Ph.D. dissertation, Department of Anthropology, University of New Mexico, Albuquerque.

Rappaport, R. A.
1979 Ecology, Meaning, and Religion. Richmond, Calif.: North Atlantic Books.

Reilly, F. K., III
2004 People of Earth, People of Sky: Visualizing the Sacred in Native American Art of the Mississippian Period. In *Hero, Hawk, and Open Hand*, edited by R. F. Townsend and R. Sharp, pp. 124–137. Chicago: Art Institute of Chicago.

Renfrew, C.
1986 Introduction: Peer Polity Interaction and Socio-Political Change. In *Peer Polity Interaction and Socio-Political Change*, edited by C. Renfrew and J. F. Cherry, pp. 1–18. Cambridge: Cambridge University Press.

Rice, P. M.
1998 Contexts of Contact and Change: Peripheries, Frontiers, and Boundaries. In *Interaction, Culture Change, and Archaeology*, edited by J. G. Cusick, pp. 44–66. Occasional Paper 25. Carbondale, Illinois: Center for Archaeological Investigations, Southern Illinois University.

Richards, J. D.
1992 Ceramics and Culture at Aztalan, a Late Prehistoric Village in Southeastern Wisconsin. Unpublished Ph.D. dissertation, Department of Anthropology, University of Wisconsin-Milwaukee.

Robertson, J. A.
1980 Chipped Stone and Socio-Cultural Interpretations. Unpublished M.A. thesis, Department of Anthropology, University of Illinois, Chicago.

Rodning, C. B.
1996 Towns and Clans: Social Institutions and Organization of Native Communities on the Appalachian Summit. Unpublished paper submitted to the Department of Anthropology, University of North Carolina, Chapel Hill.
1999 Archaeological Perspectives on Gender and Women in Traditional Cherokee Society. *Journal of Cherokee Studies* 10: 3–27.
2001 Mortuary Ritual and Gender Ideology in Protohistoric Southwestern North Carolina. In *Archaeological Studies of Gender in the Southeastern United States*, edited by J. M. Eastman and C. B. Rodning, pp. 77–100. Gainesville: University Press of Florida.
2005 The Cherokee Town at the Coweeta Creek Site. Unpublished Ph.D. dissertation, Department of Anthropology, University of North Carolina, Chapel Hill.

Rogers, J. D.
1996 Markers of Social Integration: The Development of Centralized Authority in the Spiro Region. In *Political Structure and Change in the Prehistoric Southeastern United States*, edited by J. F. Scarry, pp. 53–68. Gainesville: University Press of Florida.
2006 Chronology and the Demise of Chiefdoms: Eastern Oklahoma in the Sixteenth and Seventeenth Centuries. *Southeastern Archaeology* 25: 20–28.

Rohrbaugh, C. L.
1982 Spiro and Fort Coffee Phases: Changing Cultural Complexes of the Caddoan Area. Unpublished Ph.D. dissertation, Department of Anthropology, University of Wisconsin, Madison.
1984 Arkansas Valley Caddoan: Fort Coffee and Neosho. In *Prehistory of Oklahoma*, edited by R. E. Bell, pp. 265–285. Orlando, Florida, Academic Press.

Rose, J. C.
1999 Mortuary Data and Analysis. In *The Mound 72 Area: Dedicated and Sacred Space in Early Cahokia*, by M. Fowler, J. Rose, B. Vander Leest, and S. Ahler, pp. 63–82. Reports of Investigations, No. 54, Springfield: Illinois State Museum.

Rosenwig, R. M.
2000 Some Political Processes of Ranked Societies. *Journal of Anthropological Archaeology* 19:413–460.

Rothschild, N. A.
1979 Mortuary Behavior and Social Organization at Indian Knoll and Dickson Mounds. *American Antiquity* 44:658–667.

Rowe, C. W.
1958a A Crematorium at Aztalan. *Wisconsin Archeologist* 39: 101–110.
1958b The Use of Earth Moving Machinery at Aztalan. *Wisconsin Archeologist* 36: 63–65.

Rowe, C. W., and A. Whiteford
n.d. Unpublished field notes for the 1942 Zimmerman's Island site (40JE2) excavations. Manuscript on file at the Frank H. McClung Museum, University of Tennessee, Knoxville.

Rudolph, J. L.
1984 Earthlodges and Platform Mounds: Changing Public Architecture in the Southeastern U.S. *Southeastern Archaeology* 3: 33–45.

Sabo, George, III
1998 The Structure of Caddo Leadership in the Colonial Era. In *The Native History of the Caddo: Their Place in Southeastern Archeology and Ethnohistory*, edited by T. K. Perttula and J. E. Bruseth, pp. 159–174. Studies in Archeology 30. Austin: Texas Archeological Research Laboratory, University of Texas.

Salo, L. V.
1969 *Archaeological Investigations in the Tellico Reservoir, Tennessee, 1967–1968: An Interim Report*. Department of Anthropology Report of Investigations No. 7. Knoxville: University of Tennessee.

Sattler, R. A.
1995 Women's Status among the Muskogee and Cherokee. In *Women and Power in Native North America*, edited by L. F. Klein and L. A. Ackerman, pp. 214–229. Norman: University of Oklahoma Press.

Saxe, A. A.
1970 Social Dimensions of Mortuary Practices. Unpublished Ph.D. dissertation, Department of Anthropology, University of Michigan, Ann Arbor.

1971 Social Dimensions in a Mesolithic Population from Wadi Halfa, Sudan. In *Approaches to the Social Dimensions of Mortuary Practices*, edited by J. A. Brown, pp. 39–57. Memoir 25. Salt Lake City: Society for American Archaeology.

Scarry, C. M.
1986 Change in Plant Procurement and Production During the Emergence of the Moundville Chiefdom. Unpublished Ph.D. dissertation, Department of Anthropology, University of Michigan, Ann Arbor.
1992 Political Offices and Political Structure: Ethnohistoric and Archaeological Perspectives on the Native Lords of Apalachee. In *Lords of the Southeast: Social Inequality and the Native Elites of Southeastern North America*, edited by A. W. Barker and T. R. Pauketat, pp. 163–179. Archeological Paper Number 3. Washington, D.C.: American Anthropological Association.
1995 *Excavations on the Northwest Riverbank at Moundville: Investigations of a Moundville I Residential Area.* Report of Investigations 72. Tuscaloosa: University of Alabama Museums, Office of Archaeological Services.
1996 The Nature of Mississippian Societies. In *Political Structure and Change in the Prehistoric Southeastern United States*, edited by J. F. Scarry, pp. 12–24. Gainesville: University Press of Florida.

Scarry, J. F.
1999 Elite Identities in Apalachee Province: The Construction of Identity and Cultural Change in a Mississippian Polity. In *Material Symbols: Culture and Economy in Prehistory*, edited by J. Robb, pp. 342–361. Occasional Paper 26. Carbondale, Illinois: Center for Archaeological Investigations, Southern Illinois University.

Scarry, J. F. (editor)
1996 *Political Structure and Change in the Prehistoric Southeastern United States.* Gainesville: University Press of Florida.

Schama, S.
1995 *Landscape and Memory.* New York: Knopf.

Schiller, A.
2001 Mortuary Monuments and Social Change among the Ngaju. In *Social Memory, Identity, and Death: Anthropological Perspectives on Mortuary Rituals*, edited by M. S. Chesson, pp. 70–79. Archeological Papers 10. Arlington, Virginia: American Anthropological Association.

Schortman, E. M., and P. A. Urban
1987 Modeling Interregional Interaction in Prehistory. *Advances in Archaeological Method and Theory* 11: 37–95.
1998 Culture Contact Structure and Process. In *Interaction, Culture Change, and Archaeology*, edited by J. G. Cusick, pp. 102–125. Occasional Paper 25. Carbondale, Illinois: Center for Archaeological Investigations, Southern Illinois University.

Schroeder, S.
2004a Power and Place: Agency, Ecology, and History in the American Bottom, Illinois. *Antiquity* 78: 812–827.

2004b   Current Research on Late Precontact Societies of the Midcontinental United States. *Journal of Archaeological Research* 12: 311–372.
2006   Walls as Symbols of Political, Economic, and Military Might. In *Leadership and Polity in Mississippian Society*, edited by B. Butler and P. Welch, pp. 115-141. Occasional Paper 33. Carbondale: Center for Archaeological Investigations, Southern Illinois University.

Schroedl, G. F.
1998   Mississippian Towns in the Eastern Tennessee Valley. In *Mississippian Towns and Sacred Spaces*, edited by R. B. Lewis and C. Stout, pp. 64-92. Tuscaloosa: University of Alabama Press.

Schurr, M. R., and M. J. Schoeninger
1995   Associations between Agricultural Intensification and Social Complexity: An Example from the Prehistoric Ohio Valley. *Journal of Anthropological Archaeology* 14: 315–339.

Scott, G. T., and R. R. Polhemus
1987   Mortuary Patterning. In *The Toqua Site: A Late Mississippian Dallas Phase Town*, edited by R. R. Polhemus, pp. 378-432. Publications in Anthropology 44. Knoxville: University of Tennessee, Department of Anthropology.

Sears, W. H.
1961   The Study of Social and Religious Systems in North American Archaeology. *Current Anthropology* 2:223–246.

Service, E. R.
1962   *Primitive Social Organization*. New York: Random House.
1971   *Primitive Social Organization*. 2nd ed. Originally published 1962. New York: Random House.
1975   *Origins of the State and Civilization*. New York: W. W. Norton.

Sewell, W. H., Jr.
2005   *The Logics of History: Social Theory and Social Transformation*. Chicago, University of Chicago Press.

Sharp, R., A. King, C. Walker, C. Schultz, F. K. Reilly, III, J. Jacobs, and T. Thompson
2006   A Sacred Precinct on the Summit of Etowah's Mound A. Paper presented at the 63rd Annual Meeting of the Southeastern Archaeological Conference, Little Rock, Arkansas.

Shennan, S. J.
1993   After Social Evolution: A New Archaeological Agenda? In *Archaeological Theory: Who Sets the Agenda?* edited by N. Yoffee and A. Sherratt, pp. 53–59. Cambridge: Cambridge University Press.
1997   *Quantifying Archaeology*. 2nd ed. Iowa City: University of Iowa Press.

Shennan, S.
1975   The Social Organization at Branc. *Antiquity* 49:279–288.

Sherrat, A.
1982   Mobile Resources: Settlement and Exchange in Early Agricultural Europe. In *Ranking, Resource, and Exchange*, edited by C. Renfrew and S. Shennan, pp.13–26. Cambridge: Cambridge University Press.

Sherrod, P. C., and M. A. Rolingson
1987 *Surveyors of the Ancient Mississippi Valley*. Research Series 28. Fayetteville: Arkansas Archeological Survey.

Sherwood, S. C., B. Driskell, A. Randall, and S. Meeks
2004 Chronology and Stratigraphy at Dust Cave, Alabama. *American Antiquity* 69: 533–554.

Shryock, A. J.
1987 The Wright Mound Reexamined: Generative Structures and the Political Economy of a Simple Chiefdom. *Midcontinental Journal of Anthropology* 12: 243–268.

Simek, J. F., and A. Cressler
2001 Issues in the Study of Prehistoric Southeastern Cave Art. *Midcontinental Journal of Archaeology* 26: 233–250.
2005 Images in Darkness: Prehistoric Cave Art in Southeastern North America. In *Discovering North American Rock Art*, edited by L. Loendorf, C. Chippendale and D. Whitley, pp. 93–113. Tucson: University of Arizona Press.

Simek, J. F., and A. Cressler
2008 On the Backs of Serpents: Prehistoric Cave Art in the Eastern Woodlands. In *Cave Archaeology of the Eastern Woodlands: Essays in Honor of Patty Jo Watson*, edited by D. H. Dye, pp. 169–191. Knoxville: University of Tennessee Press.

Simek, J. F., A. Cressler, and E. Pope
2004 Association Between a Southeastern Rock Art Motif and Mortuary Caves. In *The Rock-Art of Eastern North America: Capturing Images and Insight*, edited by C. Diaz-Granados and J. R. Duncan, pp. 159–173. Tuscaloosa: University of Alabama Press.

Simek, J. F., C. H. Faulkner, T. Ahlman, B. Cresswell, and J. D. Franklin
2001 The Context of Late Prehistoric Southeastern Cave Art: The Art and Archaeology of 11th Unnamed Cave, Tennessee. *Southeastern Archaeology* 20: 142–153.

Smedal, O. H.
1989 *Order and Difference: An Ethnographic Study of Orang Lom of Bangka, West Indonesia*. Occasional Papers in Social Anthropology No. 19. Oslo: Department of Social Anthropology, University of Oslo.

Smith, B. D.
1978 Variation in Mississippian Settlement Patterns. In *Mississippian Settlement Patterns*, edited by B. D. Smith, pp. 479–503. New York: Academic Press.
1986a A Comparison of the Exploitation of Animal Species by Middle Mississippi and Fort Ancient Groups. *Southeastern Archaeological Conference Newsletter* 28: 19–22.
1986b The Archaeology of the Southeastern United States: from Dalton to de Soto, 10,500–500 B.P. In *Advances in World Archaeology*, edited by F. Wendorf and A. E. Close, pp. 1–92. New York: Academic Press.
1992 Mississippian Elites and Solar Alignments: A Reflection of Managerial Necessity, or Levers of Social Inequality? In *Lords of the Southeast: Social Inequality*

and the Native Elites of Southeastern North America, edited by A. W. Barker and T. R. Pauketat, pp. 11–30. Archeological Papers 3. Washington, D.C.: American Anthropological Association.

Smith, M. O.
2004 Gunpowder. In *Encyclopedia of Cave and Karst Science*, edited by J. Gunn, pp. 410–411. New York: Fitzroy Dearborn.

Smith, M. T.
1987 *Archaeology of Aboriginal Culture Change in the Interior Southeast*. Gainesville: University Press of Florida.
1994 Archaeological Investigations at the Dyar Site, 9GE5. Report Number 32. Laboratory of Archaeology, University of Georgia, Athens.

Smith, M. T., and J. B. Smith
1989 Engraved Shell Masks in North America. *Southeastern Archaeology* 8(1): 9–18.

Sollors, W.
1996 Foreword: Theories of Ethnicity. In *Theories of Ethnicity: A Classical Reader*, edited by W. Sollors, pp. x–xliv. Ipswich, Suffolk: Ipswich Book Company.

Somers, A. N.
1892 Prehistoric Cannibalism in America. *Wisconsin Archeologist* 19: 18–19.

Speck, Frank G.
1979 [1909] *Ethnology of the Yuchi Indians*. Atlantic Highlands, New Jersey: Humanities Press.

Spence, M. W.
1994 Mortuary Programmes of the Early Ontario Iroquoians. *Ontario Archaeology* 58: 6–26.

Stein, G. J.
2002 From Passive Periphery to Active Agents: Emerging Perspectives in the Archaeology of Interregional Interaction. *American Anthropologist* 104: 903–916.

Steponaitis, V. P.
1978 Location Theory and Complex Chiefdoms. In *Mississippian Settlement Patterns*, edited by B. D. Smith, pp. 417–453. New York: Academic Press.
1983 *Ceramics, Chronology, and Community Patterns*. New York: Academic Press.
1986 Prehistoric Archaeology in the Southeastern United States, 1970–1985. *Annual Review of Anthropology* 15: 363–404.
1991 Contrasting Patterns of Mississippian Development. In *Chiefdoms: Power, Economy, and Ideology*, edited by T. Earle, pp.193–228. Cambridge: Cambridge University Press.
1998 Population Trends at Moundville. In *Archaeology of the Moundville Chiefdom*, edited by V. J. Knight, Jr., and V. P. Steponaitis, pp. 26–43. Washington, D.C.: Smithsonian Institution Press.
2004 The Meaning and Use of Etowah Palettes. Paper presented at 61st annual meeting of the Southeastern Archaeological Conference, St. Louis, Missouri.

Steponaitis, V. P., M. J. Blackman, and H. Neff
1996 Large-Scale Patterns in the Chemical Composition of Mississippian Pottery. *American Antiquity* 61: 555–572.

Sterling, W. T.
1920 A Visit to Aztalan in 1838. *Wisconsin Archeologist* 19: 18–19.

Steward, J.
1955 *Theory of Culture Change*. Urbana: University of Illinois Press.

Stickel, E. G.
1968 Status Differentiations at the Rincon Site. *Archaeological Survey Annual Report* 10:209–261. Los Angeles: University of California, Los Angeles.

Strathern, Marilyn
1988 *The Gender of the Gift: Problems with Women and Problems with Society in Melanesia*. Berkeley: University of California Press.

Strezewski, M.
2003 Morton Mound 14 and Mortuary Ceremonialism in the Central Illinois Valley. *Midcontinental Journal of Archaeology* 28: 7–32.

Stubblefield, J. R.
1885 Letter to the Editor. *Nashville Union* [Nashville, Tennessee].

Stuiver M., P. J. Reimer, E. Bard, J. W. Beck, G. S. Burr, K. A. Hughen, B. Kromer, G. McCormac, J. van der Plicht, and M. Spurk.
1998 INTCAL98 Radiocarbon Age Calibration, 24000–0 cal BP. *Radiocarbon* 40(3): 1041–1083.

Sullivan, L. P.
1986 The Late Mississippian Village: Community and Society of the Mouse Creek Phase in Southeastern Tennessee. Unpublished Ph.D. dissertation, Department of Anthropology, University of Wisconsin-Milwaukee.
1987 The Mouse Creek Phase Household. *Southeastern Archaeology* 6: 16–29.
1989 Household, Community, and Society: An Analysis of Mouse Creek Settlements. In *Households and Communities: Proceedings of the 21st Annual Chacmool Conference*, edited by S. MacEachern, D. Archer, and R. Garvin, pp. 317–327. Calgary, Alberta: University of Calgary.
1995 Mississippian Household and Community Organization in Eastern Tennessee. In *Mississippian Communities and Households*, edited by J. D. Rogers and B. D. Smith, pp. 99–123. Tuscaloosa: University of Alabama Press.
2001 Those Men in the Mounds: Gender, Politics, and Mortuary Practices in Late Prehistoric Eastern Tennessee. In *Archaeological Studies of Gender in the Southeastern United States*, edited by J. M. Eastman and C. B. Rodning, pp. 101–126. Gainesville: University Press of Florida.
2006 Gendered Contexts of Mississippian Leadership in Southern Appalachia. In *Leadership and Polity in Mississippian Society*, edited by B. M. Butler and P. D. Welch, pp. 264–285. Occasional Paper 33. Carbondale: Center for Archaeological Investigations, Southern Illinois University.

2007a Revised Chronology for the Chickamauga Basin. Paper presented at Current Research in Tennessee Archaeology, Nashville, Tennessee.
2007b Shell Gorgets, Time, and the SECC in Southeastern Tennessee. In *Southeastern Ceremonial Complex: Chronology, Content, Context*, edited by A. King, pp. 107–133. Tuscaloosa: University of Alabama Press.
2009 Archaeological Time Constructs and the Construction of the Hiwassee Island Mound. In *75 Years of TVA Archaeology*, edited by E. Pritchard and T. Ahlman, pp. 181–209. Knoxville: University of Tennessee Press.

Sullivan, L. P., and C. B. Rodning
2001 Gender, Tradition, and the Negotiation of Power Relationships in Southern Appalachian Chiefdoms. In *The Archaeology of Traditions: Agency and History Before and After Columbus*, edited by T. R. Pauketat, pp. 107–120. Gainesville: University Press of Florida.
2007 Residential Burial, Gender Roles, and Political Development in Late Prehistoric and Early Cherokee Cultures of the Southern Appalachians. Paper presented at the 72nd Annual Meeting of the Society for American Archaeology, Austin, Texas.
2010 Residential Burial, Gender Roles, and Political Development in Late Prehistoric and Early Cherokee Cultures of the Southern Appalachians. In *Residential Burial: A Multi-Regional Exploration*, edited by R. L. Adams and S. M. King. Archeological Papers of the American Anthropological Association. Washington, D.C.: American Anthropological Association. In press.

Swanton, J. R.
1911 *Indian Tribes of the Lower Mississippi Valley and Adjacent Coast of the Gulf of Mexico*. Bureau of American Ethnology, Bulletin 43. Washington: Government Printing Office.
1928 Social Organization and Social Usages of the Indians of the Creek Confederacy. In *Bureau of American Ethnology, Forty Second Annual Report*, pp. 23–472. Washington: Government Printing Office.
1979 *The Indians of the Southeastern United States*. Washington: Smithsonian Institution Press. Originally published 1946 as Bulletin Number 137 Bureau of American Ethnology.
1993 *Source Material for the Social and Ceremonial Life of the Choctaw Indians*. Birmingham, Alabama: Birmingham Public Library Press. Originally published 1931 as Bulletin Number 103 Bureau of American Ethnology.

Tainter, J. A.
1975a Social Inference and Mortuary Practices: An Experiment in Numerical Classification. *World Archaeology* 7:1–15.
1975b The Archaeological Study of Social Change: Woodland Systems in West-Central Illinois. Unpublished Ph.D. dissertation, Department of Anthropology, Northwestern University, Evanston.
1977 Woodland Social Change in West-Central Illinois. *Midcontinental Journal of Archaeology* 2:67–98.

1978   Mortuary Practices and the Study of Prehistoric Social Systems. *Advances in Archaeological Method and Theory* 1: 105–141.

Tainter, J. A., and R. H. Cordy
1977   An Archaeological Analysis of Ranking and Residence Groups in Prehistoric Hawaii. *World Archaeology* 9:95–112.

Tavaszi, M. M.
2004   Stylistic Variation in Mortuary Vessels from Upper Nodena (3MS4) and Middle Nodena (3MS3). Unpublished M.A. thesis, Department of Anthropology, University of Arkansas.

Thomas, C.
1894   *Report on the Mound Explorations of the Bureau of Ethnology.* Smithsonian Institution, Bureau of Ethnology, Twelfth Annual Report. Washington: Government Printing Office.

Thomas, L.
2001   The Gender Division of Labor in Mississippian Households. In *Archaeological Studies of Gender in the Southeastern United States*, edited by J. M. Eastman and C. B. Rodning, pp. 27–56. Gainesville: University Press of Florida.

Townsend, R. F., R. V. Sharp, and G. A. Bailey (editors)
2004   *Hero, Hawk, and Open Hand.* New Haven, Conn.: Yale University Press.

Trinkaus, K. M.
1984   Mortuary Ritual and Mortuary Research. *Current Anthropology* 25:674–679.

Trocolli, R.
1999   Women Leaders in Native North American Societies: Invisible Women of Power. In *Manifesting Power: Gender and the Interpretation of Power in Archaeology*, edited by T. L. Sweely, pp. 49–61. London: Routledge.

Tuan, Y.-F.
1977   *Space and Place: The Perspective of Experience.* Minneapolis: University of Minnesota Press.

Turner, Christy G. II
1983   Taphonomic Reconstructions of Human Violence and Cannibalism Based on Mass Burials in the American Southwest. In *Carnivores, Human Scavengers & Predators: A Question of Bone Technology*, edited by G. M. LeMoine and A. S. MacEachern. Calgary: University of Calgary.

Tuttle, M. P., J. D. Sims, K. Dyer-Williams, R. H. Lafferty, III, and E. S. Schweig, III
2000   *Dating of Liquefaction Features in the New Madrid Seismic Zone.* NUREG/ GR-0018. Washington: United States Nuclear Regulatory Commission.

Ubelaker, D. H.
1974   *Reconstruction of Demographic Profiles from Ossuary Skeletal Samples.* Smithsonian Contributions to Anthropology 18. Washington, D.C.: Smithsonian Institution Press.

Upham, S.
1990   Decoupling the Process of Political Evolution. In *The Evolution of Political Systems: Sociopolitics in Small-Scale Sedentary Societies*, edited by S. Upham, pp. 1–17. Cambridge: Cambridge University Press.

Varner, J., and J. Varner
1951 *The Florida of the Inca*. Austin: University of Texas Press.

Vickery, K. D., T. S. Sunderhaus, and R. A. Genheimer
2000 Preliminary Report on Excavations at the Fort Ancient State Line Site, 33 Ha 58, in the Central Ohio Valley. In *Cultures Before Contact: The Late Prehistory of Ohio and Surrounding Regions*, edited by R. A. Genheimer, pp. 272–328. Columbus: Ohio Archaeological Council.

Vietzen, R., and R. Vietzen
1956 *Saga of Glovers Cave, Kentucky*. Wahoo, Nebraska: Ludi.

Wagner, R.
1991 The Fractal Person. In *Big Men and Great Men: Personifications of Power in Melanesia*, edited by Maurice Godelier and Marilyn Strathern, pp. 159–173. Cambridge: Cambridge University Press.

Walthall, J. A., and D. L. DeJarnette
1974 Copena Burial Caves. *Journal of Alabama Archaeology* 20: 1–62.

Waring, A. J., Jr., and P. Holder
1945 A Prehistoric Ceremonial Complex in the Southeastern United States. *American Anthropologist* n.s. 47:1–34.
1968 The Southern Cult and Muskhogean Ceremonial: General Considerations. In *The Waring Papers*, edited by S. Williams, pp. 30–69. Papers of the Peabody Museum of American Archaeology and Ethnology, no. 50. Cambridge: Peabody Museum.

Waselkov, G. A., and K. E. H. Braund (editors)
1995 *William Bartram on the Southeastern Indians*. Lincoln: University of Nebraska Press.

Watson, P. J.
1969 *The Prehistory of Salts Cave, Kentucky*. Springfield, Illinois: Illinois State Museum.
1974 *Archaeology of the Mammoth Cave Area*. New York: Academic Press.

Watson, R. J.
2000 Sacred Landscapes at Cahokia: Mound 72 and the Mound 72 Precinct. In *Mounds, Modoc, and Mesoamerica: Papers in Honor of Melvin L. Fowler*, edited by S. R. Ahler, pp. 227–243. Scientific Papers, Volume 28. Springfield: Illinois State Museum.

Webb, W. S., and D. L. DeJarnette
1942 *An Archaeological Survey of Pickwick Basin in Adjacent Portions of the States Alabama, Mississippi, and Tennessee*. Bureau of American Ethnology Bulletin 129. Washington: Government Printing Office.

Webb, W. S., and C. E. Snow
1945 *The Adena People*. University of Kentucky Reports in Anthropology and Archaeology, Volume 6. Lexington: University of Kentucky.

Welch, P. D.
1991   *Moundville's Economy.* Tuscaloosa: University of Alabama Press.
2006a Interpreting Anomalous Mississippian Settlements: Leadership from Below. In *Leadership and Polity in Mississippian Society*, edited by B. M. Butler and P. D. Welch, pp. 264–285. Center for Archaeological Investigations Occasional Paper 33. Carbondale, Illinois: Southern Illinois University.
2006   *Archaeology at Shiloh Indian Mounds, 1899–1999.* Tuscaloosa: University of Alabama Press.

Welch, P. D., and B. M. Butler
2006   Borne on a Litter with Much Prestige. In *Leadership and Polity in Mississippian Society*, edited by B. M. Butler and P. D. Welch, pp. 1–15. Center for Archaeological Investigations Occasional Paper 33. Carbondale, Illinois: Southern Illinois University.

Weltfish, G.
1977   *The Lost Universe: Pawnee Life and Culture.* Lincoln: University of Nebraska Press.

Wesler, K. W.
1991   Ceramics, Chronology, and Horizon Markers at Wickliffe Mounds. *American Antiquity* 56:278–290.

Wesson, C. B.
1998   Mississippian Sacred Landscapes: The View from Alabama. In *Mississippian Towns and Sacred Spaces: Searching for an Architectural Grammar*, edited by R. B. Lewis and C. Stout, pp. 93–122. Gainesville: University of Alabama Press.

Whalen, M. E., and P. E. Minnis
2002   Leadership at Casas Grandes, Chihuahua, Mexico. In *Alternative Leadership Strategies in the Prehispanic Southwest*, edited by B. J. Mills, pp. 168–179. Tucson: University of Arizona Press.

Wheelersburg, R. P.
1992   An Archaeobotanical Study of Fort Ancient Subsistence in Southwestern Ohio: The State Line Site. *Pennsylvania Archaeologist* 62: 45–65.

White, Tim D.
1992   *Prehistoric Cannibalism at Mancos 5MTUMR-2346.* Princeton, New Jersey: Princeton University Press.

Whyte, T. R., and L. R. Kimball
1997   Science versus Grave Desecration: The Saga of Lake Hole Cave. *Journal of Cave and Karst Studies* 39:143–147.

Wilk, R. R., and R. M. Netting
1984   Households: Changing Forms and Functions. In *Households: Comparative and Historical Studies of the Domestic Group*, edited by R. M. Netting, R. R. Wilk, and E. J. Arnould, pp. 1–28. Berkeley: University of California Press.

Willey, P., G. Crothers, and C. H. Faulkner
1988   Aboriginal Skeletons and Petroglyphs in Officer Cave, Tennessee. *Tennessee Anthropologist* 13: 51–75.

Williams, S.
1957 James Kelly Hampson Obituary. *American Antiquity* 22: 398–400.
1980 Armorel: A Very Late Phase in the Lower Mississippi Valley. *Southeastern Archaeological Conference Bulletin* 22:105–110.
1990 The Vacant Quarter and Other Events in the Lower Valley. In *Towns and Temples Along the Mississippi*, edited by D. Dye and C. Cox, pp. 170–180. Tuscaloosa: University of Alabama Press.
1999 A Discussion of Phases in Southeast Missouri. Paper prepared for the Beckwith Archaeological Conference, Southeast Missouri State University, Cape Girardeau.

Williams, S., and J. M. Goggin
1956 The Long Nosed God Mask in Eastern United States. *Missouri Archaeologist* 18: 1–72.

Williamson, R. A., and C. R. Farrar (editors)
1992 *Earth and Sky: Visions of the Cosmos in Native American Folklore*. Albuquerque: University of New Mexico Press.

Williamson, R. F., and S. Pfeiffer
2003 *Bones of the Ancestors: The Archaeology and Osteobiology of the Moatfield Ossuary*. Mercury Series Paper 163. Ottawa: Archaeological Survey of Canada.

Wilson, G. D.
2001 Crafting Control and the Control of Crafts: Rethinking the Moundville Greenstone Industry. *Southeastern Archaeology* 20: 118–128.
2005 Between Plaza and Palisade: Household and Community Organization at Early Moundville. Unpublished Ph.D. dissertation, Department of Anthropology, University of North Carolina, Chapel Hill.
2008 *The Archaeology of Everyday Life at Moundville*. Tuscaloosa: University of Alabama Press.

Wilson, G. D., J. B. Marcoux, and B. Koldehoff
2006 Square Pegs in Round Holes: Organizational Variation Between Moundville and Cahokia. In *Leadership and Polity in Mississippian Society*, edited by B. M. Butler and P. D. Welch, pp. 43–72. Carbondale, Illinois: Center for Archaeological Investigation, Southern Illinois University.

Winter, M. C.
1976 The Archeological Household Cluster in the Valley of Oaxaca. In *The Early Mesoamerican Village*, edited by K. V. Flannery, pp. 25–31. New York: Academic Press.

Wobst, H. M.
1977 Stylistic Behavior and Information Exchange. In *For the Director: Essays in Honor of James B. Griffin*, edited by C. E. Cleland, pp. 317–344. Anthropological Papers of the Museum of Anthropology 61. Ann Arbor: University of Michigan.

Wolf, E. R.
1999 *Envisioning Power: Ideologies of Dominance and Crisis*. Berkeley: University of California Press.
2001 *Pathways of Power: Building and Anthropology of the Modern World*. Berkeley: University of California Press.

Worth, J. E.
1998 *The Timucuan Chiefdoms of Spanish Florida*. Vol. 1, *Assimilation*. Gainesville: University Press of Florida.

Wyckoff, D. G., and T. G. Baugh
1980 Early Hasinai Elites: A Model for the Material Culture of Governing Elites. *Midcontinental Journal of Archaeology* 5: 225–288.

Yerkes, R. W.
1983 Microwear, Microdrills, and Mississippian Craft Specialization. *American Antiquity* 48: 499–518.
1989 Mississippian Craft Specialization on the American Bottom. *Southeastern Archaeology* 8: 93–106.

Yoffee, N.
1993 Too Many Chiefs? (or, Safe Texts for the '90s). In *Archaeological Theory*, edited by N. Yoffee and A. Sherratt, pp. 60–78. Cambridge: Cambridge University Press.
2005 *Myths of the Archaic State: Evolution of the Earliest Cities, States, and Civilizations*. Cambridge: Cambridge University Press.

Young, Bilone W., and Melvin L. Fowler
2000 *Cahokia: The Great Native American Metropolis*. Urbana: University of Illinois Press.

List of Contributors

Edmond A. Boudreaux III
Assistant Professor
Department of Anthropology
East Carolina University
Greenville, North Carolina 27858–4353

James A. Brown
Professor
Department of Anthropology
Northwestern University
Evanston, Illinois 60208 1330

Robert A. Cook
Assistant Professor
Department of Anthropology
The Ohio State University
Columbus, Ohio 43210

Alan M. Cressler
Hydrologist
United States Geological Survey
Atlanta, Georgia

Jay D. Franklin
Associate Professor
Department of Anthropology
East Tennessee State University
Johnson City, Tennessee 37614

Rita Fisher-Carroll
Program Director
School of Medical Imaging
St. Mary's Medical Center
Huntington, West Virginia 25702

Lynne G. Goldstein
Professor
Department of Anthropology
Michigan State University
East Lansing, Michigan 48824

Michaelyn S. Harle
Ph.D. candidate
Department of Anthropology
University of Tennessee
Knoxville, Tennessee 37996

Keith Jacobi
Osteologist
Office of Archaeological Research
Alabama Museum of Natural History
University of Alabama
Tuscaloosa, Alabama 35487–0340

Adam King
Research Associate Professor
South Carolina Institute of Archaeology and Anthropology
University of South Carolina
Columbia, SC 29208

Lucinda M. Langston
Department of Anthropology
East Tennessee State University
Johnson City, Tennessee 37614

Robert C. Mainfort, Jr.
Professor
Arkansas Archeological Survey
Department of Anthropology
University of Arkansas
Fayetteville, Arkansas 72701

Jon Bernard Marcoux
Senior Archaeologist
Brockington and Associates, Inc.
Mount Pleasant, South Carolina 29464

Timothy R. Pauketat
Professor
Department of Anthropology
University of Illinois
Urbana, Illinois 61801

Elizabeth K. Price
Department of Anthropology
East Tennessee State University
Johnson City, Tennessee 37614

Jan F. Simek
Professor
Department of Anthropology
University of Tennessee
Knoxville, Tennessee 37996

Lynne P. Sullivan
Curator of Archaeology and Adjunct Professor
Frank H. McClung Museum
University of Tennessee
Knoxville, Tennessee 37996

Vincas P. Steponaitis
Professor and Director
Research Laboratories of Archaeology
University of North Carolina at Chapel Hill
Chapel Hill, North Carolina 27599-3120

Gregory D. Wilson
Assistant Professor
Department of Anthropology
University of California at Santa Barbara
Santa Barbara, California 93106–3210

Index

Agency theory, 9, 16
Altars. *See* palettes, stone
Ancestors, 9, 11, 17, 26, 33, 86, 128, 148, 150, 212
Archaeological phases: Angel, 123, 126; Dallas, 7, 10, 54, 97, 108, 234, 238–41, 243–44, 248–49, 252, 254–57, 260, 263, 265–67, 269; Evans, 36, 53; Fort Ancient, 10, 113–17, 123–27; Fort Coffee, 34, 38–39, 53; Harlan, 36, 53; Lamar, 248, 252; Leak, 199, 208, 216–19, 224–29; Lohmann, 21; Middle Cumberland, 123–24, 126, 297; Moorehead, 21, 22; Moundville I, 77, 84, 85; Moundville II, 77, 84, 85; Moundville III, 77, 85; Moundville IV, 77; Mouse Creek, 126, 234, 238–39, 243, 248; Nodena, 10, 128–31, 133, 135, 137, 139, 141, 143, 176, 178, 185, 189–90, 193; Pisgah, 10, 248, 252, 254–57, 263–67, 269; Plum Bayou, 36; Qualla, 249; Spiro 2, 30, 32, 34, 36, 38–39, 43, 46–49, 51–52, 54, 116, 179; Stirling, 21–22; Town Creek, 2, 8, 195–206, 208, 212–33; Wilbanks, 55, 57–61, 65–66, 69–70, 72–73, 248
Archaeological sites: 1GR2, 81; 5th Unnamed Cave, 284–85; 6th Unnamed Cave, 284–87; 7th Unnamed Cave, 288; 12th Unnamed Cave, 285, 288–90, 290; 15th Unnamed Cave, 286; 34th Unnamed Cave, 285, 287; 38th Unnamed Cave, 285, 287–89, 289; 40Hw44, 264; Annis, 126, 311; Arnold, 126, 265; ASG, 263, 264; Averbuch, 126; Aztalan, 2, 5, 12, 18, 24, 27, 90–97, 92, 99–101, 103–4, 106–12; Banks, 90, 130, 133; Bert Smith, 264; Big Bone Cave, 270–72, 274; Big Mound, 19, 22; Braden Schoolhouse, 39; Bradley, 133; Bridges, 126; Cahokia, 2, 9–10, 12, 14–15, 18–21, 20, 23–30, 32–33, 36, 38, 48, 50–52, 96, 117, 249; Campbell, 182, 185–86, 193; Cemetery Mound, 19, 22; Cobb Island, 252, 254, 265; Coleman Cave, 279; Dickson Mounds, 18, 24, 27; Dunbar Cave, 281; Dust Cave, 280; Etowah, 2, 45, 54–57, 55, 64, 66, 69–70, 72–73, 116, 248; Fains Island, 2, 237–48, 241, 254, 265; Fatherland, 33, 35; Galley Pond, 33; Ganier, 126; Glover's Cave, 276, 278; Goforth Saindon, 48; Harding ("Rattlesnake") Mound, 20, 21; Hazel, 133; Hixon, 260; Holliston Mills, 2, 250–69, 251; Indian Cave, 283; John Chapman, 18, 24, 27; Jonathan Creek, 99; Junkyard Mound, 19, 21–22, 25, 27; Kellogg, 81; King, 117, 124, 125, 126; Koger's Island, 2, 6, 145–46, 147, 149–53, 159–61, 163–69, 171–73; Lake Hole Cave, 281; Ledford Island, 2, 126, 237–40, 240, 242–48; Loy, 254, 265; Macon Plateau, 18; Madisonville, 126; McCullough Bend, 254, 265; McMahan, 269; Middle Nodena, 10, 129–44, 184–85, 191–92; Mitchell Mound, 19, 22–23; Moore, 39; Morton Mound, 33; Moundville, 2, 7, 10, 12, 48, 54, 74–89, 76, 108, 116, 133, 148–50, 152, 155, 157, 172, 178–80, 189, 193, 232; Mouse Creek, 244, 246; Nelson, 265; Nodena, 2; Pecan Point, 2, 7, 133, 137–38, 174–76, 177, 178–93; Picture Cave, 288; Plum Grove, 265–66; Powell Mound, 19; Rotherwood, 264; Russell Cave, 280; Rymer, 244; Saltpeter Cave,

346   Index

Archaeological sites—*continued*
280; Schild, 18, 33, 110; Schomaker, 126; Shiloh, 18–19, 24; Southwind, 129; Spiro, 2, 30, 32, 34, 36, 38–39, 43, 46–49, 49, 51–52, 54, 116, 179; State Line, 126; SunWatch, 2, 113, 115, 117–21, 118, 123–27, 125; Taylor, 126; Toltec, 36; Town Creek, 2, 8, 195–97, 198, 199–201, 203–4, 212–16, 219, 221–33; Turpin, 126; Upper Nodena, 10, 128–44, 174, 176, 178–81, 184–85, 187, 190–93, 259; Warren Wilson, 256, 260, 265–67; Wilson Mound, 21, 33; Yokem, 18, 33; Zimmerman's Island, 262
Ascribed (ascriptive) status, 83, 85, 120, 149, 160, 228

Barrett, Samuel A., 17–18, 90, 93–96, 99, 101, 104, 106, 108, 110, 294
Baskets, 34, 41–44, 53, 291
Binford, Lewis R., 4–6, 31, 33, 54–55, 74, 83, 145–46, 148, 151, 171, 179, 199
Birdman, 41, 44, 71, 261
Braden style, 36, 71
Bundles, medicine or sacred, 17, 41–43, 45–46, 69
Burials: bundle, 78, 108, 111, 277, 280; disarticulated, 23, 39–40, 46, 48, 50, 52, 104, 211; residential, 11; secondary (reburial, disposal), 5, 18–19, 30–33, 52, 70, 78, 94, 106, 108, 112, 163. *See also* charnel houses; crematories; ossuaries

Caddo, 23, 34, 36, 49
Cannibalism, 12, 93, 95, 104, 108
Celts, 58–59, 71, 84, 141, 143, 154, 158, 160, 169, 180, 188, 255–57, 262, 266
Ceramic vessels, 39, 131, 135–37, 142–43, 181–82, 184–85, 188, 190–91, 210, 257, 275; headpots, 175; negative painted, 117, 123
Charnel houses or structures, 18–19, 23, 25, 33, 94–95, 106, 108, 109, 111. *See also* burials; crematories; ossuaries
Cherokee, 10–11, 215, 236, 248–49, 271
Chickasaw, 151
Chiefdoms, 6–9, 12, 55, 98, 110, 113, 115, 178–79, 193, 195, 262–63, 267, 269
Chunkey (chunky) game, 124; stone, 23, 84, 124; stick, 24

Circle with cross (cross-in-circle) motif, 40, 44, 53, 64, 260, 262, 287, 288
Clans, 8, 56, 65–66, 75–76, 88–89, 148, 150, 186, 212–13, 215, 221, 223
Collective representation, 34, 39, 43, 45
Copper artifacts, 1, 23–25, 38, 42, 44, 45, 46, 53n4, 58, 59, 60, 69–71, 85, 108, 141–43, 152–54, 159–60, 169, 172n2, 179–80, 189, 206–7, 209–10, 214–16, 222–23, 226, 228, 230, 254–57, 262, 275
Corporate groups, 10, 14, 19, 25, 28, 46, 60, 65–66, 69, 72, 74, 86–89, 97, 103, 124, 148, 168–69, 171, 172n1, 201, 215, 221, 231–32, 267–69, 291
Cosmos, 9, 15, 24, 26, 30, 32, 48–50, 62–65; cosmogram, 38, 46, 48, 52, 63, 65; cosmological plan, 32, 34, 38–39, 41, 46, 49, 52, 53, 59
Creek, 2, 8, 61–62, 66, 99, 126, 150, 195–206, 208, 212–34, 238–39, 243–48, 260, 266
Crematories, 94; and cremated remains, 46, 277, 283; and cremations, 277, 280, 281, 286–87, 291. *See also* burials; charnel houses; ossuaries
Crystals, 24, 46
Cultural pluralism, 9

De Soto, Hernando, 254
Discoidal (stone or ceramic), 60, 84–85, 117, 119, 124, 138–43, 181–84, 186–89, 192, 257
Dogs, 25, 44, 275, 277

Earspools, 25, 69, 103, 108, 179, 188, 192, 209, 255, 256, 262
Earth Mother, 41, 44
Effigies, 46, 101, 138–39, 142, 154, 181–84, 186–87, 189, 284–85, 287, 291
Ethnicity, 10–11, 31, 144, 190, 192, 235–36; ethnic groups, 9, 114, 236, 269

Feasts/feasting, 28, 51, 94, 225
Feathers, 58, 271–72
Figurines, 41, 44

Gender, 8, 10–11, 28, 31, 74, 109, 111, 133, 212, 234, 236, 239, 246–47, 283, 291
Greenstone, 84–85, 141–42, 154, 156, 158, 160, 169, 192, 287, 307, 339

Hasinai, 340
Hawks. *See* raptors
Headresses, 58–60, 66, 69, 70, 255; headbands, 40, 45
Heterarchies, 8, 230
Hightower style, 70–71
Holder, Preston, 21, 25
Holmes, William H., 174, 313
House society (social house), 11–12, 56, 66
Huron, 51

Iroquois, 27, 63, 40

Kroeber, Alfred L., 17

Lapham, Increase A., 90, 92, 101
Litters, 38, 40–41, 44–48, 51

Masks, 42, 142, 188, 260–61, 266
Mica, 60, 208, 228–29, 257, 266, 275, 280
Mississippianization, 16, 127
Monolithic ax, 58–60
Moore, Clarence B., 174
Morning Star (Morningstar), 24, 32, 72
Mounds, 72, 10, 12–13, 15, 18–19, 21–27, 23, 30, 32–33, 48–52, 96; platform, 1, 24, 90, 94, 101, 116, 195–96, 231, 239; ridgetop, 15, 18–19, 21–23, 25–29
Mummies, 273, 274, 283
Muskogean, 62–64

Natchez, 6, 34, 151
Norris, Philetus, 175

Ogee, 139, 183–84, 187–89
Osage 56, 72
Ossuaries, 36, 38–40, 45–46, 51. *See also* burials; charnel houses; crematories

Palettes, stone (portable stone altars), 58–59, 60, 152–54, 159–60, 169
Palmer, Edward, 174–76
Pawnee, 72
Pearls, 42–43, 70, 65, 179
Pee Dee, 199, 214
Personhood, 12, 15–17, 27, 29, 46
Pipes, 19, 36, 41, 44, 60, 103, 121, 139, 141–42, 154, 181–82, 207–8, 229, 256–57, 275

Platform mounds. *See under* mounds
Posts/poles/wooden markers, 17,18–19, 22–24, 26, 28, 33, 37–38, 40–42, 63, 65, 77, 84, 93–94, 98, 112, 116, 124, 126, 128, 160, 201, 209, 216, 221, 226, 228, 278, 280, 283
Power, 8, 10–12, 17, 26, 31–32, 38, 40, 46, 50, 63, 66, 73, 96–99, 110, 117, 123, 195–97, 212–13, 222, 224, 230–31, 268
Prestige goods, 110, 116, 268

Raccoons, 153–54, 159–60, 166, 184, 186–87, 189, 208, 229–30
Ranked society, 6, 145–46, 148–51
Raptors, 44, 186, 288, 58, 149, 152–54, 159–60, 166, 169
Rattles, 24, 149, 159–60, 166, 208–9, 228–30, 266
Red ochre, 121, 182–84, 229, 275
Ridgetop mounds. *See under* mounds
Ritual landscape, 12, 291
Role theory, 3–4

Sacrifices, 18, 23–28, 71–72
Saxe, Arthur A., 3–6, 54–55, 74, 87, 145–46, 148, 171, 179, 199
Shamans, 46, 50, 186
Sharks' teeth, 60
Shell artifacts, 38, 120, 256; beads, 18, 23–25, 42–44, 70–71, 85, 103, 108, 119–20, 139–43, 152, 154, 156–60, 169, 179, 182–84, 187–89, 192, 206–11, 214, 244, 255–57, 259–60, 266, 275–76, 280; bracelets, 121, 140, 142, 181, 188, 191 ; cups, 36, 40, 46–47, 70, 117, 154, 160, 169; ear pins, 208–9, 244; earplugs, 140, 142, 181–84, 186–89, 191–92, 276; gorgets, 36, 63, 179, 188, 209–10, 244, 256–57, 260–62, 266–67, 275–76; necklaces, 23, 139, 140, 142, 181–84, 186–89, 191–92; pendants, 42, 119, 121, 206, 244, 280, 287
Shrines, 33–35, 48
Shrouds/shrouding, 23, 25, 271
Siouan, 23, 27
Snakes/serpents, 41, 47, 289; rattlesnakes, 44, 47, 47, 256, 260–61, 266
Sociogram, 75, 88–89
Souls, 17, 28, 47, 70, 72; Path of Souls, 70, 72; soul adoption, 27

Southeastern Ceremonial Complex, 9, 57, 99; Southern Cult, 9, 61
Spatulate celt (ax), 84–85, 141, 143, 182, 188
Square ground, 61–65, 62, 69
Stockades/palisades, 90, 94, 99, 101, 106, 109, 112
Swanton, John, 34, 61, 66, 201, 215, 228, 230, 235

Tableaus 9, 15, 25, 38, 51–52
Tainter, Joseph A., 3–4, 128, 335–36
Temples, 22, 26–28, 65
Textiles (cloth, fiber), 43, 44, 53n5, 178, 272, 273, 274, 289

Thomas, Cyrus, 57, 137, 175–76, 181, 336
Thunderer, 24, 27
Timucua, 151
Turkeys, 152–53, 158–60, 169, 182, 186, 260–61, 288

Underworld, 12, 292

Vacant Quarter, 115, 126, 300, 339

Wealth, 31, 40, 44, 66, 99, 179, 267–69
White, John, 33, 42
Works Progress Administration (WPA), 39, 51, 238–39

Ripley P. Bullen Series
FLORIDA MUSEUM OF NATURAL HISTORY

Tacachale: Essays on the Indians of Florida and Southeastern Georgia during the Historic Period, edited by Jerald T. Milanich and Samuel Proctor (1978)
Aboriginal Subsistence Technology on the Southeastern Coastal Plain during the Late Prehistoric Period, by Lewis H. Larson (1980)
Cemochechobee: Archaeology of a Mississippian Ceremonial Center on the Chattahoochee River, by Frank T. Schnell, Vernon J. Knight Jr., and Gail S. Schnell (1981)
Fort Center: An Archaeological Site in the Lake Okeechobee Basin, by William H. Sears, with contributions by Elsie O'R. Sears and Karl T. Steinen (1982)
Perspectives on Gulf Coast Prehistory, edited by Dave D. Davis (1984)
Archaeology of Aboriginal Culture Change in the Interior Southeast: Depopulation during the Early Historic Period, by Marvin T. Smith (1987)
Apalachee: The Land between the Rivers, by John H. Hann (1988)
Key Marco's Buried Treasure: Archaeology and Adventure in the Nineteenth Century, by Marion Spjut Gilliland (1989)
First Encounters: Spanish Explorations in the Caribbean and the United States, 1492–1570, edited by Jerald T. Milanich and Susan Milbrath (1989)
Missions to the Calusa, edited and translated by John H. Hann, with an introduction by William H. Marquardt (1991)
Excavations on the Franciscan Frontier: Archaeology at the Fig Springs Mission, by Brent Richards Weisman (1992)
The People Who Discovered Columbus: The Prehistory of the Bahamas, by William F. Keegan (1992)
Hernando de Soto and the Indians of Florida, by Jerald T. Milanich and Charles Hudson (1993)
Foraging and Farming in the Eastern Woodlands, edited by C. Margaret Scarry (1993)
Puerto Real: The Archaeology of a Sixteenth-Century Spanish Town in Hispaniola, edited by Kathleen Deagan (1995)
Political Structure and Change in the Prehistoric Southeastern United States, edited by John F. Scarry (1996)
Bioarchaeology of Native Americans in the Spanish Borderlands, edited by Brenda J. Baker and Lisa Kealhofer (1996)
A History of the Timucua Indians and Missions, by John H. Hann (1996)
Archaeology of the Mid-Holocene Southeast, edited by Kenneth E. Sassaman and David G. Anderson (1996)
The Indigenous People of the Caribbean, edited by Samuel M. Wilson (1997)
Hernando de Soto among the Apalachee: The Archaeology of the First Winter Encampment, by Charles R. Ewen and John H. Hann (1998)
The Timucuan Chiefdoms of Spanish Florida, by John E. Worth: vol. 1, *Assimilation*; vol. 2, *Resistance and Destruction* (1998)
Ancient Earthen Enclosures of the Eastern Woodlands, edited by Robert C. Mainfort Jr., and Lynne P. Sullivan (1998)
An Environmental History of Northeast Florida, by James J. Miller (1998)
Precolumbian Architecture in Eastern North America, by William N. Morgan (1999)
Archaeology of Colonial Pensacola, edited by Judith A. Bense (1999)
Grit-Tempered: Early Women Archaeologists in the Southeastern United States, edited by Nancy Marie White, Lynne P. Sullivan, and Rochelle A. Marrinan (1999)
Coosa: The Rise and Fall of a Southeastern Mississippian Chiefdom, by Marvin T. Smith (2000)
Religion, Power, and Politics in Colonial St. Augustine, by Robert L. Kapitzke (2001)
Bioarchaeology of Spanish Florida: The Impact of Colonialism, edited by Clark Spencer Larsen (2001)

Archaeological Studies of Gender in the Southeastern United States, edited by Jane M. Eastman and Christopher B. Rodning (2001)
The Archaeology of Traditions: Agency and History Before and After Columbus, edited by Timothy R. Pauketat (2001)
Foraging, Farming, and Coastal Biocultural Adaptation in Late Prehistoric North Carolina, by Dale L. Hutchinson (2002)
Windover: Multidisciplinary Investigations of an Early Archaic Florida Cemetery, edited by Glen H. Doran (2002)
Archaeology of the Everglades, by John W. Griffin (2002)
Pioneer in Space and Time: John Mann Goggin and the Development of Florida Archaeology, by Brent Richards Weisman (2002)
Indians of Central and South Florida, 1513–1763, by John H. Hann (2003)
Presidio Santa Maria de Galve: A Struggle for Survival in Colonial Spanish Pensacola, edited by Judith A. Bense (2003)
Bioarchaeology of the Florida Gulf Coast: Adaptation, Conflict, and Change, by Dale L. Hutchinson (2004)
The Myth of Syphilis: The Natural History of Treponematosis in North America, edited by Mary Lucas Powell and Della Collins Cook (2005)
The Florida Journals of Frank Hamilton Cushing, edited by Phyllis E. Kolianos and Brent R. Weisman (2005)
The Lost Florida Manuscript of Frank Hamilton Cushing, edited by Phyllis E. Kolianos and Brent R. Weisman (2005)
The Native American World Beyond Apalachee: West Florida and the Chattahoochee Valley, by John H. Hann (2006)
Tatham Mound and the Bioarchaeology of European Contact: Disease and Depopulation in Central Gulf Coast Florida, by Dale L. Hutchinson (2006)
Taino Indian Myth and Practice: The Arrival of the Stranger King, by William F. Keegan (2007)
An Archaeology of Black Markets: Local Ceramics and Economies in Eighteenth-Century Jamaica, by Mark W. Hauser (2008)
Mississippian Mortuary Practices: Beyond Hierarchy and the Representationist Perspective, edited by Lynne P. Sullivan and Robert C. Mainfort Jr. (2010; first paperback edition, 2012)
Bioarchaeology of Ethnogenesis in the Colonial Southeast, by Christopher M. Stojanowski (2010)
French Colonial Archaeology in the Southeast and Caribbean, edited by Kenneth G. Kelly and Meredith D. Hardy (2011)
Late Prehistoric Florida: Archaeology at the Edge of the Mississippian World, edited by Keith Ashley and Nancy Marie White (2012)

www.ingramcontent.com/pod-product-compliance
Lightning Source LLC
Chambersburg PA
CBHW070749230426
43665CB00017B/2298